BITS OF HONEY

SOUTH FLORIDA STUDIES IN THE HISTORY OF JUDAISM

Edited by
Jacob Neusner
William Scott Green, James Strange
Darrell J. Fasching, Sara Mandell

Number 74
BITS OF HONEY
Essays for Samson H. Levey

edited by
Stanley F. Chyet
and
David H. Ellenson

BITS OF HONEY
Essays for Samson H. Levey

edited by

Stanley F. Chyet
and
David H. Ellenson

Scholars Press
Atlanta, Georgia

BITS OF HONEY

©1993
University of South Florida

Publication of this book was made possible by a grant from the Tisch Family Foundation, New York City. The University of South Florida acknowledges with thanks this important support for its scholarly projects.

Library of Congress Cataloging in Publication Data
Bits of honey: essays for Samson H. Levey/ edited by Stanley F. Chyet and David H. Ellenson.
   p. cm. — (South Forida studies in the history of Judaism; no. 74)
  Includes index.
  ISBN 1-55540-850-8
  1. Judaism—History. 2. Rabbinical literature—History and criticism. 3. Judaism—Essence, genius, nature. 4. Bible. O.T.—Criticism, interpretation, etc.   I. Levey, Samson H.   II. Chyet, Stanley F.   III. Ellenson, David Harry, 1947–   . IV. Series: South Florida studies in the history of Judaism, 74.
BM160.B55   1993
296'.09—dc20   93-21881
                                            CIP

Printed in the United States of America
on acid-free paper

דִּבְרֵי תּוֹרָה, שֶׁנֶּאֱמַר בָּהֶם ְ וְנֹפֶת צוּפִים ֹ

. . . the words of the Torah, of which it is said,
Sweeter also than honey and the honeycomb – noḟet ẓufim
(Psalm 19:11)

– B're>shit Rabah 71:8

Table of Contents

Foreword ix
The Editors

Note on Transliteration xi

Part One
ANTIQUITY

1. Textual Transformations: Rabbinic Exegesis of Genesis 22:14 3
   Lewis M. Barth

2. Yohanan Ben Zakkai at Yavneh: Merkavah and Messiah 25
   Uri D. Herscher

3. Introductory Poems (R'shuyot) to the Targum of the Haftarah in Praise of Jonathan Ben Uzziel 43
   Michael A. Klein

4. The Priestly Consecration (Leviticus 8): A Rite of Passage 57
   Jacob Milgrom

5. The Greco-Roman Philosophy of Judaism: The Mishnah in Context 63
   Jacob Neusner

6. Gentiles and Israelites in Mishnah-Tosefta>: A Study in Ethnicity 93
   Gary G. Porton

7. A New Interpretation of "V'Hinam Shol'ḥim >Et-Ha-Z'morah >El->apam" (Ezekiel 8:17) 113
   Melvin S. Sands

8. Understanding a Midrash Text: The Case of the Inhabitants of Nineveh 121
   Lou H. Silberman

9. Geomessianism: Why Did the Essenes Settle at Qumran? ... 131
   Ben Zion Wacholder

Part Two
THE MEDIEVAL CENTURIES

10. Speculations on the Passover 141
    Lee T. Bycel

11. Yehuda Halevi: The Consolations of Utopia 147
    Stanley F. Chyet

12. Abortion and the Emergence of Human Life: Maimonides and the Judaic View 163
    Lenn E. Goodman

13. Flexibility in Halakhah: Jewish Authorities at Work – Former Days 191
    Edward Zipperstein

Part Three
THE MODERN WORLD

14. Translation and the Project of Culture: On Transferring Western Literature into Hebrew 1893-1930 209
    William Cutter

15. A Note on Peter Berger's "Charisma and Religious Innovation: The Social Location of Israelite Prophecy" 229
    David H. Ellenson

16. The Use of Reason in Maimonides – An Evaluation by Ahad Ha-Am 233
    Alfred Gottschalk

17. Freud, Moses and the Law 243
    Norman B. Mirsky

18. The Good Life 255
    J. Wesley Robb

19. The Stranger in Our Mirror 265
    Harold M. Schulweis

20. Judaism as Interpretation: Text and Spirit 277
    Michael A. Signer

21. Segregation or Unity in Diversity: The Controversy between Samson Raphael Hirsch and Seligmann Bär Bamberger and Its Significance 289
    Leo Trepp

Afterword 311
    Samson H. Levey

Note on Contributors 313

Index: Persons and Places 315

Index: Subjects 325

Foreword

Rabbi Dr. Samson Halevi Levey, scion of a distinguished rabbinical family, is a native of Benton Harbor, Michigan, and an alumnus of the University of Chicago, Dropsie College, Hebrew Union College (Cincinnati), and the University of Southern California. He is founding (now emeritus) director of the Edgar F. Magnin School of Graduate Studies on the Los Angeles Campus of Hebrew Union College, served many years on the Los Angeles faculty, and since 1978 has been Professor Emeritus of Rabbinics and Jewish Religious Thought. Prof. Levey is himself exemplary of two crucial qualities in Jewish intellectual life: *b'qi>ut*, an enviable knowledge of classical Jewish – and other – sources, and *ḥarifut,* a rigorously analytical – but also imaginative – approach to the phenomena which command scholarly interest. These qualities have been fully evident in his teaching and in his publications – we are thinking of such works as *The Messiah: An Aramaic Interpretation*, which appeared in 1974, and *The Targum of Ezekiel,* which appeared in 1986, or essays like "The Best Kept Secret of the Rabbinic Tradition" (*Judaism,* 1972), "Ben Zoma, the Sages, and Passover" (*Journal of Reform Judaism,* 1981), and "Amos in the Rabbinic Tradition" (*Willis W. Fisher Tribute Volume,* 1983). He has been and continues to be significant for students and colleagues alike as *moreh* and *manhig ruḥani,* mentor and spiritual guide.

When Uri Herscher asked us to undertake the production of a Festschrift honoring Samson Levey on his eightieth birthday and when Prof. Levey supplied a list of the scholars he wanted us to invite, we had no idea what to expect – except that the results were sure to be interesting. As indeed they are, reflecting in their heterogeneity not only Prof. Levey's wide acquaintance and intellectual catholicity but also something of the prodigious range which typifies Judaic studies as the 20th century fades into the 21st.

We are grateful to the scholars who have responded so generously to our invitation, and we are grateful also to the many who have helped us bring this endeavor to fruitful issue – and to none more than to Marian Thomas, Secretary both to the faculty of the Los Angeles School and to the Director of the Magnin School. Her patience and expertise have been indispensable, to say the very least.

Stanley F. Chyet
David H. Ellenson
Los Angeles, Summer 1991

A Note on Transliteration

(From Hebrew and Aramaic)

CONSONANTS:		VOWELS:	
>alef	= >	shva> na<	= '
bet	= b	ẓéreh yod	= é
vet	= v̄	pataḥ, qamaẓ	= a
ġimel	= ġ	segol, ẓéreh	= e
dalet	= d	shuruq, qubuẓ	= u
hé	= h	qamaẓ qaṭan, ḥolam	= o
vav	= v	ḥiriq, ḥiriq yod	= i
zayin	= z		
ḥet	= ḥ		
ṭet	= ṭ		
yod	= y		
kaf	= k		
khaf	= kh		
lamed	= l		
mem	= m		
nun	= n		
samekh	= s		
<ayin	= <		
pé	= p		
ƒé	= f		
ẓadi	= ẓ		
quf	= q		
resh	= r		
śin	= ś		
shin	= sh		
tav	= t		

Gemination is generally disregarded. Names are, for the most part, left free of diacritical marks.

Part One
ANTIQUITY

1

Textual Transformations: Rabbinic Exegesis of Genesis 22:14

By Lewis M. Barth

This paper engages with three types of Rabbinic texts: Midrash, Talmud and Targum. These texts represent the areas and disciplines which Samson Levey opened up to my classmates and me over thirty years ago as our first teacher of Rabbinics. They have remained the central focus of his scholarly activity and continue to shape and nourish the religious dimensions of his life and teaching. For that early instruction and for his gracious sharing of Torah and Wisdom over many years, this is offered with thanks and appreciation.

Scholars have long noted the fact that a single Rabbinic tradition is often repeated within the same document or in several different documents. There does not appear to be any restriction on the type of material which is repeated. An exegetical comment, *mashal* or story can show up in formally and programmatically diverse Rabbinic texts in connection with quite different characters, verses, or subject matter, provided a key word or situation allows for the link to be made.[1] In the case of some traditions, all repetitions nearly match word for word. In the case of others, there are differences of great magnitude. At times one is compelled to wonder if the repetitions are intended to represent the same original statement.

---

[1] In his introduction to Midrash B're>shit Rabah, Chanoch Albeck referred to traditions repeated within the same text as doublets. See Albeck, "Mavo> L'Midrash B're>shit Rabah," in Judah Theodor and Ch. Albeck, eds., *Bereschit Rabbah* (Jerusalem: Sifré Wahrman, 1965), III, 1-11. Jacob Neusner describes the same traditions found in various documents as "peripatetic materials ... that is to say, a handful of sayings and stories travel from one document to the next"; see his *Canon and Connection: Intertextuality in Judaism* (New York: University Press of America, 1987), p. 31.

When we compare one occurrence of a repeated tradition to another, what accounts for observed differences? This question is meant to point beyond variations based on prior oral transmission, scribal characteristics or broad redactional traits of documents. It will be argued here that some variations can be accounted for only by assuming that they reflect decisions regarding the content of a tradition which are made by those who re-use it. On the basis of such decisions, writers transform texts, at times so significantly that the content found in the repetition consciously contradicts what it repeats.

This paper will analyze one tradition in several of the contexts in which it appears as an example of this phenomenon. It is found in the Theodor-Albeck *Midrasch Bereschit Rabbah* (*BR*) 56:10, p. 607; the Margulies *Midrash Wayyikra Rabba* (*LR*) 29:9, p. 682; T. Y. Ta<aniyot 65d and later parallels to these passages.[2] It also informs the Aramaic translation of Genesis 22:14 found in the targums *Pseudo-Jonathan* (*PsJ*), *Neophyti* (*N*), and the *Fragment-Targums* published by Michael Klein. The examples to be discussed here have been selected from four formally different types of Rabbinic compositions: *BR*, an "exegetical midrash"; the Talmud of the Land of Israel (the Palestinian or Yerushalmi); *LR,* a "homiletical midrash"; and the targums *PsJ* and *N*.

In four out of five of these documents the tradition appears as an exegetical comment on, or a translation of, or contains a reference to, Genesis 22:14. Modern biblical scholarship has pointed to various problems in construing this verse. Van Seters, in his provocative work on the Abraham traditions, describes the verse as "enigmatic," but offers no explanation of the enigma.[3] Speiser, in the comment to his Anchor

---

[2]Abbreviations and editions used in this paper: *BR* = *Midrasch Bereschit Rabbah*, ed. Theodor and Albeck. *LR* = *Midrash Wayyikra Rabba*, ed. Mordecai Margulies, Vols. I-III (Jerusalem: American Academy for Jewish Research, 1953-1960). *PRK* = *P'siqta> d'Rav Kahana>*, ed. Bernard Mandelbaum, Vols. I-II (New York: Jewish Theological Seminary of America, 1962). *FT* = *The Fragment-Targums of the Pentateuch According to their Extant Sources*, ed. Michael Klein, 2 vols. (Rome: Biblical Institute Press, 1980). *N* = *Neophyti 1: Targum Palestinense MS de la Biblioteca Vaticana* (Madrid-Barcelona: Consejo Superior de Investigaciones Cientificas, 1968-1978), 5 vols. *PsJ* = *Targum Pseudo-Jonathan of the Pentateuch: Text and Concordance*, ed. E.G. Clarke (Hoboken: Ktav, 1984). *TO* = *The Bible Is in Aramaic*, I, The Pentateuch according to Targum Onkelos, ed. Alexander Sperber (Brill: Leiden, 1959).

Other parallels to the passages mentioned here appear in *PRK* 23:9, p. 34; Tanḥuma> Vayera>, 23; Buber, Tanḥuma> Vayera> 46; *P'siqta> Rabati (PRI)* 41:6, p. 171a and Midrash T'hilim 29:1.

[3]John Van Seters, *Abraham in History and Tradition* (New Haven: Yale University Press, 1975), p. 248.

Bible translation of Genesis, refers to Genesis 22:14 as "this parenthetical notice" and suggests that it

> ...embodies two separate allusions. One, *Yahweh yir'ê*, points back to *Elohim yir'ê*, in vs. 8; the other is connected with the Temple Hill in Jerusalem. As now vocalized, the verb in the descriptive clause is pointed as a passive, i.e., *yērā'ê* ... "(Yahweh) is seen, appears," ...which accords with Mount Moriah, but obscures the allusion to vs. 8. If we repoint the verb to *yir'ê*, the balance will shift the other way.[4]

Gunkel and von Rad both emphasized the importance of the act of naming in the verse, but argued that the actual name of the site is absent from the text. Gunkel also held the view that site naming in the Hebrew Bible always indicated an old saga. These factors, plus the differences in divine name between verses 22:8 and 22:14, >*elohim* and *yhvh* respectively, led him to conclude that the verse had been significantly reworked.[5]

A sample of modern biblical translations reflects the diversity of scholarly opinion:

1. And Abraham named that site Adonai-yireh [*i.e., "the Lord will see"; cf. v. 8*], whence the present saying, "On the mount of the LORD there is vision": the 1985 Jewish Publication Society *Tanakh*[6];

---

[4]*The Anchor Bible: Genesis*, trans. E. A. Speiser (Garden City: Doubleday, 1964), pp. 163-64. The second allusion mentioned by Speiser is quite ancient and already attested in the LXX, in which *yera>eh* is translated *ōphthē*.

[5]Hermann Gunkel, *Genesis* (Göttingen: Vanden Hoeck and Ruprecht, 1969), p. 239; Gerhard von Rad, *Genesis: A Commentary* (Philadelphia: Westminster Press, 1972), p. 242. Von Rad's full comment:

> The naming of the place, which Abraham now does, was an important matter for the ancients; for a place where God had appeared in so special a fashion was consecrated for all future generations. Here God will receive the sacrifices and prayers of coming generations, i.e., the place becomes a cultic center. It is strange, to be sure, that the narrator is unable to supply the name of a better-known cultic center. He gives no place name at all, but only a pun which at one time undoubtedly explained a place name. But the name of the place has disappeared from the narrative; only the pun is left, and it now lends itself all the more to a subtle playful change of the supposedly basic word "see" from active to passive (God sees, God is seen, i.e., he appears). The thoughts are not precise...

[6]*Tanakh: A New Translation of The Holy Scriptures, According to the Traditional Hebrew Text* (Philadelphia: Jewish Publication Society, 1985). This translation is followed here as the meaning of the Masoretic Text (MT), to be distinguished from the various Rabbinic (midrashic or targumic) translations of the verse. This translation is very close to that of Speiser: "And Abraham named

2. Abraham named that shrine "The LORD will provide"; and to this day the saying is: "In the mountain of the LORD it was provided": the 1989 Oxford/Cambridge *Revised English Bible (REB)*[7];
3. So nannte Abraham diesen Ort: "....." denn "er sprach": heute, "auf dem Berge hier" "ersah sich" Jahve!: the 1969 Gunkel *Genesis*, p. 239.

I

The first text to be analyzed is *BR* 56:10. The decision to begin with *BR* does not conform to the generally accepted relative chronological dating which places the Talmud of the Land of Israel first (early fifth century), followed by *BR, LR* and *P'siqta> d'Rav Kahana> (PRK)*.[8] However, this is the earliest example from midrashic and talmudic literature in which the tradition transmitted by R. Bibi in the name of R. Yohanan appears as an exegetical comment to Genesis 22:14.[9] It will be argued that the comment in *BR* represents an early formulation of R. Bibi/R. Yohanan's words in response to which all the other examples were constructed.

---

the site Yahweh-yireh [Yahweh sees/finds; cf. v. 8], hence the present saying, On Yahweh's mountain there is vision" (Speiser, p. 162).
[7]*The Revised English Bible: With the Apocrypha* (New Rochelle: Oxford and Cambridge University Presses, 1989). See also, with explanatory note for the place name, *The New English Bible* (New York: Oxford University Press, 1976).
[8]For classic formulation of arguments on the dating of *BR* and its relation to other Rabbinic documents, see: Ch. Albeck, "Mavo>," *BR*, III, 44-89 and esp. 93-96, and Margulies, in his "Mavo>" to *LR*, part five, pp. ix-xxxiii. On the dating of *PRK*, see Lewis M. Barth, "'The Three of Retribution and Seven of Consolation' Sermons in the Pesikta deRav Kahana," *Journal of Jewish Studies*, XXXIII (Spring-Autumn, 1982), 504, n. 2, and 505.
[9]In *BR*, T. Y. Ta<aniyot, *LR, PRK* and *PR*, the tradition is transmitted by R. Bibi Rabba or Rubba, a third generation Palestinian >amora>, c. 300-350. His name also appears as R. Bibi bar Abba and in other forms in various mss. and printed editions containing these texts. It is attributed to R. Yohanan, a second generation Palestinian >amora>, c. 250-300.

Textual Transformations: Rabbinic Exegesis of Genesis 22:14 7

B're>shit Rabah, MS Vat. 30 (see p. 607):[10] "And Abraham named that site Adonai-yireh (Gen. 22:14)."[11] R. Bibi Rabba in the name of R. Yohanan: He [Abraham] said before Him, "Master of the Universe, from the moment You said to me, 'Take, etc. (Gen. 22:2)', I had what to answer you. Previously you said to me, 'for it is through Isaac that offspring shall be continued for you (Gen. 21:12)'; and now You say to me 'Take your son, your favored one (Gen. 22:2)'! But, God forbid, I didn't do that; instead I subdued my compassion to do Your will. Thus, may it be Your will, that when the descendants of Isaac come to the fouling of bad deeds,[12]

---

[10] Ms. Vat. 30 represents probably the earliest complete version of *BR*. Michael Sokoloff has pointed out that it is a copy of a text found in fragments of a Christian palimpsest which has now received considerable scholarly attention. See his remarks on this text and references in *The Geniza Fragments of Bereshit Rabba*, ed. Sokoloff (Jerusalem: Israel Academy of Sciences and Humanities, 1982), pp. 19-20. The fragment underlying this portion of Vat. 30 is found on p. 138 of this work. An expanded version in Vat. 60 ms. of *BR* is similar to the comment in *PRK*.

[11] The midrashic translation of the verse, based on its being reread in light of the comment which follows, will be found at the conclusion of the comment to this section.

[12] The translation, "the fouling of bad deeds," is based on the reading in Vat. 30 and the important palimpsests discussed by Sokoloff, *op. cit.*, text p. 138, and comments on ms., pp. 19-20. The problem is whether one is to read: <akirut, as in Vat. 30 and the palimpsest, or <averot, as in many of the other witnesses. The issue depends on whether the second letter is *kaf*, as in Vat. 30 and the palimpsest, or *bet*, which is the reading of the majority of witnesses. The two letters can be nearly indistinguishable. In the course of transmission, this reading was taken as <averot, as is found in the more common phrase <averot uma<aŝim ra<im, "transgressions and evil deeds."

Marc Bregman shared the following response to the translation presented here, and I am most grateful for his insights which strengthen the argument in this analysis:

> What you have noted in BR MS. VAT. 30 and the Geniza fragments simply – and very significantly – documents this word <akhirut for Rabbinic Hebrew (at least Amoraic). The most important parallel to the usage in BR is found in Rabbenu Bachaye Commentary to the beginning of Parashat VaYishlaḥ (ed. Chavel), p. 274-5. There you find a *mashal* about a spring in which someone swishes the water with his foot, the water becomes turbid (<akur) for a short time [i.e., the muddy sediment is stirred up making the water murky for a time] *she->oto* <akhirut éno l'<olam, (but this murkiness is not forever). The *nimshal*, based on Prov. 25:26, is to a Tzadik who is humiliated by a Rasha; he soon returns to his "purity" (z'liluto). In light of this the idea in BR (according to the correct reading you point out) is that the offspring of Isaac will come to "stirring up" evil deeds. The image I think this is supposed to elicit is Israel muddying the normally clear water of their faithfulness to God's commandments by occasionally "fouling" their ways (as you said). The turbid waters will clear by themselves in the normal process of sedimentation. The use of this phrase, <akirut ma<aŝim

may You remember for them the Binding and be filled with compassion concerning them.

In *BR*, this passage is the first section of a three part exegetical composition on Genesis 22:14.[13] If the comment of R. Bibi/R. Yohanan is severed from the verse to which it is attached, it provides us with no information about when in the unfolding story Abraham was to have spoken these words. Clearly the speech was uttered after Isaac was spared, but there is no internal indication of how long. The problem of the connection of the passage with Genesis 22:14 is exacerbated by the fact that this verse is not cited within the comment. So, for example, it might be argued that the comment would have served as well to respond to the question introduced in *BR* 56:11 on Genesis 22:15-16 or in the *LR* passage to be discussed below: "What need was there for this promise?" Typical of midrashic literature, the link between verse and comment is to be puzzled out.

This section can broadly be described as a prayer addressed by Abraham to God.[14] The prayer is comprised of an address, an argument and a petition. Abraham addresses God as "Master of the Universe" and states that, at the very moment God commanded him to offer up Isaac, he "had what to answer," i.e., he had an argument which he did not use. He could have pointed out the contradiction between God's promise of progeny through Isaac (Genesis 21:12) and His command to offer Isaac up as a burnt-offering (22:2). This previously unused but now stated argument is quite remarkable and serves several functions within the passage. In revealing what Abraham did not say at the time of the original command (22:2), the narrator has Abraham reveal something of his character as well as his initial reaction. But the argument also discloses a strategy and an assumption concerning the relationship between Abraham and God.

---

ra<im, is meant to admit that occasionally Israel goes astray, but to give the best possible construction to it and de-emphasize its moral implications as much as possible. See also the comment of Theodor on BR 47:7, p. 475, note to line 5, in which he mentions Loew's suggestion to emend that text to read *<akhirut ma<asim*.

[13]Part two is an exegetical aggadah on the naming of Jerusalem by God; the name of the city reflects God's attempt to effect a compromise between Abraham having named it >*adonai-yir>eh* and Shem calling it *Shalem*. Part three utilizes Genesis 22:14 to project midrashically that God showed Abraham the Temple built, destroyed and permanently rebuilt in the Future to Come.

[14]It might also be described as a monologue. If it is taken as one half of a dialogue between Abraham and God, the other half, God's response, is obviously not included. Two reasons may account for this: 1) as Abraham's statement is about the future, it could only be answered in the future, or 2) the implied answer is to be found in the following biblical verses, Genesis 22:16 ff.

Abraham, of course, is projected as a man accustomed to arguing with God.[15] The narrator appears to suggest that, from Abraham's perspective, he had sufficient rhetorical ammunition at his disposal to cancel or block the command.[16] This representation requires that we alter our view of the patriarch's immediate acceptance of the command to offer Isaac as well as our sense of the balance of power between Abraham and God. The detail of the argument conveys the image of an Abraham in full possession of himself and capable of perceiving the stated contradiction between promise and command as if it were between two biblical verses, in typical Rabbinic fashion. There is another dimension as well: had Abraham used his argument, its content would have indicated the paradoxical nature of the command, indeed its absurdity, thereby reflecting negatively on the Commander. Whatever the implications of this affirmation through denial, the narrator has Abraham make clear that he did not initially respond. He consciously suppressed his rational and emotional responses, his argument and his compassion, in order to do God's will.

The narrator has laid the basis for Abraham's petition in this now highly charged and exceedingly complex opening. The patriarch then requests that, when Isaac's descendants come to "the fouling of bad deeds,"[17] God should remember for them the <aqedah and be filled with compassion. What is it about the <aqedah that God should remember? If we limit our inquiry to this passage, the answer is that God should remember those aspects of the <aqedah which center on and reflect Abraham's reactions: suppression of argument and compassion, obedience, and follow through in response to God's command. In contrast to other representations of the <aqedah, this passage contains no suggestion of the idea of sacrificial atonement, i.e., that Isaac's sacrifice atones for all Israel.[18]

---

[15]This image has its biblical source in the exchange over Sodom in Genesis 18:16-33, but also is reflected in such Rabbinic passages as *BR* 46:3, in which Abraham challenges God concerning the command to become circumcised. In contrast to our passage, in these examples God responds, and in the case of *BR* 46:3, the response is built on the exploitation of an exegesis of the verse, Genesis 17:1.

[16]The image of Abraham having the power to overcome God's decree has its parallels in Rabbinic stories of charismatic Rabbis and their miraculous interventions.

[17]See note 12, above, on translation.

[18]See especially Geza Vermes, *Scripture and Tradition in Judaism* (Leiden: Brill, 1967), pp. 193-227.

The conclusion of Abraham's petition ends abruptly, "and be filled with compassion concerning them."[19] We want some expression of completion such as the one found in the targums *PsJ* and *N* ("and save them") or those in the homiletical midrashim (*LR*: "... and provide atonement for them"; *PRK*: "... and transform for them the Attribute of Judgment into the Attribute of Compassion").[20] However, the argument as we have it is complete. It conforms to a rhetorical pattern which has been described as "an argument from reciprocity," which aims "at giving the same treatment to two situations which are counterparts of each other": i.e., when God commanded Abraham to offer up Isaac, Abraham suppressed his compassion to do God's will; when Isaac's descendants make trouble, God should remember the <aqedah for them and be filled with compassion.[21] From this, of course, we may infer that, when God's compassion is activated and God fulfills Abraham's request, the continuity of Abraham and Isaac's descendants will be assured – thus fulfilling the earlier divine promise. There are several elements of symmetry in the argument, both explicit and implicit:

ABRAHAM	GOD
Assumption: Isaac precious to Abraham	Assumption: Descendants precious to God
Abraham requests	God commands
Didn't speak	Should remember
Abraham did God's will	May it be God's will...
Human compassion	Divine compassion
Abraham subdues his compassion	May God be filled with compassion
Assumption: Willing to sacrifice what is precious	Implication: Should save what is precious

These symmetries suggest a coherent tradition represented here in literary form, crafted to create a unified impression of the characters, the situation and its implications.

---

[19]The same conclusion is found in T. Y. Ta<aniyot 65d, within a exegesis of >adonai yir>eh, which appears to be tacked on to T. Y. Ta<aniyot's version of R. Bibi/R. Yohanan's comment. See below.
[20]*PRK* implies the unstated divine alternative: that in response to Israel's sins, God would exercise His attribute of justice and exact punishment.
[21]See Ch. Perelman and L. Olbrechts-Tyteca, *The New Rhetoric: A Treatise on Argumentation* (Notre Dame: University of Notre Dame Press, 1969), pp. 223 ff. Note the role symmetry plays in "Arguments of Reciprocity" and also the discussion of argumentation by sacrifice, pp. 248 ff.

Finally, the passage does not contain any response from God. In argumentation, the artfully disingenuous stating of the unstated typically invites the response, "Well, had you really said it, then I would have said...," of which there is no trace here. The absence of a response will be treated in the re-presentations of this material in T. Y. Ta<aniyot and *LR*.

Based on this reading of R. Bibi/R.Yohanan's comment, the Rabbinic translation of Genesis 22:14 is approximately as follows: And Abraham prayed to God (first stating his "argument"), that God remember the <aqedah and be filled with compassion. The presuppositions of this translation are minimally 1) that the verb *qara*>, "called" [*Tanakh*: "named"] is to be understood as "called upon" or "prayed"; 2) that the content of the prayer needed articulation; and 3) that the phrase *yhvh* [read: >*adonai*] *yir*>*eh* is to be understood as "May the Lord see = remember." As we shall see later, each element of this reconstruction is assumed in the targums *PsJ* and *N*, both of which have also absorbed and transformed much of the material found in the comment of R. Bibi.[22]

II

T. Y. Ta<aniyot 65c-d to Ta<anit 2:4[23]:

Mishnah:

After the first he says, May He who answered Abraham at Mt. Moriah answer you and hear the sound of your cry this day. Blessed are You, O Lord, Redeemer of Israel.

G'mara>:

1. Wasn't it Isaac who was redeemed? Since Isaac was redeemed, it is as if all Israel was redeemed.
2. R. Bibi the son of Abba in the name of R. Yohanan: Abraham said before the Holy One Blessed be He, "Master of the Universe, it was revealed and known before You that at the very moment that You told me to offer up Isaac my son, I had what to answer and to say before You. Previously you said to me, 'for it is through Isaac that offspring shall be continued for you (Gen. 21:12)'; and now You say to me 'and offer him there as a burnt-offering (Gen. 22:2)'! God forbid, I didn't do that but subdued my inclination and did Your will. Thus, may it be Your will, that when the descendants of Isaac my

---

[22]So also the *FT*. See Michael Klein, *op. cit.*, I, 54 and 140. The same structural elements are found in *TO*, but the content is different. See below.

[23]The translation is based on the Krotoshin edition and the text published by Louis Ginzberg in *Yerushalmi Fragments from the Geniza* (New York: Jewish Theological Seminary, 1909), I, 176.

son enter into trouble and have no one who will plead on their behalf, may You plead on their behalf."
3. >adonai yir>eh: may You remember for them the Binding of Isaac their father and be filled with compassion concerning them.

Ta<anit 2 deals with the order and detail of the liturgy to be utilized during public fasts. Mishnah 2:4 contains the endings or "seals" of several special liturgical compositions previously listed in 2:3, which were to be inserted into the daily eighteen benedictions. T. Y. Ta<aniyot 65c-d is an extended comment on the opening section of Ta<anit 2:4.

The G'mara> poses a literalizing question: "Wasn't it Isaac who was redeemed?" The focus of this query is the reference to God as the "Redeemer of Israel" which appears at the conclusion of the seventh benediction, into which the first additional prayer for the fast is inserted. The question is also linked to the reference in Ta<anit 2:4 that God answered Abraham at Mt. Moriah. If it is true that God responded to Abraham by saving Isaac, why is God here referred to as Redeemer of Israel and by implication why is he not called Redeemer of Isaac? The G'mara>'s answer is: "Since Isaac was redeemed, it is as if all Israel was redeemed." But what does this answer mean? A reasonable explanation is that since Isaac was the ancestor of Israel, had he been slaughtered, there would have been no Jewish people. But this "reasonable" answer is neither spelled out nor dealt with yet.

Two unstated questions now explain the inclusion of R. Bibi/R. Yohanan's comment in the G'mara>: 1) since Ta<anit 2:4 relates that God answered Abraham, what was it that Abraham said, and 2) in what way did the saving of Isaac have an impact on the redemption of all Israel? As we shall see, the "fit" of the passage here is problematic. The immediate association one might have with the Mishnah passage and the G'mara>'s literalizing question and answer is that Abraham must have offered a prayer that God spare Isaac's life. Yet neither the biblical text nor the midrashic commentaries indicate that Abraham pleaded for Isaac! At most, Rabbinic expansions of Genesis 22:2 emphasize delaying tactics.[24] As in *BR*, Abraham's prayer reflects a temporal sequence in which Isaac has already undergone the <aqedah, eliminating any possibility of connecting it with some hypothetical prayer at the point of Genesis 22:2.

---

[24]A prayer in which Abraham pleads for Isaac is mentioned in the late Midrash Va-Yosha. See *Bet ha-Midrasch*, ed. Aldolph Jellinek (photo-offset; Jerusalem, 1967), I, 3. I thank Marc Bregman for calling it to my attention. On Midrash Va-Yosha, see Moshe David Herr in *Encyclopaedia Judaica*, XVI, 1517. On delaying tactics, see *BR* 55:7, p. 590, lines 1-3; p. 592, lines 4-5, and parallels.

The opening of R. Bibi bar Abba/R. Yohanan's comment is roughly identical with what we found in *BR*. Four variations deserve comment. First, in contrast to *BR*, the narrator here has Abraham expand his address: "it was revealed and known before You that at the very moment that You told me to offer up Isaac my son...," i.e., that God knew that Abraham had a response to His command to offer up Isaac as a burnt-offering. The phrase "it was revealed and known before You" is an ubiquitous formula in Rabbinic literature.[25] However, this acknowledgment of God's omniscience here is also the first hint of an attempt to soften the daring aspects of the *BR* narrative. Second, in contrast to *BR*, Abraham bases his plea on the fact that he had suppressed his "inclination" to do what God wanted. Why does the writer utilize "inclination" rather than "compassion," found in *BR*? From the context it is clear that the "argument" which popped into Abraham's mind and now pops out of his mouth, which he did not and now does use, is unacceptable to the writer both in terms of his conception of Abraham's character and theologically. Since it is found in Abraham's mouth, i.e., it already existed as an essential element in the tradition, it could not be eliminated but rather explained by attributing its source to the "evil inclination" which Abraham subdued. Third, in contrast to *BR*, T. Y. Ta‹aniyot states the problem Abraham foresees in this language: "that when the descendants of Isaac my son enter into trouble." The vague phrase "into trouble" contrasts sharply with the reference to the "fouling of bad deeds" of Isaac's descendants in *BR*. Potentially it shifts blame from the Israelites to the nations who subjugate and oppress them, a theme also alluded to in both *PsJ* and *N*. In that regard, it is appropriate wording to introduce what follows. Fourth, in contrast to *BR*, T. Y. Ta‹aniyot concludes "and have no one who will plead on their behalf, may You plead on their behalf." The expression *l'lamed ‹aléhem sanegoryah*, "to plead on behalf of," is common to the courtroom context and also typically used in settings in which God defends His people before the Princes of the Nations. It is also symmetrically appropriate for what Abraham might have done on

---

[25]Because *PsJ* and *N* contain a parallel to this as a comment to the first occurrence of >*adonai yir>eh*, it might be argued that its inclusion here is an echo of earlier exegesis. However, the acknowledgment of God's knowledge, by human beings or by God, is found throughout Rabbinic literature. See, for example, *BR* 92:9, Exodus Rabah 2:5, Numbers Rabah 21:2, Deuteronomy Rabah 11:10, Esther Rabah 8:7, Ruth Rabah 7:1, Ecclesiastes Rabah 7:24 and comment on *PsJ* below. Note: the phrase appears in only two of the mss. cited by Theodor. See *BR*, p. 607, variants to line 4. See conclusion.

behalf of Isaac[26]; and it fits the academy/court environment of talmudic debate. Whatever the reason, the terminology suggests a line of thinking quite distinct from that of *BR*.[27]

The brief exegesis of Genesis 22:14 which follows appears to have been cited in order to solidify, explain or "prove" why God should plead for Isaac's descendants. In fact, as a separate exegetical unit it appears to have existed prior to the formulation of R. Bibi/R. Yohanan's comment here. Its language so closely parallels that of the lemma and conclusion of Abraham's prayer in *BR* that it is as if the redactor had abbreviated that text by blocking and deleting the body of the comment. The technique and meaning of the exegesis parallels the third element in the midrashic translation of Genesis 22:14 stated above. *>adonai yir>eh* is understood to mean: "May God see = remember." The object of the verb is the <*aqedah*[28]; and the hope is that God will become filled with compassion for the Israelites. As in *BR*, T. Y. Ta<anyiot emphasizes Abraham's role in the <*aqedah*, this time with the superhuman act of suppressing his inclination. Finally, this exegesis concludes with the same abruptness as *BR*. The G'mara> continues with an aggadic reference to the ram's horn as the vehicle to bring God to save the Israelites. This comment is clearly interpolated as it inverts the order of the biblical text to comment on Genesis 22:13 after Genesis

---

[26]Is the argument of reciprocity which we found in *BR* employed here, and are the same symmetrical components utilized? In general the structure of the argument is the same: i.e.,because Abraham didn't argue for Isaac, but did God's will, God should plead for Isaac's descendants. But not all the elements found in *BR* appear here and the symmetry is different:

ABRAHAM	GOD
Assumption: Isaac precious to Abraham	*Assumption: Descendants precious*
Acknowledgment of God's knowledge	*to God*
Abraham requests	*God commands*
Subdued inclination to save	*[Should subdue inclination to punish]*
Didn't speak/argue	*Should plead on behalf*
Assumption: Willing to sacrifice	*Assumption: Should save what is*
what is precious	*precious*

[27]Urbach places this passage into the context of a discussion of "the atonement of Isaac," and cites a number of significant parallels. As will be indicated, however, the emphasis remains on the narrative describing Abraham's actions. See, Urbach *The Sages* (Jerusalem: Magnes Press, 1969), p. 448 and n. 57.

[28]If we were to assume the comment is on the second occurrence, vocalized *>adonai yera>eh*, it might be translated "O Lord, may it appear [to You; i.e., may the <*aqedah* be recalled by You]," the subject of the verb being the <*aqedah*. However, there is no way to determine here how to vocalize *yr>h* or whether the citation refers to the first or second occurrence of the phrase in Genesis 22:14. And, the comment has no relation to the ways in which the targums deal with the second occurrence.

22:14. However, it contains what *BR* lacks, God's response to Abraham's plea.

The analysis of this passage suggests that the redactor of the G'mara> in T. Y. Ta<aniyot responded to and transformed R. Bibi/R. Yohanan's comment either as found in *BR* or in a similar form. He changed it to diminish the unacceptable aspects of Abraham's response to God and to make it fit the needs of the talmudic discussion. His use of the brief exegesis indicates either that he abbreviated the lemma and comment or that it existed as a separate unit of tradition prior to its inclusion at this point in the text. In either case, the exegesis presumes the version of the comment in *BR*, in which Abraham suppressed his "compassion," and not the version here.

III

Leviticus Rabah 29:9: Another Interpretation: "In the seventh month (Lev. 23:24)."

1. R. Berechya used to call it the month of the promise. A month in which the Holy One Blessed be He promised to our father Abraham that "I'm going to redeem your descendants," for thus it is written, "By Myself I swear," the LORD declares (Gen. 22:16).
2. What need was there for this oath?
3. R. Bibi the son of Abba in the name of R. Yohanan: Abraham said before the Holy One Blessed be He, "Master of the Universe, it was revealed and known before Your Throne of Glory that at the very moment You said to me, 'Take your son, your favored one, Isaac. (Genesis 22:2),' I should have answered you and said to you: 'Previously you said to me, 'for it is through Isaac that offspring shall be continued for you (Gen. 21:12)'; and today [*ha-yom!*] You say to me 'Take your son, your favored one (Gen. 22:2).' Rather, just as I should have answered you, but didn't answer you, so when the descendants of Isaac come to transgressions and bad deeds, may You remember for them the Binding of Isaac their father and provide atonement for them."

LR 29 is a literary homily on Leviticus 23:24, the reading for Ro>sh Ha-shanah according to the Palestinian custom. This passage is a section of the *gufa>*, the "body" or exegetical portion of the homily, and is one of a series of comments on the verse.[29]

---

[29] On the term *gufa>*, see the references in N. Weider, "Three Sermons for the Fast for Rain from the Geniza," in *Tarbiz*, LIV (1985), 38, n. 100.

The section is composed of three parts: 1) an opening interpretation of the lemma in Aramaic by R. Berechya, followed by an independent elaboration of his comment in Hebrew which concludes with the citation of Genesis 22:16; 2) a question on the verse; and 3) the comment of R. Bibi/R. Yohanan. R. Berechya interprets "In the seventh (*sh'ūi<i*) month (Leviticus 23:24)" as "the month of the promise (*sh'ūu<ta>*)." This re-reading establishes the theme of the entire passage as that of God's oath (Genesis 22:16), which is understood as signifying God's promise to "redeem Abraham's descendants." The question which follows provides the transition to the rest of the passage, shifts our focus to the oath in Genesis 22:16 and represents a "traditional" query to this verse.[30] The comment of R. Bibi/R. Yohanan is cited to answer this question by indicating that God's promise was a direct response to this prayer.

The formulation of the comment here both parallels and differs from that in *BR* and T.Y. Ta<aniyot. *LR* expands the trope found in T. Y. Ta<aniyot, "it was revealed and known," by adding "before Your Throne of Glory." Although this addition is not unique to this passage, it is the first of several variations which make it appropriate to its liturgical setting in a homily for the New Year. The shift in Abraham's introduction from "I had what to answer You" to "I should have answered you," reflects the continuing tendency to diminish the daring representation of Abraham in the other two sources by focussing on Abraham's duty rather than on his strategy or the content of his argument. Within the argument, the use of "today" in place of "now" is an allusion to the New Year, and may be one of the sources of the later comment that the <aqedah took place on this date.[31] In contrast to the two other sources, *LR* merely states that, although Abraham should have responded to God, he didn't. Finally, *LR* includes an addition, "and provide atonement for them," which further links the passage with the festival period.

This passage is significantly less powerful than the versions we find in *BR* or T. Y. Ta<aniyot. There is no reference to the suppression of compassion or inclination, nor to the desire to do God's will, significant omissions from a dramatic and religious perspective. The symmetry of

---

[30]The question elicited various aggadic responses. See, for example, *BR* 56:11, 608.

[31]*Pesikta Rabbati*, ed. M. Friedmann (Vienna: Privately Published, 1880), 171b; "Lection for the Second Day of Rosh Hashanah: A Homily Containing the Legend of the Ten Trials of Abraham [Hebrew texts]", ed. Lewis M. Barth, *Hebrew Union College Annual*, LVIII (1987), Hebrew Section: p. 40, 60r,12; and *Midrash B're>shit Rabati*, ed. Ch. Albeck (Jerusalem: M'qiẓé Nirdamim: Jerusalem, 1940), p.91.

human and divine compassion is altogether lacking, as is the assumed symmetry of the "evil inclination" and God's Attribute of Judgment/ Justice.[32] Apart from the general context of *LR* 29, the application of the passage to the theme of "atonement" is not prepared for, nor is it clear why, if God remembers the <aqedah, He should provide "atonement" for Isaac's descendants. These differences seem to be the result of the decision to make this passage fit the "liturgical" context of the literary homily.

IV

Scholars have developed a considerable body of evidence that the targums retain traces of the earliest strata of Palestinian biblical exegesis, i.e., prior to the first century C.E.[33] But it is equally true that targumic texts contain additions to the biblical material of which there are numerous parallels in Rabbinic and especially midrashic literature. In such cases, do the targums reflect the creative source of the elaborations found in midrashic collections, or do they serve as a kind of "reader's digest" of midrashic discussions, encapsulating these discussions as well as the exegetical issues on which they are based?

The following discussion of Targum *Pseudo-Jonathan* and Targum *Neophyti* to Genesis 22:14 will be preceded by a brief analysis of this verse in Targum *Onqelos (TO)*. This procedure is not based on the assumption that *TO* precedes *PsJ*, nor is its use intended to resolve the exceedingly complex issues of the dating and relationship between *TO*,

---

[32] How does the argument of reciprocity work here, and what are the symmetrical components? The structure of the argument is broadly the same as in the two other sources, but the justification is different. Thus, because Abraham didn't argue for Isaac, God should atone for Isaac's descendants. In addition, there is some difference in symmetry:

ABRAHAM	GOD
Assumption: Isaac precious to Abraham	Assumption: Descendants precious to God
Acknowledgment of God's knowledge	
Abraham requests	Implied: God promises
Should have answered	Should remember
Didn't answer	Should provide atonement
Assumption: Willing to sacrifice what is precious	Should forgive

[33] However, the pre-Rabbinic material on Genesis 22:14 is limited. For the early witnesses, see *Biblia Hebraica Stuttgartensia* (Stuttgart: Württembergische Bibelanstalt, 1977), to 22:14. Jubilees adds to its repetition of the verse, on the phrase "in the mountain the Lord has seen," the comment "It is Mount Zion," which will be echoed in the reference to the Sanctuary in *N* and *FT*. "Jubilees," in *The Old Testament Pseudepigrapha*, ed. James A. Charlesworth (Garden City: Doubleday, 1985), II, 91, v. 19:13.

PsJ and *N*.³⁴ The purpose of this procedure is to allow us to see at work common assumptions in the targumic process, even where the collections are significantly different in time, place and language and where similar exegetical assumptions lead to quite opposite conclusions.

> 1.) *Onqelos*³⁵: Abraham worshipped and prayed. There, in that place, he said before YVY, "Here may the [future] generations worship." Thus it shall be said – as is still the case – "In this mountain, Abraham worshipped before YVY."

TO transforms the verse from a naming event marking the location of a theophany to a scene linking Abraham's worship with the site. The prayer Abraham uttered at that moment is fulfilled, and the later generations for whom he prayed respond by acknowledging what Abraham did.

TO translates *qara>*, "called" [*Tanakh*: "named"], with a doublet and understands it to refer to "calling upon" God, in worship and prayer.³⁶ It reads *shem* [lit. "the name of"] as *sham*, "there," and takes the next phrase in its simple sense "in that place." *TO*'s rendering "he [Abraham] said before YVY," typically de-anthropomorphizes the Hebrew by having Abraham pray before God, and also serves to introduce the prayer which is the targumist's addition to the text: "Here may the generations worship." The word *ha-yom* – "whence the present (*ha-yom*)" - is translated *ka-yoma> haden*. This phrase is used rather frequently to translate *ka-yom ha-zeh*, which often has the sense "as is now/still the case."³⁷ De-anthropomorphization continues with

---

³⁴See the summary of the scholarly literature in R. T. White's unpublished doctoral dissertation, *A Linguistic Analysis of the Targum to Chronicles with Specific Reference to its Relationship with Other Forms of Aramaic* (Oxford University, 1981), pp. 7-36; Shirley Lund and Julia Foster, *Variant Versions of Targumic Traditions within Codex Neofiti 1* (Missoula: Scholars Press, 1977), pp. 1-18; Gerald J. Kuiper, *The Pseudo-Jonathan Targum and its Relationship to Targum Onkelos* (Rome: Institutum Patristicum Augustinianum, 1972), pp. 6-41. On *PsJ* and its place within targumic literature, see Michael Sokoloff, *A Dictionary of Palestinian Jewish Aramaic* (Ramat-Gan: Bar Ilan University Press, 1990), p. 20, n. 2, and E. M. Cook, *Rewriting the Bible: the Text and Language of the Pseudo-Jonathan Targum* (Ph.D. diss. UCLA, 1986), pp. 40-53, 105-6.
³⁵*The Bible in Aramaic*, ed. Alexander Sperber (Leiden: Brill, 1959), Vol. I: The Pentateuch According to Targum Onkelos.
³⁶On targumic doublets, see the comment of Michael Klein, *Geniza Manuscripts of the Palestinian Targum to the Pentateuch* (Cincinnati: Hebrew Union College Press, 1986), I, xxxi.
³⁷See Genesis 50:20, and esp. Deuteronomy 2:30; 4:20; 4:38; 8:18; 10:15; 29:27. It is to be noted that some manuscripts of *TO* read *b'yoma> haden*, which would definitely emphasize both the specific day of the <*aqedah* and later celebrations.

the substitution of Abraham's actions for God's at the end of the translation of the verse. This conclusion indicates that later generations still acknowledge that this was the site upon which Abraham worshipped.[38]

TO appears to remove the verse from its context; the <aqedah is not mentioned. The hypothetical historical stance of the narrator is in a period in which the Temple still stood in Jerusalem. *TO* shares with *BR* the interpretation that Genesis 22:14 means that Abraham prayed, and similarly conveys the content of the prayer, although it has no relation to the content of the prayer in R. Bibi/R. Yohanan's comment.

> 2.) Targum *Pseudo-Jonathan*[39]: And Abraham confessed and prayed there, in that place. And he said, "I plead before YYY. It is revealed before You that there was no guile in my heart, and that I desired to perform your decree joyfully. Thus, when the descendants of Isaac, my son, enter into a time of trouble [affliction], You will remember for them and answer them, and save them. And all those [future] generations which are going to arise shall say, 'in this mountain Abraham bound Isaac his son, and there the Shekinah of YYY was revealed upon him.'"

PsJ shares material with *TO*, but also diverges from it.[40] In addition, it appears to echo and transform elements of R. Bibi/R. Yohanan's comment, whether in *BR* or T. Y. Ta<aniyot. It continues the doubling of *qara>* found in *TO*, but in place of *plḥ*, "worshipped," *PsJ* reads *>odi*, which I have translated "confessed."[41] The verb is used to underline Abraham's strikingly self-justifying remark "there was no guile in my heart."

Why does the targumist feel the need to insert this apology in Abraham's speech? It is not prepared for in the biblical text, in *TO* or in *PsJ*'s extensive midrashic translation of the previous verses of Genesis 22. As the remainder of Abraham's plea found here is roughly identical with Abraham's prayer in R. Bibi/R. Yohanan's comment, the most likely hypothesis is that the targumist is either responding to the text as we find it in *BR* or T. Y. Ta>aniyot, or to some oral embodiment of it. He

---

This phrase translates *ba-yom ha-zeh*, "On that [this] very day"; see Genesis 17:11; Exodus 19:1, etc. For variants, see Sperber, I, p. 32, to Genesis 22:14

[38]Does this refer to biblical generations or *TO*'s own contemporaries?

[39]Clarke, *op. cit.*

[40]See note 33, above. Also, Klein, *FT*, 1-24 ("Introductory Essays"), for arguments on the relationships between the targumim.

[41]It is also possible to translate the verb as a Hebraism, "gave thanks," in which case it might imply an unstated prayer of thanksgiving that Isaac's life was spared, although this is unlikely. The same verb is used in *PsJ*'s translation of Leviticus 26:40 ff., where it is found in a context with the phrase *sha<at >aniki*, "time of trouble," and God remembering covenants.

has evaluated the representation of Abraham's argument and strategy in those texts and replaces them with a phrase which denies what R. Bibi/R. Yohanan's comment affirms: "there was no guile in my heart." He also adds the term "joyfully," perhaps to further undercut the emotion of anger which might be read into Abraham having suppressed his compassion, as in *BR*, or the possibility that the "evil inclination" might have gotten the best of Abraham, as in T. Y. Ta<aniyot. From the perspective of translation, *PsJ* renders the first occurrence of >*adonai yir>eh* as "It is revealed before You..." and places it in the introduction to Abraham's plea. As previously noted, the acknowledgment of God's omniscience is typical of Rabbinic aggadah and common to *PsJ* and *N* as well.[42] Used here, the phrase continues the tendency to transform Abraham, theologically sanitize his argument, and remove from him any of the negative connotations which might be inferred from the formulation found in the midrashic source.

Abraham's petition here differs significantly in its opening part from *TO*; although it repeats the reference to location, there is no trace of the hope that future generations will pray in this place. Nor is there any direct hint of Abraham's argument, as found in *BR* and T. Y. Ta<aniyot. Further, it is of note that God is called upon simply to remember; the <*aqedah* is not mentioned! The immediate referent of "remember" must be Abraham's lack of guile and willingness to perform God's command joyfully as a basis for saving Isaac's offspring in the future.

The concluding midrashic additions and translation, "And all those ...revealed upon him," may be understood either as the continuation of Abraham's prayer, as translated above, or as the targumist's addition. In this two-fold conclusion, *PsJ* stresses Abraham's role in the <*aqedah* and the ancient understanding of the location as one in which a theophany occurred. First, although it appears to build on *TO*'s reference to "generations," it replaces the generalizing comment that "Abraham worshiped" with the specific reference to his act of binding Isaac. Second, it re-introduces in Rabbinic language the ancient interpretation found in the LXX, "God appeared," but relates this directly to Abraham: "there the Shekinah of YYY was revealed upon him."

> 3.) Targum *Neophyti*[43]: And Abraham worshipped and prayed in the name of the *memra>* of the Lord, and he said: "I beg mercy from before You; everything is manifest and known before You, [including] that there was no doubt in my heart the first time that

---

[42]See Clarke, *op. cit.* Key-Word-In-Context Concordance, p. 142, and the same verses in *N*.

[43]*N*, p. 129. I have consulted, but not followed the English translation on p. 552.

You told me to offer up Isaac my son, and to make of him dust and ashes before You; rather, I immediately rose up early in the morning, and immediately performed Your *memra>* joyfully, and I fulfilled Your decree; and now, when his children will stand in an hour of oppression, You will remember the binding of Isaac their father, and hear the sound of their prayers and answer them and save them from all distress; for the generations that are destined to rise after him will say; 'On the Mount of the Holy Temple of the Lord that Abraham offered up Isaac his son; and on this mountain the *<iqar sh'khinta>* of the Lord was revealed.'"

N's translation strongly links Abraham's prayer to the *<aqedah*, while retaining some of the layers of the tradition which are present in *BR, TO* and *PSJ*. For example, *N* utilizes the same initial verbs as *TO*, but understands *shem ha-maqom* as "the name of God," and then uses the typical targumic circumvention, *memra>*, to introduce the prayer. In so doing, *N* contains no trace of the emphasis on location found in *TO* and echoed in *PsJ* at the beginning of their translations. *N* then continues parallel to *PsJ* in the presentation of Abraham's introduction to his prayer, with the exception that he uses *palgu*, which I have translated "doubt," rather than *PsJ*'s "guile." The lexical range of this word includes "difference of opinion," and it appears in legal contexts which convey the technical sense of "argument."[44] The choice of the term by *N* confirms an opposition to the representation of Abraham in *BR* and T. Y. Ta<aniyot which focuses on and denies what those texts explicitly say, that Abraham did have an argument which he could have used, but did not use. Now, in place of *PsJ's* general statements regarding Abraham's willingness to perform God's decree, *N* explicitly mentions the content of the decree, to offer up Isaac, and details Abraham's actions by paraphrasing targumic translations of Genesis 22:3. With minor differences and some significant additions, *N* then continues to parallel *PsJ* from Abraham's request that God save Isaac's children through the conclusion of the passage. In agreement with *BR* and *LR*, but in contrast to *PsJ*, *N* relates that God should remember "the Binding of Isaac."[45] He also adds the identification of the mountain as the Holy Temple of the Lord, and the emphasis that Abraham *qrb*,

---

[44]See Sokoloff, *Dictionary*, p. 434. For an example of a parallel use in Hebrew, see *BR* 1:7. In that passage it is argued that no creature is *ḥaluqah*, i.e., no one would hold the untenable position that two deities created the world. Note that the word is used in same context as the term *g'zerah*, "heavenly decree," i.e., an act perceived as punishment from a human perspective. The same term appears in *PsJ* to describe God's command in Genesis 22:2.

[45]*BR* has simply "the *<aqedah*"; *LR* and *N* have the full phrase "*<aqedat Yiẓḥaq*." These terms are used interchangeably, and the difference is not significant for the argument presented here.

"offered up" his son Isaac there, rather than *kpt*, "bound him." The idea that God should remember the "Binding of Isaac" as the basis for saving the generations from distress reinforces the centrality of this event, yet the translation still focuses the justification for God to save Isaac's descendants on Abraham's character and action as the central meaning of the <*aqedah* itself.[46]

Conclusions

The transformations of *BR* 56:10 reflect the conscious decisions of writers or redactors who reflected on and were uncomfortable with aspects of the representation of Abraham in this tradition. Evidence for the beginning of this process is already found in T. Y. Ta<aniyot 65d, *LR* 29:9 and *PRK* 23:9. The writers or redactors of *PsJ* and *N* carry the process to its conclusion by denying what the midrashic and talmudic texts affirm. The remaining question has to do with the utilization of R. Bibi/R. Yohanan's statement in *BR* as an exegetical comment on Genesis 22:14. We have seen that the statement works equally well in *LR* 29:9. Therefore, it is appropriate to ask if the juxtaposition of verse and comment in *BR* 56:10 assumes an understanding of the verse which is logically and chronologically prior to the original creation of R. Bibi's comment and without which the placement of this comment with the verse in *BR* makes no sense. Any answer to this question must reflect the complex interaction between targumic translation and midrashic imagination, as well as the problematic relationship between the targum texts and the texts of Midrash and Talmud.

In his introduction to *BR*, Albeck already examined the citations of targum in *BR*. He concluded that *BR* utilized ancient targumic material which was similar to but not identical with *TO* and the later "Palestinian" targums, *PsJ* and presumably the *Fragment-Targums* (*FT*) published by Kahle. His excellent analysis did not deal with the issue raised here. From the material presented above, it would appear that the author of *BR* has reread the opening of Genesis 22:14 in light of an ancient tradition of translation reflected in the targums we have discussed. Where *qr*> is used in the biblical text in a phrase in which God is invoked, the targums translate with the following words: *plḥ*, *ẓli*

---

[46]Avigdor Shinan, *The Aggadah in the Aramaic Targums to the Pentateuch* (Jerusalem: Hebrew University, 1979), p. 324, cites this passage and parallels as one of the many examples of *z'khut* >*aōot*, "the merits of the Ancestors," in targumic literature; and following him, B. Barry Levy, *Targum Neophyti 1: A Textual Study* (New York: University Press of America, 1986), pp. 165-66. The probable source of the comments of Shinan and Levy is the analysis of T. Y. Ta<aniyot 65d by Urbach, who discussed this passage in relation to Rabbinic attitudes toward *z'khut* >*aōot*. See Urbach, *op. cit.*, p. 448 and note 57.

and >*odi*, either alone or in combination with one another, as we found in their rendering of Genesis 22:14. Examples include: Genesis 4:26, *TO*; 12:8, *TO, PsJ, N*; 13:4, *TO, PsJ, N*; 21:33, *TO, PsJ,N,FT*; Genesis 26:25, *TO, PsJ, N*; Genesis 33:20, *TO, N*; Genesis 16:13, *TO, PsJ, N,FT*. Consequently, it is reasonable to think that this is a relatively early translation which precedes *BR* 56:10 and is the pretext for bringing the comment of R.Bibi/R. Yohanan there. Incidentally, it should be noted that by the end of the Amoraic period this ancient and traditional translation has led to the identification of *q'ri>ah* as one of the terms to denote prayer.[47]

However, the direction of the exegetical process is reversed regarding the phrase >*adonai yir>eh*. As previously mentioned, the acknowledgment of God's omniscience, expressed in the phrase "it is revealed and known before You," is found frequently in midrashic texts as well as in both Talmuds. Clearly, it is not used in T. Y. Ta<aniyot as an exegetical echo of Genesis 22:14. It is reasonable to assume that the phrase, in a modified form, is absorbed into the targumic translation of Genesis 22:14 from the elaboration of R.Bibi/R. Yohanan's comment in T. Y. Ta<aniyot, *LR* and *PRK*, and is not an original targumic rendering of >*adonai yir>eh*. The phrase, of course, also fits nicely the typical targumic pattern of circumventing anthropomorphisms.

In regard to technique, it is as if *PsJ* and *N* exploit >*adonai yir>eh* as an unstated lemma to which is attached the affirmation of God's omniscience and denial of Abraham's "guile" or "doubt."

Finally, *PsJ* and *N* are allied with T. Y. Ta<aniyot in the image of the projected problem to be faced by the descendants of Isaac: it is either "trouble" or "oppression" or being saved from "distress," but not the "bad deeds" of *BR* or *LR*. There is no echo in *PsJ* or *N* to Genesis 22:14 of a Ro>sh Ha-shanah connection as we found in *LR*. Nevertheless, the reference to the >*aqedah* found in *BR* and *LR* resurfaces, along with a Rabbinic rephrasing of *TO*'s emphasis on place.

The complex interaction which is reflected in the above description suggests the need for further close examination and comparison of texts both within *and* between Rabbinic documents and literary genres.

---

[47] See Lamentations Rabah 3:15:60, citing Isaiah 65:24, and later parallel Deuteronomy Rabah 2:12; see also Deuteronomy Rabah 2:1, citing Psalm 18:7, which is not found in Lieberman's edition of Deuteronomy Rabah, p. 36.

2

Yohanan Ben Zakkai at Yavneh: Merkavah and Messiah

By Uri D. Herscher

A generation ago the messianic idea seemed on the wane in Jewish life; at most and at best it was felt as an historical memory, not a contemporary impulse in the Jewish street. Surely there were some souls who read in the horrors visited on European Jews during the first half of the century a prefiguring of the messianic advent – the *hevlé mashiah*, as it were – but Jewry as a whole exhibited scant interest in such expectations. Not even the rebirth of Jewish political independence in 1948 stirred much by way of messianic fancies: with Jerusalem all but cut off from the rest of the State and with the Jewish Quarter in the Old City obliterated and the Western Wall in enemy hands, who could anticipate a messianic denouement? But the 1967 war changed all that, and in the years since "Messiah Now!" has become an increasingly insistent craving in certain prominent circles. Today, it seems no exaggeration to say, a new messianic movement has taken shape in the Jewish street, not only in Israel but in the Diaspora, too.

What such a development portends for the Jewish future can only be guessed at, but no doubt many Jews will see in the future a messianic threat rather than a messianic hope. They will have in mind the messianic movements of past generations and the consequences these movements had for Jewish life. Those who today easily restrain their messianic enthusiasm will find these historical "proof texts" instructive. The present essay, dedicated to a great teacher, Samson Levey, a man with a messianic memory, will seek to understand how a much earlier – a first-century – generation related to the messianic prospect, and negotiated its way through the fearful difficulties inherent in an upsurge of messianic passion. The question is central to the experience of the first-century patriarch and tana> Rabban Yohanan ben Zakkai.

Yohanan is reputed to have predicted the fall of the Jerusalem Temple years before its occurrence. The prediction – if indeed he made it – may suggest supernatural powers on his part. If, however, Yohanan was less a visionary than a masterful analyst of political events and social upheaval, and if he was knowledgeable about Roman intentions and military might, there is no need to assume that he displayed superhuman abilities.

Many Jerusalemites before the revolution of 66 C.E. thought contemporary Jewish society on the verge of a complete collapse. They anticipated the ruination of their national and cultural life.[1]

It was clear to them that the Zealots, driven by what appear to have been messianic urgencies, would force the Roman authorities into a position necessitating retaliation. Given her inveterate practice of draining subject provinces of their economic resources, Rome could not tolerate a rebellious Judaea. Yohanan ben Zakkai understood this and divined the probable finale of the drama.

He must also have sensed that the Temple was diminishing as a relevant institution in Jewish life. As a new post-biblical elite, the Pharisees, gained power and as the people became increasingly disenchanted with the Sadducees, the traditional priesthood, and with the difficulties posed by a strict pentateuchal law, which had much more to do with an already obsolete agrarianism than with the commercial society of the Greco-Roman Mediterranean Basin, the Temple lost its vital role and became increasingly vestigial, a testimony to the glorious past. Therefore, Yohanan's prediction that the Temple was going to fall may very well have resulted from an insightful understanding of the contemporary situation. The fall of the Temple appeared imminent both in a physical and a social sense.[2] This was even more evident when the Roman armies under Vespasian and his son Titus marched on Jerusalem and finally laid the city under siege. It was their inevitable response to the rebellion which had spread throughout Judaea. As each succeeding stronghold of the Zealots fell, refugees from the war-torn villages streamed into Jerusalem in order to find sanctuary in the continuing war.

We do not know the complete make-up of the Jerusalem community and its leadership during these years (69-70), although we can be sure that the spectrum ranged from the hard-core Zealots to the conservative

---

[1] T. B. Yoma> 39b; cf. Mark 13:1-2, and see also E. E. Urbach, *The Sages: Their Concepts and Beliefs* (Jerusalem: Magnes Press, 1975), I, 666.
[2] H. S. Hoenig, *The Great Sanhedrin* (Philadelphia: Dropsie College, 1953), p. 112. Hoenig dates the fall of the Temple as occurring four years after the Sanhedrin was disbanded. The termination of the Sanhedrin would provide evidence for the impending doom of the Temple.

pro-Roman element.³ There was constant friction between the various groups as each attempted to exert influence over the community. Cecil Roth, in describing how the Qumran scrolls mirror the story of the fall of Jerusalem, paid close attention to the opposing factions.⁴

One of the more extreme of the Zealot groups with real influence in Jerusalem was led by Abba Sikra, Yohanan's nephew. Roth asserts that Yohanan himself had Zealot tendencies which he effectively suppressed. It was, Roth states, Yohanan's ability to overcome his own anti-Romanism which assured Jewish life a post-*Ḥurban* future.⁵

Before the destruction of the Temple the Zealots could claim wide popular support.⁶ The best evidence for this lies in the fact that Jerusalem did not capitulate, although a small, yet significant portion of the population thought that surrender would be the best course. Political conditions were such that inside Jerusalem the Zealots were preparing to battle the Roman legions. Outside the city, the Roman armies prepared an all-encompassing siege of the city. Undoubtedly the Roman armies were more in accord as to their course of action than the numerous factions among the Jerusalemites could ever be. In every account of Yohanan's escape, for instance, we are told how a Zealot group took the extreme and controversial action of setting the Jerusalem storehouses aflame.⁷

It was this very tumultuous and bitter atmosphere which set the scene for Yohanan's escape from Jerusalem. In view of everything that has been said, the legends surrounding Yohanan's departure from the besieged city tell a bizarre and extraordinary story. But, then, the total image of Yohanan ben Zakkai is extraordinary. As a member of the Jerusalem community, Yohanan was familiar with various members of the political structure. On the one hand, he was the uncle of Abba Sikra ben Battiah, who headed one of the Zealot factions, and, on the other hand, he signed the *k'tubah* of the daughter of the conservative Nakdimon ben Gurion, one of the four councilors of the city. The interests of Abba Sikra and Nakdimon were in extreme conflict, but

---

³Cecil Roth, "The Zealots, a Jewish Religious Sect," *Judaism*, VIII, 33. Roth divides the different political tendencies among Jews during the rebellion into five categories: a) Pro-Roman; b) "Moderate" revolutionaries (including Yohanan ben Zakkai); c) Nationalists; d) Zealots; and e) Hard-core Zealots.
⁴Roth, "The Jewish Revolt against the Romans in the Light of the Dead Sea Scrolls," *Palestine Exploration Quarterly*, July-December 1958, p. 103. This is especially true of the Habakkuk commentary dated 66-73 C.E., which covers these important years.
⁵Roth, "Zealots," *loc. cit.*; see also Urbach, I, 298, 370, 596.
⁶Roth, "Jewish Revolt," points out that the Habakkuk commentary shows Zealot oppression of the moderates.
⁷Lamentations Rabah 1:5.31.

Yohanan was involved with both of them. If there was one common denominator for these three men, it was the wealth and power they commanded in Jerusalem.

Nakdimon represented the top level of society. He would have the most to lose from the rebellion against Rome. In fact, Yohanan is said to have found his daughter – it was surely after the cataclysm of 70 – picking barley from animal droppings along the road.[8] The rebellion had clearly and most adversely affected Nakdimon's fortunes. Abba Sikra's wealth was not so great, but ambition led him to covet the power he could attain as the leader of the Jerusalem masses. He could win glory as the outstanding Zealot. Indeed, until the rebellion was crushed, Abba Sikra did appear to represent the primary leadership element in Jerusalem.

Yohanan himself also possessed substantial wealth. As a member of the moderate Hillelite faction, he surely spoke for the upper crust of the Pharisaic party. Although he himself was a man of property, his distinction would stem from other roots, for he was spokesman and formulator of an ideology around which the people rallied. He would make his mark as judge, interpreter of law, and teacher. He would leave the shattered Judaism of his day a source of life and regeneration – his students, who were to provide the leadership for the rebuilding of Judaism after the destruction of Jerusalem and the elimination of the Temple cult. The primary concern of the Hillelites during the siege was survival. As the Zealots grew in strength, Yohanan's group found itself relegated to a minority position. The alternatives open to them were limited. Remaining in doomed Jerusalem would not benefit Yohanan's cause or his party's; there could be no future for them there. Even if the Zealots were successful in defending the city, there would be no place for the Hillelite party, which had advocated peace with Rome. If, as was most likely, the Romans defeated the Jews, Roman mistrust of anyone found in the city would prevent Judaea's future administration by any group which had elected to stay in Jerusalem.

Thus, the tenuous nature of Hillelite authority at this time persuaded Yohanan to negotiate with the Zealots.[9] There are three different accounts of Yohanan's escape from Jerusalem. They are found in >Avot d'Rabi Natan, Version A, chapter 4; in Lamentations Rabah 1:5.31; and in the Babylonian Talmud, Giṭin 56b. That there are

---

[8] >Avot d'Rabi Natan [ADRN], Version A, Ch. 17; K'tubot 66b.
[9] Lamentations Rabah 1:5.31. Neusner views the Zealot willingness to negotiate with Yohanan as proof that Yohanan was not as opposed to the war as he was to the Zealots' handling of it. See Jacob Neusner, *A Life of Rabban Yohanan Ben Zakkai* (Leiden: Brill, 1962), p. 116, n. 3.

multiple versions of the episode indicates a lack of certainty as to how, in fact, Yohanan did effect his escape from Jerusalem, to whom he fled, and at what point in the siege his escape was accomplished.[10] However, there are certain factors that can be considered indisputable and these must occupy our attention.

By the time Jerusalem was seriously threatened by Roman forces, Yohanan had already attained a dominant position of leadership in his own party, if not in the structure of the entire government. Therefore, in any case, he had to employ a devious method of escape, or his departure would have been prevented by the Zealot group, which would have seen in it a serious loss of prestige. Yohanan's escape, that is to say, would expose the Zealots' lack of control over rival forces in the beleaguered city. To have a man of such high position flee besieged Jerusalem would result in a much diminished morale. His flight would underscore Yohanan's opposition to Zealot policies and would document his willingness to forsake Jerusalem for the soon to be victorious Roman camp. Thus, any pact Yohanan concluded with Abba Sikra would not have been made public at that time. It may be assumed that once Yohanan was established in Yavneh, the story of a pact with Abba Sikra would be publicized to show that the Zealots – some Zealots at any rate – had been interested in aiding Yohanan and fostering his policy of moderation.

However Yohanan left Jerusalem, it is unlikely that he took such a step before the city was close to collapse. This question has been debated by scholars, yet there are elements common to all three accounts of the escape: Yohanan left at great peril, under much difficulty, using devious means. This could have happened only at a time when a regular means of exit from the city had been sealed off.

Given the available evidence, one cannot be faulted for asserting that the glorification of Yohanan's escape was undertaken only later, after he had established himself at Yavneh. Only then could any such action be justified by Rabbinic tradition and validated by Jewish history.

Following the defeat of Jerusalem, the destruction of the Temple, and the end of the rebellion, Rome's best interests lay in the early reconstruction of Judaea. Rome could not tax a barren land and a disorganized population. Therefore, the Roman authorities in Judaea grasped at every means to make the land and its population productive again, so that the desired funds could once again be collected. Simon Dubnow points out that Rome, as one would expect, quickly

---

[10]For clarification of these question, see Neusner, pp. 113-14.

reestablished taxation following the rebellion.¹¹ In order to accomplish the difficult task of reconstructing the Judaean economy, Rome looked to cooperative Jewish leaders. Any conquering nation knows the benefit to be derived from ruling through members of the conquered community. The Roman governors always wanted the members of the Sanhedrin to serve as their spokesmen. A subjugated people would resent foreign domination, but would react more favorably to what it construed as rule by its own countrymen.¹²

Having the insight provided by her long imperial experience, Rome looked to Yohanan and his Hillelite party to take a leading part in the country's rebuilding. The people needed a focal point once the Temple had been destroyed. They now turned to Yavneh and to Yohanan ben Zakkai. Rome could be sure of Yohanan's allegiance. He had revealed a marked pro-Roman inclination prior to the war, and there was no need for him to abandon his Roman allegiance, especially since he was now in authority. Even if Roman officials nursed some doubts about Yohanan's allegiance, they comforted themselves with the understanding that his new position depended entirely on their support. Yohanan, they calculated, was not likely to forfeit his newfound eminence in the post-Ḥurban government.¹³ There is some evidence that Yavneh was the site of the Roman garrison, and it was also the private property of the Roman emperor.¹⁴ Hence, Yohanan and his new government would have been very much under the watchful eye of the Roman eagle. We see the new balance of forces in the land. Rome needed Yohanan and the Hillelites to lead the Judaean community after the rebellion. Yohanan and the Hillelites needed Rome to endorse their right to govern at Yavneh.

There is some controversy among scholars about the nature of the Yavneh community. Menahem Stein, for example, proposes that Yavneh was already an important seat of learning. As the private property of the emperor, it had had its own special form of government and also a *Sanhedra* or court in the days of the early Roman emperors.¹⁵

---

¹¹Simon Dubnow, *History of the Jews* (New York: Thomas Yoseloff, 1968), p. 27.
¹²Adolf Buechler, *The Economic Conditions of Judaea after the Destruction of the Second Temple* (London: Jews College Publications, 1912), p. 18. Many people survived the destruction of Jerusalem. Some kept their wealth, but there was tremendous poverty in the land.
¹³G. F. Moore, *Judaism in the First Centuries of the Christian Era* (Cambridge: Harvard University Press, 1944), I, 131; II, 116.
¹⁴Buechler, p. 18; H. Revel, "Yohanan ben Zakkai," *Universal Jewish Encyclopedia*, VI, 164-66.
¹⁵M. Stein, "Yavneh and Its Scholars," *Ziyon*, n.s., III (1937), 118-22.

Therefore, it was an excellent location in which to establish Yohanan's new pro-Roman government.[16] Gedaliah Allon, however, attempts to show that, according to Josephus, Rome was accustomed to exile recalcitrants and intern them in certain cities, Yavneh among them. This was especially true for important fugitives. Allon also asserts that Rome was not fighting against the rebels alone, but against the entire Jewish nation; he offers as evidence the Roman terrorist activities against towns not known to harbor rebels. Therefore, Allon concludes, it is unlikely that the Roman government aided Yohanan in establishing a Jewish community at Yavneh. Yohanan, he believes, was sent to Yavneh to be interned there.[17]

Whether Yohanan was at Yavneh by his own choice or by force of internment, it is clear that his major role there was to avert another revolt against the Romans. The war had resulted in Ḥurban, the all but total economic as well as spiritual devastation of the entire Jewish populace. How Jewish despair and rage were to be deflected from forming the focus of another revolt against the Romans was the major task confronting Yohanan at Yavneh. How would he have hoped to accomplish it? It is my contention that Yohanan effectively utilized esoteric speculation as a means of diverting an embittered and emotionally downtrodden people from embarking on, or nursing hopes for, another revolt against the Romans. It is surely no surprise to discover the possibility of occult interests on Yohanan's part. Such interests characteristically flourish in periods of social and economic instability, and the world in which Yohanan and his contemporaries lived provided fertile ground for the growth of metaphysical doctrines.[18] Not only was Yohanan successful at the task he undertook for himself, but at the same time he was able to maintain the Jewish hope, a messianic hope, of eventual redemption – and he accomplished it all without alienating the Roman overlord.

The main talmudic source which deals with Yohanan's involvement in esoteric speculation is the famous Ḥagigah passage depicting Yohanan riding on a mule and followed by his close disciple, Eleazar ben Arak. The disciple turns to his master and asks him to share his knowledge of

---

[16]Stein is joined in his opinion by Revel, who shows: 1) Yavneh was the private property of the Roman emperors (Josephus, *Antiquities of the Jews*, Book 17, Ch. 8:1 and Book 18, Ch. 6:3); 2) Yavneh was populated by Jewish Zealots (Philo, *Embassy to Gaius*, IV, 144); 3) there was an independent Sanhedrin in Yavneh (Sanhedrin 89).

[17]Gedaliah Allon, *Meqarim b'Toldot Yiśra>el* (Tel Aviv: Ha-qibuẓ Ha-m'>uḥad, 1957-58), I, 219-38. Neusner also joins Stein in disproving Allon's argument: see Neusner, p. 124.

[18]See Urbach, I, 578; Moore, I, 411-13.

ma‹aśeh merkaōah. To which Yohanan replies in effect: Only those select few who qualify can enter the realm of esoteric speculation. At this point, Eleazar ben Arak begins to discourse on ma‹aśeh merkaōah in his teacher's presence; Yohanan, sensing that Eleazar not only qualified but was fully capable of understanding the intricacies of ma‹aśeh b're›shit as well, dismounts, sits by the side of the road, and listens to his disciple's comments on mysticism. At the conclusion of Eleazar's discourse, Yohanan praises his disciple as one who not only understands the realm of the esoteric, but as one who honors God in Heaven by his words.

> Our Rabbis taught: Once R. Yohanan b. Zakkai was riding on a mule when going on a journey, and R. Eleazar b. Arak was driving the mule from behind. [R. Eleazar] said to him: Master, teach me a chapter of the "Work of the Chariot." He answered: Have I not taught you thus: "Nor [the Work of] the Chariot in the presence of one, unless he is a Sage and understands of his own knowledge"? [R. Eleazar] then said to him: Master, permit me to say before you something which you have taught me. He answered: Say on! Forthwith R. Yohanan b. Zakkai dismounted from the mule and wrapped himself up, and sat upon a stone beneath an olive tree. Said [R. Eleazar] to him: Master, why did you dismount from the mule? He answered: Is it proper that while you are expounding the "Work of the Chariot," and the Divine Presence is with us, and the ministering angels accompany us, I should ride on the mule! Forthwith, R. Eleazar b. Arak began his exposition of the "Work of the Chariot," and fire came down from heaven and encompassed all the trees in the field; [thereupon] they all began to utter [divine] song.... An angel [then] answered from the fire and said: This is the very "Work of the Chariot." [Thereupon] R. Yohanan b. Zakkai rose and kissed him on his head and said: Blessed be the Lord God of Israel, Who has given a son to Abraham our father, who knows how to speculate upon, and to investigate, and to expound the "Work of the Chariot." There are some who preach well but do not act well, others act well but do not preach well, but you preach well and act well. Happy are you, O Abraham our father, that R. Eleazar b. Arak has come forth from your loins.

This brief passage suggests how pervasive was Yohanan's influence upon his disciple.

There are three versions of the episode. The first version is found in Tosefta› Ḥagigah 2:1. The first part of chapter 2 of Tosefta› Ḥagigah is a clarification and expansion of Mishnah Ḥagiga 2:1. The Mishnah forbade public exposition of esoteric doctrines like ma‹aśeh b're›shit and ma‹aśeh merkaōah – whatever may have been the precise meaning of these terms. Only individuals who had the ability to grasp these teachings should be exposed to them. After clarifying the wording of the Mishnah, the Tosefta› then proceeds to give several stories and parables which illustrate the qualifications held necessary for esoteric speculation and the dangers involved therein. Tosefta> Ḥagigah 2:1 relates the story just recounted above of how Eleazar ben Arak proved to Yohanan's satisfaction that he was qualified to enter the dangerous realm of speculative thought. The qualification he exhibited – the ability to understand the essence of such esoteric material – enabled him to avoid the major danger inherent in an exposure to esoteric speculation: the adverse effect of such speculation on one's "orthodox" beliefs and behavior. While most of those who expounded *ma<aśeh b're>shit* and *ma<aśeh merkaṿah* ceased to observe Jewish law, Eleazar was described as *na>eh doresh v'na>eh m'qayem*, one who "preaches well and practices well" (2:1). In the next section of the Tosefta> (2:2), we find a report of three other disciples who were also considered qualified to lecture on *ma<aśeh merkaṿah* before their teachers and, like Eleazar, were not led astray by their involvement in esoterica. One of these disciples was Joshua ben Hananiah, who is depicted discussing *ma<aśeh merkaṿah* with Yohanan ben Zakkai. Unlike the Tosefta>, the Ḥagigah passage found on page 77a of the Krotoshin edition of the Palestinian Talmud begins with a discussion of whether the halakhah outlined in Mishnah Ḥagigah 2:1 follows Akiba or Ishmael. Though the Mishnah is said to be the opinion of Rabbi Akiba, the thrust of the developing halakhah seems to be in agreement with Rabbi Ishmael – who did not prohibit the expounding of esoteric material. Again, however, we see certain restrictions placed upon involvement in esoteric speculation, guidelines which would naturally limit esoterica to the few deemed qualified. It is stated that only those disciples who prove to their teachers that they are so qualified may venture into this dangerous realm.

It is at this point that the series of master-disciple stories enters to illustrate the experience both of those who had success and of those who met with failure in the realm of expounding the esoteric. To exemplify those who fared well in expounding esoterica, the Palestinian Talmud first repeats the story of Eleazar and Yohanan and then adds information about R. Jose Hakohen and R. Shimon ben Netanel, two other close disciples of Yohanan. They were so successful that they were eventually invited to sit before the *Sh'khinah* and study the hidden matters.

Like the Palestinian before it and following the Tosefta>, the Babylonian Talmud intended to stress that qualified individuals alone were to be exposed to the mysteries of *ma<aśeh b're>shit* and *ma<aśeh merkaṿah*. The version of the passage which is to be found in the Babylonian Talmud, Ḥagigah 14b, once again presents a series of illustrations of the success and failure of individuals who entered the

world of these mysteries. At first we are given three illustrations of individuals who were not negatively influenced by their involvement in esoteric speculation. The initial example is our story of Yohanan ben Zakkai and Eleazar ben Arak. The unique aspect of this version of the story is that the episode itself has for its context a very graphic description of how the angels came down from Heaven and they, too, rejoiced to hear Eleazar ben Arak expound the ma<aseh merkavah. This mystical setting itself shows the importance the Rabbis attached to Yohanan's involvement in mysticism with his disciples; it highlights the close relationship between Yohanan and his disciples within the realm of esoterica. Following the Yohanan-Eleazar story is another passage which describes two other of Yohanan's disciples, Rabbi Joshua ben Hananiah and Rabbi Jose Hakohen, who, when walking on the road, overheard the conversation between Yohanan and Eleazar and witnessed Eleazar's discourse on ma<aseh merkavah. As a result, they, too, desired to enter the realm of esoteric speculation. The Babylonian passage then repeats the Tosefta> section regarding the three disciples who expounded the ma<aseh merkavah in the presence of their teachers, and in this version also Rabbi Joshua ben Hananiah is depicted as lecturing in his master's presence. The three versions underline the Rabbinic conviction that Yohanan ben Zakkai was intimately involved with his close disciples in esoteric speculation. This particular involvement is depicted by the Rabbis as something quite positive.

Yohanan is also seen as a key figure in the chain of mystical tradition. Another of Hillel's disciples, an older peer of Yohanan's, Yonatan ben Uzziel, was reportedly also involved in mysticism. Yonatan's experience in esoteric speculation is described in the Babylonian Talmud, Megillah 3a. It is probable, therefore, that Yohanan stood in a chain of tradition passed initially from Hillel down to Yonatan ben Uzziel, a tradition of mystical speculation which Yohanan himself transmitted to his own disciples. Yohanan's closest disciples – in this realm of mysticism at least – seem to have been Eleazar ben Arak, Joshua ben Hananiah, Jose Hakohen, and Shimon ben Netanel, but the passages cited about his relations with his disciples suggest that Yohanan exposed his entire circle to esoterica.

One of the main disciples involved in the mystical coterie surrounding Yohanan was Eliezer ben Hyrkanus. Y.D. Gilat, an Israeli scholar, in a work entitled *Mishnato shel R. Eliezer ben Hurkanus*, concludes that Eliezer ben Hyrkanus possessed a highly negative attitude towards Gentiles in general. His halakhic decisions tended to negate all dealings with them, both in the political and the economic spheres.[19] Gilat cites a passage in the Babylonian Talmud, <Avodah Zarah 23a, in which Rabbi Eliezer rejects any sacrifice coming from a Gentile. In Mishnah Ḥulin 2:7, Eliezer is reported forbidding Jews to slaughter meat for non-Jews, while Mishnah Ḥalah 4:7 records his insistence that the produce of a Jew who is a tenant farmer for a Gentile landowner in Syria is subject to the laws of tithing and the sabbatical year. The Palestinian Talmud sees Eliezer's injunction as a kind of fine to be imposed upon Jews who are employed by Gentiles. Another passage which reflects Eliezer's anti-Gentile attitudes is Tosefta> Sanhedrin 12:2, which quotes him as stating that the Gentiles have no place in the World to Come. Finally, there is the passage in *Seder >Eliyahu Zuṭa*, chapter 20, in which Eliezer flatly asserts that God will punish all the nations which have made Israel suffer.

Eliezer ben Hyrkanus' *halakhot* also manifested an overwhelming zeal for the honor and sanctity of Jerusalem, a belief in the superiority of >Ereẓ Yiśra>el, an impatient expectation of a restored Kingdom of David, and a certainty that the Temple would be rebuilt momentarily. Tosefta> Megillah 4:4 supports this view of Eliezer as a representative of nationalistic feelings reflective of the tradition bearing Shammai's name. On one occasion, the Tosefta> recalls, a Jew read in the presence of Eliezer ben Hyrkanus the prophetic passage which states that one should make known to Jerusalem her abominations. Eliezer's caustic rejoinder was: "While you are investigating the abominations of Jerusalem, go and investigate the abominations of your own mother." Not only does the passage evince Eliezer's tremendous pride in Jerusalem and >Ereẓ Yiśra>el; it also suggests that, according to him, the destruction of Jerusalem had in no way been due to the sins of the Jews. A key passage cited by Gilat as proof for Eliezer's hope and belief that the Temple would be rebuilt momentarily and Jewish independence restored is found in the Babylonian Talmud, B'rakhot 48b, which declares that, if one does not use the phrase "a desirable, good and extensive land" in describing >Ereẓ Yiśra>el and also fails to mention the restored Kingdom of the House of David in reciting the *birkhat hamazon*, the postprandial grace, then he has not fulfilled his obligation.[20]

Most scholars would concur that Eliezer ben Hyrkanus exhibited at least very strong Zealotic tendencies and was certainly anti-Roman in his feelings. Two sources in particular indicate the strength and vitality of these feelings: in Leviticus Rabah 35:9, Eliezer stated that revenge

---

[19] Y. D. Gilat, *Mishnato shel R. Eliezer ben Hurkanus u-M'qomah B'Toldot Ha-Halakhah* (Tel Aviv: D'vir, 1968). See, in particular, pp. 300 ff. See also b. Ḥagigah 14b, quoted here *in extenso*.
[20] Gilat, pp. 305 f.

against Edom was in the hands of God "by means of Israel." According to the Rabbis, Edom was incontestably synonymous with Rome, and it is significant that Eliezer added the phrase "by means of Israel" – intimating that revenge would take the form of Israel's outright military revolt against the Romans. The most famous passage indicating Eliezer's Zealotic connections is a story told in the Babylonian Talmud, ʿAvodah Zarah 16b, which depicts Eliezer's arrest by the Romans and his subsequent trial. It seems quite reasonable to conjecture that Eliezer owed his arrest as much to his anti-Roman expressions as to a suspicion that he harbored Christian leanings.

Scholars have noted that virtually all of Eliezer's halakhic opinions are linked explicitly to the tradition of Yohanan ben Zakkai or quote him directly.[21] Clearly the relationship between the two was very close; especially where the sharing of opinions was concerned, it was a relationship between a master and his disciple. Is it fair to suggest at this point that the sharing of opinions must have been almost without limit and included, therefore, the anti-Roman sentiments voiced by Eliezer ben Hyrkanus? Quite possibly, but Yohanan ben Zakkai was much too astute a politician to articulate in public anything resembling Eliezer's anti-Roman polemics, and there can be little question that Yohanan must have seen it as imperative to avert another revolt. It was Yohanan's role to discourage the highly nationalistic anti-Gentile and anti-Roman feelings of his student as well as similar views held by other disciples in his circle.

Yohanan's task at Yavneh, it is quite clear, was immense. Not only did he have to deal with a depressed populace, but he also had to maintain his control over a group which obviously cherished a militant anti-Romanism and was very eager for another revolt. Yohanan's political sense convinced him that a renewed rebellion would have constituted a disaster for Judaea and her people – indeed, for all Judaism. Yohanan's task was in a way one of manipulation, of uplifting the spirits of a depressed populace to give them some hope and at the same time silencing those voices which called for revolt. In some cases, as just noted, the voices were those of his closest disciples. What Yohanan did was to utilize his knowledge and experience in esoteric speculation to carry out his difficult political task, ultimately with a great deal of success: a revolt did not immediately take place. In other words, Yohanan meant to keep alive the hope of Jewish redemption, but to avoid encouraging specificity as to the date of the messianic advent.

---

[21]Note, for example, Wilhelm Bacher's characterization of Eliezer in his work *Aggadot ha-Tannaim* (Berlin: D'vir, 1922), I (Part 1), 92-114. See also *Encyclopaedia Judaica*, VI, 622.

A willingness to accept postponement was necessary. Immediate political messianism would have been at the least counterproductive.

There are in Rabbinic literature passages which reflect Yohanan's genius in moralizing the literally downtrodden and curbing those who wished for immediate revolt. >Avot d'Rabi Natan, version A, chapter 14, depicts Yohanan discussing with his five immediate disciples the question of the best way one may enter – secure one's share in – the World to Come.[22] Of the responses of his five disciples, Yohanan clearly agrees with Eleazar ben Arak's view. He wants his disciples to cleave to Eleazar's view that the World to Come can best be achieved through devotion towards Heaven as well as good-heartedness towards humankind in general. The use in the passage of the Hebrew word *davaq* – "to cleave to" – indicates a tremendously intense concern about the World to Come within the circle of Yohanan ben Zakkai and his disciples. The reason for the concern is obvious. They were all searching for a better tomorrow. A militant's formula for a better tomorrow would have prescribed immediate revolt, but Yohanan and Eleazar ben Arak saw that particular solution as self-destructive. While the Romans were so securely in power, appeasement had to be the path to follow. The Romans most probably and correctly interpreted the statements of Yohanan and Eleazar as being rather favorable to the Gentiles and to themselves, but one wonders to what degree such a pro-Roman stance was in fact more than a ploy, a manoeuvre as it were, to appease the Romans and counter the militants.

A passage which beautifully depicts Yohanan's brilliance in uplifting the spiritually depressed is found in the following post-*Ḥurban* scene: In >Avot d'Rabi Natan, version A, chapter 4, Yohanan is pictured coming forth from Jerusalem followed by his disciple Joshua ben Hananiah. Both behold the Temple in ruins and Joshua bemoans the fact that, with the Temple laid waste and the sacrificial cult suspended, there is no longer a place where the iniquities of Israel can be atoned for. Yohanan consoles his disciple by observing that there is another kind of atonement which is just as effective – *g'milut ḥasadim,* acts of loving kindness – and then cites a prooftext in Hosea 6:6: "for I desire mercy and not sacrifice." Yohanan's emphasis in his reply to Joshua is that, as circumstances dictate, the path to be followed is *g'milut ḥasadim* rather than vengeful adventures.[23]

Understandably enough, the Romans would have been rather anxious had the philosophy of Yavneh specified a particular date for the

---

[22]In quoting passages from ADRN, the Schechter edition (New York, 1967) was utilized: see p. 58.
[23]See Urbach, I, 434, 667.

coming of the messiah. Talk of an imminent deliverance would have been interpreted by the Roman authorities as anticipated revolt. Yohanan, therefore, had to guard against feeding Roman suspicions on this score, but at the same time he needed to give his people hope. A passage which beautifully reflects Yohanan's attempt to discourage any consideration of an early deliverance is found in >Avot d'Rabi Natan, version B, chapter 31: if a man has a sapling in his hand and someone says to him: "Behold, there is the messiah!" he should go on with his planting and only afterwards go out to greet the redeemer. The messianic idea is by no means abandoned, but its retention in this form would not have been encouraging to the heirs of the Zealots or threatening to the Romans.

In this context, Yohanan's deathbed scene is most revealing. It underscores his political brilliance in appeasing the Romans by refraining from statements which they might interpret as seditious and, at the same time, voicing sentiments which his own people could interpret as sustaining their hopes for a better future. Again, there are three versions of the story. One is found in the Palestinian Talmud, Soṭah IX.16; a second appears in the Babylonian Talmud, B'rakhot 28b, and a third in >Avot d'Rabi Natan, version A, chapter 25. Yohanan is represented in all three texts as speaking to his disciples who come to visit him while he is lying on his deathbed. Yohanan, weeping, addresses himself to the prospect of soon meeting God, his Creator, and obviously receiving either reward or punishment for his life; then he utters his last request – his closest disciples are bidden to remove all the vessels of uncleanliness and to prepare a throne for Hezekiah, the king of Judah, "who is coming." Only the version in the Babylonian Talmud includes the phrase "who is coming" in the reference to King Hezekiah. The Palestinian version and the version in >Avot d'Rabi Natan both read simply: "prepare a throne for Hezekiah, the king of Judah." This shorter version seems to be the more authentic and clearly leaves open the question of the messianic advent. What Yohanan ben Zakkai is likely to have urged on his disciples was the need to keep on working and preparing the way for the messiah, who would come at some *quite indefinite* time in the future.

The throne of Hezekiah was certainly to be seen as a messianic allusion, and Hezekiah himself was to be understood as a messianic figure. Abba Hillel Silver, in his *History of Messianic Speculation in Israel*, dealt at length with Hezekiah's messianic dimension.[24] A further

---

[24] A. H. Silver, *A History of Messianic Speculation in Israel* (Boston: Beacon Press, 1959), p. 13. See also Joseph Klausner *Ha-Ra<ayon Ha-M'shiḥi b'Yiśra>el* (Jerusalem: Dfus Ha-Po<alim, 1927), pp. 252f.; Urbach, I, 668.

corroboration of Hezekiah as a messianic figure is offered by Jacob Neusner in *A Life of Rabbi Jochanan ben Zakkai*, where he notes that the second-century Christian Church Father Justin Martyr's *Dialogue with Trypho* construes Hezekiah as a symbol of Christ.[25] If Christians held Hezekiah to be a messianic symbol, it is certainly not hard to believe that this tradition must initially have pervaded Jewish life. The Romans, of course, might not have felt it necessary to interpret the words *kise> Ḥizqiyahu* as a messianic utterance. The passage gave encouragement to Yohanan's people at the same time that it denied the Romans any reason for suspicion as to its immediate messianic import.

Yohanan's ability to communicate with his people, to give them courage for the future and at the same time avoid sparking Roman suspicion, is cleverly depicted in the following passage couched in mystic terms. The passage, rather esoteric in nature, was to be understood only by aware Jews and would have confused or at the least seemed of scant interest to the Roman authorities. This passage is extant in four versions, all of them from the Babylonian Talmud. The one to be quoted here is from Ḥagigah 13a; the other three versions are found in Pesaḥim 94a and 94b, as well as in <Eruvin 53a. The Ḥagigah version reads:

> It is taught: R. Yohanan b. Zakkai said: What answer did the *bat qol* give to that wicked one, when he said: I will ascend above the heights of the clouds; I will be like the Most High? A *bat qol* went forth and said to him: O wicked man, son of a wicked man, grandson of Nimrod, the wicked, who stirred the whole world to rebellion against Me by his rule. How many are the years of man? Seventy, for it is said: The days of our years are threescore years and ten, or even by reason of strength fourscore years. But the distance from the earth to the firmament is a journey of five hundred years, and the thickness of the firmament is a journey of five hundred years, and likewise [the distance] between one firmament and the other. Above them are the holy living creatures: the feet of the living creatures are equal to all of them [together], the ankles of the living creatures are equal to all of them; the legs of the living creatures are equal to all of them; the knees of the living creatures are equal to all of them; the bodies of the living creatures are equal all of them; the horns of the living creatures are equal to all of them. Above them is the throne of glory; the feet of the throne of glory are equal to all of them; the throne of glory is equal to all of them. The King, the Living and Eternal God, High and Exalted, dwells above them. Yet, you did say, I will ascend above the heights of the clouds, I will be like the

---

[25] Jacob Neusner, *A Life of Yohanan ben Zakkai* (2d ed.; Leiden: Brill, 1979), p. 228, n. 3.

Most High! No, you shall be brought down to the netherworld, to the uttermost part of the pit.

Several things seem quite clear from this passage. First, of course, Yohanan's reference to Nebuchadnezzar, the king of Babylonia, was a shrewd way of alluding to the Roman Empire of his own day. By referring to the historical Babylonian oppression, Yohanan would have run little risk of antagonizing the Romans, but at the same time would have communicated to his disciples his own anti-Roman feelings. Secondly, the lengthy paragraph which involves a detailed mystical description of the heavenly realm indicates that Yohanan and his disciples were thoroughly adept in many of the early mystical traditions and accounts. We even seem to find a reference to Ezekiel's vision of the Heavenly Chariot. Yohanan is portrayed as a master of the esoteric, able to draw upon mystical images and concepts in describing the difference between the heavenly and the earthly realms. Finally, and most important, is the juxtaposition in his passage of Yohanan's subtle anti-Roman views with his expression of esoterica.

Through his knowledge of mysticism and his mastery of esoteric speculation, Yohanan found a means of making endurable the Roman victory over the earthly Jerusalem. By involving his disciples in a discussion of the heavenly realm, he taught them that the Roman incursion would be better countered by an understanding of the mysteries of the Heavens than by a resort to arms. This was how Yohanan attempted to carry out his role as the head of Yavneh. The use of esoteric speculation had a two-fold purpose. On the one hand, it diverted the energies of his students from a revolt which would have been disastrous; on the other hand, it gave these same students a measure of encouragement that the future was not totally bleak, that in God's good time the yoke of Roman oppression would eventually be lifted. The latter point might well have resulted in Yohanan's arrest had the Romans understood the meaning behind the message. Or perhaps not: perhaps they, too, understood and were pragmatic enough to assess Yohanan's strategy as on balance advantageous to them.

The story of Yohanan's involvement with Abba Sikra bears repeating, especially in the light of some of the passages describing what may indeed have been Yohanan's suppressed feelings vis-à-vis Roman rule. Clearly at Yavneh, Yohanan was not able – that is, not indiscreet enough – to publicize any anti-Roman sentiments he might have harbored. Even during the war itself it would not have been politically astute of Yohanan to allow himself open expression of his anti-Roman feelings, although the relationship between Yohanan and Abba Sikra allows room to argue that the two men were devoted to the same end, if not the same means: achieving the restoration of Jewish autonomy. One of the two traditions of Yohanan's escape from Jerusalem clearly illustrates the very close relations between Abba Sikra and his uncle. As Gedaliah Allon points out, of the two basic traditions concerning escape from Jerusalem, one appears in two separate accounts found in the >Aṽot d'Rabi Natan[26]: Yohanan is portrayed as a pro-Roman who was recognized as such by Vespasian. In this version, Yohanan's escape is facilitated by his close disciples, and no mention is made of Abba Sikra. There is, however, a second tradition, which seems to be more authentic. Cited in Lamentations Rabah 1:5.31[27] as well as in T.B. Giṭin 56a-b, this version emphasizes that Yohanan decided to leave Jerusalem only *after* the Zealots had burned the food stores. It appears, then, that Yohanan was not so much opposed to fighting a defensive war, but when the food stores were no longer available, it was clear that holding out against the Romans had become hopeless, a desperate folly. It was at this point that Yohanan turned not to his disciples, but to Abba Sikra, for aid in escaping Jerusalem. After a lengthy conversation in which Yohanan complained about the tactics of the Zealots, tactics which he was convinced could lead only to the death of the Jewish people, Yohanan urged his nephew to enable him, Yohanan, to leave Jerusalem and then perhaps pursue a course which would bring salvation to the people. According to the passage cited, the plan Abba Sikra devised proved successful, and Yohanan escaped from Jerusalem to Yavneh.

The anti-Roman feelings which political necessity forced Yohanan to conceal during his tenure in Yavneh come to the fore in a passage cited in three separate versions in the Talmud and Midrash.[28] The passage offers a discussion between Yohanan and his disciples as to the meaning of the verse from Proverbs 14:34: "Righteousness exalts a nation and the kindness of the peoples is sin." In the series of answers given by the disciples, Eleazar interprets the verse as meaning: "Righteousness exalts a nation and so does kindness (this refers to Israel), but to the nations of the world belongs sin." Yohanan responds to Eleazar's words by saying: "I prefer the words of Eleazar to my words and to your words, for he assigns righteousness and kindness to Israel and sins to the nations of the world." To what could "the nations of the world" refer in this case? Only to Rome.

---

[26]Allon, "Halichato shel Rabban Yoḥanan ben Zakai l'Yaṽneh," Ẓiyon, III (1938), 213; ADRN, Version A, Chapter 4; ADRN, Version B, Chapter 6.
[27]*Lamentations Rabbah*, trans. by H. Freedman and Maurice Simon (London, 1951).
[28]T. B. Baba> Batra> 10b; *P'siqta> d'Raṽ Kahana>* (Buber ed.), 12b; *Yalkut Shim<oni* II, *Remez* 952.

The version in *Yalqut Shim<oni* II, *Remez* 952, reflects upon Yohanan's seeming changing of attitude to the Romans: previously Yohanan's interpretation of the same verse had been that, just as the sin offering made atonement for Israel, so charity made atonement for the heathen. Why the radical shift from one position to another, from an earlier pro-Roman to a later anti-Roman outlook? Most probably, the change came toward the end of Yohanan's life.

In this as in every other case, Yohanan was not explicit in his condemnation of Roman authority or Roman policy. He never failed to speak in terms of indirection and circumlocution, even when he was willing to allow his associates to detect in him a degree of anti-Romanism. The Roman governors could have asked for nothing more: Yohanan's strategy reduced the prospects for Jewish messianic passion and the military adventurism associated with it, but at the same time moralized the Jews by making them hopeful of the future and thus willing for the time being to assent to Roman rule. What in the end undoubtedly held paramount importance in his eyes was preservation – even in veiled form – of the messianic promise. That promise, he would have been convinced, did not have to be fulfilled in his generation or in the near future, but it had to be kept alive, a legacy to be bequeathed future generations of Jews and to inform every future expression of Judaism until the Holy One Blessed Be He determined that the time was ripe for its fulfillment.[29]

---

[29]See Samson H. Levey's suggestive "The Messiah Idea," in *Keeping Posted*, February 1977, especially p. 5.

3

Introductory Poems (*R'shuyot*) to the Targum of the *Haftarah* in Praise of Jonathan Ben Uzziel

By Michael L. Klein

לשמשון לוייא
מתורגמן דנבייא

The two most popular talmudic legends about Jonathan ben Uzziel (first century B.C.E. - first century C.E.) relate to his study of Torah and to his translation of Torah. Both stories contain supernatural motifs that endeared them to the people and eventually led to their inclusion in Aramaic introductory poems, *r'shuyot*, to the targum of the *haftarot*.

The first story[1] tells that Jonathan ben Uzziel delivered the Targum of Prophets as received from the mouths of Haggai, Zechariah and Malachi[2]; and the entire Land of Israel trembled on that day. A heavenly voice (*bat-qol*) called out, "Who is it that revealed my secrets unto mankind?" To which Jonathan boldly responded, "It is I who revealed your secrets. Surely you realize that I did it neither for personal honor nor for the honor of my father's house – but that there not increase dispute among Israel" (Rashi *ad loc.*: over the interpretation of obscure biblical passages).

---

[1]T. B. M'gilah 3a:
תרגום של נביאים יונתן בן עוזיאל אמרו מפי חגי זכריה ומלאכי ונזדעזעה ארץ ישראל ארבע מאות פרסה על ארבע מאות פרסה יצתה בת קול ואמרה מי הוא זה שגילה סתריי לבני אדם עמד יונתן בן עוזיאל על רגליו ואמר אני הוא שגליתי סתריך לבני אדם גלוי וידוע לפניך שלא לכבודי עשיתי ולא לכבוד בית אבא אלא לכבודך עשיתי שלא ירבו מחלוקת בישראל ועוד ביקש לגלות תרגום של כתובים יצתה בת קול ואמרה דייך מאי טעמא משום דאית ביה קץ משיח.

[2]Also compare the Aramaic poem from Maḥzor Vitry, par. 168, in the Appendix below. The legend ignores the chronological gap of over 500 years between these prophets and the tana>; for our present purposes, we, too, suspend disbelief.

He further wished to reveal the targum of the Hagiographa, but the heavenly voice called out, "Enough!" And why was that? Because it contains the fixed time (for the coming) of the Messiah (Rashi: in the Book of Daniel).[3]

The second story speaks of the eighty disciples of Hillel the Elder (first century B.C.E. - first century C.E.), the greatest of whom was Jonathan ben Uzziel and the smallest of whom, Yohanan ben Zakkai. "It was said of Jonathan ben Uzziel that, when he was involved in the study of Torah, any bird that flew over him was immediately burnt" (Rashi: from the fire of the divine angels that gathered about, to listen to his exposition of the Torah).[4]

Introductory poems to the *haftarah* as collected from Mahzor editions and manuscripts were first listed by Leopold Zunz in his *Literaturgeschichte der Synagogalen Poesie*.[5] In that monumental work, Zunz merely cited opening and closing phrases of poems; and in this manner, he lists the poem איסב רשות מכולכון ("Let me obtain permission from all of you...") among three Aramaic introductory poems for the *m'turg'man* (i.e., translator) of the festival *haftarah*. Zunz noted that his sources for this poem are Mahzor Vitry and some (unidentified) French manuscripts. He divided this short poem into its three components and elsewhere offered a probable date of composition as the Geonic period.[6]

The other two poems listed by Zunz are איסב רשו מן קדם אלהא רמא... ("Let me obtain permission from the exalted God...") and אילו פמי כל נימי... ("If my mouth were all musical strings..."). Yet a fourth composition listed by Zunz and recognized by Bacher as belonging to the same genre,

---

[3] I will not deal here with the obvious problem, namely, that in fact there are targumim to the entire Hagiographa except Daniel and Ezra-Nehemiah, presumably because they were originally composed partially in Aramaic. The talmudic story would seem to apply the prohibition to the entire K'tuvim. Yet, it is well-known that fragments of two exemplars of Targum to Job have survived among the Dead Sea Scrolls and antedate Jonathan ben Uzziel by some 200 years. Likewise, another talmudic story relates that Rabban Gamliel I (early first century C.E., and possibly a younger contemporary of Jonathan ben Uzziel) tried to suppress an existent Targum of Job (T. B. Shabat 115a; Sof'rim 5:15; and elsewhere).

[4] T. B. Sukah 28a; Baba> Batra> 134a ... שמונים תלמידים היו לו להלל הזקן גדול שבכולם יונתן בן עוזיאל קטן שבכולם רבן יוחנן בן זכאי אמרו עליו על עוזיאל בן עוזיאל בשעה שיושב ועוסק בתורה כל עוף שפורח עליו מיד נשרף. On the comparison of Torah to fire, see, for example, Jeremiah 23:29, "Behold, My word is like fire, declares the Lord...," and the many Rabbinic homilies on this and similar verses.

[5] (Berlin, 1865), pp. 79-80.

[6] *Ibid.* p. 9.

Introductory Poems (R'shuyot) to the Targum of the Haftarah

is אנקוט בריש הרמנא מקמי רחמנא ("Let me first obtain authority from before the Merciful One...").[7]

The texts of these Aramaic introductory poems to the *haftarot* were first published towards the end of the nineteenth century, within the editions of two other works:

1. As an appendix to his edition of the Targum to the Prophets, based upon Codex Reuchlinianus, P. de Lagarde published the poems that appear at the end of that manuscript.[8] The eight compositions in that collection were published, categorized and described by W. Bacher almost immediately after their first appearance.[9]

2. In 1889, S. Hurwitz produced the first edition of Maḥzor Vitry. The section of that work devoted to the Sabbath liturgy contains a series of introductory passages to be recited on the festivals "after reading the targum to the first three verses of the haftarah."[10]

In the course of preparing the catalogue *Targumic Manuscripts in the Cambridge Genizah Collections*,[11] I recently came upon three fragments containing Aramaic introductory poems in praise of Jonathan ben Uzziel. Two of the fragments preserve complete and distinct compositions, whereas the third contains an identical copy of a portion of one of the other two poems, followed by the targum of Isaiah 5:30–6:1.

The following is a brief physical description of the manuscripts:

1. T-S AS 71.64

Paper; 2 leaves (1 bifolium); mutilated; 16.2 x 12.0 cm (per leaf); 1 column; 13-15 lines; Oriental semi-cursive script; 13th cent.; Tiberian vocalization; folio 1 contains Onqelos with Hebrew lemmata to Exodus 12:21-31; folio 2r contains a Hebrew poem for the return to the Land of

---

[7]*Ibid.*, p. 569, item no. 11, composed by a poet named Yosef, of unknown date. In an article to which we will refer at length, Wilhelm Bacher gives the full text of this introductory poem: "Alte aramäische Poesien zum Vortrage des Haphtara-Targum," *Monatsschrift für Geschichte und Wissenschaft des Judenthums*, XXII (= N.F. 5; 1873), 220-28.

[8]*Prophetae Chaldaice* (Leipzig, 1872), pp. 490-93.

[9]See n. 7, above, and n. 14, below.

[10]S. Hurwitz, *Machsor Vitry* (2nd ed.; Nürnberg, 1923), pp. 158-65, paragraphs 167-79. At the end of par. 166, we find the instructions: וביום טוב שנהגו לומר תרגום של הפטרה אומר המפטיר ג' פסוקים ואחר יאמר המתרגם רשויות ואלו הן. This rule is, presumably, in order to avoid an interruption between the opening benediction to the *haftarah* and the actual reading of a minimal passage.

[11](Cambridge: Cambridge University Press for Cambridge University Library, 1992). My thanks to Dr. Stefan C. Reif, Director of the Taylor-Schechter Genizah Research Unit, for his kind assistance in every matter.

C.U.L. T-S AS 71.64, folio 2, verso
Courtesy of the Syndics of
Cambridge University Library

Introductory Poems (R'shuyot) to the Targum of the Haftarah

Israel and the coming of the Messiah and Elijah the prophet; folio 2v contains an introductory poem to the targum of the *haftarah*.[12]

2. T-S B 11.17

Paper; 1 leaf, 12.8 x 9.1 cm; 1 column; 14-15 lines; Oriental semi-cursive script; 13th cent.; Tiberian vocalization; recto contains the end of an introductory poem to the targum of the *haftarah* (=T-S AS 71.64); bottom of recto and entire verso contain Targum Jonathan with Hebrew lemmata to Isaiah 5:30 - 6:5.

3. T-S H 15.27

Paper; 1 leaf; 18.2 x 14.1 cm; 1 column; 14 + 2 lines; Oriental semi-cursive script; 12th cent.; unpointed; recto contains an Aramaic introductory poem to the targum of the Torah and *haftarah* plus two unidentified incomplete lines at the bottom; verso blank.

The following are the texts, English translations and some explanatory notes. I have also appended several relevant passages from the above mentioned and previously published poems, so as to complete the picture and facilitate comparative study of the genre.

C.U.L. T-S AS 71.64, folio 2v

1. רשות לל הפטרות
2. אסב רשות מן כלכון]   רברבניכון עם זעיריכון
3. כען הבו ש[רויא   ] דמביני עממיא אתרעי
4. בכון]   מנו] מצראי אפיק ית[כון] יי
5. אלהא דאב[התכון] יוסף עליכון כות[כון] אלף
6. זמנין [ויברך יתכ]ון כמא ד[מליל לכון]
7. דאמיר על ידי יהושע [   ] ופריש יהונ[תן]
8. בר עוזיאל רב חכימיא ובמימר חגי זכריה
9. ומלאכי נבייא דבשעתא דהוה לעי באוריתא
10. כל ציפר גפא ד[הו]ה פרח עלוהי באויר רקיע שמיא
11. הוה מתוקד משלהובית יקרא דשרי עלוהי
12. [ופ]ריש יאות והכי קא אמר:

Translation

C.U.L. T-S AS 71.64, folio 2v

1.   Permission for the *Haftarot*
2. Let me obtain permission from all of you – your old and your young.
3. Grant now permission, [you] whom He has chosen from among the nations.

---

[12] I wish to thank Mrs. Edna Engel of the Institute of Microfilmed Hebrew Manuscripts at the Jewish National and University Library in Jerusalem, for providing the dating of all three manuscripts.

4. He brought you forth from among the Egyptians. May the Lord,
5. God of your fathers, increase you a thousandfold,
6. and bless you as He promised you.
7. That which was spoken by Joshua and interpreted by Jonathan
8. ben Uzziel, master of the scholars, under the instruction of Haggai, Zechariah
9. and Malachi, the prophets; (that) when he [i.e., Jonathan] was toiling in the [study of] Torah,
10. any bird of wing that flew over him in the air of the heavenly firmament
11. would be burnt from the flame of the Glory that rested upon him.
12. And interpreting correctly, here is what he said:

Explanatory Notes

2. אסב...זעיריכון] This opening phrase is almost identical with that of Mahzor Vitry (= MV), par. 167. A similar formula for obtaining permission from young and old (lit., great and small) is found at the beginning of the second poem in Codex Reuchlinianus (=Cod. Reuch.): ברשותכון רברבייא וזעירייא.[13]

3-4. דמביני...בכון] Cf. targumim to Deuteronomy 7:6 and 14:2: בך/בכון, אתרעי...מכל עממיא and the Hebrew benediction for reading the Torah אשר בחר בנו מכל העמים, which would have been recited several times in the synagogue, only a short while before the recitation of this poem. Cf. MS T-S H 15.27, below, ואתרעי בבניהון בתריהון מכל עממיא. Also, cf. Cod. Reuch. poem no. 8: בגין כן מחייבינן למיתן ברכתא ברישא ובסופא דאתרעי בנא מן כל עממיא.

4. מצראי] The toponymic מצרים would have been expected, rather than the gentilic form, especially in conjunction with the verb אפיק. Contrast MS T-S H 15.27, ואפקנן ממצרים. The gentilic in the present MS reflects the concept of לקחת לו גוי מקרב גוי (Dt. 4:34). It may also be under the influence of the preceding phrase מביני עממיא.

4-6. יי...לכון] = Onqelos Deuteronomy 1:11. This verse is also included in MV, par. 167.

7. יהושע] This introductory poem was intended for the first day of Passover, for which the *haftarah* is from the Book of Joshua. Folio 1 of the present manuscript contains Onqelos to Exodus 12:21-31, which is part of the Torah reading for that day. Moreover, in MV, the targum of the *haftarah* for the first day of Passover, beginning with the words ויאמר יהושע, follows immediately after the various introductory poems (par. 180). In Cod. Reuch. poem no. 6, Joshua is singled out as first of the prophets: כל מיליהון דנביאיא דאיתנביאו מן יהושע משמשניה דמשה עד מלאכי כהנא.

---

[13]Further references to parallel poetic compositions in MV are to the edition of Hurwitz, mentioned above in n. 10.

Introductory Poems (R'shuyot) to the Targum of the Haftarah

However, most of the introductory poems do not refer to any specific prophet, but rely upon the reader to insert the appropriate name, e.g., נבואתא דאתנבי פל׳ נבייא ;or: אמיר דאיתאמר בנבואה על ידי פלוני נבייא. This indicates that the various introductory poems were intended not only for the first day of the Passover festival, but for other occasions as well.

8. רב חכימיא] Probably a reference to the legend cited above that Jonathan was the foremost disciple of Hillel the Elder (see note 4, above). Compare the superlative descriptions in other poems, such as והוא חד מתמנן תלמידי ספרייא רב על כולהון במילי חכימיא ורב רברנייא, (MV, par. 168), and רב חכימיא or רב ספרייא (Cod. Reuch. poems nos. 2 and 4). In some of the poems, this also serves as a background against which the reader himself is modestly contrasted: זוטר ברם אנא or ריבא אנא וזוטר בחברייא ורבייא ולא דאיקנא במיליהון דרבנייא and the most self-effacing description (quoting in part Daniel 2:30) ואנא לא בחכמתא די איתי בי מכל חייא אלהין לפום זעירות שכל דאלפני חכימיא (Cod. Reuch. poems nos. 2,4, and 3, resp.).

8-9. ובמימר...ומלאכי] Cf. beginning of footnote 1, above.

9-11. דבשעתא...עלוהי] Cf. footnote 4, above.

10. כל...שמיא] This is Onqelos to Deuteronomy 4:17, with minor adaptation. The form נפא, rather than גדפא, is the dominant variant among the manuscriptal sources of Onqelos.

12. [ו]פריש] The verb פרש is applied to targumic activity in Rabbinic literature, cf. T.B. M'gilah 3a, where Nehemiah 8:8 is interpreted as follows: מפרש זה תרגום.

C.U.L. T-S H 15.27

1. מרשות מלך מלכיא׳ ומרא דיניא דבמימריה
2. אתבריאו ארעא ושמיא׳ ואתרעי בתלתא אבהתא צדיקיא
3. אברהם יצחק ויעקב אבוהון דשבטיא׳ ואתרעי
4. בבניהון בתריהון מכל עממיא׳ ואפקנון ממצרים
5. באתיא ומופתיא ושקע פרעה ומשריתיה בימא׳
6. וחזו ישראל ושבחו תושבחיא וקרבנא לטורא דסיני ואשמעיננא
7. עשרה דבריא ויהב לנא אוריתא ופקודיא ודיניא׳
8. במשה אבוהון דכל נבייא יהא שמיה רבא מברך לעלמיא
9. ועלמי עלמיא׳ די חכמתא וגבורתא דיליה היא והוא
10. מהשני עדינייא וזמניא׳ ומרשות מרינו ורבינו
11. נגיד נגידיא ומרשות מר ור׳ שמואל ראש כל חכימיא
12. ומר[שות] הקהל הקדוש הזה יזכם אל לבנין אריאל וביאת הגואל
13. וקיבוץ נפוצות יהודה וישראל ברשות אתחיל ואתרגם בתורה
14. האל ואשלים בתרגום יונתן בן עוזיאל
15. //ד הזמן //יל   המכ////
16. ///////

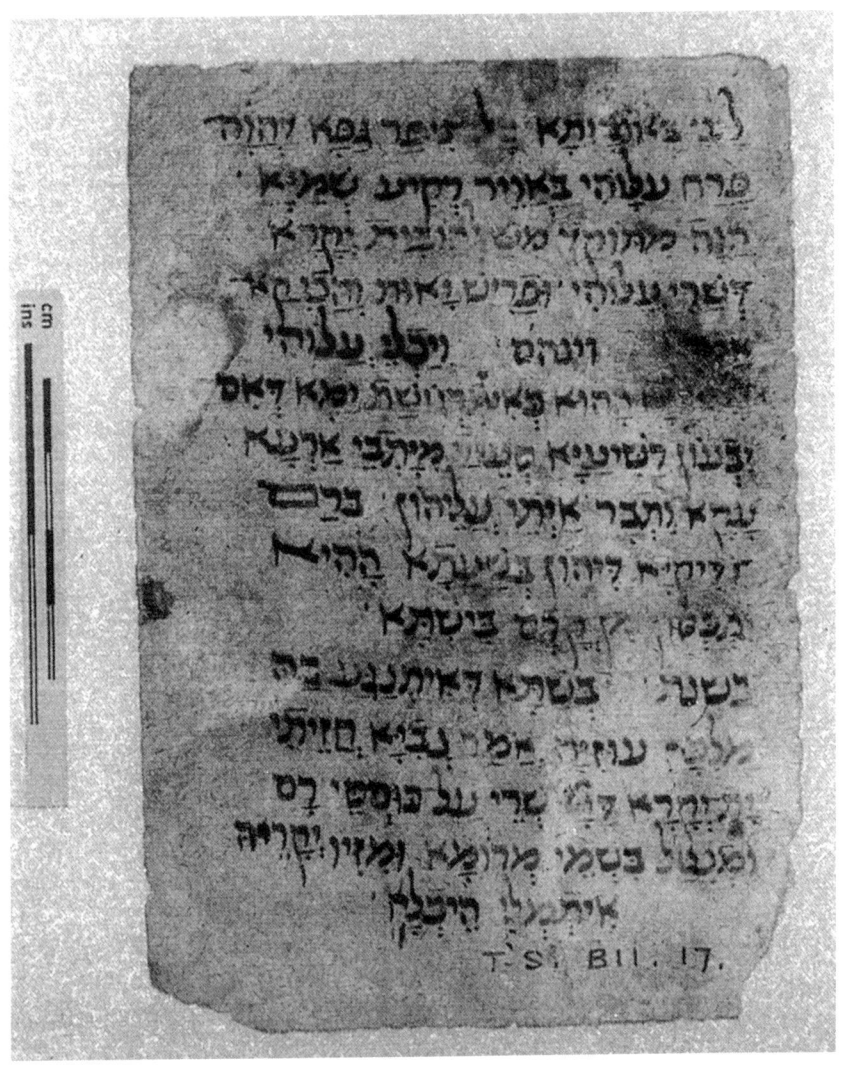

C.U.L. T-S B 11.17, recto
Courtesy of the Syndics of
Cambridge University Library

Translation
C.U.L T-S H 15.27
Permission for the Targum of Jonathan ben Uzziel
1. With permission of the King of Kings and the Master of Judges, by Whose word
2. earth and heaven were created. He chose the three righteous patriarchs
3. Abraham, Isaac and Jacob, father of the Tribes; and chose
4. their children after them from among the nations. He brought them forth from Egypt
5. with signs and wonders; and drowned Pharaoh and his army in the seas.
6. And Israel saw, and offered praises. He brought us near Mount Sinai and made us hear
7. the ten sayings. He gave us the instructions, commandments and laws
8. through Moses father of all prophets; may His great name be blessed forever
9. a..d forever after. Wisdom and might are His; He
10. alters the seasons and times. With permission of our master and teacher,
11. prince of princes, and with permission of our m[aster] and t[eacher] Samuel, head of the scholars,
12. and with permission of this holy congregation, may the Almighty grant them [to witness] the [re]building of Ariel [i..e., the Holy Temple], the arrival of the Redeemer,
13. and the ingathering of the dispersions of Judah and Israel. With permission, I will begin to translate the divine
14. Torah, and I will conclude with the Targum of Jonathan ben Uzziel
15. [   ] the time [   ]
16. [   ]

Explanatory Notes
1. מלכיא׳] Pairs of superlinear strokes are used to indicate rhymed phrases (-*ayya*) throughout the poem.
2-3. ואתרעי ב-] Cf. the beginning of MS T-S AS 71.64, for the motif of chosenness.
4. ואפקנון] Accusative and dative attached suffixes, characteristic of the dialect of Onqelos and Jonathan to the Prophets, are employed here and elsewhere in this poem: וקרבנא and ואשמעינא (line 6). Also, note the use of the verb חזו (line 6).

7. עשרה דביריה] Hebrew עשרת הדברים in Exodus 34:28; Deuteronomy 4:13; 10:4. In all of these verses the phrase is translated by Onqelos as עשרא ת/פתגמיא/ן. Only in the Palestinian targumim do we find the expression עשרתי דבירייא. Also, in Deuteronomy 4:10, ואשמעם את דברי is translated in Onqelos ואשמעינון ית פתגמי, as opposed to ואשמע יתהון ית דברי in Neofiti. The phrase ואשמעינא עשרה דבירייא in the present poem seems to be a hybrid of Onqelos and Palestinian targum dialects.

8-9. יהא...עלמיא] This clause is included under the influence of Daniel 2:20, and leads directly into the following two phrases. However, its wording has been altered to conform almost verbatim with the similar and more popularly known version in the Qadish prayer. The referent is the subject of the preceding verbs, namely God.

9-10. די...ומניא] = Daniel 2:20-21.

10-11. מרינו...חכימיא] The person described has not been identified. The juxtaposition of the title נגיד נגידיא with the personal name R. Shmuel calls to mind R. Shmuel Hanagid of Granada (993-1055 C.E.). But there is no supportive evidence for this identification, nor am I aware of any parallel for the superlative title "prince of princes."

12. ומרשות] The remainder of the composition is in Hebrew.

13-14. אתחיל...עוזיאל] This *r'shut* would seem to have been recited before the targum to the Torah reading, תורת האל, but served to obtain permission also for the targum of the hafṭarah, ואשלים בתרגום יונתן בן עוזיאל.

Introductory Poems (R'shuyot) to the Targum of the Haftarah

Appendix of Parallel Compositions from Codex Reuchlinianus (CR) [14] and from Maḥzor Vitry (MV, *apud* Hurwitz)

CR, Introductory passage

בשם עוטה כמלתחה אורה / אחרוט וגם אסדרה / רשויות קודם הפטרה

CR 1

אנקוט בריש הרמני מקמי רחמנא / בתר הכי ממרנא ורבננא /
גרסי קראי מתניתא ואולפנא / .... / סוכלתנו אפיש ליונתן רב
חכימייא / פירש תורגמן לכל מילייא ולכל נבייא /
אמיר דיתאמר בנבואה / על ידי פל' נבייא כמא דפרש /
יונתן בר עוזיאל / וכדו הוה פריש ואמר.

CR 2

אפתח פומא בשבחא דמרי דשמייא / ברשותכון רברבייא וזעירייא /
ריבא אנא וזוטר בחברייא / .... / יהוון לרעווא כל אמריא /
דאמינא קדמיכון רחומייא / מילתא דפרש יהונתן רב ספרייא /
נבואתא דאיתנבי פל' נבייא.

CR 4

שמעו שותאי רברבייא וזוטרייא / דאתן לצלאה בהדין כנסיא /
.... / מריש הרמנא נסיבית מחכימיא / והדר שריתי לתרגומי
בנביאייא / היכמא דתרגים רב חכימייא / יונתן מתורגמן וסגן
ספרייא / .... / זוטר ברם אנא ורבייא / ולא דאיקנא במיליהון
דרבנייא / קדמיכון אשכח סבר אפייא / כד אישרי לתרגומי מילייא /
דאיתאמרו בנבואה מן שמייא / על ידוי דפל' נבייא.

CR 5

אוול איסב הירמון ממרי עלמא / ברי כל דאיכא במישרא וברומא /
.... / מהרמניה אשרי לישן ואפתח פומא / נבואת עבדוהי לתרוצי
בשותא תירגומא / סוף מילייא איסב מילכא וטעמא / עתודי מרשותכון
על איסטוונא דקיימא / פשר אפטרתא לתרגומי ורזין לפרסומא /
.../ שפר מילי פשר אחוית תרגומא / לנא / היך תרגום יונתן
חכימא / מה דאיתנבי פל' נביא בנומא / היכדין אישרי לתרגומי דן יומא.

---

[14]The present transcriptions are based upon the facsimile edition published by A. Sperber, *Codex Reuchlinianus no. 3 of the Badische Landesbibliothek in Karlsruhe* (Copenhagen: Ejnar Munksgaard, 1956), pp. 769-70. There are a number of variants in Bacher's transcription. Whereas de Lagarde's readings are extremely accurate, Bacher's edition is replete with printer's errors, or unintentional "corrections" of the texts.

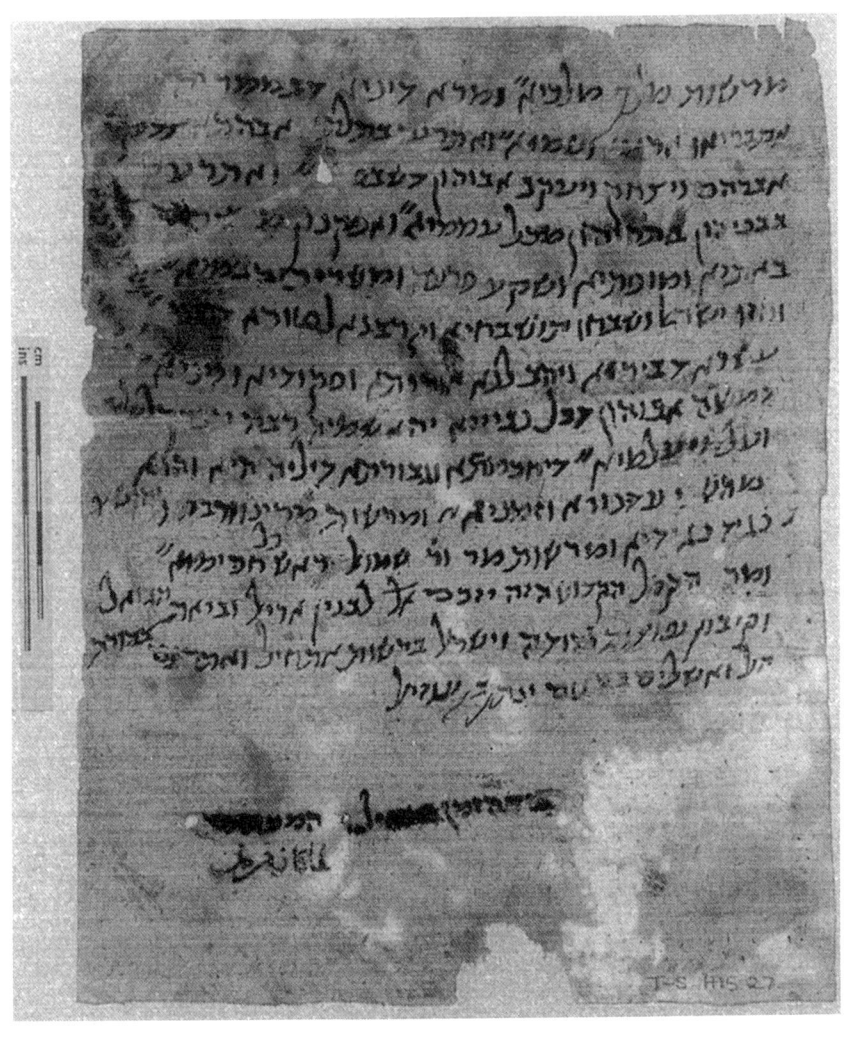

C.U.L. T-S H 15.27, recto
Courtesy of the Syndics of
Cambridge University Library

Introductory Poems (R'shuyot) to the Targum of the Haftarah

CR 6

טב לך יונתן בר עוזיאל דאיתרעי בך מרי עלמא מכל חברך תלמידי
הלל סבא וקבלתא אולפן מן פום חגי זכריה מלאכי לתרגומי כל
מיליהון דנביאיא דאיתנביאו מן יהושע משמשניה דמשה עד מלאכי
כהנא רבא וכדו תרגים ואמר בספרא דנבואת פל' באפטרתא דעניין
יומא פל' כמא דאתקינו רבני סנהדרין למיקרי בספר אוריתא
ולאפטורי בנביאיא

MV 167

איסב רשות מכולכון. מן רברבניכון ומן זעיריכון. בריכון תהוון
קדם אלהכון וידרכון רגליכון על פריקת צוארי סנאיכון: יי אלהא
דאבהתכון אסף עליכון כוותכון אלף זמנין ויברך יתכון כמא דמליל
לכון. אמיר דאיתמר בנבואה על ידי פלוני נבייא. או נגידא. או
מלכא: כמא דפריש יונתן בר עוזיאל וכדו הוה פריש ואמר:

MV 168

... מצליין וקריין באורייתא דכייא : ומתרגמן במילי בחירי נבייא:
כתרגם יונתן רב רברבניא: מפומיה דמלאכי חגי וזכריה: יאיין
שמעתתיה בסימו מילייא. והוא חד מתמנן תלמידי ספרייא: רב על
כולהון במילי חכמימא. עוף דפרח עלוהי מיקיד כעסיק בעלוקיא:
ועייפו מילוהי ארבע מאה פרסי פותחי. יסודי ושכלולי דארעא צבייא:
אתרעישו ואתרגיפו תחות קלא יקומייא. אורכא אזדעזעא ארבע מאה
פרסייא: נפקא בת קלא משמי מרומייא. מאן הוא דמגלי סודי סתרייא:
קם על ריגלוהי באימתא וזעיא. מתחנן קמי מרי מרייא: לא ליקרי
עבדית כך קדמך גלייא. ולא ליקר בית אבא ורבי ושבחייא: להן ליקרך
דר על כרוביא. בדיל דלא יסגון בעלי פלוגתייא: ותוב צבי לפרושי
כתיבי קדישיא: וקל מן שמיא נפל דיך בקדמיא: מטול דאית ב[ה]
קיצא פרקייא. קץ משיחא צדיקא דאתי לסופייא: ומטול מן ריבוני
בחיריא. ברשותכון מפטרינא בנבכי פסוקייא: ובריכין תהוון לאלהא.
ותזכון לקיומי כל פיקודייא: אמיר.

MV 173

ארו שותא בלא רשותא. .... יהונתן. גבר סוכלתן. עלי משכביה. יהי
שלמא: אמיר:

MV 174

יציב פתגם. לאת ודגם. .... כקאימנא. ותרגימנא. במילוי דבחיר
ספרין: יהונתן גבר [ענוותן]. בכן ליה ינמטי אפרין: אמיר:

MV 175

שדי עובדוהי מהחווי סגיין .... וברם. קהלא חדין על' דא אנחנא
אתיין. דנתרגם אפטרתא דאפרין נמטיין: נבייא פלנייא. בחיזא חילמא
חזיין. ויהונתן פירשה בקראי מקריין: אמיר:

MV 176

שפר ישפר מלכי. .... משיחא ייתי עינוותן. יהי לנא צוותן. כמא
דפריש יהונתן. דגליה ליה מטמרין: אמיר:

MV 177

אלהא מקמא בעינא רשותא. בתריה ממרן דהכא בי כנשתא: .... ואתינא
קמייכו תרגומי אפטרתא: .... זקוקי זכוון באישא בעורתא. פרושי
תורגמנא ומילי נביואתא. וכד פרש בר עוזיאל וגלי מסתרתא. מפומיה
דקודשא בריך הוא דדיליה מלכותא: אמיר.

MV 179

אלימו כען דמינכון כזיז. .... כדן פריש יהונתן. קבל [קהלה] דקם
קבלין. אמיר:

4

The Priestly Consecration (Leviticus 8): A Rite of Passage

By Jacob Milgrom

Arnold van Gennep has defined rites of passage as "rites which accompany every change of place, state, social position and age." They are marked by three phases: separation, margin (or *limen*, signifying "threshold" in Latin), and aggression, as illustrated by the following diagram[1]:

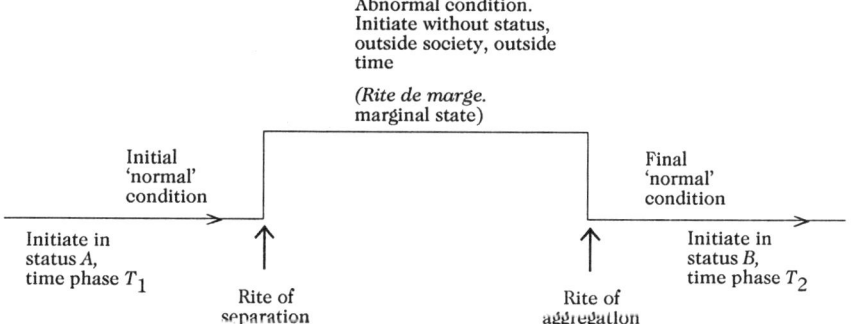

Turner characterizes the liminal phase:

> During the intervening liminal period, the characteristics of the subject (the passenger) are ambiguous: he passes through a cultural realm that has few or none of the attributes of the past or coming state... as liminal beings, they have no status, property, insignia, secular clothing indicating rank or rule, position in a kinship system – in short, nothing that may distinguish them from their fellow neophytes or initiands. Their behavior is normally

---

[1] A. Van Gennep, *The Rites of Passage* (London: Routledge and Kegan Paul, 1960); E. Leach, *Culture and Communication* (Cambridge: Cambridge University Press, 1976), p. 78.

passive or humble; they must obey their instructions implicitly, and accept arbitrary punishment without complaint.²

This description of the liminal state already bears many similarities to the biblical rite of priestly consecration. First, however, let a specific example throw these similarities into clear relief. During the installation rites of the Kanongesh (senior chief) of the Ndembu, the chief-elect is isolated in a hut called *kafwi*, a term Ndembu derive from *ku-fwa*, "to die," where he dies from his commoner state. He is clad in nothing but a ragged waist-cloth and sits crouched in a posture of shame or modesty. The officiant conducts the rite of *Kumukindyila*, which literally means "to speak evil or insulting words against him." His homily begins with these words: "Be silent! You are a mean and selfish fool, one who is bad-tempered! You do not love your fellows, you are only angry with them! Meanness and theft are all you have! Yet we have called you and we say that you must succeed to the chieftainship." After this harangue, any person who considers that he has been wronged by the chief-elect in the past is entitled to revile him, while the latter has to sit silently with head downcast. In the meantime, the officiant strikes his buttocks insultingly. The night before the rite, the chief-elect is prevented from sleeping, partly as an ordeal, partly because he may doze off and have bad dreams about the shades of dead chiefs. For the duration of the rite, he is submissive, silent and sexually continent.³

The above-cited taboos relating to the liminal state accompanying the elevation of a chief characterize many other primitive cultures as well. The chief-elect of the Swazi "remains secluded; ... all day he sits naked on a lion skin in the ritual hut of the harem or in the sacred enclosure in the royal cattle byre. Men of his inner circle see that he breaks none of the taboos."⁴ During the installation rite for the king of Gaboon, the people

> surrounded him in a dense crowd, and then began to heap upon him every manner of abuse that the worst of mobs could imagine. Some spat in his face; some beat him with their fists; some kicked him; others threw disgusting objects at him; while those unlucky ones who stood on the outside, and could reach the poor fellow only with their voices, assiduously cursed him, his father, his mother, his sisters and brothers, and all his ancestors to the

---

²V. Turner, *The Ritual Process* (Chicago: Aldine, 1969), pp. 94-95.
³*Ibid.*, pp. 100-9.
⁴H. Kuper, *An African Aristocracy* (London: Oxford, 1947), pp. 219-20, cited in Turner, *The Forest of Symbols* (Ithaca: Cornell University Press, 1967), p. 109.

remotest generation. A stranger would not have given a cent for the life of him who was presently to be crowned.[5]

Rites of passage are attested throughout the world, in every culture and age. The examples adduced above have been selected only because they have a bearing on Israel and the ancient Near East.[6] The similarities to the biblical rite of priestly consecration are quickly recognizable: the seclusion of the consecrands (in the Sanctuary court), their silence and submissiveness (they are commanded, but do not respond), their sexual continence (they are isolated within the sacred premises), and their mortal fear lest they break any of the taboos. Regarding the latter, the biblical text is frustratingly brief. It specifies only one taboo, that of leaving the Sanctuary. Clearly there were others. For example, since their status was still that of laymen, they were forbidden to officiate on the altar or enter the shrine (cf. Numbers 18:3), and they cooked and ate the sacrificial portions reserved for the laity in the area reserved for the laity[7] rather than eating the priestly prebends[8] in the inner court – the exclusive preserve of the priests. Moreover, being in the Sanctuary, they would have taken precautions against the occurrence of ritual impurity. The chief-elect of the Ndembu was prevented from sleeping the night before his installation because of the fear of a polluting dream. The high priest of Israel was kept awake Yom Kippur night for fear of a polluting emission. "If he sought to slumber, young members of the priesthood would snap their middle finger before him and say to him, 'My lord, high priest, get up and drive away [sleep] this once [by walking] on the [cold] pavement.' And they used to divert him until the time of slaughtering drew near" (m. Yoma> 1:7). One must presuppose that equally effective measures were enjoined for the priestly consecration.

It is, however, the Babylonian New Year Festival that provides the most illuminating parallels to the cases cited above. For the Babylonians, New Year was a momentous rite of passage. The fate of the nation was decreed during this period: "He (the šešgallu-priest) shall strike the king's cheek. If, when [he strikes] the king's cheek, the tears flow, (it means that) the god Bel is friendly: if no tears appear, the god Bel is angry: the enemy will rise up and bring about his downfall."[9]

---

[5]P.B. Du Chaillu, *Explorations and Adventures in Equatorial Africa* (New York: Harper, 1868), pp. 43-44, cited in Turner, *Ritual Process*, p. 171.
[6]Cf. also R. Patai, *Man and Temple in Ancient Jewish Myth and Ritual* (London: Thomas Nelson and Sons, 1947), p. 183.
[7]Leviticus 8:31.
[8]Leviticus 8: 26-29.
[9]J.E. Pritchard, *Ancient Near Eastern Texts* (Princeton: Princeton University Press, 1955), p. 334.

Moreover, the studied humiliation of the king is a prominent feature of the festival:

> When he (the king) reaches [the presence of the god Bel], the *šešgallu*-priest shall leave the (sanctuary) and take away the scepter, the circle, and the sword [from the king]. He shall bring them [before the god Bel] and place them [on] a chair. He shall leave (the sanctuary) and strike the king's cheek....He shall accompany him (the king) into the presence of the god Bel...he shall drag (him by) the ears and make him bow to the ground.[10]

The similarities and, more important, the differences between the Babylonian New Year Festival and Israel's Yom Kippur are discussed elsewhere,[11] but the parallels between the Babylonian king and the Ndembu chief in their respective liminal states need to be underscored here. Both are stripped of their clothing – their symbols of authority – and are subjected to rites of humiliation. Nothing of this sort obtains in the consecration ceremonies for Aaron and his sons. To the contrary, Aaron is explicitly anointed while wearing his ornate robes; so, too, his sons after they don their official garments. Yet this may be the biblical method of accentuating this liminal state: dressed as priests, they may not serve as priests; they are in effect laymen and their priesthood still lies ahead. They truly are in passage. During the seven-day dedication of the temple built by Gudea of Lagash, all ranks are abolished.[12] One can only recall that on Yom Kippur the high priest is indeed divested of his princely garments and dressed in simple linen vestments (Leviticus 16:4), a requirement which has been variously interpreted. But on this annual day when the welfare of the nation hangs upon the efficacy of his ritual, he is literally engaged in a rite of passage, entering and exiting the Holy of Holies, into which no man – not even a Moses – may enter. Even so, no act of self-deprecation was instituted for the priestly investiture. Did perhaps a ritual of verbal humiliation obtain? The Bible is silent.

Thus anthropology helps illumine the priestly consecration ceremony. The virtual quarantining of the consecrands within the sanctuary court and the admonition that they must observe the restrictions imposed upon them (as laymen) give the unshakable impression that we have to do here with a rite of passage where the

---

[10]*Ibid.*
[11]J. Milgrom, *Leviticus I. AB 3* (Garden City: Doubleday, 1991), chapter 16, Comment C.
[12]A. Falkenstein and W. von Soden, *Sumerische und Akkadische Hymnen und Gebeten* (Zürich: Artemis, 1953), I, 180: Gudea Cylinder B xvii; G. A. Barton, *The Royal Inscriptions of Sumer and Akkad* (New Haven: Yale University Press, 1929), p. 187: Statue B vii, 26-43.

The Priestly Consecration (Leviticus 8): A Rite of Passage

priestly consecrands and their ordination offering share a transitional, liminal status. The priestly consecration, therefore, begs for anthropological analysis. (An attempt was made by Leach[13], but it is flawed by a multitude of exegetical errors.)

Why the liminal state is always a perilous one is difficult to answer. Perhaps the establishment, entrenched outside, regards the anarchical, amorphous state of the consecrands as a danger to societal law and order.[14] Mary Douglas' investigation[15] would, rather, point to the anomalous position of the consecrands which, by the very fact that it defies classification, is feared as dangerous. In either case, there would be complete agreement that Aaron and his sons underwent a transformation during their rite of passage. Henceforth they are priests; however, their acquired privileges and prestige are matched by greater responsibilities and restrictions.

---

[13]Leach, *op. cit.* (n. 1), pp. 77-93.
[14]Turner, *Ritual Process*, pp. 108-9.
[15]M. Douglas, *Purity and Danger* (London: Routledge and Kegan Paul, 1966).

5

The Greco-Roman Philosophy of Judaism: The Mishnah in Context

By Jacob Neusner

I

At stake in the philosophy of Judaism represented by the Mishnah, a philosophical system in the form of a law code brought to closure in the Land of Israel ca. 200 C.E., is not merely analysis of how things are, but a proposition on why they are the way they are, what it means that things are this way, rather than some other. Accordingly, the philosophy of Judaism demonstrates – predictably, through a plethora of detailed cases – that all things in place, in proper rank and position in the hierarchy of being, point to, stand for, one thing. I suppose that, in the context of Scripture, with its insistence that Israel's God is one and unique, we may take as the unarticulated premise a theological position, and, it would follow, identify as premise that fundamental and ancient affirmation of Israel.

But we deal with a composition that is everywhere systematically philosophical and only rarely, and then episodically, theological. Two-thirds of all tractates focus upon issues of philosophy, and scarcely a line of the Mishnah invokes the word "God" or the active presence of God. More to the point, the philosophy never addresses in philosophical terms such theological questions as the meaning and end of history, the nature of prophecy, nature and supernature, the being of God, miracles, and the like.[1] True, answers to these questions assuredly lie at, or even lay, the foundations for the philosophical structure. But the system and

---

[1] The suspicious attitude toward miracles, expressed in the famous story about Ḥoni the Circle-drawer, forms a very minor footnote (Ta‹anit 3:8). Silences testify far more eloquently than occasional observations or pointed stories.

structure ask the questions philosophers ask concerning the nature of things, and answer them in the way the philosophers answer them, through orderly sifting of data in the process of natural philosophy. The only point of difference is subject-matter, but, after all, philosophers in the great tradition took up multiple questions; some worked on this, some on the other thing, and no single question predominated.

We address in particular the *telos* of thought. To state the Mishnah's philosophical method and proposition simply, many things are made to say one thing, which concerns the nature of being, and the philosophy of Judaism must be deemed ontological. For it is a statement of an ontological order that the system makes when it claims that all things are not only orderly, but ordered in such wise that many things fall into one classification, and one thing may hold together many things of a single classification. These two contrary propositions – many things are one, one thing is many – complement each other, because, in forming matched opposites, the two provide a complete and final judgment of the whole.

That judgment faces forward and backward. The framers of the Mishnah set forth a substantial judgment concerning order and the rationality that identifies what is orderly. For this philosophy, rationality consists in hierarchy of the orders of things. That rationality is revealed by the possibility always of effecting the hierarchical classification of all things: each thing in its *taxon*, all *taxa* in correct sequence, from least to greatest. And showing that all things can be ordered, and that all orders can be set into relationship with one another, we transform method into message. The message of hierarchical classification is that many things really form a single thing, the many species a single genus, the many genera an encompassing and well-crafted, cogent whole. Every time we speciate, we affirm that position; each successful labor of forming relationships among species, e.g., making them into a genus, or identifying the hierarchy of the species, proves it again. Not only so, but when we can show that many things are really one, or that one thing yields many (the reverse and confirmation of the former), we say in a fresh way a single immutable truth, the one of this philosophy concerning the unity of all being in an orderly composition of all things within a single *taxon*. The species point to the genus, all classes to one class, all *taxa* properly hierarchized then rise to the top of the structure and the system forming one *taxon*. So all things ascend to, reach one thing. All that remains is for the theologian to define that one thing: God. But that is a step that the philosophers of the Mishnah did not take. Perhaps it was because they did not think they had to. But I think there is a different reason altogether. It is because, as a matter of fact, they were philosophers.

And to philosophers, as I said at the outset, God serves as premise and principle (and whether or not it is one God or many gods, a unique being or a being that finds a place in a class of similar beings is hardly germane!), and philosophy serves not to demonstrate principles or to explore premises, but to analyze the unknown, to answer important questions.

In such an enterprise the premise, God, turns out to be merely instrumental, and the given principle, to be merely interesting. But for philosophers, intellectuals, God can live not in the details, but in the unknown, in the as-yet unsolved problem and the unresolved dilemma. In the philosophy of Judaism, God lives, so to speak, in the excluded middle. God is revealed in the interstitial case. God is made known through the phenomena that form a single phenomenon. God is perceived in the one that is many. God is encountered in the many that are one. For that is the dimension of being – that, so I claim, immanental and sacramental dimension of being – that defines for this philosophy its statement of ultimate concern, its recurrent point of tension, its generative problematic.

That then is the urgent question, the ineluctable and self-evidently truthful answer: God in the form, God in the order, God in the structure, God in the heights, God at the head of the great chain of hierarchical being. True, God is premise, scarcely mentioned. But it is because God's name does not have to be mentioned when the whole of the order of being says that name, and only that name, and always that name, the name unspoken because it is always in the echo, the silent, thin voice, the numinous in all phenomena.

Among the philosophers of that time and place, which is to say, within important components of the philosophical tradition that sustained the Greco-Roman world, however arcane the subject matter of the philosophy of Judaism, the philosophers of Judaism can claim a rightful, and honored, place. Among the philosophers, Judaism's philosophy can be and should have been perceived not merely as philosophical, but, indeed, as philosophy. The basis for that claim is simple: whether or not philosophers can have understood a line of the document (and I doubt that they would have cared to try), the method and the message of the philosophy of Judaism fall into the classification of philosophical methods and messages of the Greco-Roman philosophical tradition. The method is like that of Aristotle; the message, congruent to that of neo-Platonism.

To state the upshot of the proposition at hand, Judaism's first system, the Mishnah's, finds its natural place within philosophy first because it appeals to the Aristotelian methods of natural philosophy – classification, comparison and contrast – and the media of expression of philosophy – *Listenwissenschaft* – to register its position. And, second, that proposition, on the essential unity or the hierarchical nature of all being, falls into the classification of philosophy, since, as we shall see, it forms one important, generative premise of neo-Platonism. But in registering these twin-claims as to the philosophical character, in philosophical context, of the philosophy of Judaism, I have moved well ahead of my story. Let us start from the beginning and move onward, first to method, then to proposition.

II

Let me then ask, is this Judaism philosophical not in *its* context[2] but in the setting of philosophy? I mean: by the criteria of method and message dictated by what persons or movements generally acknowledged as philosophical deemed philosophical, can we classify the method as philosophical? And can we identify the message as philosophical? What I wish to know, then, is the answer to two simple questions:

As to method, can we classify the taxonomic method – premises and rules – of the Sages in the same category as the method of Aristotle?

As to substance, can we identify the fundamental propositions of the philosophy of Judaism with the premises and points of acute engagement of Plato in the version that would emerge in the third century as neo-Platonism?

These are the questions that yield answers on the context in which the philosophy of Judaism is to be located. And, in this setting, by "context" is meant something piquantly appropriate to our results: the classification of the philosophy. For, as I shall now show, our back-country philosophers in a fairly primitive way replicated the method of Aristotle in setting forth the single paramount proposition of neo-Platonism.[3]

---

[2]Whatever we deem that context to have been, and scarcely a word in the entire Mishnah suggests what it was, or what it was supposed to have been.

[3]I leave for Philonic scholarship the comparison of the Mishnah's neo-Platonism with that of Philo. Philo's mode of writing, his presentation of his ideas, seems to me so different from the mode and method of the Mishnah that I am not sure how we can classify as Aristotelian (in the taxonomic framework of natural philosophy, which seems to me the correct framework for the Mishnah's philosophical method) the principal methodological traits of Philo's thought. But others are most welcome to correct what is only a superficial impression. I think the selection for comparison and contrast of Aristotle and neo-Platonism – first method, then proposition – is a preferable strategy of analysis (and exposition, as a matter of fact), and I willingly accept the onus of criticism for not comparing and contrasting the method and message of Philo with those of the Mishnah. I mean only to suggest that the questions Wolfson's Philo raised

The issue is not one of direct connection. None conjure up the fantasy and anachronism of the Mishnah's authors tramping down a Galilean hill from their yeshiva to the academy in a nearby Greek-speaking town, Caesarea or Sepphoris, for example, there studying elementary Aristotle and listening to the earliest disclosures of neo-Platonism, then climbing back up the hill and writing it all up in the crabbed back-country idiom made up of the cases and examples of the Mishnah.

But, as a matter of fact, in its indicative traits of message and method, the Mishnah's philosophical system is a version of one critical proposition of neo-Platonism, set forth and demonstrated through a standard Aristotelian method.[4] And that is what an examination of the philosophical context will show us. But – as I cannot overstress – these judgments rest upon not a claim of direct connection but an exercise of simple, inductive comparison and contrast, that is to say, of mere classification.[5] I propose now only in an entirely inductive manner to

---

may well be reopened, but within an entirely fresh set of premises and in accord with what I conceive to be a more properly differentiated and therefore critical reading of the data.

[4]I need hardly add that the very eclecticism of the philosophy of Judaism places it squarely within the philosophical mode of its time. See J. M. Dillon and A.A. Long, eds., *The Question of "Eclecticism." Studies in Later Greek Philosophy* (Berkeley: University of California Press, 1988).

[5]I hasten to add that further studies of the Mishnah's philosophical context are about to make much more precise any judgment about the philosophical context of the document and its system. For this initial account, it seems unnecessary to do more than argue, as I do, that the Mishnah's fundamental intellectual structure in its method and message fall into the classification, defined by circumstance and context, of philosophy. The method, I shall show, is standard for natural philosophy, exemplified by Aristotle, and the proposition proves entirely congruent with one principal conception of Middle Platonism, exemplified by Plotinus. At the same time, I point out, the components of congruence, method and message alike yield far more specific results. If we ask, does the Mishnah's theory of mixtures coincide with that of a specific philosophy of the larger tradition, the answer is, indeed so: the Stoic. But do other components of the Mishnah's metaphysics fit together with the rest of Stoic physics, e.g., theories of space and time? So, too, if Middle Platonism will have found entirely familiar the Mishnah's keen interest in showing how one thing yields many things, in demonstrating a hierarchical unity of being through the ordering of all classes of things (that is to say, the ontological unity of things proven on the basis of the natural world), does that make the Mishnah's philosophy in general a form of Middle Platonism? If we ask about the concept of space of place, we look in vain for a familiar conception; cf. S. Sambursky, *The Concept of Place in Late Neoplatonism* (Jerusalem: Israel Academy of Sciences and Humanities, 1982). My general impression is that, when all is said and done, the philosophy of Judaism is far less abstract, even at its most abstract level, than any other philosophy of the same tradition and temporal

classify the system by the indicative traits of philosophical systems. In that simple way I shall show that, in two fundamental aspects, this system shares traits important to systems all deem philosophical. Therefore, this system by the criteria of philosophy and in the specific and explicit context of philosophy must be classified as philosophical. That is my simple argument. But it is fundamental to my purpose, which is to show that in the Mishnah's system, both as to mode of thought and as to message, we deal with a philosophy – philosophy in an odd idiom, to be sure, but philosophy nonetheless.[6]

True, none can seriously admit a claim of diachronic let alone synchronic intersection. The Mishnah as a representation of the philosophy of Judaism links itself with no prior writing but Scripture, hence we exclude diachronic connection ("tradition"). And it is a commonplace of scholarship that the Sages at hand never cite a line of a philosophical text of their own day or of any other time, hence we exclude synchronic relationship. So how shall I show that Judaism's system as the Mishnah portrays it is a philosophy – that is to say, is to be classified as philosophy?

Let me ask the question in its simplest form: by appeal to the paramount taxic traits of Aristotelian method and neo-Platonic message, can we classify the method as Aristotelian, the proposition as neo-Platonic? If we can, then my purpose, which is to demonstrate that the Judaism of the Mishnah is a philosophy, will have been accomplished. That is as far as we can go: no further. But it suffices to accomplish the goal of demonstrating that, as to classification, the system of the Judaism of the Dual Torah is a philosophical system. That fact established, the characterization of the second system of the Judaism of the Dual Torah will become possible.

Let me explain first of all why I place severe limits upon what is to be claimed: classification through comparison and contrast, *that* alone.

---

setting; as to the issue of space or place, my sense is that the Judaic philosophers were deeply concerned with *what* things are, not where they are; Jerusalem, for instance, is a profoundly abstract, taxic indicator. That conforms to the larger Aristotelianism of the system. Here, I prove only that by the synchronic and even diachronic standards of philosophy, Judaism – method, message, if not medium – in this system is philosophical. These preliminary remarks are meant only to point the way toward a further range of inquiry into the philosophy of Judaism: the comparison and contrast in detail of that philosophy with other philosophies of the Greco-Roman tradition.

[6]And no less than Philo's philosophy was a philosophy. My sense is that these results, when properly digested and refined, as noted above (n. 3), must reopen the questions addressed by the great Harry A. Wolfson in his *Philo: Foundations of Religious Philosophy in Judaism, Christianity, and Islam* (Cambridge: Harvard University Press, 1947).

Why do I insist that what I undertake is mere comparison, without a claim as to direct contact, of two philosophical worlds? And how come I undertake only the goal of showing that one of the worlds is sufficiently like the other to be classified with the other, the mishnaic with the Aristotelian in method and with the neo-Platonic in message? The reason is simple. Contexts both diachronic and synchronic prove notoriously difficult to specify. The reason is that the one book our philosophers have given us, the Mishnah, identifies no author or authority, specifies no context in its own time or in times past, and lacking beginning and ending seems indifferent to all questions of circumstance and setting. We do not know the books that our authors consulted, the modes of thought and media of inquiry that they found helpful. Our inductive inquiry has permitted an outline of a philosophy of hierarchical classification of all things within a single structure, but the same inductive method that must govern contains scarcely a suggestion on the context in which the philosophy has found its intellectual nurture.

And yet, of course, that is not entirely true, so an important qualification is required. While our authors set forth their system in a document mostly indifferent to issues of context, whether intellectual or social, there is one prior writing the presence of which is acknowledged, and that is Scripture. Where the Mishnah contains language that is different from the prevailing syntax and morphology, word-choices and even mode of discourse, we can always identify the source of that language by reference to a single piece of writing, which is the Scripture. And the authors of the Mishnah acknowledge that fact with key-language such as "as it is said" or "as it is written." It is not common, but it is there. Accordingly, the inquiry into the context in which the first philosophy of Judaism came to formation and expression begins with Scripture.

But the search for context turns up little of consequence. To account for the distinctive character of Mishnah, with its now-demonstrated concern properly to classify all things in hierarchical order, we look in vain to Scripture. For there, among the diverse writings collected as the Mosaic Pentateuch, while assuredly we find sustained interest in the problem of order, we cannot identify at any point passages that set forth or even adumbrate the method of hierarchical classification. The Priestly authorship in Genesis 1:1-24 sets forth the myth of creation as an exercise in bringing order out of chaos through the hierarchical classification of all things. When order is attained, then God calls creation very good and blesses and sanctifies what has been ordered. So, in a very general sense, the Priestly creation-myth invites deep thought on the principles of hierarchical classification of the natural and social world. An interest in the good and stable order of society in the image of Heaven characterizes other passages of the Priestly Code as well, and in that Code, as many have observed, e.g., with reference to the taboo against sowing mixed seeds, interstitial cases form a source of danger. But scarcely a line in Scripture prepares us for what we find in the Mishnah, and, conversely, the authors of the Mishnah only occasionally and episodically acknowledge the presence of Scripture.

Given the sustained and pervasive interest in hierarchical classification through appeal to the traits of things, moreover, how shall we have expected otherwise? For if Scripture's Priestly Code has asked the question of order, on the one side, and classification on the other, and if the Code likewise identifies interstitial cases as problems, the Priests have no solution to offer as to how these problems are to be solved and questions to be answered. But the Mishnah's sagacious authors do, and that solution draws them across the frontier that separates intuitive or poetic from philosophical and systematic thought. And, as we now recognize full well, the Mishnah is nothing if not systematic, and, in a very general sense, philosophical in its method. To state matters baldly, if the authors of the Mishnah had turned to Scripture for guidance on *how* to accomplish their goal, which is the ordering of all things in a single manner and construction, they simply could not have found the required method for doing so. Accordingly, Scripture did not teach the lessons that have guided the formation of the philosophy of Judaism. No wonder that the Priestly authors of the Creation-myth attributed to God and not to the human being the power to endow all things with their rightful name and to set them forth each in its correct position and order in relationship to all other things. God could do it, humanity could not.

It follows that the diachronic inquiry leads elsewhere than to Scripture. But where? If the answer is to be gained principally through showing how the authors of the Mishnah cited and made use of other writings than Scripture, then there is no answer to be found. For, as I have underlined just now, the philosophers whose system comes to expression in the Mishnah set forth a seamless system, lacking antecedents, acknowledging only Scripture, if that. So if our philosophers read books other than Scripture, we cannot say what they might have been. Nor does appeal to the particular historical circumstances of the document and its writers help. For, it is generally assumed, these later second-century back-country Galilean intellectuals, conducting their reflections in the aftermath of two violent wars against Rome, cannot be supposed to have had ready access to the great libraries of the age, or, if they did, to have read enough Greek to learn the rules of classification and hierarchization that Greco-Roman philosophy had long since worked out. The simple facts of the matter deny our identifying as the philosophy's diachronic context the ancient heritage of Greco-Roman philosophy.

The way beyond the impasse – the utter absence of pertinent data permitting allegations of intersection and filiation – lies through the simple comparison, out of all concrete context, of what our philosophers have done with what others had in mind in the making of the rules of natural philosophy. While we cannot show, and therefore do not know, that the Mishnah's philosophers read Aristotle's work on natural history or his reflections on scientific method, e.g., the *Posterior Analytics*,[7] we can compare our philosophers' method with that of Aristotle, who also, as a matter of fact, set forth a system that, in part, appealed to the right ordering of things through classification by correct rules. As to propositions about the hierarchical ordering of all things in a single way, the unity of all being in right order, while we cannot show and surely do not know that the Mishnah's philosophers knew anything about Plato, let alone Plotinus' neo-Platonism (which came to expression only in the century after the closure of the Mishnah!), we can compare our philosophers' proposition with that of neo-Platonism. For that philosophy, as we shall see, did seek to give full and rich expression to the proposition that all things emerged from one thing, and one thing encompasses all things, and that constitutes the single proposition that animates the system as a whole.

The work of comparison need not appeal for justification to context. I do not have to claim that, because the Sages read Aristotle, we can compare their method of classification with that of Aristotle, and because the Sages knew about the ideas that Plotinus ultimately expressed, a comparison between the neo-Platonism of the Mishnah and the neo-Platonism of Plotinus is in order. Methods of classification define their own category, and diverse methods, emerging in different circumstances, sustain comparison on their own simply because each method among many, coming from a variety of settings, shows a means of answering a single question or solving a single problem. The endpoint, therefore, the problem that is solved, justifies ignoring differences as to circumstance or setting among the starting-points, those who solve the problem. A fixed repertoire of rules – rationalities, in this context – defines the intellectual conventions, and in inquiring into the nature of those conventions, we compile a catalogue of possibilities only when we

---

[7]See Jonathan Barnes, *Aristotle's Posterior Analytic* (Oxford: Clarendon Press, 1975).

move beyond the specificities of intersection and context, e.g., who read whose book.

That explains the reason that without for one minute claiming the Mishnah's Sages read Greek philosophy, past or present or future, I turn to Aristotle and to neo-Platonism. Comparison and contrast by definition acknowledge no boundaries of culture or historical context. By rights and by simple logic we can compare anything that falls into the same classification as anything else, and contrast the things that do; and since people in widely separated places may and often do come to the same conclusions about the same things, we commit no act of violence against common sense by invoking in this context the names of Aristotle as to method and Plato and particularly Plotinus as to proposition. What we seek, as a matter of fact, is nothing more than the classification of the philosophy of Judaism among philosophies of the same kind, that is, philosophies that, wholly or partly, ask the same types of questions and pursue the same means for answering them.

Now to the specific task at hand. A brief account, based upon the standard textbook picture, of the taxonomic method of Aristotle permits us to compare the philosophical method of the methodologically-paramount philosophy of Judaism with that of the methodologically-paramount natural philosophy of the Greco-Roman world.[8] We begin with the simple observation that the distinction between genus and species lies at the foundation of all knowledge. Adkins states the matter in the most accessible way, "Aristotle, a systematic biologist, uses his

---

[8]See A.W.H. Adkins, *From the Many to the One. A Study of Personality and Views of Human Nature in the Context of Ancient Greek Society, Values, and Beliefs* (Ithaca: Cornell University Press, 1970); D.J. Allan, *The Philosophy of Aristotle* (London: Oxford University Press/Geoffrey Cumberlege, 1952); A.H. Armstrong, "Platonism and Neoplatonism," *Encyclopaedia Britannica* (1975), XIV, 539-45, and "Plotinus," *ibid.*, pp. 573-74; Emile Bréhier, *The History of Philosophy. The Hellenistic and Roman Age*, translated by Wade Baskin (Chicago: University of Chicago Press, 1965); Harold Cherniss, *Selected Papers*, edited by Leonard Tarán (Leiden: Brill, 1977); Louis H. Feldman, "Philo," *Encyclopaedia Britannica* (1975), XIV, 245-47; Erwin R. Goodenough, *An Introduction to Philo Judaeus*, second edition (Lanham: University Press of America Brown Classics in Judaica, 1986); P. Merlan, "Greek Philosophy from Plato to Plotinus," in A. H. Armstrong, ed., *The Cambridge History of Later Greek and Early Medieval Philosophy* (Cambridge: Cambridge University Press, 1967), pp. 14-136; Lorenzo Minio-Paluello, "Aristotelianism," *Encyclopaedia Britannica*, I, 1155-61; Joseph Owens, *A History of Ancient Western Philosophy* (New York: Appleton, Century, Crofts, 1959); G.F., Parker *A Short History of Greek Philosophy from Thales to Epicurus* (London: Edward Arnold, 1967); Giovanni Reale, *A History of Ancient Philosophy. III. The Systems of the Hellenistic Age*, edited and translated from the third Italian edition by John R. Catan (Albany: State University of New York Press, 1985).

classification by genera and species, itself developed from the classificatory interests of the later Plato, to place man among other animals...The classification must be based on the final development of the creature...."⁹ But to classify, we have to take as our premise that things are subject to classification, and that means that they have traits that are essential and indicative, on the one side, but also shared with other things, on the other. The point of direct contact and intersection between Judaism's philosophy of hierarchical classification and the natural philosophy of Aristotle lies in the shared, and critical, conviction concerning the true nature or character of things. Both parties concur that there *is* such a true definition – a commonplace for philosophers, generative of interesting problems, e.g., about Ideas, or Form and Substance, Actual and Potential, and the like – of what things really are.[10]

But how are we to know the essential traits that allow us to define the true character of, e.g., to classify, things? And this is the point at which our comparison becomes particular, since what we need to find out is whether there are between Aristotle's and Judaism's philosophies only shared convictions about the genus and the species or particular conceptions as to how these are to be identified and organized. The basic conviction on both sides is that: objects are not random, but fall into classes and so may be described, analyzed, and explained by appeal to general traits or rules.

The component of Aristotelianism that pertains here is "the use of deductive reasoning proceeding from self-evident principles or discovered general truths to conclusions of a more limited import; and syllogistic forms of demonstrative or persuasive arguments."[11] The goal is the classification of things, which is to say, the discovery of general rules that apply to discrete data or instances. Minio-Paluello states,

> In epistemology...Aristotelianism includes a concentration on knowledge accessible by natural means or accountable for by reason; an inductive, analytical empiricism, or stress on experience in the study of nature...leading from the perception of contingent individual occurrences to the discovery of permanent, universal patterns; and the primacy of the universal, that which is

---

⁹Adkins, *op. cit.*, pp. 170-71.
[10]But only Aristotle and the Mishnah carry into the material details of economics that conviction about the true character or essence or definition of things. The economics of the Mishnah and the economics of Aristotle begin in the conception of "true value," and the distributive economics proposed by each philosophy then develops that fundamental notion. The principle is so fundamental to each system that comparison of one system to the other in those terms alone is justified.
[11]Minio-Paluello, *op. cit.*

expressed by common or general terms. In metaphysics, or the theory of Being, Aristotelianism involves belief in the primacy of the individual in the realm of existence; in correlated conceptions allowing an articulate account of reality (e.g., 10 categories; genus-species-individual, matter-form, potentiality-actuality, essential-accidental; the four material elements and their basic qualities; and the four causes-formal, material, efficient and final); in the soul as the inseparable form of each living body in the vegetable and animal kingdoms; in activity as the essence of things; and in the primacy of speculative over practical activity.

The manner in which we accomplish this work is to establish categories of traits, and these will yield the sought rules for generalizations that make possible both classification, and, in the nature of things, therefore also hierarchization.

The work of classification is not simple. What we deal with is not a simple scheme of mutually exclusive and independently existent genera and species. We distinguished among causes in existing and mutable things, and that is what permits the differentiation of the subject-matters of the natural sciences.[12] At work is a triple scheme of classification. The first involves causes, the second, substance, and the third, change. As to causes, there are the formal, efficient, and final causes, which can coincide. In physics there are three classifications of substance: things incapable of motion, things that move and are indestructible, and destructible things. In change there is generation and destruction, and there are three kinds of motion: alteration in the category of quality, increase and diminution in the category of quantity, and locomotion in the category of place.[13]

While, as a matter of fact, "the world is composed of individuals, no two of whom are precisely alike,"[14] the correlated categories, matter and form, allow us to establish categories that encompass individual or distinct terms. Allan states:

> The wood which is potentially a table is also the matter upon which the carpenter will impress the form of a table...Matter and form are relative terms, in the sense that a thing which has some degree of form may serve as the matter upon which a new form is imposed...It is Form...which imparts structural unity to a single individual. Various materials are required in order to build a house...what holds them together is the Form of the house... Form...tends to unity of design, matter to plurality...[15]

---

[12]*Encyclopaedia Britannica*, I, 1167-68.
[13]*Ibid.*
[14]Allan, *op. cit.*, p. 42.
[15]*Ibid.*, p. 39.

On the matter of form and matter, G.F. Parker further explains, "The matter is the basic stuff which makes it possible for the Form to have existence at all."[16] The Form represents what is particular to a given instance.

Parker proceeds, "Coupled with the concept of Matter and Form in every substance we find that other typically Aristotelian pair, Actual and Potential." Parker continues:

> "Typically Aristotelian" because it is here we see the outlook of one deeply immersed in Natural History, of one who has studied with minute care the development of living organisms from embryo to old age, of one who attempts to oppose a dynamic to a static view of things.... Matter is potential, embryo is actual; the embryo in turn is potential, the baby is actual...The Potential is eternally moving, eternally changing into the Actual. Equally, Matter is eternally moved into Form.[17]

What Aristotle seeks to know is causes: "to know that something happens is mere shallowness unless one probes deeper and reveals the reason why." The answer to the question of why derives from the famous "four causes." Taking as the question, what has "caused" the famous status of Zeus in his temple at Olympia, a statue "made of ivory and gold on a core of wood by Phidias, the foremost sculptor of his time...placed in the central shrine of Olympia...," we have these four causes in play:

1. The material cause: the gold, the ivory, and the wood
2. The efficient cause: the hands and tools of Phidias
3. The formal cause: what the thing represents; in this case the figure of Zeus
4. The final cause: the purpose and meaning of the thing; in this case the greater glory of Zeus and the improvement of man.

We may draw these four causes into relationship with the issue of the potential and the actual: "The whole end and purpose of an acorn is to grow into an oak; and the efficient cause, that which gave an acorn the opportunity of taking on the form of an oak, was a parent oak. ... Each cause plays its part in the process which makes a thing become what it is."

Clearly, when we review some of the more obvious characteristics of Aristotle's logical and taxonomic principles, in specific terms we find only occasional points of contact with the principles we have laboriously uncovered in our inductive inquiry into the Mishnah's philosophical structure. Only in general does the manner in which Aristotle does the

---

[16] Parker, *op. cit.*
[17] *Ibid.* p. 142.

work of definition through classification also characterize the way in which Sages do the same work. But these points of intersection in detail are of special interest. For instance, while the actual and the potential form critical taxic categories for Aristotle, they prove subsidiary, though pertinent, in the Mishnah. While, for the Mishnah, the matter of mixtures defines a central and generative problematic, for Aristotle, the same matter is subsumed into other compositions altogether. It constitutes a chapter in the story of change, which is explained by the passage of elements into one another. That will help us to account for the destruction of one element and the creation of another. In this connection, Allan says: "Aristotle does not mean by 'mixture' a mere shuffling of primary particles, as if the seeds of wheat and barley were mixed in a heap, but genuine change of quality resulting in a new 'form,' towards which each component has made a contribution."[18] The consideration of the classes of mixtures plays its role in Aristotle's account of the sublunary region; it is not, as represented by Allen, a point at which Aristotle repeatedly uncovers problems that require solution, in the way in which the issue of mixtures forms the source for the Mishnah's solution of urgent problems.

Enough has been said to justify comparing Aristotle's and Judaism's philosophies, but I have yet to specify what I conceive to be the generative point of comparison. It lies in two matters, first, the paramount one of the shared principles of formal logic, which I find blatant in the Mishnah and which all presentations of Aristotle's philosophy identify as emblematic. The second, as is clear, is the taxonomic method, viewed from afar. Let us turn to the former. When we follow a simple account of the way in which we attain new truth, we find ourselves quite at home. Allan's account follows[19]:

> Induction...is the advance from the particular to the general. By the inspection of examples...in which one characteristic appears conjoined with another, we are led to propound a general rule which we suppose to be valid for cases not yet examined. Since the rule is of higher generality than the instances, this is an advance from a truth "prior for us" toward a truth "prior in nature."

My representation of the mishnaic mode of presentation of cases that, with our participation, yield a general rule, accords with this logic, which is inductive. But that impression requires qualification:

> On the other hand, sometimes two general truths, which are self-evident or not open to reasonable doubt, necessarily imply a third

---
[18]Allan, p. 60.
[19]*Ibid.* pp. 126ff.

truth, of more limited scope. Such a procedure is deduction or demonstration. It advances from what is prior in nature towards what is prior for us, and, because it does this, has a completeness and a constraining force which is always missing in induction. It shows not merely that a fact is true but why it is true.

The theory of deduction forms the center piece of Aristotle's logic, so Allan maintains. Have we instances of the same deductive reasoning in the Mishnah?

In my judgment, the exemplary case of the comparison of the king and the high priest forms precisely such a deductive and, as a matter of fact, syllogistic statement. By syllogism is meant "discourse in which, certain things being stated, something other than what is stated follows of necessity from their being so."[20] When we establish the general truths concerning the high priest and the king, we identify a third truth, concerning the priority of the latter over the former, and that truth is one of deduction.

And that observation carries us to the more important of the two principles of sound intellectual method, the taxonomic interest in defining through classification. This definitive trait of natural philosophy is what we find in common between Aristotle's and the Mishnah's philosophical method, and the points in common prove far more than those yielded by the general observation that both systems appeal to the identification of genera out of species. In fact, what philosophers call the dialectical approach in Aristotle proves the same approach to the discovery or demonstration of truth as that we find in the Mishnah. Owens sets the matter forth in the following language: "Since a theoretical science proceeds from first principles that are found within the thing under investigation, the initial task of the philosophy of nature will be to discover its primary principles in the sensible things themselves."[21] I cannot imagine a formulation more suited to the method of the Mishnah than that simple statement.

The philosophers whose system is set forth in the Mishnah appeal to the traits of things, deriving their genera from the comparison and contrast of those inherent or intrinsic traits. This I take to be precisely what is stated here. "In accordance with the general directives of the Aristotelian logic, the process of their discovery will be dialectical, not demonstrative." This distinction is between genuine reasoning and demonstration. Demonstration proceeds from truth known as such, while dialectic deals with reasoning from opinions.

---

[20]Owens, *op. cit.*, p. 340.
[21]*Ibid.*, p. 304.

Dialectical reasoning works with opinions "that are generally accepted, though not recognized definitely by the reasoner as truth on the strength of their own proper evidence."[22]

> Though the dialectic itself does not yield knowledge in the full sense of the term, it is of the utmost importance for the acquisition of knowledge and for meeting other people on their own ground...dialectic may be said to contain the path to the first principles of all the sciences. Hence arises its indispensable function "in relation to the ultimate bases of the principles used in the several sciences. For it is impossible to discuss them at all from the principles proper to the particular science in hand, seeing that the principles are the primus of everything else; it is through the opinions generally held on the particular points that these have to be discussed, and this task belongs, properly, or most appropriately, to dialectic: for dialectic is a process of criticism wherein lies the path to the principles of all inquiries."[23]

Dialectical procedure yields not knowledge but the quest for knowledge. Aristotle's interest is in "thinking processes" that make possible various types of dialectic.

When Aristotle pursues the dialectical approach to knowledge, like Sages in the Mishnah, he deals with the physical world:

> The universe is a plurality. It consists of substance and accidents. Sensible substance itself is found to be a plurality. Change is seen as a process from one contrary to another....contraries do not constitute the substance of anything. They are accidents and so should require a substrate.

Here we see the work of comparison and contrast, but of course the subject-matter is hardly congruent with that taken up by the Mishnah's authors. Yet do we distinguish, in the Mishnah, accidents from essential qualities? And do we recognize the plurality of data and the parlous character of our taxonomic labor with it? I can open any page of the Mishnah for examples of precisely those distinctions and recognitions.

What is at stake in dialectic is stated by Allan as follows:

> Dialectic will find some common foundation for those unproved assumptions upon which all scientific reasoning is based, and, in general, will make our fragmentary experience part of one coherent system, not by assembling the fragments and piecing them together, but by an intuitive grasp of a central necessary truth...from which all partial truth can be deduced without risk of error.[24]

---

[22]*Ibid.*, pp. 309ff.
[23]Owens, p. 305, citing Aristotle, as indicated in his notes.
[24]Allan, p. 145.

The Greco-Roman Philosophy of Judaism: The Mishnah in Context

On the one side, we find ourselves at home with a philosophy that aims at imparting coherence to knowledge and experience. On the other, in the Mishnah we find ourselves worlds away from Aristotle. Aristotle's goal and that of the Mishnah's philosophers simply do not relate, however, for while the former is aiming at discovering the final causes of things, their purpose and the source of their movement and change, the latter have a different objective in mind. For Aristotle, the aim of science "is to produce a body of judgments which, in their connection with each other, reflect the necessary connections between substances and properties in the real world."[25] For the philosophy of Judaism, the aim of science, that is to say, learning, is quite different.

The following summary of what is at stake for Aristotle appeals to the methods shared by Aristotle and the philosophers of Judaism to reach a conclusion that simply has no bearing upon the interests of the latter:

> The primary immobile movent that Aristotle has in mind is evidently enough the soul of the outermost heaven. Any animated thing, plant or animal, is a self-movent, and its soul originates motion. Such perishable self-movents, however, require a higher and imperishable efficient cause to account for the eternal series of generations and passings-away. The operative notion in the Aristotelian demonstration of the primary efficient cause is therefore the eternity of the cosmic process. The first efficient cause is necessary, not to explain the existence of things, but to account for the eternal character of their motion. The argument is based clearly upon the eternity of cosmic motion and of time. Without that basis it is no longer the Aristotelian proof.[26]

If I may now specify the point at which the philosophy of Judaism in its first principles takes its leave from Aristotle's philosophy, it is not merely in the subject-matter, even in the level of abstraction and generalization characteristic of Aristotle, though such a mode of mathematical thought seems to me unimagined by the philosophers of the Mishnah. It is that the goal of Aristotle's system, the teleological argument in favor of the unmoved mover, and the goal of Judaism's system, the demonstration of the unity of being, are essentially contradictory, marking utterly opposed positions on the fundamental character of God and the traits of the created world that carries us upward to God. So we establish our first point, concerning the philosophical character of the method of the Mishnah's system, only at the cost of uncovering a major contradiction: the proposition that animates the one system stands in direct opposition, as to its premises,

---

[25]*Ibid.*, p. 147.
[26]Owens, p. 317.

implications, and explicit results, with the results of the other. Aristotle's God attained through teleological demonstration accomplished through the right classification of all things and the Mishnah's God, whose workings in the world derive from the demonstration of the ontological unity of all things, cannot recognize each other. And that is the case even though they are assuredly one.

Judaism's philosophy as to its basic proposition thus forms a different quest altogether, and that simple contrast moves us from the matter of method, shared with the philosophical tradition of the Greco-Roman world in general and Aristotle in particular, to the issue of proposition. The method is standard Aristotelianism, the medium familiar, and some of the propositions entirely acceptable to the philosophical tradition. But the message runs along the lines of important fundamentals of the philosophy of Plotinus (204-270) in the name of Plato, and to that message we have now to turn.[27] What we shall see is that the principal proposition of the Mishnah, concerning the ontological unity of being, with many things forming one thing, and one thing yielding many things, proves entirely congruent with one important conception of Middle Platonism concerning the unity of all being.

Let us begin with a general description of Middle, or Neo-Platonism, and proceed to a specific figure, Plotinus. The great Bréhier introduces the philosophy in the following words:

> Neo-Platonism is essentially a means of approaching an intelligible reality and a construction or description of this reality...In Neo-Platonism what matters most is passage from a sphere where knowledge and happiness are impossible to one where they are possible... The philosophy of the age is in a sense a description of

---

[27] See A. Hilary Armstrong, *Plotinian and Christian Studies* (London: Variorum Reprints 1979); A.H. Armstrong, *The Architecture of the Intelligible Universe in the Philosophy of Plotinus. An Analytical and Historical Study* (Amsterdam: Adolf M. Hakkert, 1967); Émile Bréhier, *The Philosophy of Plotinus*, translated by Joseph Thomas (Chicago: University of Chicago Press, 1958); J.M. Dillon and A.A. Long, *op. cit.*; Joseph Katz, *The Philosophy of Plotinus. Representative Books from the Enneades.* (New York: Appleton-Century-Crofts, 1950); Elmer O'Brien, *The Essential Plotinus. Representative Treatises from the Enneads* (Repr., Hackett Publishing Co., 1975); J.M. Rist, *Plotinus: The Road to Reality* (Cambridge: Cambridge University Press, 1967); Samuel Sambursky, *The Concept of Place in Late Neoplatonism, op. cit.*; Samuel Sambursky and S. Pines, *The Concept of Time in Late Neoplatonism* (Jerusalem: Israel Academy of Arts and Sciences, 1971); Grace H. Turnbull, *The Essence of Plotinus. Extracts from the Six Enneads and Porphyry's Life of Plotinus*, based on the translation by Stephen Mackenna (New York: Oxford University Press, 1948).

the metaphysical landscapes through which the soul is transported as it undergoes what might be described as spiritual training.[28]

On the face of matters, the philosophers of Judaism offer not the slightest hint that they concern themselves with such matters; "the soul" scarcely appears in the hundreds of chapters of which the Mishnah is composed.

But the reflections concerning unity that form the centerpiece of Plotinus' thought prove remarkably interesting and pertinent:

> We can conceive of a unity that increases to the point where the parts of a being fuse and become almost inseparable. For instance, we cannot speak in the same sense of the parts of a living body and of the parts of a science; in a living body the parts are solitary but are locally separated, whereas in a science a part is a theorem and each theorem contains potentially every other theorem. Thus we see how an additional degree of unification takes us from the corporeal to the spiritual.[29]

Here we see, in abstraction, considerations that we locate in very concrete terms in the progress from classification of things to their hierarchization and finally to their unification, shown in the fact that as one thing is made up of – holds together in unity – many things, so many things emerge from one thing. That, in abstract language, forms the centerpiece of the mishnaic interest in classification. So, too, as Bréhier says, "every imperfect reality or union of parts implies a more complete unity beyond itself...In the absence of the higher unity, everything disperses, crumbles and loses its being. Nothing is other than through the One." As to method, what is at hand is "explaining a particular aspect of reality by relating it to a more perfect unity." What we find in the Mishnah is the distinctive definition of those components of reality that are to be taken up in the quest for ontological unity: the this and that of the every day and the here and now, precisely what Plotinus finds of no consequence whatsoever, but what Aristotle in his scientific writings took as the focus of analytical interest.[30]

---

[28]Bréhier, *The History of Philosophy. The Hellenistic and Roman Age, op. cit.*, p. 182.
[29]*Ibid.*, p. 184.
[30]I find the mishnaic discourse far closer to Aristotle's than to Plotinus's. Bréhier notes (p. 187):

> Plotinus reminds us that Platonic dialectic does not proceed through additions, like Aristotelian logic, and simply adding specific differences in order to define the species; it proceeds instead through division, and this means that the genus is a concrete whole selected for division into species in much the same way that we might divide the world into sky and sublunar regions. Progress from genus to species is not an

Specifically, Plotinus in the name of Plato[31] set forth a doctrine of the hierarchial order of being, in which many things are subsumed within one thing, and one thing yields many things, from the lowest order, which is diverse, to the highest, which is unified. The doctrine of the One in Plotinus may be best summarized as follows:

> The One is infinite, the others finite; the One is creator, the others creatures; the One is entirely itself, entirely infinite, the others are both finite and infinite...the One has no otherness, the others are other than the One. It is not the case that while the Forms exist, the One does not. Rather the One exists in an infinite way, the others finitely...[32]

The centerpiece of the system then is the conception of the One, and, as we shall now see, the fundamental hierarchical unity of being in the orderly world that descends from the One.

Accordingly, moving from Aristotle to neo-Platonism opens the way to the rough and ready comparison between the philosophical message of a critical and paramount philosophical system, that of Plotinus in the middle of the third century, and the philosophical message of the Mishnah, at the end of the second century or beginning of the third. Let me begin with a simple definition of "Platonism and neo-Platonism,"

---

enrichment but rather a passing from the whole to parts which still preserve the richness of the whole. One important consequence issues from Plotinus' line of reasoning. The Aristotelian intelligible designated only genera and species, and the individual realized in the sensible world therefore contained all the characteristics of its specific form, to which were added an indeterminate number of other characteristics attributable to its realization in matter and responsible for its true individuality. It is possible to think "man" but not "Socrates," whose individuality is attributable to the myriad accidents that have befallen the specific form of man during his realization. Thus according to Aristotle, in certain aspects the sensible world would be greater than the intelligible world! Plotinus holds on the contrary that the individual exists in the intelligible world, or that there are "ideas of individuals."

But my program does not require this kind of detailed comparison of specifics. Let it suffice to underline here that matters are far more complex than this preliminary inquiry is meant to suggest. All I wish to prove is that I deal with intellectuals whom (other) philosophers, properly instructed as to the details of discourse, will have classified as philosophers, like themselves.

[31]My argument has no bearing on the relationship between Plato and Middle Platonism in general, or Plotinus in particular. See A. Hilary Armstrong, "Elements in the Thought of Plotinus at Variance with Classical Intellectualism," *Plotinian and Christian Studies* (London: Variorum Reprints, 1979), paper XVI. Note also R.T. Wallis, *Neoplatonism* (London: Duckworth, 1972).
[32]J.M. Rist, *Plotinus: The Road to Reality, op. cit.*, p. 37.

that supplied by A. H. Armstrong, as follows (with the pertinent points given in italics, supplied by me):

> Neoplatonism, the form of Platonism developed by Plotinus in the third century A.D., contains among its leading ideas the following:
> 1. *There is plurality of spheres of being, arranged in hierarchical descending order, the last and lowest comprising the universe, which exists in time and space and is perceptible to the senses.*
> 2. Each sphere of being is derived from its superior, a derivation that is not a process in time or space.
> 3. Each derived being is established in its own reality by turning back toward its superior in a movement of contemplative desire, which is implicit in the original creative impulse of outgoing that it receives from its superior...
> 4. Each sphere of being is an image or expression on a lower level of the sphere above it.
> 5. *Degrees of being are also degrees of unity; in each subsequent sphere of being there is greater multiplicity, more separateness, and increasing limitation, – till the atomic individualization of the spatiotemporal world is reached.*
> 6. The supreme sphere of being, and through it all of what in any sense exists, derives from the ultimate principle, which is absolutely free from determinations and limitations and utterly transcends any conceivable reality, so that it may be said to be "one being." As it has no limitations, so it has no division, attributes, or qualifications; it cannot really be named but may be called "the One" to designate its complete simplicity. It may also be called "the Good" as the source of all perfections and the ultimate goal of return; for the impulse of outgoing and return that constitutes the hierarchy of derived reality comes from and leads back to the Good.
> 7. Since this supreme principle is absolutely simple and undetermined (or devoid of specific traits), man's knowledge of it must be radically different from any other kind of knowledge: it is not an object (a separate, determined, limited thing) and no predicates can be applied to it; hence it can be known only if it raises the mind to an immediate union with itself, which cannot be imagined or described.[33]

The point at which I find an important common proposition is, as is surely self-evident, the conviction of a hierarchical order of being, in which, as one ascends, one moves ever toward a more unified realm of being. This conception here is expressed in the reverse order: as one descends, things become more complex, so the one yields the many. The differences in detail – as any scholar of Middle Platonism must remind us – are stupefying. But I see no fundamental difference

---

[33] Armstrong, "Platonism and Neoplatonism," *op.cit.*

between the two positions on the unity of being and subordinated matters I should classify as ontological. Armstrong's points 1 and 5 thus appear to me to coincide with the Mishnah's fundamental and repeatedly demonstrated proposition about the unity of being, attained through the hierarchical classification of all things. Bréhier states the matter in the simplest possible way: "...the universe appears as a series of forms each of which depends hierarchically on the preceding, and the universe can be the object of rational thought."[34] Exactly how this is demonstrated is hardly our problem, since Plotinus' way of showing the ordered hierarchy of being is not the same as Aristotle's, and as to mode of thought it is Aristotle's and not Plotinus' (or Plato's!) that served our philosophers.

It is the proposition of the One that matters, and here I find an identity of viewpoint between the two philosophies, the pagan and the Judaic. A. H. Armstrong's account of the One[35] leaves no doubt of the complexity of what is at stake for Plotinus in thought about that fundamental subject. But the basic point serves our purpose full well: the first aspect of the One is "as conclusion of the metaphysical and religious search for a primary reality which can act as explanation of the universe." The One of course is transcendent and absolute. The One is "not only self-thinking but self-willing and self-loving." We need not venture into the neo-Platonic metaphysics and cosmology, with their interest in an astronomical theory of the sensible world.[36] These have no bearing upon our interest. Nor do I appeal to a shared concept of the soul, e.g., as suggested by Plotinus' "If all souls are one,"[37] since in the Mishnah we find no doctrine of the soul or the person or person-hood of the human being. And that is not the only proposition that is not only not shared but, from the perspective of the Judaic philosophy,

---

[34]Bréhier, p. 43.

[35]A. H. Armstrong, *The Architecture of the Intelligible Universe in the Philosophy of Plotinus, op. cit.,* pp. 1-48. Armstrong maintains: "Behind this stands the systematic theology of Aristotle," and he finds in the *Metaphysics* and *De Anima* influences of the *Enneads*: "This transcendent self-sufficing God, pure and self-directed Act, the supreme object of desire but himself desiring nothing but himself, appears in philosophy before Plotinus only in Aristotle and in the Platonic literature of the Imperial period." Since the importance of Aristotle in my account pertains to method, not the doctrine of the One (or of God), all of this is of only tangential interest. So far as the philosophy of Judaism proposes to deal with the unity of God, it is by showing the hierarchical order, therefore the unity, of the world, and, as I shall point out below, the polemic addresses the pagan, not the Christian-philosophical, ontology of God.

[36]*Ibid.,* p. 44.

[37]Cf. Armstrong, "The Apprehension of Divinity in Plotinus," *Plotinian and Christian Studies, op. cit.,* paper XVIII.

incomprehensible. Then what is at stake? Once more the answer is the same, but now in greater specificity. It is the proposition that "above this multiple unity, which constitutes the intelligible world, we must posit...the absolute One without distinction and without variety,"[38] that I find pertinent to the simple case at hand. And, I add, *that alone.*

For Plotinus set forth a way of life, not only a doctrine, and the way of life posited by the philosophers of Judaism contained their doctrine too. But the respective ways of life bore nothing in common, so that is not to represent the Sages of Judaic philosophy as precursors of Plotinus' mystics, portrayed as living in "the solitude of the sage who is alone with the supreme principle which he has attained because he has successively abandoned all finite and definite reality."[39] To the contrary, the more we examine the concept of the unity of all being as expressed in the Mishnah's hierarchical order of all things, the less Middle or neo-Platonic the Mishnah's ontological system appears in detail to be.

Certainly there is no basis for suggesting that the philosophers of Judaism behind the Mishnah's system aimed through philosophy at attaining mystical union with God or set forth in mundane garb an essentially mystical Judaism. It is only to claim that the critical proposition of this Judaism is a philosophical proposition, and the basis for the claim is that philosophers of the same span of time – the late second and third centuries – took the same position and deemed it an appropriate one for philosophy to entertain. That, and that alone, is what is subject to demonstration in the allegation that the one and the many of the philosophy of Judaism portrays a proposition strikingly congruent with the unity of being set forth by Middle Platonism.

Yet having set in a prominent place the obvious and fundamental differences, let me turn to a brief component of Bréhier's moving account and see how far apart the two systems really are:

> To think, for Plotinus, is then to comprehend the unity of a composition of which sensations acquaint us only with the dispersed elements – the intention of the dancer in the multiplicity of movements in a dance figure, the living unity of the circular course of a star across the infinity of positions it occupies successively. It is to proceed toward a reality which, far from from losing anything of the richness of sensation, quite to the contrary goes beyond it and uncovers its depth.[40]

---

[38]Armstrong, *Architecture*, p. 45.
[39]Bréhier, p. 5.
[40]*Ibid.*, p. 11.

Here, I would claim, the Judaic philosophers would concur in detail. They expressed the counterpart to the multiplicity of movements in a dance figure, the infinity of positions the star occupies. And then, in the detail, they recover not intention but rule, not circular course but the laws of motion.

This movement from detail, within detail, through detail, toward the sense of the unity of things – the rule, the order – in my judgment is gained by the philosophy of Judaism in a way different from the way that it is gained in Plotinus' thought as Bréhier interprets it. For he says,

> The contemplation of the intelligible proceeds along the same line as the contemplation of the sensible. It extends contemplation of the sensible directly without passing in any way through the intermediary of logically connected ideas; for it is not through reasoning and induction that one ascends from the first to the second but only through a more collected and intense contemplation.[41]

Here our Sages would have to part company; they remain wholly within the limits of the sensible world, uncovering what is intelligible within what is sensible, there alone. There is no bypassing of reasoning and induction, but rather a focus upon the reasoning of classification and the induction of hierarchization of what is classified, that alone. But that observation only confirms my proposition, which is that the method is that of Aristotle, in behalf of the proposition important to Plotinus, within Middle Platonism overall.

What then can we say of that proposition concerning the ontological unity of being? Here we turn again to Bréhier's exposition, which emphasizes how Plotinus joined religious problems to Greek philosophizing[42]:

> True to the tradition of Plato, adopted by the Neo-Pythagoreans, the One is in Plotinus the ultimate condition of the spiritual life, the principle thanks to which Intelligence provides itself with objects and contemplates them...[43] ...for Plotinus, there is never any intellectual knowledge without spiritual life. The soul, for example, is aware of Intelligence only in uniting with it. True realities are not inert objects of knowledge but subjective spiritual attitudes.[44]

---

[41]*Ibid.*
[42]*Ibid.*, p. 19.
[43]*Ibid.*, p. 141.
[44]*Ibid.*, p. 148.

Having come this far, I may say very simply that not a single category or concept in the foregoing, and the vast structure to which Bréhier alludes, finds a counterpart in the philosophy of Judaism.

And yet, if in detail we find ourselves far from the Mishnah, whether in method or medium or message, in the main point we are entirely at home; as Bréhier says in a stunning generalization of his own:

> A true philosophical reform, such as that of a Socrates or of a Descartes, always takes for its point of departure a confrontation of the needs of human nature with the representation the mind forms of reality. It is the sense of a lack of correspondence between these needs and this representation which, in exceptionally endowed minds, awakens the philosophical vocation. Thus, little by little, philosophy reveals man to himself. It is the reality of his own needs, of his own inclinations, which forms the basis of living philosophical thought. A philosophy which does not give the impression of being indispensable to the period in which it appears is merely a vain and futile curiosity.[45]

By the definition, I should claim, the philosophy of Judaism indeed is a philosophy: it reveals that correspondence between the givens of the everyday and their representation in the ordered rules by which they are placed into hierarchy that for those to whom the philosophers meant to speak formed reality: in proportion, in balance, in proper place: the reality of Israel's own needs and inclinations.[46] And that draws us to the end of this inquiry into the philosophical context. None can reasonably doubt that in the philosophy of Judaism we have an authentic philosophy, by the standards of the context of the Greco-Roman philosophical tradition, all the more so by the standard Bréhier sets forth for all time: "little by little, philosophy reveals man to himself. It is the reality of his own needs, of his own inclinations, which forms the basis of living philosophical thought."

Shall we now conclude that in the Mishnah we have a Judaic version of the method of Aristotle and the message of Plotinus? I think that judgment carries us far beyond the limits of our evidence and is contradicted by most of that evidence. So I have to underline for both Aristotle and Plotinus that the method of the one and the proposition of the other hardly exhaust what they said. Nor were these necessarily the most important things that they did (for method) or said (for message). Were I to list all of the methodological principles of Aristotle's analysis

---

[45]*Ibid.*, pp. 183-84.
[46]The comparison of the Judaic, Christian, and pagan systems of Middle Platonism seems to me made possible, in a very preliminary way, to be sure, by Armstrong in his "Man in the Cosmos," *Plotinian and Christian Studies,* paper XVII, p. 11.

and all of the substantive propositions of Plotinus' *Enneads*, we should readily recognize a simple fact. The Sages of the Mishnah intersect at only a few, very specific points with the philosophical method and message I have identified.[47] The entire medium through which the unity of being was expressed, the system of three hypostases that interested Plotinus for example, not to mention Plotinus' doctrine of the soul, these seem to me remote from the thought-processes and propositions of the Judaic philosophers. But the proposition I have identified as common to the two systems of thought – so I repeat – was the same. And that justifies my calling the one system of thought, the Mishnah's, philosophical in its proposition as much as in its method and mode of thought.

Accordingly, to conclude, I invoke Aristotle's method and Plotinus' proposition simply to show that other people – our authors specifically – who pursue intellection in the manner of the one or set forth a proposition important to the other were saying philosophical things and saying them in accord with a philosophical method. That is my claim, and I believe that what has been said establishes it beyond any reasonable doubt.[48] The method, Aristotelian, and the propositions, congruent with the Middle Platonism of Plotinus, were philosophical in the way in which (other) philosophers achieved their results and set forth their propositions.

If, as I claim, the Mishnah sets forth a system that philosophers of the day, properly instructed, can have identified as philosophical in method and message, though (obviously) not in medium, then we must ask ourselves, *cui bono*? Or more precisely, not to whose advantage, but rather, *against* whose position, did the Judaic philosophical system propose to argue? When we realize that at stake is a particular means for demonstrating the unity of God, we readily identify as the principal focus the pagan reading of the revealed world of the here and the now, and, it must follow, Judaism as a philosophy stood over against the pagan philosophy of the world of its time and place. The fundamental argument in favor of the unity of God in the philosophy of Judaism is by

---

[47]That fact underlines my earlier observation on how valuable detailed studies of where there are, and are not, points of confluence and congruence are going to be. My sense is that a study of like and not alike in the matters of method and message will allow us much more precisely to situate the philosophy of Judaism within – and not only as part of – the philosophical world: like in what ways, not like in what ways, hence with what concrete results?

[48]I concede that more concrete and specific studies of comparison and contrast between the mishnaic philosophers and those under study here are entirely called for and will yield considerable refinement in my representation of matters.

showing the hierarchical order, therefore the unity, of the world. The world, therefore, is made to testify to the unity of being, and – to say the obvious with very heavy emphasis – *the power of the philosophy derives from its capacity for hierarchical classification.* When we compare the pagan and the Christian philosophical ontology of God, we see that it is the pagan position, and not the Christian one, that forms the target of this system. The Christian position is simply not perceived and not considered.

The comparison of the Judaic, Christian, and pagan systems of Middle Platonism seems to me made possible, in a very preliminary way to be sure, by Armstrong:

> The difference here between pagans and Christians...is a difference about the degree of religious relevance of the material cosmos, and, closely connected with this, about the relative importance of general, natural, and special, supernatural, divine self-manifestation and self-communication. On the one side, the pagan, there is the conviction that a multiple self-communication and self-revelation of divinity takes place always and everywhere in the world, and that good and wise men everywhere...have been able to find the way to God and the truth about God in and through rational reflection on themselves and on the world, not only the heavens but the earth, and the living unity of the whole. On the other side, the Christian, there is indeed a readiness to see the goodness and beauty of the visible cosmos as a testimony to God's creation...but the religious emphasis lies elsewhere. Saving truth and the self-communication of the life of God come through the Incarnation of God as a man and through the human...society of which the God-Man is the head, the Church...It is only in the Church that material things become means of revelation and salvation through being understood in the light of Scripture and Church tradition and used by God's human ministers in the celebration of the Church's sacraments. It is the ecclesiastical cosmos, not the natural cosmos, which appears to be of primary religious importance for the Christian.[49]

If God is revealed in the artifacts of the world, then, so pagans in general considered, God must be multiple. *No,* the philosophy of Judaism is here seen to respond. Here we find a Judaic argument, within the premises of paganism, against paganism. To state with emphasis what I conceive to be that argument: *the very artifacts that appear multiple in fact form classes of things, and, moreover, these classes themselves are subject to a reasoned ordering, by appeal to this-worldly characteristics signified by properties and indicative traits.* Monotheism hence is to be demonstrated by appeal to those very same data that for paganism prove the opposite.

---

[49]Armstrong, "Man in the Cosmos," *op. cit.*

The medium of hierarchical classification, which is Aristotle's, conveys the message of the unity of being, which is Plato's and Plotinus', in the this-worldly mode of discourse formed by the framers of the Mishnah. The way to one God, ground of being and ontological unity of the world, lies through "rational reflection on themselves and on the world," this world, which yields a living unity encompassing the whole. That claim, conducted in an argument covering overwhelming detail in the Mishnah, directly faces the issue as framed by paganism. Immanent in its medium, it is transcendent in its message. And I hardly need spell out the simple reasons, self-evident in Armstrong's words, for dismissing as irrelevant to their interests the Christian reading of the cosmos. To the Mishnah's Sages, it is not (merely) wrong, it is insufficient.

And yet, that is not the whole story. For the Mishnah's Sages reach into Scripture for their generative categories and, in doing so, address head-on a Christianity that Armstrong centers, with entire soundness, upon the life of the Church of Jesus Christ, God-Man.[50] We do well here to review Armstrong's language: "It is only in the Church that material things become means of revelation and salvation through being understood in the light of Scripture and Church tradition and used by God's human ministers in the celebration of the Church's sacraments."

The framers of the Mishnah would have responded. *"It is in the Torah that material things are identified and set forth as a means of revelation."*

Again Armstrong: "It is the ecclesiastical cosmos, not the natural cosmos, which appears to be of primary religious importance for the Christian."

To this the philosophers of Judaism would reply, *"It is the scriptural account of the cosmos that forms our generative categories, which, by the power of intellect, we show to constitute an ordered, hierarchical unity of being."*

So the power of this identification of "the ecclesiastical cosmos" is revealed when we frame the cosmos of the Mishnah by appeal to its persistent response to the classifications and categories of Scripture. If the Church, as Armstrong portrays matters, worked out an ecclesiastical cosmos, only later on producing the Bible as it did, for its part the philosophy of Judaism framed a scriptural cosmos – and then read it

---

[50]That judgment does not contradict the argument of my *Uniting the Dual Torah: Sifra and the Problem of Mishnah* (Cambridge: Cambridge University Press, 1990) concerning the Sifra> authorship's critique of the mishnaic philosophers' stress upon classification through intrinsic traits of things as against through classes set forth solely by the Torah. I mean only to stress the contrast between appeal to Scripture and to nature, which I find in the philosophy of Judaism, and appeal to the ecclesiastical cosmos.

philosophically in the way in which I have explained matters. We may therefore identify three distinct positions on the reading of the natural world: the pagan, the Christian, and the Judaic. The one reads nature as a source of revelation. The other two insist on a medium of mediation between nature and intellect. For Christianity it is, as Armstrong says, ecclesiastical, and, as I claim, for Judaism, the medium of mediation of nature lies through revelation, the Torah.

Given their circumstance, the philosophers' reach into Scripture's entire practical program, as worked out in Exodus, Leviticus, Numbers, and Deuteronomy, for the many things that they would show are really one, is not only indicative. It also is to be predicted. But – so I claim – that is not for traditional or merely cultural reasons. True, since our philosophers were part of the Israel that had received and revered as God's word the Written Torah of Sinai, we cannot be surprised that they have adopted as their agenda of things to be analyzed in one way and shown to be really one thing the list of things that Scripture treats. And, further, since these same philosophers were part of the living Israel that lived by Scripture, the culture of their time and place surely will have made quite natural the address to the scriptural program.

But there is a philosophical reason, which I deem paramount and which explains my insistence that this Judaism is a philosophy, a philosophy – not a theology – in its message and its mode of thought. It is that by merely appealing to the authority of Scripture, but by themselves analyzing the revealed truths of Scripture, that the intellects at hand accomplished their purposes. By themselves showing the order and unity inherent within Scripture's list of topics, the philosophers on their own power meant to penetrate into the ground of being as God has revealed matters. This they did by working their way back from the epiphenomena of creation to the phenomenon of Creation – then to the numinous, that is, the Creator. That self-assigned challenge forms an intellectual vocation worthy of a particular kind of philosopher, an Israelite one. In my view, it explains also why in the Mishnah philosophers produced their philosophy in the form that they chose.

For the form, so superficially unphilosophical in its crabbed and obsessive mode of discourse, proves in the end to form a philosophy. Judaism in the system of the Mishnah is philosophical in medium, method, and message. But then philosophy also is represented as, and within, the Torah in topic and authority. The union then of the Torah's classifications and topics, philosophy's modes of thought and propositions – that marriage produced as its first fruits a philosophical Judaism, a Judaic philosophy: the Torah as Moses would have written it at God's instructions, had Moses been a philosopher. But the offspring of the happy marriage was not to live long, and the philosophy of

Judaism would soon give way to the theology of Judaism: theology, not philosophy, dictated the future for a thousand years.

6

Gentiles and Israelites in Mishnah-Tosefta>: A Study in Ethnicity

By Gary G. Porton

I

It is a privilege to be able to participate in a volume honoring Samson H. Levey. His dedication as a rabbi, scholar, and teacher places him among the best of the sages of our generation. Although he has played an important role in the life of generations of Reform rabbis and educators, I personally owe him a great deal. Professor Levey was the first to introduce me to the wonders of Rabbinic literature and to the value of serious scholarship on the Rabbis, their culture and their literature. Without his care, understanding, and dedication, I would not have been able to pursue my future education and to achieve my role as a teacher in Israel.

II

Mishnah and Tosefta>, the foundation documents of Rabbinic Judaism, are notoriously parochial. These two collections, edited in the first half of the third century C.E., contain comments attributed to Sages who supposedly lived from the Maccabean revolt in the 160's B.C.E. through the beginning of the third century C.E. They were composed in a Palestinian environment which experienced the invasion of Rome, the rise and fall of Herod and his dynasty, Jerusalem's conquest by the Parthians, the destruction at Roman hands of the Temple and the Holy City, the flourishing of the Essenes at Qumran, the massacre of the Sicarii on Massada, and the rise and expansion of Christianity. And yet, if all we had were these two Rabbinic texts, we would know next to nothing about the most important form of non-Rabbinic Judaism of the period, Christianity, or of the less popular examples of non-Rabbinic

Judaism, the Essenes, the Sicarii, or the Zealots. Even the Pharisees' major adversary, the Sadducees, appear about as frequently in the New Testament as they do in Mishnah and Tosefta>. Similarly, from the Rabbinic collections we discover little about the destruction of the Holy City or the Temple, and they are almost silent about the Roman rule of Palestine. Mishnah-Tosefta> focus their attention on the minutiae of Rabbinic Judaism. Therefore, while we learn a good deal about the Temple ritual which ended approximately 150 years before these collections were edited, we hear virtually nothing about the Great Revolt which resulted in a major influx of Gentiles into Palestine about 110 years before our documents were compiled. Although we have detailed discussions of the mildew which grows on clothes or on buildings, we learn nothing about the spread of Christianity throughout the contemporary Roman Empire.[1] Given these facts, we would expect that the Gentiles, the *goyim*, would receive little attention in our documents. In fact, it might cause us to wonder that they are discussed at all. But they are treated in our documents and for reasons and in ways which are repeated, in general terms, throughout the world, in many different localities, and by many different peoples, cultures, and religions.[2] In the following discussion we shall see that the Rabbinic treatment of the non-Israelites, the *goyim*, is in no way different from, let us say, the British treatment of the French, the American treatment of the Blacks or Asians, or the Catholic treatment of the Protestants.

Peoples, nations, ethnic groups, tribes, cultures, religions, and the like do not exist in vacuums. Each unit interacts with other sets and subsets of peoples on various levels and in several contexts, and each grouping's identity is partially created and influenced by these contacts.[3] Each community understands itself, at least partially, in terms of the other society. In order to act, human beings must categorize, classify, and symbolize all reality, including themselves; as Rodney Needham argues, the creation of "binary opposites is an

---

[1] For a convenient discussion of the content and ideas of the Mishnah, see Jacob Neusner, *Judaism: The Evidence of the Mishnah* (Chicago: University of Chicago Press, 1981). For an informative summary of the history of the period, see Shaye J.D. Cohen, *From the Maccabees to the Mishnah* (Philadelphia: Westminster Press, 1987).

[2] For a full treatment of the issues discussed in this essay, see Gary G. Porton, *Goyim: Gentiles and Israelites in Mishnah-Tosefta* (Atlanta: Scholars Press, 1988).

[3] Fredrik Barth writes, "ethnic distinctions do not depend on an absence of social interaction..., but are quite to the contrary often the very foundation on which embracing social systems are built." See his *Ethnic Groups and Boundaries: The Social Organization of Cultural Difference* (Bergen-Oslo: Universitets Forlaget, 1969), p. 10.

elementary and universal mode of classification."[4] Although this need not be the case, for there is no inherent reason for a classification system to stop at the creation of pairs or opposites,[5] it is common for an aggregate of individuals to divide the human community into "us" and "them." While the Rabbis differentiated among various types of Israelites of whom they disapprove,[6] they had only one term for all non-Israelites, whether idolaters or farmers, liars or trustworthy, Greeks or Romans, worshipers of Jesus or atheists. While internally "we" might be variegated, from "our" point of view, "they" form an undifferentiated "them." The world's population was divided into two peoples, "us" and "them," *b'né yiśra>el* and *goyim*.

George Devereux argues that the statement "A is not a non-X (they) is prior to the statement A is an X (we)," so that "specifications as to what constitutes ... identity develop only after a ... group recognizes the existence of others who do not belong to the group."[7] According to Devereux, a "we" cannot describe itself until after it has identified and classified a "they," a "not-we." Following Devereux's insights, we understand that, while the Rabbis did not need to have dwelt extensively upon the Gentiles, they could not have ignored them. If the Sages wished to develop a definition of the People Israel, they had to make reference to the non-Israelites. Following both Devereux and Needham, we see that an attempt by the Rabbis to treat the Israelites without any mention of the non-Israelites would have been doomed to failure. Therefore, on a theoretical level, the Rabbis could not have constructed a definition of the People Israel or clearly delineated the ways in which they were to relate to one another and to the central symbols and institutions of their group without reference to those who stood outside the unit. This explains why documents as parochial, and at times as theoretical, as Mishnah-Tosefta> took up the question of the Gentile at all. Both Needham and Devereux explain why parochial texts can remain ethnocentric in their outlook and still be cognizant of the

---

[4] Rodney Needham, *Symbolic Classification* (Santa Monica: Goodyear, 1979), p. 32. Cf. his *Primordial Characters* (Charlottesville: University Press of Virginia, 1978), p. 35.
[5] Needham, *Symbolic Classification*, pp. 57-58.
[6] William S. Green, "Otherness Within: Toward a Theory of Difference in Rabbinic Judaism," in Jacob Neusner and Ernest S. Frerichs, eds., *"To See Ourselves as Others See Us": Christians, Jews, "Others" in Late Antiquity* (Chico: Scholars Press, 1985), pp. 57-59.
[7] George Devereux, "Ethnic Identity: Its Logical Foundations and Its Dysfunctions," in George De Vos and Lola Romanucci-Ross, *Ethnic Identity: Cultural Continuities and Change* (Palo Alto: Mayfield, 1975), p. 54.

"other."⁸ Given their claims, if there had been no non-Israelite inhabitants of Palestine, the Rabbis and the Israelites would have had to invent them.⁹

But there were non-Israelites in Palestine, especially after the failure of the Bar Kokhba Revolt. Michael Avi-Yonah estimates the population of Palestine on both sides of the Jordan after the Bar Kokhba War, that is after 135 C.E., at 2,500,000 of which at most 800,000 were Jews, and 300,000 to 400,000 of these lived in Galilee. This means that about two thirds of the population was Gentile.¹⁰ Thus, Israelites and Gentiles daily confronted one another in Palestine, and were presumed to have done so by the Rabbis, so that rules and procedures had to be set forth to regulate their interaction. This was of immediate importance because both groups interacted with important elements in the Rabbis' symbolic system – the Land of Israel, the Israelite periods of sacred time, and the Temple – and the Rabbis had to explain how these units should differ in their responses to those entities.

Although the realities of life in Palestine mandated that the non-Israelites had to be dealt with in Mishnah-Tosefta>, the Gentiles are not the subject of one of the six major divisions of our documents or the sixty-three smaller units, the *masekhtot*. Nor did they engender unique literary creations or receive a distinctive treatment in these by our authors or editors.¹¹ The Gentiles were an element in the Sages' environment, to be catalogued, interpreted and regulated through the existing categories of Rabbinic deliberation. But the Gentiles in no case define an area of legislation unto themselves.¹² Not only did the Rabbis view everything from their own point of view, but they also limited their attention to matters they believed essential in constructing and defining the People Israel and in maintaining their unique character. The Gentiles were an issue for attention primarily because they, actually or potentially, came into contact with the People Israel and the latter's ethnic symbols and institutions. It is in terms of these symbols and institutions that the Gentiles are discussed. The treatment of the

---

⁸Similarly, Michael Fischer states that "ethnicity is a process of inter-reference between two or more cultural traditions and that these dynamics of intercultural knowledge provide reservoirs for renewing human values." See his "Ethnicity and the Post-Modern Arts of Memory," in James Clifford and George E. Marcus, eds., *Writing Culture* (Berkeley and Los Angeles: University of California Press, 1986), p. 201.
⁹Cf. Green, p. 52.
¹⁰Michael Avi-Yonah, *The Jews of Palestine: A Political History from the Bar Kokhba War to the Arab Conquest* (New York: Schocken, 1976), p. 19.
¹¹Porton, pp. 13-144.
¹²A significant amount of the legislation concerning idols and idolatry in Mishnah-Tosefta> deals with Israelites, and not with Gentiles.

Gentiles has been Rabbinized in the sense that it has been framed in the same literary terms and around the same basic symbols and concepts which were used for the other topics taken up in Mishnah-Tosefta>. This means that we see the Gentiles through the eyes of the authors of these documents and that we know about them only what the Sages behind Mishnah-Tosefta> thought was important from their point of view and according to their agenda. We see the Gentiles only in light of YHWH, his Land, his People, and his Residence. We do not see them on their own terms. We see the non-Israelites primarily only as a counterpart to the Israelites.

The discussions of the Gentile in Mishnah-Tosefta> derive from three sources: 1) The Torah, 2) the Sages' imagination, and 3) the Rabbis' Palestinian environment. In several places the biblical images of the non-Israelite inform the passages in Mishnah-Tosefta>. For example, our texts consistently refer to a non-Israelite servant as a "Canaanite," an image perhaps derived from Genesis 9:25-26.[13] Moreover, on the basis of Deuteronomy 23:4-9, the Sages discuss the entrance of biblical peoples, such as Moabites, Edomites, Ammonites, and Egyptians, into the congregation of Israel,[14] even though the Rabbis themselves admitted that these peoples, with the exception of the Egyptians, no longer existed. Furthermore, the >*Asherah* of the Bible and the biblical Molekh are as real to the Rabbis of Mishnah-Tosefta> as the Roman god Mercury.[15] In light of the role that biblical ideas and conceptions played in the formulation of the ideas in Mishnah-Tosefta>, we encounter exactly what we expect to find.[16]

Distinguishing those matters in Mishnah-Tosefta> which resided only, or primarily, in the minds of the authors of these texts from those which existed in the world outside of the Sages' imagination is difficult, if not impossible. However, the Rabbis' attempts to regulate the marriage practices among the Gentiles,[17] to limit situations in which Israelites had to follow the rulings of the *Gentile* courts,[18] to legislate the business practices of *non-Israelite* merchants,[19] to set the amount of

---

[13]Ephraim E. Urbach, "The Laws Regarding Slavery as a Source for Social History of the Period of the Second Temple, the Mishnah and Talmud," in J.G. Weiss, ed., *Papers of the Institute of Jewish Studies London* (Jerusalem: Magnes Press, 1964), p. 31.
[14]m. Y'vamot 8:3 and t. Y'vamot 8:1.
[15]Porton, *passim*
[16]Neusner, pp. 167-229.
[17]m.Qidushin 4:3 and t.Qidushin 5:1.
[18]m.Giṭin 9:8 and t.Y'vamot 12:13.
[19]t.<Avodah Zarah 2:1.

compensation *Gentiles* should pay for injury done to an Israelite,[20] and to require *Gentiles* to free a slave they had purchased from an Israelite[21] – these probably reflect wishful thinking on the part of the Sages and not the actual authority they had in these situations. Furthermore, the stereotyping of the Gentiles as dangerous,[22] sexually "uncivilized,"[23] and untrustworthy[24] is reflective of intellectual constructions.

Clearly, the Bible and the Rabbinic imagination are important elements in the descriptions of the Gentiles found in Mishnah-Tosefta>. However, the catalyst for these discussions most likely was the presence of the non-Israelites in the Rabbis' Palestinian environment and the Rabbis' need to define the nature of the People Israel in this environment. Those statements which are attributed to known Sages are assigned primarily to Rabbis who lived during the period following the Bar Kokhba revolt,[25] a time when, as we have seen, the Gentile population and its influence in Palestine achieved new importance.[26] Furthermore, virtually all of the *sugyot* in Mishnah-Tosefta> which discuss the Gentiles assume that non-Israelites and Israelites regularly interacted with one another on a daily basis. On the one hand, the Sages attempted to regulate the Gentiles as well as the Israelites, while, on the other hand, they recognized the authority that the Gentile rulers had over the Rabbis and their followers.[27] While the Sages viewed the Gentiles in abstract stereotypical terms, they also saw them as individuals whom they had to support and with whom the Israelites had to live in peace.[28] In addition, some of the discussions about the Gentiles and wine are based on far-fetched situations, such as what

---

[20] m.Baba> Qama> 4:3, t.Baba> Qama> 4:1 and 4:3.
[21] t.<Avodah Zarah 3:16.
[22] t.T'rumot 8:12, m.<Avodah Zarah 2:1 and t. <Avodah Zarah 3:3.
[23] m.<Avodah Zarah 2:1 and t.Avodah Zarah 3:2.
[24] t.Pe>ah 4:1 and t.D'ma>y 5:2.
[25] Porton, pp. 145-72.
[26] However, the frequency of the names of Sages from this period may be a result of the editing of Mishnah-Tosefta>, for these Sages predominate throughout. See Abraham Goldberg, "The Mishna – A Study Book of Halakhah," and "The Tosefta – companion to the Mishna," in Shmuel Safrai, ed, *The Literature of the Sages First Part: Oral Torah, Halakha, Mishna, Tosefta, Talmud, External Tractates, Compendia Rerum Iudaicarum ad Novum Testamentum* Section 2, 3, First Part (Philadelphia: Fortress Press, 1987), pp. 215-22, 293-98.
[27] m. <Eduyot 7:7.
[28] t. Pe>ah 3:1, m. Sh'viit 4:3, t. Gitin 3:13-14.

happens when a Gentile falls into a vat of Israelite wine,[29] while others are derived from the practical needs of the Palestinian economy.[30]

The Rabbinic comments on the Gentiles paint a varied and complex picture of the non-Israelites, one which seems to reflect the diversity of the situation confronting, or imagined by, the authors of Mishnah-Tosefta>. <Avodah Zarah devotes a good deal of attention to the Gentiles as idolaters, worshipers of divinities other than YHWH, perhaps the feature which most readily comes to the minds of most of us when we hear the term "Gentile." But Mishnah-Tosefta> recognize the Gentiles as much more than idolaters. They are also farmers, landowners, and tenants who could perhaps own a parcel of the Land of Israel, work her soil, and benefit from her crops; they are merchants and customers who trade in produce grown on the Land or in goods which are susceptible to the Israelite purity laws, agricultural gifts, and other dietary restrictions; and they are neighbors, fellow citizens, rulers, soldiers, and commoners, who must function alongside the Israelites in the legal, political, economic, and social systems of Palestine, all of which fall under YHWH's concern and which the Rabbis interpret and regulate according to the Revelation at Sinai.

We have, then, a limited, highly selective and interpreted description of the Gentiles. The picture reflects both the Gentiles as they existed solely in the minds of the Rabbis and the Gentiles as the Rabbis saw them in everyday life. The Gentiles are not merely projections from the Bible, imagined or theoretical others, or normal human beings. They are all three. However, the Gentiles do not demand the Rabbis' interest or attention on their own terms. They are important only because they served the authors of Mishnah-Tosefta> as a means of defining the People Israel. The one point made over and over again in Mishnah-Tosefta> is that *the Gentiles are not Israelites*. For this reason, rules which apply to Israelites *do not* apply to non-Israelites, and common activities are performed in *dissimilar ways* by members of each group. Gentiles were of interest to the Rabbis because they interacted with Israelites on a daily basis, and the Sages treated them in such a way so as to make the distinctions between Israelites and Gentiles clear and definite. It appears, then, that the discussions of the Gentiles provided the Rabbis with a means of constructing and defining the People Israel as an ethnic unit, so that the Rabbis dealt with the non-Israelites in the same manner that all other peoples deal with their neighbors.

---

[29]m. Avodah Zarah 4:10.
[30]t. <Avodah Zarah 7:17.

III

Israelite culture of Mishnah-Tosefta> is heavily influenced by the religious ideas of their authors. It is obvious that one way we can learn about these ideas is to turn to the study of the important symbolates of these cultures: YHWH, the Land of Israel, Sacred Time, the People Israel, and the Temple and its cult. Normally, these symbolates have been approached through examining the ways in which the Israelites respond to them. However, assuming that Needham and Devereux are correct in their claim that a group defines itself by reference to "outsiders," we should be able to learn a good deal about the basic elements of this earliest form of Rabbinic Judaism by approaching these symbols through the patterns of behavior Mishnah-Tosefta> allow to the Gentiles. The following analyses must of course remain tentative, for we do not yet have thorough studies of these symbolates, so that it is impossible to compare the conclusions reached here with those which might be drawn if we had studied all of the discussions of these symbolates throughout Mishnah-Tosefta>.

There is no doubt that YHWH has a special relationship to the People Israel or that Mishnah-Tosefta> are intent upon making him the exclusive object of worship among the Israelite people, so that one of the main thrusts in the discussions of the Gentiles' religious practices is to keep the Israelites from worshipping, appearing to worship, or contributing to the worship of foreign deities. However, YHWH is seldom discussed in these texts. His attributes and activities are presumed throughout, but they are seldom detailed. Similarly, the direct responsibilities that human beings have toward YHWH and their relationship to him most often are expressed in Mishnah-Tosefta> in terms of the other basic symbolates: The Land, the People, the Holy Times, and the Temple. However, the exclusiveness of YHWH's relationship to the Israelites finds some expression in the discussions of the Gentile.[31] Objects owned by Gentiles may not be used in the worship of YHWH, nor may YHWH's blessings be called upon them.[32] The issue here is probably the assumption that Gentiles' possessions could have been used in an idolatrous ritual, so that they were unfit to be used in the worship of YHWH.

Most relevant in the present context is t. M'gilah 2:16[33]:

---

[31] Gentiles may not be included in the recitation of the Grace after meals, but neither may women, slaves, or minors – see m. B'rakhot 7:1-2 – so that this is irrelevant to our discussion.

[32] m. B'rakhot 8:6 and t. B'rakhot 5:31.

[33] A slightly different version appears in T. B. <Arakhim 6a. Cf. Saul Lieberman, *Tosefta Ki-fshutah: A Comprehensive Commentary on the Tosefta Part V*,

If a Gentile sanctified a beam for a synagogue and on it was written "For the Name," they examine him. If he vowed it for the "Holy Name," they store it away. If he vowed it for the sake of the synagogue, they plane off the Name, store away the chips, and use what is left of the beam.

The force of the passage is that the Gentile cannot dedicate something to YHWH or apply YHWH's name to an object dedicated to YHWH. On the other hand, the Gentiles were allowed to bring free-will offerings to the Temple, so that some of the Sages believed that the non-Israelites were free to worship YHWH if they chose.[34]

A major symbolate in the framework of Mishnah-Tosefta> is the Land of Israel.[35] For some, the Land was to be an exclusive Israelite possession, an exclusive gift from YHWH, and there are texts which seem to question the right of the Gentile to own property in the Land of Israel.[36] Much of what Mishnah-Tosefta> have to say about the Land and its produce is derived from the beliefs that the Land of Israel belongs to YHWH and that it is holy. The agricultural gifts which Israelites separate from their crops were a means of recognizing YHWH's ownership of the Land, and in the Torah it appears that *all* of the agricultural gifts were related to this single idea.[37] However, upon examining the Gentiles in relationship to the agricultural gifts, one discovers that the authors of Mishnah-Tosefta> attributed more than one meaning to some of the agricultural gifts. On the one hand, many Sages held that the Gentile, like the Israelite, could recognize YHWH's stewardship of the Land of Israel through the separation of the heave-offering and the tithes.[38] The Land was holy, it was a gift from YHWH,

---

Order Mo'ed (New York: Jewish Theological Seminary of America, 1962), p. 1156.
[34]Porton, pp. 259-68.
[35]On the importance of the Land in Judaism, see Lawrence A. Hoffman, ed., *The Land of Israel: Jewish Perspectives* (Notre Dame: University of Notre Dame Press, 1986), and William D. Davies, *The Gospel and the Land: Early Christianity and Jewish Territorial Doctrine* (Berkeley: University of California Press, 1974). Cf. Porton, pp. 173-203.
[36]See, for example, m. D'ma>y 6:1-2 and the discussion in Richard Sarason, *A History of the Mishnaic Law of Agriculture. Section Three: A Study of Tractate Demai. Studies in Judaism in Late Antiquity* (Leiden: Brill, 1979), pp. 205-6. Cf. Daniel Sperber, *Roman Palestine: 200-400, the Land* (Ramat-Gan: Bar-Ilan University, 1978), pp. 160-76.
[37]On the importance of the Land of Israel in the Bible, see Harry M. Orlinsky, "The Biblical Concept of the Land of Israel," in Hoffman, *op. cit.*, pp. 27-64, and Davies, *op. cit.* See also Hoffman, "Introduction: Land of Blessing and 'Blessings of the Land' " in Hoffman, *op. cit.*, pp. 1-23.
[38]m. T'rumot 3:9, t. T'rumot 4:12, t. Halah 2:6, t. T'rumot 4:13; Porton, pp. 189-93.

and even non-Israelites should acknowledge this fact. On the other hand, the Gentile could not separate the gifts for the poor, such as the gleanings,[39] forgotten sheaves,[40] or "corners."[41] In the Sages' minds these gifts had become ethnic obligations only. While in the Torah they reflected the fact that YHWH owned the Land and cared for the poor, in Mishnah-Tosefta> they represent only the Israelites' responsibility to care for one another. The Land, in Mishnah-Tosefta>, becomes a means of expressing YHWH's greatness *and* a symbol through which the ethnic unity of the People Israel is maintained. In these instances, the Land thus appears to be a medium through which the Gentiles could approach YHWH if they chose because, for some Sages, the sacred nature of the Land of Israel which was derived from its relationship to YHWH was important no matter who worked the soil and benefitted from her produce. For others, however, the Land was sacred only for Israelites; therefore, only Israelites were required to separate the agricultural gifts. Furthermore, the Land had become a means through which the mutual responsibility of the People Israel could be expressed. The Land provided the means, through YHWH's beneficence, for the Israelites to care for one another. The Land of Israel provided the People Israel not only with geographical unity, at least symbolically, but also with the means for assuring material unity, through the sharing of her bounty. In fact, Israelites were theoretically prohibited from eating grain produced by Gentiles, unless the Israelites could be certain that the grain had been tithed; that is, that it had been made the same as Israelite produce.[42]

Above all else, Mishnah-Tosefta> focus on the nature of the People Israel, and this concern stands behind most of the discussions of the Gentile and the Land. We discover that while Israelites and Gentiles both worked the Land of Israel, they did so differently. Israelites could not work the soil in the Seventh Year while Gentiles could.[43] Israelites were required to separate a number of agricultural gifts for use by the poor among them, but these were not required of non-Israelites. Some held that the laws of the Fourth Year applied to Gentiles, while others limited its applicability to Israelites alone.[44] It appears that the laws of

---

[39] t. Pe>ah 2:11, m. Pe>ah 4:6, t. Pe>ah 3:1.
[40] m. Pe>ah 6:6-8; Porton, pp. 183-84.
[41] t. Pe>ah 3:1, m. Pe>ah 4:6, t. Pe>ah 2:10.
[42] m. Ma<šrot 1:1, m. Pe>ah 4:9, t. Pe>ah 2:11. On the agricultural laws in Mishnah-Tosefta>, see Alan J. Avery-Peck, *Mishnah's Division of Agriculture: A History and Theology of Seder Zeraim*. Brown Judaic Studies 79 (Chico: Scholars Press, 1985), and the literature cited there.
[43] m. Sh'viit 5:7, 5:9, 4:3, t. Sh'viit 3:12.
[44] m.<Orlah 1:2, t.<Orlah 1:5, m.T'rumot 3:9, t. T'rumot 2:13.

mixed-kinds also did not apply to Gentiles.[45] Furthermore, only Israelites were required to separate the dough-offering.[46]

Two points should be made. First, despite the fact that Israelites and Gentiles had to follow different practices when planting and harvesting their fields, the texts assume that they might jointly own property, buy and sell land from each other,[47] or rent property to and from each other. Therefore, the differences in agricultural practices did not prevent their interaction in the agricultural sphere, it only regulated it. Second, in many cases, the different ways in which the Gentiles and Israelites treated their harvested grain would not be obvious to the Gentiles; they were internal Israelite matters.[48] This suggests that it was important only from the Israelites' point of view to mark out their uniqueness. For example, an Israelite might purchase grain from a Gentile and then separate the tithe after he left the Gentile's presence, so that the Gentile might never know that the Israelite had treated his grain differently from grain purchased from another Israelite.

The situation with regard to the Gentiles' relationship to the Israelites' periods of Sacred Time is fairly straightforward.[49] The periods of time which receive the most attention in our documents are the Sabbath and Passover. Overall, the Gentile has no responsibility on his or her own for observing the periods of Israelite sacred time. The rites, rituals, and alterations of normal activity which are incumbent upon Israelites *do not* apply to Gentiles. If, however, a Gentile comes into contact with an Israelite, especially on the Sabbath, the former must alter his or her activity, so that the *Israelites'* observance of the Sabbath may cause the Gentiles to alter their own activities. Limiting the observance of the Sabbath exclusively to the Israelites reflects a conscious choice by the Rabbis. In the Torah, the Sabbath has both a cosmic and an ethnic meaning.[50] In Genesis and Exodus, one rests on

---

[45]t. Kil>aim 2:15, t. T'rumot 2:13. The rules concerning mixed-kinds are complex because they are viewed both as an ethnic issue and as a set of rules connected to the holiness of the Land. See Porton, pp. 184-85, and Samuel Cooper, "The Law of Mixture: An Anthropological Study in Halakhah," in Harvey E. Goldberg, *Judaism Viewed From Within and From Without: Anthropological Studies* (Albany: State University of New York Press, 1987), pp. 55-74.

[46]t. Ḥalah 1:3, 2:12, 2:6, t. T'rumot 4:13, m. Ḥalah 3:5-6.

[47]Some held that Gentiles could not own property in the Land of Israel, but Mishnah-Tosefta> assume that they did.

[48]I owe this insight to Professor Alan Avery-Peck.

[49]Porton, pp. 205-20.

[50]Both of these are reflected in the Sabbath liturgy. For example, in the Sabbath *qidush*, the Sabbath commemorates both the creation of the world and the Israelites' departure from Egypt.

the Sabbath because YHWH rested when he finished creating the universe.[51] However, in Deuteronomy, Israelites rest because they were once slaves in the Land of Egypt.[52] The Sages' decision to apply the Sabbath-restrictions to Israelites alone reflects their following Deuteronomy's ethnic explanation of the Sabbath, for the universalistic view of Genesis and Exodus could have caused matters to be worked out differently.[53]

When the Israelite restriction on working on the Sabbath is applied to Gentiles, it is done so because the issue is the work, and not who performs it.[54] Furthermore, these restrictions are applied only from the Israelite point of view and only when the activity impinges, or might impinge, upon the Israelites. This means that the concerns with the Gentiles' working on the Sabbath focus on the relationship of ideas of work and rest to the Israelite. This explains why in some cases one may benefit from a Gentile's activity if done without any regard for the Israelite.[55] The ethnic character of the Sabbath would have been obvious to all, for Israelites alone altered their activity on the Sabbath, even with regard to Gentiles with whom they might have come into contact.[56]

The ethnic quality of Passover is also emphasized in Mishnah-Tosefta>. Abstention from possessing and eating leaven became the central feature of Passover for the Sages of Mishnah-Tosefta>.[57] The texts which discuss the Gentile make it clear that an Israelite is a person

---

[51] Genesis 2:1-4, Exodus 20:8-12, 31:14-17, 34:17.
[52] Deuteronomy 5:12-15.
[53] For a discussion of the Sabbath in Rabbinic literature, see Robert Goldenberg, "The Jewish Sabbath in the Roman World up to the Time of Constantine the Great," in H. Temporini and W. Haase, eds., *Aufstieg und Niedergang der römischen Welt* (Berlin and New York: De Gruyter, 1979), II.19.1, 414-44.
[54] m. Shabat 16:8, t. Shabat 13:12, t. Shabat 17:15, m. Shabat 23:4, t. Shabat 17:14 list activities done by a Gentile for his own benefit from which an Israelite may benefit; m. Shabat 1:7 and t. Shabat 1:22 define a situation in which an Israelite may not aid a Gentile in the latter's work on the eve of the Sabbath; m. Shabat 16:6 and t. Shabat 13:9 state that one may not tell Gentile fire fighters to put out a fire or to ignore a fire on an Israelite's property during the Sabbath.
[55] There is, however, the curious case in m. Shabat 24:1 and t. Shabat 7:20 in which an Israelite is allowed to give his purse to a Gentile to carry so that he will not violate the Sabbath if he is travelling along with a Gentile on a Friday afternoon.
[56] Note, however, t. Mo<ed Qatan 2:14-15, which tells us that Gamliel permitted Israelites to sit on the chairs near Gentile shops on the Sabbath, even though it might appear that they were engaging in business. On the Gentiles' views of the Israelite Sabbath, see John G. Gager, *The Origins of Anti-Semitism: Attitudes Toward Judaism in Pagan and Christian Antiquity* (New York: Oxford University Press, 1985), *passim*, as well as Goldenberg.
[57] Baruch M. Bokser, *The Origins of the Seder: The Passover Rite and Early Rabbinic Judaism* (Berkeley: University of California Press, 1984).

who *does not possess* leaven during Passover, while the Gentile is *one who does* retain leaven during this period. In fact, the *Gentile* is pictured as the mirror-image of the Israelite, with the possession of leaven being the crucial element which distinguishes the two peoples.[58] Thus, the periods of sacred time become a uniquely Israelite manner of approaching YHWH and of distinguishing between the Israelites and the non-Israelites. The treatment of the Gentiles in this context serves solely as a means of stressing the uniqueness of the Israelites.

The distinction between Israelites and Gentiles is further drawn in the discussions of the holy days in three ways. First, the Gentiles receive little attention in this major division of Mishnah-Tosefta>. Second, in the treatment of Passover, the holiday which celebrates the creation of the People Israel, the sharpest distinctions between the Israelites and the Gentiles are drawn. Baruch Bokser[59] has demonstrated that the Rabbis' central concern with reference to Passover was with leaven, and it is exactly here that the differences between Israelites and non-Israelites are most sharply drawn in our texts. Third, during the intermediate days of Passover and Sukot an Israelite may engage in activities with Gentiles in which he may not be occupied with another Israelite or he is forbidden to do things for Gentiles which he may do for other Israelites.[60] This means that, when Israelites and non-Israelites met each other during the Israelite holidays, the Gentiles would see that they were being treated differently from Israelites.

When we examine the Temple and its cult from the perspective of the discussions of the Gentile in Mishnah-Tosefta>, it becomes clear that it is a symbolate with multiple meanings.[61] The two relevant meanings for our purposes are the Temple as YHWH's residence and the Temple as the Israelites' ethnic shrine. The Gentiles were allowed only limited access to the precincts of the Israelite ethnic shrine.[62] Furthermore, they could not contribute to its upkeep by dedicating items for its repair, or by paying the half-*sheqel* tax.[63] These restrictions on the Gentiles' activity with regard to the Temple probably

---

[58]m. P'saḥim 2:1-23, t. Pisḥa> 2:5-15. See Porton, pp. 212-13, 219-20.
[59]See note 57, above.
[60]t. Mo<ed 1:2, t. Ṭ'vul Yom 2:6.
[61]Porton, pp. 259-68.
[62]On this issue, see Shmuel Safrai, "Temple," in Safrai and M. Stern, eds., *The Jewish People in the First Century: Historical Geography, Political History, Social, Cultural and Religious Life and Institutions, Compendia Rerum Iudaicarum ad Novum Testamentum* Section 1, 2 (Philadelphia: Fortress Press, 1974-1976), pp. 866, 878.
[63]m. Sh'qalim 1:5.

derived both from the concept of the Temple as an ethnic shrine and from the idea that YHWH was first and foremost the divinity of the Israelites. However, even Gentiles could express their adoration for YHWH through separating the heave-offering and the tithes. This finds further expression in the fact that Gentiles were allowed to bring free-will offerings to the Temple and that the Israelite community could support these offerings, by providing the drink-offerings if the Gentiles had not supplied them.[64] The point here is that Gentiles were allowed *limited* access to YHWH through the Temple. However, even when the Gentiles brought offerings, the complex rules which applied to Israelites' offerings were not applied to the Gentiles' sacrifices.[65] The result was that, even when Gentiles presented offerings to YHWH, they did so differently from the way in which Israelites would have made those same sacrifices. Furthermore, the Rabbinic texts and Josephus make it clear that the Gentiles were allowed only limited access to the Temple Mount. In fact, the tablets which defined the border beyond which the Gentiles could not pass have been found. This means that, even when they brought offerings to the Temple, the Gentiles occupied a different space from that in which the Israelites stood.[66]

When the Gentiles approached the Temple or sought to participate in its cult, they would have been cognizant of the fact that they were different from Israelites. They would have been barred from entering certain areas of the Temple Mount, they were limited in the sacrifices and offerings they could present to YHWH, and they were limited in the rites they could perform over their sacrifices. It would have been obvious to all that Jerusalem's Temple was an Israelite institution and that YHWH was primarily a deity of the Israelites. When this is combined with the legislation in Mishnah-Tosefta> concerning Gentile religious practice, it would have been clear to both Gentiles and Israelites that they represented two completely different religions.

With reference to the Gentiles' celebrations of religious practices, the lines between Israelites and non-Israelites were sharply drawn.[67] The authors of Mishnah-Tosefta> did everything they could to prevent the Israelites from participating in, or appearing to engage in, any form of worship of a deity other than YHWH.[68] It would have been obvious to the Gentiles that during their periods of religious activity they were treated differently by the Israelites from the way they were treated at

---

[64]m. Sh'qalim 1:5, t. Sh'qalim 1:7, m. Sh'qalim 7:6.
[65]m. M'naḥot 9:8. t. M'naḥot 10:13, m. Z'vaḥim 4:5, t. Z'vaḥim 5:6.
[66]Safrai, "Temple," *op. cit.*, p. 866.
[67]Porton, pp. 241-58.
[68]For a discussion of the many passages which cover this issue, see Porton, pp. 243-40.

other times. Mishnah-Tosefta> seek to make it clear that from the point of view of the religious Gentiles they were completely distinct from Israelites.

In the minds of the authors of Mishnah-Tosefta>, Gentiles and Israelites were totally different people, originating from different ancient ancestors.[69] They could not intermarry, nor could they engage in sexual activities with each other.[70] Furthermore, different laws and regulations concerning testimony in the courts,[71] the application of the laws of damage,[72] and the like applied to each group. Our texts indicate also that the Rabbis believed they could, or should be able to, regulate the activities of the Gentiles as well as those of the Israelites. Again, this is an area of activity in which the Gentiles would recognize that they were treated differently from Israelites *if any* of the rules in Mishnah-Tosefta> were actually put into practice.

Perhaps the most complex area to understand revolves around the Israelite purity laws.[73] On the one hand, the Israelite purity laws did not apply to the Gentiles.[74] Of course, this would have meant nothing to the non-Israelites. On the other hand, some held that Gentiles were treated as if they were unclean.[75] Whether or not either of these positions would have been obvious to the Gentiles is unclear. However, the two positions would have caused the Israelites to treat the Gentiles very differently. If the latter position held, social interaction between the groups would have been limited, while the former position would have resulted in easy daily social intercourse. Perhaps the disagreement in this area reflects the reality that, while some wished to limit severely the interaction between Israelites and non-Israelites, others realized that this could not be done. The need to deal with the actual situation

---

[69]Porton, pp. 221-39.
[70]m. Sanhedrin 9:6, t. Qidushin 5:1, m. Qidushin 1:1, t. K'tubot 1:3 and 5:1, t. Y'vamot 4:6, m. Y'vamot 2:8, t. Y'vamot 4:6, m. Giṭin 9:2, m. Y'vamot 7:5. See also Porton, pp. 222-23.
[71]t.Y'vamot 12:13, m. Giṭin 9:8, t. Sh'vu<ot 2:5, 2:14, 5:10.
[72]Porton, p. 225. t. Baba> Qama> 1:1-2, m. Baba> Qama> 4:1-3, t. Baba> Qama> 4:1-3, m. Baba> Qama> 4:2-3.
[73]Porton., pp. 269-83.
[74]t. >Ahilot 1:4, t. Z'vaḥim. 2:1, m. N'ga<im 3:1 and 7:1, t. N'ga<im 2:14-15, m. N'ga<im 11:1, t. N'ga<im, 7:10, 7:15, m. N'ga<im, 12:1, t. N'ga<im 6:4.
[75]m. >Ohalot. 18:7ff and t. >Ahilot 18:6ff assume that the dwelling-places of Gentiles are unclean: m. >Ohalot 5:8, 7:6, t. Z'vaḥim 2:1. Gedalyahu Alon, "The Levitical Uncleanness of the Gentiles," in his *Jews, Judaism and the Classical World*, translated by Israel Abrahams (Jerusalem: Magnes Press, 1977), pp. 146-89. Adolf Buechler, "The Levitical Impurity of the Gentile in Palestine Before the Year 70," in *Jewish Quarterly Review*, New Series, XVII (1926-1927), 1-81. Jacob Neusner, *The Idea of Purity in Ancient Judaism. Studies in Judaism in Late Antiquity* (Leiden: Brill, 1973).

in Palestine is evident throughout our documents, and it may apply here.

From the point of view of the authors of Mishnah-Tosefta>, Israelites were different from Gentiles, and these differences had important ramifications in all areas of activity. In fact, it appears that one major reason that the Gentiles appear in our texts at all is to make this point and to serve as a means for setting forth the ethnic borders of the Israelites: Israelites treat the crops that grow in the Land of Israel in their own way, they observe their own periods of sacred time and ignore those of their neighbors, they engage in sexual activity only with other Israelites, they have their own legal system, they alone perform the rites at the Temple of Jerusalem, and they alone are concerned with ritual purity and only of other Israelites. When they come into contact with Gentiles and when they interact with them, they are constantly aware that they are dealing with non-Israelites so that all of their activities are altered.[76]

IV

The best means to understand the ways in which the Gentiles are discussed in Mishnah-Tosefta> is by recourse to the information we have about the ways in which ethnic groups form themselves and respond to "outsiders." From this perspective, the treatment of the Gentiles in Mishnah-Tosefta> is completely expected and normal. The discussions of the Gentiles do not reflect anything unique to the Israelites and are not deemed to affect their culture, or their religious beliefs; they merely result from an ethnic group's attempt to understand itself and to set itself off from those with whom it shares territory. Throughout, the Gentiles are presented only from the Israelites' point of view; the former have no inherent importance in themselves.

Our texts are complex, and the discussions of the Gentiles reflect this complexity. On the one hand, some of our material suggests that the Rabbis had complete control over all of the Israelites and Gentiles in Palestine. Other texts even indicate that the Gentiles have no rights to property within the Land of Israel and that the Gentiles and Israelites should remain entirely separate. On the other hand, there are passages which indicate that, whatever the ideal might have been, Israelites and Gentiles lived close to one another and interacted on a daily basis, and that this interaction should be allowed to occur: wine merchants do not have to worry about selling wine to Gentiles, even though we assume that they will make a libation with any wine with which they come into

---

[76]On the question of borders, see Yehudi A. Cohen, "Social Boundary Systems," *Current Anthropology* (February, 1969), X, 1, 103-26.

contact.[77] Israelites should not sell Gentiles any items, which they might use to worship their deities; however, one believes them if they say that they will not use the items they have purchased in this manner.[78] An Israelite should not attend the amphitheater, but he may if required to do so by the state.[79] Above all, Israelites should attempt to create a peaceful environment in which they and the Gentiles might live together in peace.[80]

However they interacted or remained apart, the point of Mishnah-Tosefta> is that Israelites had constantly to be aware of the fact that they were different from Gentiles. This was not a value judgment. It was what it meant to be an Israelite, and this is the overriding point of the images of the Gentile which appear in Mishnah-Tosefta>.

In Mishnah-Tosefta>, the Gentile is primarily the "other." At times the term *goy* symbolizes that part of humanity not represented by the term *b'né yiśra>el*. In other places, the Gentile is merely one of the several groups which occupy the Land of Israel, but do not adhere to the Rabbinic practices, such as tithing. As the "other," Gentiles may be characterized as dangerous and sexually deviant. In a word, they are "uncivilized." Although the Rabbis describe the Gentiles as vulgar and uncivilized, this is to be expected, for as Needham writes, "It is a frequent report from different parts of the world that tribes call themselves alone by the arrogant title 'man,' and that they refer to neighboring peoples as monkeys or crocodiles or malign spirits."[81] Norman R. Yetman writes that "ethnic groups are inherently ethnocentric, regarding their own cultural traits as natural, correct, and superior to those of other ethnic groups, who are perceived as odd, amusing, inferior, or immoral."[82] Similarly, Barbara Babcock's work on cultural reversal presents numerous examples in which the "other" is pictured as the exact opposite of the members of the group drawing the comparison, some even claiming that those on the other side of the

---

[77] For example, see t.<Aⱴodah Zarah 7:17.
[78] For example, see Judah's comment in t. <Aⱴodah Zarah 1:21. See Porton, "Forbidden Transactions: Prohibited Commerce with Gentiles in Earliest Rabbinism," in Neusner and Frerichs, *op. cit.*, pp. 321-23.
[79] t. <Aⱴodah Zarah 2:5-7 and 6:1.
[80] t. <Aⱴodah Zarah 1:33, m. >Aⱴot 3:2, t. Giṭin 3:13-14, m. Sh'ⱴiit. 4:3, 5:9, m. Giṭin 5:8-9.
[81] Needham, *Primordial Characters*, p. 5.
[82] Norman R. Yetman, *Majority and Minority: The Dynamics of Race and Ethnicity in American Life*, Fourth Edition (Boston: Allyn and Bacon, 1985), p. 7.

border must walk on their hands, for surely they could not walk on their feet as "we" do.[83]

The detailed protocols concerning the interactions of Israelites and Gentiles in specific settings are also characteristic of ethnic groups. The differences which an ethnic group sees between itself and another human aggregate have ramifications in the areas of human activity, so that the interaction between the two groups is highly regulated.[84] Therefore, we expect to find, and in fact do find, discussions concerning how an Israelite treats a Gentile who eats in his house, which Gentile professionals an Israelite may employ, how one deals with Gentile employees and employers, how Gentiles and Israelites should interact in the marketplace, and the like.[85]

The prohibition of sexual activity between the two groups also reflects a normal expression of ethnicity. Chester Hunt and Lewis Walker write that "an ethnic group is a collection of people whose membership is largely determined by ancestry."[86] Gerald Berreman accepts H.S. Morris' statement that an "ethnic group consists of people who conceive of themselves as being alike by virtue of a common ancestry, real or fictitious. . ."[87] De Vos also points to the importance of common ancestry for an ethnic group's sense of itself. In one place he lists "common ancestry" as one among the "set of traditions" which an ethnic group holds in common.[88] Keyes writes that "ethnicity derives from a cultural interpretation of descent ... [which] presupposes socially validated parent/child connection."[89] For Keyes, "kin selection provides the underlying motivation that leads human beings to seek solidarity

---

[83] Barbara A. Babcock, *The Reversible World: Essays in Symbolic Inversion* (Ithaca: Cornell University Press, 1978).
[84] Barth, pp. 15-166, writes that the formation of ethnic groups leads to

a systematic set of rules governing inter-ethnic social encounters, a structuring of interactions, a set of prescriptions governing situations of contact and allowing for articulation in some sectors or domains of activity and a set of proscriptions on social situations preventing inter-ethnic interaction . . . .

Cf. Gunnar Halaand, "Economic Determinants in Ethnic Processes," in Barth, *op. cit.* p. 61.
[85] See, especially, Porton, *Goyim*, pp. 221-39.
[86] Chester L. Hunt and Lewis Walker, *Ethnic Dynamics: Patterns of Intergroup Relations in Various Societies* (Homewood: Dorsey Press, 1974), p. 3.
[87] Gerald B. Berreman, "Race, Caste, and Other Invidious Distinctions in Social Stratification," in Yetman, *op. cit.*, p. 23.
[88] George De Vos, "Ethnic Pluralism: Conflict and Accommodation," in De Vos and Romanucci-Ross, *op. cit.* p. 9.
[89] Charles F. Keyes, *Ethnic Change* (Seattle: University of Washington Press, 1981), p. 5.

with those whom they recognize 'as being of the same people'...."[90] And finally, van den Berghe claims that ethnicity is in reality an "attenuated form" of kin selection.[91] In this context it is important to remember that the Israelites of this period most often call themselves *b'né yiśra>el* – the children, descendants, of Israel, that is Jacob. They do not designate themselves as Jews, derived from the geographical area of Judaea, but the children of Israel whose unity is established by common ancestry. Given this fact, is it any wonder that Rabbis, like all other ethnic leaders, sought to prevent sexual activity with those from other ethnic units? Thus, given that endogamy is a "usual" characteristic of an ethnic group,[92] it does not point to an over-expressed "particularism" of the Israelites.

The point of this analysis is simple: the descriptions of the Gentiles found in Mishnah-Tosefta> and the religious symbols of Israelite culture and the limitations placed on the interaction of Israelites and non-Israelites are not unique to our texts. Nor do they point to some distinctive characteristics of the Israelites, their religion, or their sacred texts. Rather, the treatment of the Gentiles in Mishnah-Tosefta> parallels in general and particular terms the ways in which any ethnic group treats those outside its unit. The Israelite view of the Gentile as expressed in Mishnah-Tosefta> is decidedly commonplace when viewed from the perspective of the interaction of ethnic units throughout the world and throughout history. And the discussions of the Gentiles served as a means for the Israelites to define themselves; they were not primarily meant to be an accurate description of the Gentiles.

---

[90]*Ibid.*, p. 6.
[91]Pierre L. van den Berghe, "Race and Ethnicity: A Psychobiological Perspective," in Yetman, *op. cit.*, p. 56.
[92]De Vos, p. 9.

7

A New Interpretation of *"V'hinam Shol'ḥim >Et-Ha-z'morah >El->Apam"* (Ezekiel 8:17)

By Melvin S. Sands

In 1936, Robert Gordis,[1] in his study of Ezekiel 8:17, and in particular the concluding phrase: *V'hinam shol'ḥim >et-ha-z'morah >el->apam*, described it as "one of the most interesting and baffling verses in the Bible." The phrase (hereafter referred to as: concl. phr. 17) has continued to be "puzzling,"[2] "the celebrated crux,"[3] "obscure."[4] In the absence of any scholarly consensus about its meaning, the challenge remains to find the key to this problem.

Ezekiel 8:17 *in toto*: *vayo>mer >elay ha'ra>ita ven->adam ha'naqel l'vét y'hudah me<asot >et-ha-to<evot >asher <asu-foh ki-mal'>u >et-ha>arez ḥamas vayashuvu l'hakh<iseni v'hinam shol'ḥim >et-ha-z'morah >el->apam*:

The New Jewish Publication Society version (NJPS): And He said to me, "Do you see, O mortal? Is it not enough for the House of Judah to practice the abominations that they have committed here, that they must fill the country with lawlessness and provoke Me still further and thrust the branch to their nostrils?"

NJPS reads *>apam* as "their nostrils" ("their," according to a footnote, is a euphemism for "My"); the Jerusalem Bible (JB): "their nostrils"; Jewish Publication Society (JPS, 1917) and Revised Standard

---

[1] Gordis, "'The Branch to the Nose' A Note on Ezekiel VIII 17," *Journal of Theological Studies (JTS)*, XXXVII (1936), 284.
[2] H.W.F. Skaggs, "The Branch to the Nose," *JTS*, New Series, XI (1960), 318.
[3] Nahum M. Sarna, "Ezekiel 8:17: A Fresh Examination," *Harvard Theological Review*, LVII (1964), 350.
[4] John W. Wevers, *Ezekiel, The Century Bible, New Series* (Greenwood, S.C.: Attic, 1969), p. 83.

Version (RSV): "their nose"; New American Bible (NAB): "my nose"; New English Bible (NEB): "even while they seek to appease me."

These variant readings – their nose/nostrils (>*apam*) and my nose (=>*api*, i.e., My nose, referring to God) – show that the translation and hence the meaning have remained undecided. The >*apam*->*api* question, central in every major scholarly discussion of 8:17, has its historical literary beginnings from the time of the Septuagint (LXX).

Thus, the LXX paraphrase[5] of the concl. phr. 17 – *kai idou autoi hōs muktērizōntes*[6] (*muktērizō*, "turn up the nose, sneer at, treat with contempt"[7]): "and, behold, these are as scorners"[8]/ "And, behold, they are like those who turn up their noses," or, "snort through their noses"[9] – indicates >*apam* rather than >*api*.[10] The later Greek Versions of Aquila, Theodotion, and Symmachus[11] also point to >*apam*, as do the Vulgate,[12] Peshitta,[13] Targum,[14] and Rashi.[15] Kimḥi, however, based his interpretation on >*api*, while adding that >*apam* was one of the

---

[5]William McKane, "Observations on the *Tiḳḳune Soperim*," in *On Language, Culture, and Religion: In Honor of Eugene A. Nida* (The Hague: Mouton, 1974), p. 71; cf. Carmel McCarthy, *The Tiqqune Sopherim and Other Theological Corrections in the Masoretic Text of the Old Testament* (Göttingen: Vandenhoeck & Ruprecht, 1981), p. 92.

[6]Alfred Rahlfs, *Septuaginta* (Stuttgart: Deutsche Bibelstiftung, 1935).

[7]Henry George Liddell and Robert Scott, *A Greek-English Lexicon* (Oxford: Clarendon, 1951), II, 1152: s.v. *muktērizō*; William F. Arndt and F. Wilbur Gingrich, *A Greek-English Lexicon of the New Testament and Other Early Christian Literature* (Chicago: University of Chicago, 1965), p. 531: s.v. *muktērizō*.

[8]*The Septuagint Version of the Old Testament and Apocrypha with an English Translation and with Various Readings and Critical Notes* (London: Samuel Bagster and Sons, n.d.), p. 988.

[9]Walther Zimmerli, *Ezekiel 1: A Commentary on the Book of the Prophet Ezekiel, Chapters 1-24*, trans. Ronald E. Clements (Philadelphia: Fortress Press, 1979), p. 222.

[10]Gordis, *op. cit.*, p. 286; McKane, *op. cit.* p. 71.

[11]McKane, p. 72.

[12]*Biblia Sacra iuxta latinam vulgatum versionem ad codicem fidem, Liber Hiezechielis* (Rome: Typis Polyglottis Vaticanus, 1978): *et ecce applicant ramum ad nares suas*. See also McCarthy, *op. cit.*, p. 92.

[13]See Gordis, p. 286, and McKane, p. 72.

[14]See the translation by Samson H. Levey, *The Targum of Ezekiel: Translated with a Critical Introduction, Apparatus, and Notes* (Wilmington: Michael Glazier, 1987), p. 36: "Behold, *they are bringing disgrace right in front of them*" (emphasis Levey's to indicate "Targum's departure from M [asoretic] T [ext]") and n. 13 thereto (p. 37): "MT: 'Behold, they extend the branch to their nose.' Probably an idolatrous practice. See *IB* [*Interpreter's Bible*, Vol. VI], p. 109"; Sarna, *op. cit.*, p. 352, n. 31: Symmachus, Aquila, Peshitta, and Targum all have the >*apam* reading.

[15]*Miqra>ot G'dolot*.

eighteen *tiquné sof'rim*[16] (one of the Scribal corrections or euphemisms for what was considered to be an originally offensive or blasphemous expression).

Scholars have often observed that uncertainty in translating the concl. phr. 17 is mainly due to the problem of interpreting the word *z'morah*.[17] *Z'morah*, "branch (of vine), twig, shoot,"[18] occurs only four other times in the Masoretic Texts (MT): Numbers 13:23 (*z'morah*), Isaiah 17:10 (*uz'morat zar*), Ezekiel 15:2 (*ha-z'morah*), and Nahum 2:3 (*uz'moréhem*). I suggest that *ha-z'morah >el->apam* alludes specifically to Isaiah 17:10 c,d.

> Isaiah 17:10 *in toto:* ki shakhaḥat >elohé yish<ekh v'ẓur ma<uzekh lo> zakhart <al-ken tiṭ'<i niṭ'<é na<amanim uz'morat zar tizra<enu.

We turn again to the English versions for a comparative view of Isaiah 17:10c,d, a method very useful in this type of study to highlight what otherwise might not be so apparent.

The NJPS reads: "That is why, though you plant a delightful sapling (*tiṭ'<i niṭ'<é* na<amanim), what you sow proves a disappointing slip (*uz'morat zar tizra<enu*)." The other English Versions, either by their renderings of verse 10 c,d or in footnotes thereto differ significantly from NJPS: (a) (*tiṭ'<i niṭ'<é na<amanim*, according to NEB, means planting "gardens in honour of Adonis" (similarly, JB) or, as in the RSV explanatory note, "plants dedicated to Tammuz" (with a reference to Ezekiel 8:14-18), or, as in the NAB footnote, "plants of delights, understood by some as planted in honor of the god of fertility." (b) *uz'morat zar* is rendered in the RSV as "slips of an alien god" (similarly, NEB and JB) or "foreign vine slips" (NAB). Albright[19] explains that

> It was seen long ago that the plant-beds of Na<man... in Is. 17:10 mean "plant-beds of Adonis," who may be referred to under this name in the Ugaritic texts. In any event, there can be no doubt that the designation *Na<mân - Nu<mân - Na<môn*, "the Charming One," was employed for Adonis by the Phoenicians...

---

[16]*Ibid.*
[17]Walther Eichrodt, *Ezekiel: A Commentary*, trans. Cosslett Quin (Philadelphia: Westminster, 1970), p. 108, n. *w*; Wevers, *op. cit.*, p. 83; McCarthy, p. 93.
[18]F. Brown, S.R. Driver, and C.A. Briggs, eds., *A Hebrew and English Lexicon of the Old Testament* [BDB] (Oxford: Clarendon Press, 1907), p. 274: s.v. *z'morah*; Marcus Jastrow, *A Dictionary of the Targumim, the Talmud Babli and Yerushalmi, and the Midrashic Literature* (New York: Pardes, 1950), I, 402.
[19]William Foxwell Albright, *Yahweh and the Gods of Canaan: A Historical Analysis of Two Contrasting Faiths* (Garden City: Doubleday Anchor Books, 1969), pp. 186-87.

Muilenburg[20] compared Tammuz, Sumerian Dumuzi, to Syrian Adonis and Canaanite Baal.

>el->apam

I now propose (a) that *ha-z'morah* of Ezekiel 8:17 alludes to *z'morat zar* of Isaiah 17:10d and to the parallel *niṭ'<é na<amanim*, verse 10c, the substance of which could inform the reader about the hidden content of >*el-* >*apam*; and (b) that the way to uncover this hidden content could be by understanding >*apam* to be a cipher, formed by the device of letter changing.

In Daniel 1:7, we have a likely example of this device and its usage: there are scholars who hold that Abed-nego (<*aved n'go*; <*aved n'go*> in Daniel 3:29), meaning "servant of Nego," is probably (some others: certainly) a deliberate substitution for <*aved n'vo*, "servant of Nebo" (i.e., Nebu/Nabu, the Babylonian god of wisdom; see Isaiah 46:1).[21] There are also those who think that this name change was probably intentional with the purpose of removing an idolatrous name.[22] It is noteworthy that the letter *gimel* (of *n'go*) follows immediately the letter *bet* in the Hebrew alphabet, a proximity which could suggest a deliberate, consciously planned choice of the letter *gimel* as a substitute for *bet*.

Louis Finkelstein's[23] suggestion of more than half a century ago for the meaning of Magog (Ezekiel 38:2; 39:6) also illustrates this device: "Write Magog backwards in Hebrew (*Gagam*) and substitute for each letter the one preceding it in the Hebrew alphabet, and it becomes

---

[20]James Muilenburg, "Ezekiel," *Peake's Commentary on the Bible*, eds. Matthew Black and H. H. Rowley (London: Thomas Nelson and Sons, 1963), p. 574. On Tammuz, see the comment by Levey, *op. cit.*, p. 37, n. 10:

> The older Rabbinic sources are silent on the god Tammuz, perhaps because of the embarrassment of having a memorial to a pagan god in the form of a month in the Jewish calendar, assumed, of course, from the Babylonians. There are no comments on this verse, nor on Tammuz the deity in the Talmud or Midrashim. Rashi and Kimḥi, *ad loc.*, as well as Maimonides (*Moreh* 3:29), have a number of fanciful explanations.

[21]See Charles C. Torrey, "Abednego," *Jewish Encyclopedia* [*JE*], I, 48; James A. Montgomery, *A Critical and Exegetical Commentary on the Book of Daniel* (New York: Charles Scribner's Sons, 1927), p. 130; *The Westminster Dictionary of the Bible*, ed. John D. Davis (Philadelphia: Westminster, 1944), p. 2: s.v. "Abed-nego"; JB, marg. n. c on "Abed-nego," p. 1423; André Lacocque, *The Book of Daniel*, trans. David Pellauer (Atlanta: John Knox, 1979), p. 29.
[22]Torrey, *op. cit.*, p. 48; Montgomery, *op. cit.*, p. 130.
[23]Finkelstein, *The Pharisees: The Sociological Background of their Faith* (3rd ed.; Philadelphia: Jewish Publication Society, 1966), pp. 338, 340.

Babel, Babylonia." The cipher, he maintained, enabled Ezekiel "in his later prophecies against Babylonia" to bring "his thought to his hearers without exposing himself to any danger from traducers."

The cipher >*pm*: Now if the letters of >*pm* are changed by substituting for the >*alef* the next letter of the alphabet, *bet*, and for the *pé* and *mem* the preceding letters of the alphabet <*ayin* and *lamed*, we have *b*<*1*. In the context of the idolatrous cultic rites of Ezekiel 8:3ff. and the specific mention of Tammuz (verse 14), the *b*<*l* would appropriately refer to *Ba*<*al*, the Canaanite god of storm, rain, and fertility mentioned in the Hebrew Bible[24] and the Ugaritic literature (where *Ba*<*lu* is also the war-god).[25]

There seems to be a scholarly consensus that the various references to Canaanite Baals in the Hebrew Bible (such as Baal-gad, Baal-hermon, Baal-peor, Baal-zephon) indicate, in general, several manifestations or local variations of the one and same Baal (rather than many Baals), and this Baal was worshipped in essentially the same way.[26] According to Numbers 25, Israel's first encounter with the Baal cult was at Peor in the land of Moab before the crossing of the Jordan; there, it is inferred from the context, many Israelites participated in Baal sex rites.[27] The Baal-peor incident is frequently recalled in the Bible as an example of apostasy (Deuteronomy 4:3; Joshua 22:17; Hosea 9:10; Psalm 106:28). "It was," write Francis I. Andersen and David Noel Freedman, "a major defection, soon after the covenant had been made. It was a portent and paradigm of Israel's later history...."[28]

While a Baal sex ritual at Peor is a probable inference from Numbers 25:1-3 and Hosea 9:10 especially, the Rabbinic literature is explicit about this ritual. In m. Sanhedrin 7:6, we read (cf. T.B. Sanhedrin 64a; Numbers Rabah 20:23; Sifré, Numbers, Balaq, 131): "One who uncovers

---

[24]M. J. Mulder, "Baal in the OT," III, in *Theological Dictionary of the Old Testament* [*TDOT*] (Grand Rapids: William B. Eerdmans, 1975), II, 193-95, 198-200: s.v. *ba*<*al*.
[25]J.C. de Moor, "The Canaanite Baal Outside the OT," in *TDOT*, II, 184-86, 188.
[26]Gunnar Östborn, *Yahweh and Baal: Studies in the Book of Hosea and Related Documents* (Lund: C.W. K. Gleerup, 1956), p. 37; Norman C. Habel, *Yahweh versus Baal: A Conflict of Religious Cultures* (New York: Bookman Associates, 1964), p. 25; Mulder, *op. cit.*, p. 192; J.A. Emerton, "New Light on Israelite Religion: The Implications of the Inscriptions from Kuntillet <Ajrud," in *Zeitschrift für die alttestamentliche Wissenschaft*, XCIV (1982), 11, 12.
[27]Joseph Reider, *The Holy Scriptures: Deuteronomy with Commentary* (Philadelphia: Jewish Publication Society, 1937), p. 48; Östborn, *op. cit.*, p. 37; Habel, *op. cit.*, p. 24; Robert G. Boling, *Joshua* (Garden City: Doubleday, 1982), p. 514.
[28]Andersen and Freedman, *Hosea* (Garden City: Doubleday, 1980), p. 166: on Hosea 1:2.

himself before Ba<al P'<or (*ha-po<er <azmo l'ū́a<al p'<or*) [is culpable] because this is the manner of worshipping it."²⁹ It is interesting to note here the view of Louis Ginzberg³⁰ that factual material in certain of the Rabbinic sources, e.g., Sifré, Numbers, Balaq, 131 and T. B. Sanhedrin 106a, "give the impression that it [i.e., the Baal-peor cult] existed at the time of the Tannaim." Maimonides³¹ in the *Moreh* connected this "uncovering" at Peor with the commandments of Exodus 28:42 and 20:23:

> You know likewise how widespread was the worship of *P'<or* in those times, and that it consisted in the uncovering of the nakedness. Therefore it commands the *Priests* to make themselves breeches *to cover the flesh of their nakedness* during the *divine service*. Nevertheless, they were commanded not to go up to the *altar* by steps: *That thy nakedness be not uncovered thereon*.

V'hinam shol'ḥim >et-ha-z'morah >el-ba<al

Since the Baal cult was primarily a fertility cult and Israel's idolatrous and sexual sinning at Baal-peor, the paradigm of Israel's apostasy in the Hebrew Bible, was traditionally connected with "the uncovering of the nakedness," I suggest that *v'hinam shol'ḥim* refers to an "uncovering" cultic act in the Jerusalem Temple precincts. This act could have been "stretching out, extending"³² to Baal (*>el-ba<al*) "the *z'morah*," the branch (of the vine, twig, shoot, slip), a symbol of or euphemism for the male phallus.³³ The cultic purpose of this phallic rite could have been to pay homage to the generative power of the rain and fertility god Baal and/or to stimulate this god to provide fertility (human, animal, plant).

---

²⁹Philip Blackman, *Mishnayoth*, Vol. IV: Order *Nezikin* (New York: Judaica, 1963), p. 270.

³⁰"Baal-peor: In Rabbinical Literature," *JE* II, 382. See also Saul Lieberman, *Hellenism in Jewish Palestine* (New York: Jewish Theological Seminary, 1962), p. 131: "According to the Rabbis the heathen of their time did homage to Pe<or by uncovering themselves, by purging themselves and by similar indecencies..."

³¹Moses Maimonides, *The Guide of the Perplexed*, translated by Shlomo Pines (Chicago: University of Chicago, 1964), 578: III. 45 (in explanation of the italics, Pines notes in the Preface that "italic type has been reserved to indicate Maimonides' use of words that are clearly identifiable as being Hebrew or Aramaic").

³²BDB, p. 1018: s.v. *shalaḥ*; W. L. Holladay, *Lexicon*, p. 371: s.v. *shalaḥ*.

³³For excellent summaries and discussions of the many explanations of the *z'morah* in the long interpretative history of Ezekiel 8:17, including the phallus one, see especially McKane, pp. 73-75; McCarthy, pp. 91-96; and Yitzhak Avishur, "The Duties of the Son in the Story of Aqhat and Ezekiel's Prophecy on Idolatry (Ch. 8)," *Ugarit-Forschungen*, XVII (1986), 59-60.

What the Greek historian Diodorus Siculus (first century B.C.E.)[34] described about the Egyptian forty-day ceremonies for a carefully chosen young bull to succeed the dead bull-god Apis at the Memphis sanctuary, offers a ritual parallel to what I have proposed above, especially when it is known that the Apis bull was originally a fertility god: "During these forty days only women may look at it; these stand facing it and pulling up their garments show their genitals, but henceforth they are forever prevented from coming into the presence of this god."

I propose, therefore, (a) that the concl. phr. 17 means: "And, lo, they uncover (stretch out, extend) the phallus (branch/vine-branch, twig, shoot, slip) to Baal"; (b) that the "abominations" in the Temple precincts ended with this fifth and climactic idolatrous rite (and not with a fourth, verse 16, as has been frequently maintained); and (c) that the key word in this phrase, ba<al, could have been changed to >apam to avoid what was considered to be a most offensive idolatrous name and cultic rite.

---

[34]*Diodorus of Sicily*, Loeb Classical Library, Vol. I, Book I, 85 (p. 291).

8

Understanding a Midrash Text: The Case of the Inhabitants of Nineveh

By Lou H. Silberman

In chapter 24 of *P'siqta>d'Rav̄ Kahana>*[1] – *shuv̄ah* – there is a series of midrashim with a similar structure, formulated as a divine reply to Israel's query whether indeed its response to the prophetic call of Hosea, *shuv̄ah yiśra>el*, will be accepted by God:

> *>am'ru yiśra>el lif'né ha-qadosh barukh hu> ribon ha-<olamim >im <ośin >anu t'shuv̄ah m'qablénu >amar lahem t'shuv̄ah shel ... qibalti u-t'shuv̄atkhem >éni m'qabel she-nigz'rah <aléhem (<alav̄) g'zerah qashah, hada> hu> dikh'tiv̄...* (Israel said unto the Holy One blessed be He, Master of the worlds, if we repent will you receive us? Said He to them, the repentance of ... I accepted, will I not accept yours? For a severe decree was entered against them (him), as it is written...)

This is followed by the scriptural passage with midrashic expansions indicating the person(s) and recounting the events. Each pericope concludes with a reprise of the initial rhetorical question: *t'shuv̄atkhem >éni m'qabel*, "will I not accept yours?"

What generates the tremulous question to which the examples are given as reassuring answers arises out of the verse (Hosea 14:1), "Samaria shall bear her guilt," that precedes the opening verse of the *haftarah* (Hosea 14:2). What does the juxtaposition of this verse with the call to repentance, *shuv̄ah yiśra>el*, intend? The reply is given by R. Samuel bar Naḥman in the form of a parable in which the king's representative puts down the rebellion in one province by pointing to the fate of another, its destruction. Hosea, like the king's agent, calls for repentance by pointing to Samaria's fate. "Thus says Hosea to Israel,

---

[1] Ed. B. Mandelbaum (New York: Jewish Theological Seminary of America, 1962), II, 361-64.

'My children, repent so that what happened to Samaria and its allies will not happen to you.'"

Some of these same midrashim, without the formulaic introduction and conclusion and, indeed, used for other purposes, are found in other collections. This allows one to conclude that these formulae are from the hand of the redactor. He, it would seem, sought various examples of repentance from available sources to include, from his particular theological perspective, in a chapter dealing with that subject. The occasion was the sabbath between Rosh Ha-shanah and Yom Kippur on which the prophetic reading is Hosea 14, beginning with verse 2.[2]

The midrash from this series dealing with the repentance of the inhabitants of Nineveh is found, lacking the introductory and concluding formulas, in the Palestinian Talmud, Ta<anit 2:1[65b]:

T.Y. Ta<anit 2:1	P'siqta> d'Rav̄ Kahana> 24:11
מתני: סדר תעניות כיצד מוציאים	תשובתן של אנשי נינוה
התיבה לרחובה של עיר נותנין אפר	קיבלתי ותשובתכם איני מקבל,
קלה על גבי התיבה ובראש הנשיא	שגזרה עליהם גזירה קשה, הד"ה
ובראש אב בית דין וכל אחד	דכת' ויחל יונה לבוא בעיר מהלך
ואחד נוטל ונותן בראשו	וגו' ויגע הדבר אל מלך נינוה
הזקן שבהן אמר לפניהם דברי	ויקם מכסאו וגו' ויאמר בנינוה
כיבושין: אחינו לוא נאמר	מטעם המלך וגדליו לאמר וגו' [יונה
באנשי נינוה 'וירא אלהים	ג:ד - ז]
את שקם ואת תעניתם' אלא 'וירא	
אלהים את מעשיהם כי שבו מדרכם	
הרעה ובקבלה מהו אומר?	
'וקרעו לבבכם ואל בגדיהם	
ושבו אל ה' אלהיכם.'	
גמרא	
אמר ר' שמעון	אמר ריש לקיש תשובה של
בן לקיש: תשובה של רמיות עשו	רמיות עשו אנשי נינוה. מה עשו,
אנשי נינוה. מה עשו? ר' חונה	ר' חוניה בש"ר שמעון בן חלפותא,
בשם ר' שמעון בן חלפותא: העמידו	העמידו העגלים מבפנים ואמותיהם
עגלים מבפנים ואימותידם מבחוץ	מבחוץ, שהיו אילו גועים מבפנים

---

[2]For a discussion of the redactor's attitudes, see Lou H. Silberman, "A Theological Treatise on Forgiveness: Chapter Twenty-tree of *Pesiqta Derab Kahana*," in J.J. Petuchowski and E. Fleischer, eds., *Studies in Aggadah, Targum and Jewish Liturgy in Memory of Joseph Heinemann* (Jerusalem: Magnes Press, Hebrew Union College Press, 1981), pp. 95-107; "Challenge and Response: Pesiqta Derab Kahana, Chapter 26 as an Oblique Response to Christian Claims," in George W. E. Nickelsburg and George W. MacRae, eds., *Christians Among Jews and Gentiles* (Philadelphia: Fortress Press, 1986), pp. 247-53.

ואימותיהן מבחוץ, והוון אילין
מגעיי מיכה ואילין מיכה, אמרין
אין לית את מרחם עלינו לית אנן
מרחמין עליהון. אמר ר' אחא אף
בערביא עבדין כן. מה נאנחה בהמה
נבוכו עדרי בקר וגו' [יואל א:יח].
ויתכסו שקים האדם והבהמה ויקראו
אל אלהים בחזקה [יונה ג:ח], מהו
בחזקה, אר' שמעון בן חלפתא חציפה
נצח לבישה, כל שכן לטובתו של
עולם. וישובו איש מדרכו הרעה
וגו' [שם ג:י]. א' ר' יוחנן מה
שהיה בכף ידיהם החזירו ומה
שהיה בשידה תיבה ומגדל לא
החזירו. וקרעו לבבכם ואל
בגדיכם וגו' [יואל ב:יג] אר'
יהושע בן לוי אם קרעתם לבבכם
בתשובה אין אתם קורעים
בגדיכם על בניכם ובנותיכם. למה,
כי חנון ורחום הוא ארך אפים
[שם]: ר' אחא ור' תנחום בשם
ר' חייא בשם ר' יוחנן ארך אף
אין כתוב כאן אלא ארך אפים,
מאריך רוחו עם הצדיקים ומאריך
רוחו עם הרשעים. מאריך רוחו עם
הצדיקים וגובה מהם מעוט מעשים
רעים שעשו בעולם הזה בשביל ליתן
שכרן משלם לעתיד לבוא ומשפע
שלווה לרשעים בעולם הזה ומשלם
להם מעוט מעשיהם טובים בעולם הזה
בשביל ליפרע מהם חוב משלם לעתיד
לבוא. ר' שמואל בר נחמן בשם ר'
יוחנן ארך אף אין כת' כאן אלא
ארך אפים, מאריך רוחו עד שלא
יגבה, בא לגבות מאריך וגובה. אר'
חנינא מאן דאמ' דרחמנא וותרן
יתוותרנין בני מעוי, אלא
מאריך רוחא וגובה דידיה. אר' לוי
מהו ארך אפים, רחיק רגיז.
למלך שהיה לו ליגיונות קשים, אמר
המלך אם דרים הם עמי במדינה
עכשיו בני מדינה מכעיסין אותי
והם עומדים מאיליהן עליהון

והוון אילין געיי מן הכא ואילין
געיי מן הכא. אמרין: אין לית
מתרחם עלינו לינן רחמין
עליהון, הה"ד 'מה נאנחה בהמה
נבכו עדרי בקר וגו' אר' אחא:
בערביא עבדין כן. 'ויתכסו שקים
האדם והבהמה ויקראו אל אלהים
בחזקה.' מהו בחזקה? אר' שמעון
בן חלפותא: חציפא נצח לכשירא,
כלשכן לטובתו של עולם. 'וישבו איש
מדרכו הרעה ומן החמס אשר
בכפיהם': אר' יוחנן: מה
שהיה בכף ידיהם החזירו.
מה שהיה בשידה תיבה ומגדל
לא החזירו. כתיב: 'וקרעו לבבם
ואל בגדיהם ושבו אל יי
אלהיכם כי חנון ורחום הוא'
אריב"ל: אם קרעתם לבבכם בתשובה
אין אתם קורעין בגדיכם לא על
בניכם ולא על בנותיכם אלא על יי
אלהיכם. למה? כי חנון ורחום הוא
ארך אפים ורב חסד ונחם על הרעה.
ר' שמואל בר נחמן בשם ר' יונתן
ארך אף אין כתיב כאן אלא ארך
אפים מאריך רוחו עם הצדיקים
ומאריך רוחו עם הרשעים. ר' אחא
ר' תנחום בי ר' חייא בשם ר'
יוחנן ארך אף אין כתיב כאן אלא
ארך אפים מאריך רוחו חד שלא
יגבה, התחיל לגבות מאריך רוחו
וגובה. אמר ר' חנינא: מאן דאמר
דרחמנא וותרן יתווהרון בני מעוי
אלא מאריך רוחיה וגבי דידיה. אמר
ר' לוי: מהו ארך אפים?
רחיק רגיז. למלך שהיו לו שני
ליגיונות קשים; אמר המלך, אם
דרים הן עמי במדינה עכשיו בני
המדינה מכעיסין אותי והן עומדין
אותן אלא הכיני שלחן לדרך רחוקה
שאם הכעיסו אותי בני המדינה עד
שאני משלח אחריהם בני המדינה
מפייסין אותי ואני מקבל
פיוסן. כך אמר הקב"ה, אף והמה

מלאכי חבלה הן, הרי אני	ומכלים אותן, אלא הרי אני
משלחן לדרך רחוקה שאם מכעיסין	משלחן לדרך רחוקה, אם מכעיסין הם
אותי ישראל עד שאני משלח אצלן	אותי בני מדינה עד שאני משלח
ומביאן, ישראל עושין תשובה ואני	אצלן הם באין ומפייסין אותי ואני
מקבל תשובתן הה״ד באים מארץ מרחק	מקבל פיוסים, הד׳ דכת׳ באים מארץ
מקצה השמים וגו׳ אמר ר׳ יצחק:	מרחק מקצה השמים וגו׳ [ישעיה יג:
ולא עוד אלא שנעל בפניהן חה״ד	ה]. א״ר יצחק ולא עוד שנועל
פתח יי את אוצרו ויוצא את כלי	בפניהם, פתח י״י את אוצרו ויוצא
זעמו עד דו פתח עד דו	את כלי זעמו [ירמיה נ:כה] עד
טרד רחמוי קריבין תני בשם ר׳	דהוא טריד רחמוי קריבין. תני
מאיר כי הנה ה׳.	בשם ר׳ מאיר כי הנה י״י יוצא
יצא ממקומו יוצא לו	ממקומו [ישעיה כו:כא], יוצא
ממידה למידה יוצא לו ממידת הדין	ממידת הדין למידת רחמים על יש׳,
למידת רחמים על ישראל.	ותשובתכם איני מקבל.

Before examining the argument of the texts, the following differences are to be noted:

In Ta<anit, Joel 1: 18 precedes R. Aha's comment and is introduced by the technical phrase hh"d (hada> hu> dikh'tiv̄), "as it is written," i.e., as the prooftext for the treatment of the cattle.[3] R. Simeon's second comment reads *k'shirah* rather than *bishah*.[4] The two chains of tradents reporting slightly different versions of R. Johanan's statement are exchanged. Again, more significantly, the conclusion of the royal parable lacking in *P'siqta>* is found in T.Y. Ta<anit:

> Kakh >amar ha-qadosh barukh hu> >af v'ḥémah mal'>akhé ḥabalah hen haré >ani m'shal'ḥakhan l'derekh r'ḥoqah she->im makh<isin >oti yiśra>el <ad she->ani m'shaléaḥ >eẓlan u-m'v̄i>an yiśra>el <osin t'shuv̄[ah] va>ani m'qabel t'shuv̄at[an] hh"d ba>im mé>ereẓ merḥaq miq'ẓeh ha-shamayim ... (Isaiah 13:5).

The real difference between the two texts lies in their settings. As noted above, the *P'siqta>* version occurs in a series of interpretations that underscore the effectiveness of repentance. In Ta<anit, it is found in the *g'mara>* that discusses the procedures for a public fast in the event of the failure of winter rains. The relevant part of the mishnah reads:

> ha-zaqen she-bahen >omer lifnéhem div̄'ré kibushin >aḥénu l>o ne>emar b'>anshé nin'veh vayar> >elohim >et šaqam v'>et

---

[3] Mandelbaum notes that Ms. Parma introduces the verse with *she-n'* (=*she-ne>emar*). It is, however, out of place after R. Aha's comment. The repetition in Aramaic of R. Simeon's comment spells out this implication.

[4] To this, see below.

Understanding a Midrash Text: The Case of the Inhabitants of Nineveh 125

ta<anitam >ela> vayar> >elohim >et ma<aséhem ki shaṽu midarkam ha-ra<ah u-ṽiq'ṽalah mahu >amar v'qir'<u l'ṽaṽ'khem v'>al big'dékhem v'shuṽu >el h' >elohékhem.

These verses, however, are not discussed immediately in the *g'mara>*. First, the public activities mentioned in the mishnah are enlarged upon. This is followed by a series of midrashic explorations of the efficacy of prayer, *ṣ'daqah* and repentance. It is only with R. Simeon b. Lakish's comment that there is any reference to the elder's citation dealing with the inhabitants of Nineveh in the mishnah and an interpretation of the verse.

The first comment in both texts of the verse(s) from Jonah is that of Resh Lakish[5]: *t'shuvah shel r'miot <aśu >anshé nin'veh*. "The lexical meaning of *r'miot* seems clear: "The repentance of the inhabitants of Nineveh was deceitful." However, in the context of *P'siqta>* and Ta<anit such a meaning seems awkward; it does not make sense, for in both texts the inhabitants are held up, seemingly, as prototypes of those who repent and whose repentance is accepted. To pause with Resh Lakish's statement alone, the evident conclusion would be that God was somehow deceived: he accepted insincere repentance. Indeed, the Parma manuscript of *P'siqta>*[6] and two texts quoting the Palestinian Talmud, *Yalqut Makhiri* and *Midrash Yonah*,[7] read *sh'lemah*, "complete," "perfect." The Braude-Kapstein paraphrastic translation reflects this discomfort with its rendering, "put on a great show of repentance."[8] In keeping with the usual text-critical procedure, however, we shall retain the hard reading. It is supported by a passage in *B're>shit Rabah* 9. There R. Hiyya, the son of R. Berechya's daughter, reports in his grandfather's name that he interpreted an obscure phrase in Ezekiel 28:14, *>at k'ruṽ mimshaḥ*, to mean that God said to Hiram he had caused Adam's death. R. Johanan asked why God had not merely decreed death for the wicked (Hiram) but not for the righteous (Adam). Was it not so that the wicked could not do *t'shuṽah shel r'miot*, so that they should not be able to say: "The righteous live only because they heap up the performance of commandments and good deeds. We too will do the same."[9] Their deeds are not disinterested.

---

[5] R. Simeon b. Lakish in the Yerushalmi.
[6] See Mandelbaum's textual variants *ad loc.*
[7] See B. Ratner, *>Ahavat Ẓion Virushalayim* (Vilna, 1913; reprint: Jerusalem, 1967), X, 72.
[8] William G. Braude and Israel J. Kapstein, *Pesikta De-Rab Kahana* (Philadelphia: Jewish Publication Society, 1975), pp. 373-74.
[9] *Bereschit Rabba,* ed. J. Theodor (Berlin, 1903; reprint: Jerusalem: Wahrmann Books, 1965), I, 30.

Further, it must be recognized that such sharp and radical statements are not unusual for Resh Lakish.

What follows appears to be an examination of the implications of the comment by way of a response to it. The question: *meh <asu* – "what did they do?" – seeks to discover what their behavior was that would deserve such opprobrium.[10] R. Huna reports R. Simeon b. Halafta's description of their action that could, at first glance, be thought of in such terms: "They put the calves in a corral with their dams outside; the calves bawled within and the mothers responded without." This is explained in an Aramaic comment that enlarges upon the thought: "When these bawled within and these without, the inhabitants of Nineveh said to God: 'If you do not have mercy upon us we will not have mercy upon them,'" followed by a prooftext: "How the beasts groan; the herds are perplexed because there is no pasture for them" (Joel 1:18). But before accepting such a conclusion, we must read further. Jonah 3:8a is quoted: *v'yitkasu śaqim ha->adam v'hab'hemah v'yiqr'>u >el >elohim b'ḥozqah,* and the question is raised: What does *b'ḥozqah* mean? Again the response is from R. Simeon b. Halafta: *ḥaẓifah neẓaḥ bishah kol she-ken l'ṭovato shel <olam.*

Before attempting to explain this interpretation, we must deal with a textual problem arising from the term *bishah*. Mandelbaum's manuscript ">alef" reads *bisha>*, as do several others, but he changed it to *bishah* in conformity to yet other manuscripts. In either case, what does it mean? Levy translates it: *"der Dreiste besiegt den Bösen (sogar dieser seine Bitte gewährt) um wie viel mehr den Allgütigen der Welt."*[11] Jastrow, similarly, renders it paraphrastically, "the persevering in prayer conquers even the bad man, so much more so even the Good One."[12] Marmorstein, however, translates it: "the arrogant prevails over the pious, all the more so over the Goodness of the world."[13] He, contrary to the others, follows S. Buber's note in his edition of *P'siqta>* where he reads *baysha>, bayshan,* "humble" or "pious," in place of *bishah, bisha>,* "evil" or "bad."[14] This reading is discussed in some

---

[10] In *P'siqta>* the comment follows the quotation of Jonah 3:4-7. In T.Y. Ta<anit, Jonah 3:10 is quoted in the mishnah with the comment coming in the *g'mara>* after other matters have been discussed.
[11] Jacob Levy, *Wörterbuch über die Talmudim und Midrashim*, 2nd ed. (Berlin and Vienna: B. Harz, 1924), s.v. *ḥẓf*.
[12] M. Jastrow, *A Dictionary of the Targumim, the Talmud Babli, and Yerushalmi, and the Midrashic Literature* (New York and Berlin: Verlag Choreb; London: Shapiro, Valentine, 1926), p. 495, s.v. *ḥaẓif*.
[13] A. Marmorstein, *The Old Rabbinic Doctrine of God* (London: Oxford University Press, 1927), I, 85-86.
[14] S. Buber, *Pesikta Rab Kahana* (Lyck: Merkize Nirdamim, 1868), p. 101a.

detail by Kohut in *Aruch Completum*, s.v. *bish*; Kohut quotes Moses Lonzono's stricture against reading *bishah=ra<* and refers to the reading in the Yerushalmi noted above, *k'shirah*, that is synonymous with *bayshan*.¹⁵

What, however, about *ḥaẓifah* that is, apparently, the explanation of *b'ḥozqah*? Levy's translation – *der Dreiste* – is more satisfactory than the others. Accepting Buber's reading and this understanding of *ḥaẓifah*, R. Simeon b. Halafta's explanation is to be understood: "boldness triumphs over humility, even so over the Goodness of the world." They acted boldly with their challenge to God and their repentance was accepted. He thus defends the actions of the Ninevites he has described, and refutes Resh Lakish. But is this indeed acceptable conduct? What lies behind his claim? Here we must follow Lieberman's advice about comparing pericopes in the Yerushalmi.¹⁶ There is a passage in Ta<anit 3:4 [66c-d] that provides the answer:

> R. Lazar fasted, but rain did not fall. R. Akiba fasted and rain fell. Someone came and said: I will provide you with a parable. What is this like? A king had two daughters, one bold (*ḥaẓifah*), the other humble, shy (*k'shirah*). When the bold one wanted something she came before her father, he would say that he understood what she wanted and that she could have it. Then she took her leave. When the shy one came before him, he held off because he enjoyed hearing her request. One is permitted to say this of R. Eliezer without defaming Deity.

Here the two terms in the Palestinian Talmud's version of the midrash on Jonah 3:8, *ḥaẓifah* and *k'shirah*, *bayshan* in *P'siqta>* [Buber], appear. Thus R. Simeon b. Halafta's comment is to be understood: the boldness of the inhabitants of Nineveh – like R. Akiba's boldness – succeeded. The inhabitants of Nineveh acted with *ḥaẓifah*, not with *r'miot*. Resh Lakish's charge is refuted.¹⁷

---

¹⁵A. Kohut, *Aruch Completum* (New York: Pardes, 1955; reprint of 1926 edition), III, 475, s.v. *ḥẓf*, and II, 28, s.v. *bush*.

¹⁶Saul Lieberman, *Ha-Y'rushalmi Kif'shuṭo* (Jerusalem: Darom, 1934), Introduction: "one should attend to those words that have a meaning other than the conventional, for only after comparing pericopes in Yerushalmi itself and in Palestinian midrashim is one able to recognize the correct interpretation of such words."

¹⁷In an earlier draft of this paper I suggested that *r'miot* could be taken from the root *rum* with a meaning of "high," echoing the biblical phrase *yad ramah*, "high handed," "bold." That phrase is interpreted in the *M'khilta* – see Jacob Z. Lauterbach, *Mekilta de-Rabbi Ishmael* (Philadelphia: Jewish Publication Society, 1976), I, 204 – *b'ro>sh galuy*, meaning in the context "boldly," impudently": *Qohelet Rabah* to 8:11 interprets the words *>asher >én na>aseh pitgam* to refer to sinners who are not punished immediately. "What does it say of them? *ha> rumya> <al'lin ha> rumya> nafqin* – boldly they entered, boldly

The conclusion of the midrash, R. Yohanan's comment on Jonah 3:10, is incompatible with both contexts, but given the more or less general redactoral practice of quoting an entire received block, one must disregard those portions that contradict the point the redactor is making.[18] The correct way of understanding the midrash, in this context is, then, to acknowledge Resh Lakish's negative remark, to recognize that R. Simeon b. Halafta's comments are intended to contradict him and to read R. Yohanan's comment *sotto voce*.[19]

Although this is the conclusion of the midrash on Jonah dealing with the inhabitants of Nineveh, a further midrash on Joel 2:13 follows. Its presence in *P'siqta>* was, it would seem, determined by the fact that the previous midrash ended with R. Yohanan's negative appraisal of the behavior of the inhabitants of Nineveh while that on Joel concludes on a positive note: *tané b'shem R. Me>ir ki hineh y"y yoze> mim'qomo* [Isaiah 26:21] *yoze> mimidat ha-din l'midat ha-rahamim <al yisra>el*. Hence, by quoting it, the redactor was enabled to finish with his rhetorical flourish: *u-t'shuvatkhem >éni m'qabel*. In the case of T.Y.Ta<anit, however, it belongs to the context, for it had been quoted in the mishnah as a verse to be alluded to by the elder on a fast day.[20]

Having come this far, we are now confronted by a crucial question: how does the midrash on Jonah fit into the contexts? For the *P'siqta>* the answer is not too difficult. It is proposed that the repentance of the inhabitants of Nineveh is an example of behavior acceptable to God. Resh Lakish challenges that view, but is refuted by R. Simeon b. Halafta. That is all his interpretation does. It does not deal affirmatively with the subject; its conclusion is: boldness is a positive way of approaching

---

they went forth." Thus *r'miot* and *hazifah* could be considered synonymous. Although the usage here may support the conjecture, the context is damaging to the suggestion that Resh Lakish is not condemning the inhabitants of Nineveh.

[18] R. Yohanan comments on Jonah 3:8:

"Each person shall turn from his evil behavior and from the violence in their hands." That which was in their hands [i.e., in their immediate possession] they returned. That which was in their strong-boxes, chests and towers [Jastrow: store closets] they did not return.

In other words, R. Yohanan, as frequently, is supporting Resh Lakish's contention. But, as suggested, this is entirely unsuitable in the context. I have wondered whether it would be possible to read his comment as a rhetorical question, implying an affirmative answer: they *did* return everything. That implies a harmonization of all the material in the block and that, it seems to me, is unwarranted.

[19] See below, note 23.

[20] For a suggestion concerning the function of the two midrashim in their context, see below.

God. Nothing further is said of repentance, but apparently it was assumed that somehow boldness was related to it.

The connection of the midrash with the verse cited in the mishnah is more difficult to establish. The elder tells the congregation that turning from wicked behavior, not sackcloth and fasting, is obedience to the divine demand. Boldness hardly seems to represent such. Indeed, as noted above, R. Yohanan's suggestion that they did not return all of their ill-gotten gains certainly contradicts this.

How, then, are we to reconcile the use of this block, composed of two midrashim that may stand separately, in these contexts? In *P'siqta>* the midrash on Jonah, read as suggested above, by refuting Resh Lakish, supports the idea of the efficacy of the repentance of the inhabitants of Nineveh. The inclusion of the midrash on Joel helps us to ignore R. Yohanan's negative conclusion. In Ta<anit the midrash on Joel plays the significant role. The midrash on Jonah is present because in some other context the two had been brought together for some other purpose.

Conclusion

This brief examination of a midrash used by the redactors of *P'siqta>* and of the Palestinian Talmud underscores the comments of Professors Louis Ginzberg[21] and Saul Lieberman[22] concerning the care and caution with which the Yerushalmi and its contemporary Galilean midrashim must be approached. A purely lexical/philological approach is not adequate. The meaning of a word or phrase must be sought for not merely in its paradigmatic, but in its syntagmatic role as well. The functional meaning is present only within the sentence or, indeed, the paragraph. Equally important is the recognition that the meaning of a midrash may, in a new setting, vary from its original. It is possible to assume that the Jonah midrash was, in its original setting, negative, for both the first and last comments disparage the inhabitants of Nineveh. In *P'siqta>*, however, it must be taken as positive, for the intention is to hold them up as exemplars of proper conduct. The Joel midrash, on the other hand, does not seem to have been affected by this setting, although we do not know what its original was. In Ta<anit the Jonah midrash does not in any way illumine the verse quoted in the mishnah that calls attention to the behavior of the inhabitants of Nineveh. Indeed, R. Yohanan's comment, as noted above, contradicts it. Nonetheless, it must be understood as saying something positive about

---

[21]*Yerushalmi Fragments* (New York: Jewish Theological Seminary, 1909), pp. vii-ix (English), iii-vi (Hebrew).
[22]See above, note 13.

them, however tenuous the connection. The Joel midrash, on the other hand, certainly through the comment of R. Joshua b. Levi, is apposite. In both contexts, far more is quoted than is pertinent to the matter at hand. This, as noted above, is a regular procedure in Rabbinic literature.[23]

---

[23]Many years ago Professor Jacob Z. Lauterbach explained this by comparing it to a scholar who in transcribing research notes from a 3x5 card copied off more than was necessary. To this I would add that, approaching this material as oral in its origin, one must learn when to stop listening.

9

Geomessianism: Why Did the Essenes Settle at Qumran?*

By Ben Zion Wacholder

This paper enlarges upon an hypothesis I proposed at the Haifa conference in the spring of 1988, namely, that many of the basic ideas and literary motifs of Qumran had their archetype in the Book of Ezekiel. This hypothesis supposes, in addition, that there may have existed an Ezekelian school from the time of the prophet to that of the foundation of the Qumran sect. Some of the texts uncovered at Qumran, whether written by the community which called itself the *Yaḥad* or by its antecedents, were apparently ascribed to Ezekiel himself. Examples of this are the so called 4Q Pseudo-Ezekiel, which is now being prepared by John Strugnell and Devorah Dimant, and *La Jérusalem Nouvelle* (1Q, 2Q, 5Q and 11Q Heavenly Jerusalem). Indeed, the work which Yigael Yadin called the Temple Scroll (*m'gilat ha-miqdash*) and I have entitled 11Q Torah, may best be described as an Ezekelian work set in a pentateuchal frame. In 11Q Torah, God addresses Moses on Mount Sinai. In large sections of this scroll, however, the author appears to be composing something more along the lines of neo-Ezekiel than a neo-Pentateuch. It thus seems to me that Ezekiel is for Qumran what Jeremiah and Ezra are for classical Judaism.

Three examples, one literary, the second theological, and the third historical, will demonstrate the continuum from Ezekiel to the writings of the Qumran library:

1. *Central to an understanding of the Ezekelian school* is the prophet's eschatology, or what I have called geomessianism. Geomessianism denotes the doctrine that a certain geographic area,

---

*I would like to thank Martin Abegg for his assistance in the editing and annotation of this essay.

lying between the Euphrates and the Brook of Egypt, was endowed with a special *q'dushah* or sanctity. This concept may have originated with Jacob's dream: *mah nora> ha-maqom ha-zeh,* "how inspiring is this place," and is seen frequently in the prophet Jeremiah's use of the word *maqom* when referring to both the positive and negative aspects of the Land of Israel. It is Ezekiel, however, who gives the term a sacral locution.[1] As I see it, the last nine chapters of the Book of Ezekiel contain the most elaborate depiction of geomessianism. Chapters 40-48 of Ezekiel present not only the dimensions of the Temple but also of >Erez Yiśra>el as well. Twenty-five years after the Babylonian conquest of Jerusalem, fourteen years after the destruction of the city, in 572 B.C.E., Ezekiel was transported by the spirit to >Erez Yiśra>el, and beheld *har gavoha m'>od,* "a very lofty mountain," perhaps better rendered as "the loftiest mountain of the earth," what the prophet elsewhere refers to as *ṭabur ha->areẓ,* "the navel of the earth." Atop this lofty mountain, the prophet tells us *v'<alav k'mivneh <ir minegev,* "on the mountain, from the south, was the structure of a city."[2] The prophet is then led by the supernatural messenger, detailing its measurements, rites and righteous priests.

After describing the *miqdash,* the "Sanctuary" itself, the last two chapters of the book present the measurements of >Erez Yiśra>el as a whole, its borders and tribal subdivisions. Prefacing these details, Ezekiel 47:1-12 illustrates the prophet's geomessianic visions concerning the borders of the Land. The text describes a brook whose source begins at the *miftan ha-bayit,* "the threshold of the Temple." What begins as a drip enlarges to become a mighty stream as the waters embrace the area of the Sanctuary. It then turns to the Galilee, moves east to the sources of the Jordan, goes down to the <Aravah, to the area of the Dead Sea: "from En Gedi to En Eglaim." The wilderness of this area is then transformed from salty waters into fishing grounds as abundant as the *yam ha-gadol,* the Mediterranean. Trees grow on the shores of the Dead Sea, trees whose fruits are most delightful, giving continual crops; their leaves do not wither and are even termed *lit'rufah,* that is, to serve as "medicaments."

2. *Following this supernatural and idealized depiction* of the Land, Ezekiel reveals the divisions of this geomessianic >Erez Yiśra>el as given to him by God. Although the borders themselves correspond roughly to those listed in Numbers 34, the prophet adds entirely new features, some of them quite revealing. For example, unlike the allotment of the Book of Joshua, Ezekiel apportioned identical shares to

---
[1] Cf. Ezekiel 3:12.
[2] Note that the word *<ir* denotes not the city alone, but also the Temple.

each of the twelve tribes. Ezekiel also adds that the *gerim* would receive the same portions equal to the natives. Most striking, however, is the description of the huge parcel called *t'rumah* to which we will now turn our attention.

In the midst of the tribal division is the *t'rumat ha-areẓ* whose measurements are 25,000 cubits north to south and stretching from the Jordan on the east to the Mediterranean on the west. This vast portion is assigned to the Naśi>, the priests and the Levites and located between the inheritance of Judah on the north and Benjamin on the south. Within this area Ezekiel describes a subdivision of increased holiness, an area 25,000 cubits square, termed *t'rumat ha-qodesh*. Of this area, both the Levites and the priests receive tracts of 10,000 x 25,000 cubits. These two portions are not, however, of equal sanctity. Ezekiel 48:12 labels the priestly portion as *t'rumiyah*, "*t'rumah* of *t'rumah*," or "the holiest land." It is this portion which is to be given to the priests, the sons of Zadok, who kept the precepts of the Lord when the others had gone astray. It is within this sacred portion that the Temple area, a square of 500 cubits, is to be located.[3]

This outline of Ezekiel 40-48, sketchy as it is, provides links to several Qumran works. *Shirot <olat Ha-shabat*, "the songs of the Sabbath Offering," published by Carole Newsom, presents the Temple's liturgy.[4] The visionary dimension of the eschatological Jerusalem is most graphically depicted in the extensive remains of *La Jérusalem Nouvelle*. In what is commonly called Heavenly Jerusalem (1Q, 2Q, 5Q, and 11Q), the seer, apparently Ezekiel or his ghost, devotes a lengthy description to the city's squares, which in their size exceed anything the ancients had experienced in any metropolis, even Babylon or Alexandria.

The visionary Jerusalem that emerges from Ezekiel, 11Q Torah, and Heavenly Jerusalem is of immense height and size, and subject to special legislation. What makes the city of the Temple so remarkable is its *q'dushah*, its sanctity. That is to say, it covers a spot on this earth that God, when he created the world, set apart as his dwelling place, not for the present sorry state, but for the end of time, when the city with its glorious Sanctuary would be God's divine residence. Thus, the place where Jacob dreamt of the ascending angels and Mount Moriah, where Abraham went to sacrifice Isaac, are fused into a single *locus*, embracing not only the area of the Sanctuary itself, but its city with all of its measurements as well.

---

[3]Cf. Midot 2:1.
[4]Carol Newsom, *Songs of the Sabbath Sacrifice: Critical Edition* (Atlanta: Scholars Press, 1985).

One of the themes that may best exemplify this interdependence of Ezekiel and Qumran is the visionary Sanctuary. This is not the place to deal at length with the work known as *m'gilat ha-miqdash*, "the Temple Scroll," except to say that, contrary to Yadin, the main theme of 11Q T's Sanctuary is not so much the Temple itself, but the *rites and rituals* of the Temple. Ezekiel's topos in chapters 40-48 is the same visionary Sanctuary, but only as an element of a larger theme – a theme that deals not only with the future Sanctuary, but its city as an integral part of the Land, whose area stretches from the Euphrates to the Brook of Egypt.

In the numerous discussions concerning the Temple in 11Q Torah, Yadin and other scholars have not given sufficient notice to the paramount role of <*ir ha-miqdash*, "the City of the Sanctuary." It appears to be no exaggeration of the evidence to claim that the dimensions of the City of the Sanctuary in 11Q Torah corresponds to the area of the *t'rumat ha-qodesh* in Ezekiel. Indeed, Milik reports that an unpublished fragment of Heavenly Jerusalem from cave 4 describes the circumference of the city to be nearly identical with that of the *t'rumah* of Ezekiel 48:20.[5] This note makes it certain that, in both Ezekiel and 11Q Torah, the concept of the *t'rumah* or *City of the Sanctuary* envisioned an immense piece of land that God had endowed with a special *q'dushah*, lower than that of the Temple, but much holier than that of the provinces. That Jerusalem, as the site of the Temple, possessed a special sanctity is recorded in the Mishnah and the Talmud, but these traditions have not prepared us for the extraordinary rules applicable to the <*ir ha-miqdash*, "the City of the Sanctuary," found in the Qumranic texts. CD 12:1-2 prohibits sexual cohabitation within the city. Columns 43-47 and 52 of 11Q Torah devote many of their instructions to its sanctity. Among the special rules of this Temple city are:

1. Its geographic borders extend from the outer perimeter of the Sanctuary to a distance of three days' walking (*derekh sh'loshet yamim*): 11Q Torah 52:14.
2. Not only are sexual relations prohibited within the borders of the city and three days' distance surrounding it, but menstruation or an emission of semen bars entry into the city for three days: 11Q Torah 45:7-12.
3. Meats and skins or leathers of animals slaughtered in the local settlement (*b'tokh <aréhemah*) cannot be imported into the city. Only meat products of the holy offerings of the Sanctuary have the

---

[5]M. Baillet, J.T. Milik, and R. De Vaux, *Les "Petites Grottes" de Qumrân: Exploration de la falaise, Les grottes 2Q, 3Q, 5Q, 6Q, 7Q, à 10Q, Le rouleau de cuivre* (Oxford: Clarendon Press, 1962), p. 185.

requisite holiness for nourishment or industrial production. Leather shoes and even parchments of holy texts are restricted to products manufactured within the holy city: 11Q Torah 47:7-18, 52:19-21.
4. The building of baths and privies is restricted to outside the city, in fact 3,000 cubits therefrom: 11Q Torah 46:13-16.

The city whose inhabitants would have to live under these and similar restrictions could not have been the metropolis of Judeans with its varied populations, which m. Qidushin 4:1 describes as consisting of priests, Levites, Israelites, defrocked priests, proselytes, freed slaves, bastards, and foundlings, not to mention foreigners. In the framework of 11Q Torah, the City of the Sanctuary, like the Temple itself, is an eschatological concept. The scroll extends the concepts of <ir and *miqdash* as found in Ezekiel. The City of the Sanctuary in 11Q Torah thus mirrors the prophet's *t'rumat ha-qodesh*, the sacred portion of >Ereẓ Yiśra>el.

The evidence, adduced from Ezekiel 40-48, Heavenly Jerusalem, 11Q Torah and other writings, indicates a hitherto unnoticed understanding of the meaning of *q'dushah*, or sanctity, as it relates to the Temple. Students of the Temple Scroll have taken it for granted that it was the structure of the Sanctuary, primarily its architecture, that makes the *miqdash* the locus for the divine *bayit*, "house." Actually, however, the Qumran texts tell us, the *q'dushah* consists of five elements:
1. *Divine Command*: a humanly erected structure without a prior ordinance, no matter how lofty its architecture, would not have the requisite *q'dushah*;
2. *Temporal Element*: taking their cue from Deuteronomy, which speaks of *ha-maqom >asher yivḥar yhvh >elohekha laśum sh'mo sham*, "in the place which the Lord will choose to place his name" (12:21, etc.), the Ezekelian school recognized only the Sanctuary that would be built in the future, i.e., the Temple that would be part of the eschatological ingathering;
3. *Dimensions of the House*: as frequently stressed in Exodus 25 and especially in Ezekiel, the architecture of the Sanctuary must conform to the the model presented by God;
4. *Priests and their rites*: only those priests of the line of Zadok, by their exemplary piety and ritual purity, would be worthy to serve in the Holy of Holies;
5. *The Locus of the Sanctuary*: this geographical place (*maqom*) is the highest locus of *q'dushah* on this earth.

When it is translated into Qumran doctrine, we can determine that geomessianism is divided into three levels of *q'dushah* in ascending order:
1. the sanctity of >Ereẓ Yiśra>el as a whole;
2. the city of the Temple;
3. the Temple itself.[6]

This threefold division of *q'dushah* may serve to account for the literary structure of 11Q Torah. After a general statement in column 2, columns 3-42 treat the *q'dushah* of the rites of the Sanctuary, columns 43-52 the <*ir ha-miqdash*, "the City of the Sanctuary," and columns 53-65 the *q'dushah* applicable to the settlements outside the Temple city.

The structure of 11Q Torah may thus be defined as placing the eschatological Temple of Ezekiel in a pentateuchal frame. To be sure, the prophet's threefold geomessianic division probably originated as a redefinition of the description of the Israelite camps, recorded in Numbers 2 through 5:
1. the twelve tribes;
2. the surrounding Levites;
3. the tent of meeting.

There is, therefore, a lineal progression from Numbers to Ezekiel to 11Q Torah, and if one may add, to the Apocalypse of John.[7]

3. *The understanding of Qumran as an extension* of the priestly school whose roots go back to the author of Numbers through the Book of Ezekiel and Pseudo-Ezekiel may resolve some historical questions as well. One example will suffice. Why, as has been frequently asked, did the founders of the sect known as the *Yaḥad*, or Essenes, settle in such a godforsaken area as Qumran? Why did they settle near the Dead Sea whose smelly waters were unsuitable for the indispensable ablutions of the group? The answer, it seems to me, may lie in a detail of the Holy Land's borders.

The author of the Thanksgiving Psalms (1Q Hodayot) construed his hymn beginning on column 8, commencing with the usual >*odekhah*, "I thank Thee," on Ezekiel 47. The entire composition depicts the healing living waters *(mayim ḥayim,* 8:7) on whose shores the plants listed in Ezekiel grow. What was the most desolate wilderness becomes, as in the days preceding the destruction of Sodom and Gomorrah, the Garden of Eden. These *mé qodesh,* "waters of the *Sanctuary,*" and trees of Eden (1Q H 8:20) were envisioned as the future portion of the members of the sect.

---

[6]The Temple, in turn, has its own subdivisions.
[7]Cf. Revelation 21:10-17; 22:1-2.

Geomessianism: Why Did the Essenes Settle at Qumran?

> I [thank Thee, Oh Lord,
> for] Thou hast placed me beside a fountain of streams in an arid land,
> and close to a spring of waters in a dry land,
> and beside a watered garden [in a wilderness]
> [For Thou didst set] a plantation
> of cypress, pine, and cedar for Thy glory,
> trees of life beside a mysterious fountain,
> hidden among the trees by the water
> and they put out a shoot of the everlasting plant.
> But before they did so, they took root
> and sent out their roots to the watercourse
> that its stem might be open to the living waters
> and be one with the everlasting spring.
> (1Q H 8:4-8a)[8]

It was, however, to remain as a parched wilderness to the enemies of the Lord, a desert as it was before the saltiness was transformed into life and blessing.

> No [man shall approach] the well-spring of life
> or drink the waters of the sanctuary[9] with the everlasting trees,
> or bear fruit with [the plant] of heaven
> who seeing has not discerned,
> and considering has not believed in the fountain of life.
> (1Q H 8:12b-14a)

Both the main theme and many of the main motifs appear to be borrowings from, among other sources, Ezekiel's description of the living waters emanating from the threshold of the Temple. These waters, according to the prophet, would envelop Israel's borders and transform the wilderness of the Dead Sea.

Pliny reports that the Essenes settled north of En Gedi, on the west shores of the Dead Sea.[10] Ezekiel 47:10 specifies the area of En Gedi and En Eglaim as an eschatological Garden of Eden. According to Farmer, En Eglaim corresponds to En Feshkha, a freshwater oasis one and a half miles south of the ruins of Qumran.[11] This site was evidently

---

[8]Geza Vermes, *The Dead Sea Scrolls in English* (London: Penguin Books, 1987), pp. 187-92.
[9]*Mé qodesh*, Vermes translates, "waters of *holiness*," p. 187.
[10]Pliny, *Historia Naturalis*, V. 17, 73. See also the discussion in J.T. Milik, *Ten Years of Discovery in the Wilderness of Judea* (London: SCM Press, 1958), pp. 44-45.
[11]William R. Farmer, "The Geography of Ezekiel's River of Life," *Biblical Archaeologist*, XIX (1956), 17-22.

used by the sect for agricultural purposes and possibly the preparation and tanning of skins. This area, the prophet envisioned, was to become the most fruitful spot on earth.

It appears, therefore, that the author of this >*odekhah* believed that the wilderness he was inhabiting, the godforsaken region that is Qumran and the mines of potash, was, conceivably, what Ezekiel 47:10 named as En Gedi and En Eglaim. This place would, in the >*aḥarit ha-yamim*, "soon enough," be turned into the Orchard of Eden. This Garden would be nourished by the stream flowing from the threshold of the Temple. How else could one account for Qumran as the place of choice for the settlement of the sect?

Part Two
THE MEDIEVAL CENTURIES

10

Speculations on the Passover Liturgy

By Lee T. Bycel

Miracles are not news in Jewish tradition. Age-old observances like Hanukkah, Purim, Passover, and Shavuot are all attended by an awareness of, an expectation of, *nisim*, the realm of the miraculous. Human experience, as Jewish tradition construes it, is never utterly divorced from miracle. Passover is a case in point, though by no means a simple case.

The Passover narrative as set forth in the earliest Haggadah text, probably dating from the ninth century C.E., recounts what is surely to be considered a prime miracle in Jewish history, the parting of the Red Sea.[1] Strangely enough, however, nowhere in the Haggadah do we find the blessing thanking God for performing this miracle, even though the blessing is recited on Hanukkah and Purim to commemorate *nisim* of lesser magnitude.[2]

The Hebrew Bible is of course rich in incidents and encounters, signs and wonders, signifying divine intervention in human history. The word *nes* appears in the Bible, but not until the Rabbinic period does it acquire the meaning of "miracle." Although the Talmud is replete with references to *nisim*, the blessing for miracles is actually prescribed in the liturgy only in connection with the festivals Hanukkah and Purim. The story of Hanukkah, as told in the post- (or at any rate extra-)

---

[1] See E.D. Goldschmidt, *The Passover Haggadah, Its Sources and History* (Jerusalem: Bialik Institute, 1981), pp. 3, 73, where it is pointed out that, though the Haggadah text in the *Seder Rav Amram* is about a century older than the text in the Saadya Ga>on Siddur, the Saadya text is more complete. See also P'saḥim 118a.

[2] *she<aśah nisim la>avoténu ba-yamim ha-hem ba-z'man ha-zeh.* See T. H. Gaster, *Purim and Hanukkah in Custom and Tradition* (New York: Henry Schuman, 1950), pp. 49, 107; A. Z. Idelsohn, *Jewish Liturgy and Its Development* (New York: Sacred Music Press, 1932), pp. 162-63.

biblical Book of Maccabees, celebrates the victory of Judaism over Hellenism, a military victory seen in the text of Maccabees as one of human dimensions. Only later, in the Talmud,[3] is miracle associated with the Maccabean achievement – the legend of the miracle of the oil lasting for eight nights. The Purim story as described in the biblical Book of Esther and in Rabbinic teaching focuses on the power of good triumphant over evil. Though the biblical text mentions no supernatural phenomenon, Jewish tradition – the Rabbinic imagination – saw something of *nes* in the roles of Esther and Mordecai.

It is not only modernist scholars who have noted and pondered the absence of the *she<asah nisim* benediction from the ceremony of Passover. Although the blessing *she<asah nisim* is not recited during the reading of the Haggadah, there are, as early as the period of the G'>onim, several halakhic explanations as to why *she<asah nisim* is not recited on Pesaḥ.[4] The implication – assertion of a negative halakah, an injunction not to say the blessing – is that originally the blessing was recited. Its recitation was apparently customary in the Land of Israel and in Egypt on the night of Passover. Evidence of the recitation appears in two *g'nizah* fragments in which the blessing immediately follows the *qidush*.[5] Although discovered in these fragments, the blessing is not found in any extant version of the Haggadah. Many commentators have reflected on why this blessing, which seems so clearly to belong in the Haggadah, is in fact excluded.

The blessing *she<asah nisim* is first mentioned in the Mishnah and in the g'mara>.[6] In the g'mara> the question is asked concerning the textual basis of the blessing; R. Yohanan's response is based on the biblical verse "and Jethro said Blessed be God who saved you from the hand of Egypt" (Exodus 18:10).

Rav Amram, the ninth-century Ga>on, offering his insight into why this blessing should not be included in the Passover ritual, describes the thrust or design of the seder service as progressing from the degradation of slavery to redemption: the ultimate singing of a song of praise for our freedom. To recite the blessing *she<asah nisim* at the beginning of the seder following the *qidush* would be to give praise before the story of degradation has been experienced and before the story of the miraculous liberation has unfolded.[7] Rav Amram clearly understood the need to control the narrative order of events in the Haggadah. There is

---

[3]b. Shabat 21b.
[4]Menahem M. Kasher, *Hagadah Sh'lemah* (Jerusalem: Makhon Torah Sh'lemah, 5727/1967), pp. 86-89.
[5]Goldschmidt, p. 6, n. 12.
[6]B'rakhot 9:1. See also B'rakhot 54a.
[7]Kasher, p. 88.

an order – *seder* – to the events: the plot is set (enslavement in Egypt), the action develops (the ten plagues), the exhilaration of the story comes (liberation), and finally there emerges the denouement (freedom). The Haggadah is not only folklore; it is also a literary document – high drama, sequential development. Rav Amram further argues that, before the *Halel*, in the *L'fikhakh* one says: "Therefore it is our duty to thank and praise, laud and glorify, extol and honor, exalt and adore Him who performed all these miracles for our fathers and for us." Thus, to have already expressed gratitude to God at the beginning of the seder in the form of *she<asah nisim* would make for a *b'rakhah l'vatalah*, a blessing which is needless and hence offensive.[8]

A much later sage, Rabbi Levi Yizḥaq of eighteenth-century Berdichev, argued that the miracles of Hanukkah and Purim had occurred in what he termed a natural manner and at a specific time in history, "in those days at that time," while the miracle of Pesaḥ transcended time and nature. Thus, one cannot say about it "in that place at this time of year." The Berdichever's conception of Pesaḥ, specifically of the narrative in the Haggadah, suggests a supposition that there is a hierarchy of miracles – that all miracles are not eternal and only some are not bound by time or nature.[9]

The fourteenth-century Maharil (Jacob Mollin) had earlier reasoned that one says the blessing on Hanukkah and Purim because their miracles are not pentateuchally based and therefore the verse from Exodus need not be applied to them. Where Passover is concerned, on the other hand, the story itself reflects the greatest biblical miracle recorded and there is no need to enhance it with the blessing for miracles, because the miracle is explicit in the text itself.[10]

The absence of the *she<asah nisim* in the Haggadah reflects the Rabbis' construction of the Haggadah narrative. There is a need in the Passover story to emphasize the human element because the divine role is evident from the biblical text. On Hanukkah the blessing is needed, because the miracle of Hanukkah is a later, Rabbinic introjection into the story recounted in the Book of Maccabees. There is no seder for Hanukkah, no narrative text which must be read. The ritual of kindling the lights shapes the miracle image. On Purim, there *is* a text to read, and there the blessing serves as a reminder that, according to the Rabbis, the victory of goodness over evil was not merely a human victory as the biblical text might seem to argue but that this reversal of circumstance was truly the work of God; thus, it is necessary to thank

---

[8]*Ibid.*, p. 87; P'saḥim 10:5.
[9]Kasher, pp. 88-89.
[10]*Ibid.*, p. 88.

God for these miracles prior to reading the text. Hanukkah and Purim need the blessing to place them securely in a religious context.

Ravْ Amram Ga>on again: his explanations of the development of the narrative and the recital of the *she<aśah nisim* blessing at the beginning of the seder as a *b'rakhah l'v̄aṭalah* offer legitimate justification for exclusion of the blessing. Recitation of the blessing at the beginning would impede and diminish the unfolding drama of the narrative. The Haggadah is not merely the recitation of an ancient text nor reenactment of an historical experience; it is more, an existential moment where the text serves in the main as a guide for one's own personal expression, one's own transformation from slave to free person. The Haggadah is a living document encountered by each Jew who recites from it, as indeed the Mishnah understands[11]: "In every generation, each Jew is obligated to see himself as if he went forth from Egypt, as it is said in the Scriptures, And you shall tell your son on that day, It is because of what the Lord did for me when I went forth from Egypt" (Exodus 13:8).

A modern writer, Ruth Fredman, has offered her own perspective on the nature of the seder:

> The Seder works with time on many levels, presenting the Exodus from Egypt as a historical event as well as a paradigmatic sequence explaining the experience of the Jews for all times. The Exodus is both history, a sequence of events, and myth, a timeless explanatory model for the society's existence, and this mythical history is made objective and palpable through the objects and actions of the ritual.[12]

Reciting the specific blessing even at the conclusion of the seder would limit the dimension of the experience to a particular moment in history. The Pesaḥ story, after all, as Levi Yiẓḥaq saw, transcends time and nature.

My esteemed teacher Samson H. Levey has his own illuminating speculation as to the Pesaḥ seder itself. Prof. Levey suggests that the Haggadah reflects in essence a tannaitic "response to the rising tide of Christianity during the period between 70 and 130 C.E." It is possible, he thinks, to construe the seder as a remonstration against Christian or Judeo-Christian apologies for the Last Supper. The seder with its distinctive narrative and ritual "was instituted by the Yavnian School under Rabban Gamliel II as the response of the Jewish community to counter the growing Christian threat to abolish the Passover altogether,

---

[11] P'saḥim 10:5.
[12] Ruth G. Fredman, *The Passover Seder* (Philadelphia: University of Pennsylvania Press, 1980), p. 95.

and to substitute in its place the celebration of the 'Lord's Supper' and the rituals which emerged with it."[13] In such a context as Prof. Levey hypostatizes, the she‹asah nisim benediction may have been omitted by the Rabbis for fear of its being somehow understood as an endorsement of the encroaching "Lord's Supper."

We are unlikely ever to know all we would wish to know about how the Haggadah, in itself such a marvel, took the shape it did. Whatever the complexity of challenge and response it reflects, this we can say of it in full confidence: the sacred, transcendent history of the Jews may claim no achievement of devotional brilliance to outrank it. I am very much obliged to Prof. Levey for having fostered in me the ability to gain this understanding.

---

[13] See Levey, "Ben Zoma, the Sages and Passover," in *Journal of Reform Judaism*, XXVIII (1981), 33-40.

11

Yehuda Halevi: The Consolations of Utopia

By Stanley F. Chyet*

Intellectual achievement, we have it from Sigmund Freud, is supremely the province of the individual "laboring in solitude," but perhaps, Freud went on to say, "the individual thinker or creative writer owed [something, a significant amount?] to the stimulus of the crowd" in whose midst he or she lived. Perhaps that thinker or writer was "the completer of mental work in which the others had participated..."[1] Though the present salute to Samson Levey is not meant to adumbrate Freud's suggestive observation, it seems appropriate to note that, in reflecting on Yehuda Halevi and his intellectual legacy, the question of time and place is of the first importance. Halevi did not inhabit a social or cultural vacuum, nor of course did he live his life in a psychic vacuum.

Halevi's work, in particular his Arabic masterpiece *The Kuzari*, and the state of mind in which that classic was produced may seem unduly mysterious unless one takes into account how crisis-haunted an age he lived in. It was a relatively stable and continuous life Spanish Jewry had known for some centuries under the Cordovan Ummayyad caliphs and their successors in the post-Cordovan emirates and even in the

---

*I have used the following editions of *The Kuzari*: *Sefer Ha-Kuzari* (Yehuda Ibn Tibbon's Hebrew version) (Warsaw: Traklin, 1929) and *The Kuzari: An Argument for the Faith of Israel* (Hartwig Hirschfeld's translation from the Arabic) with an introduction by Henry Slonimsky (New York: Schocken, 1964). The Arabic text is to be found in *Kitāb al-Radd wa-'l-Dalil fi 'l-Din al-Dhalil (al-Kitāb al-Khazari)*, edited by David H. Baneth (Jerusalem: Magnes Press, 1977).
[1] Cited in Peter Gay, *Freud for Historians* (New York: Oxford, 1985), p. 152. The Irish poet Yeats had the same idea: "...master works stir vaguely in many before they grow definite in one man's mind..." See *The Autobiography of William Butler Yeats* (New York: Collier Books, 1965), p. 138.

territories which had come under Christian rule as the Reconquista advanced southward. That "Golden Age" was all coming to upheaval and *finis* in the eleventh and early twelfth centuries. One cannot expect Halevi or any of his generation to have possessed an analytical grasp of the social and economic pressures afflicting an already waning feudalism in northern Europe and beginning to be felt in the Peninsula: the vagaries of an emergent, precarious money economy in tandem with the over-indebtedness and self-indulgence of the feudal elite in the north had been inducing severe disturbances in what was, after all, still a primarily agrarian society. What Braudel has called "the inelasticity of agricultural production" was paid insufficient attention, if any at all, and with ruinous results.[2]

---

[2] I am aware of course of the general tendency to credit the eleventh and twelfth centuries with economic expansiveness in northern Europe, but prosperity there seems on the whole to have been limited to the feudal and urban elite. The peasants and the lower orders of the feudality derived few benefits, suffered reduced circumstances, and became increasingly resentful. The attacks on Rhenish Jewry – the only part of the elite they dared as yet to confront – testify to the unrest already on the rise at the outset of the First Crusade (which apparently was, in part at least, an attempt to divert the unruly and disaffected elements away from northern Europe). The secular and ecclesiastical elite was outraged by these attacks, but a century later – the anti-Jewish policies adopted by the French king Philip Augustus are a case in point – the upper classes themselves felt sufficiently threatened by economic instability to begin assuming leadership of the new Judeophobic movement. See *Encyclopaedia Judaica* (Jerusalem: Keter/Macmillan, 1972), V, 1135-38; XIII, 392-93; XVI, 1278, 1283-85, 1288-92; G. Duby, ed., *A History of Private Life* (Cambridge: Harvard University Press, 1988), II, 76, 136.

See also J. M. Roberts, *The Pelican History of the World* (New York: Penguin, 1986), pp. 488, 490, 492, where feudal Europe reportedly "began to get richer" in the eleventh century, but the "increased wealth usually went to the landlord who took most of the profits," leaving his peasants to live on some 2,000 calories daily "for very laborious work." At its best, Roberts writes, the feudal "economy was never far from the edge of collapse. Medieval agriculture ... was appallingly inefficient." (One speculates that the empires ruled from Constantinople and Baghdad followed equally incautious policies with equally infelicitous results.) See also Marc Bloch, *Feudal Society* (Chicago: University of Chicago Press, 1964), II, 408 ff.; Fernand Braudel, *The Mediterranean and the Mediterranean World in the Age of Philip II* (New York: Harper and Row, 1976), I, 427; Robert Chazan, *European Jewry and the First Crusade* (Berkeley: University of California Press, 1987), pp. 50 ff.; Maurice Keen, *The Pelican History of Medieval Europe* (New York: Penguin, 1978), p. 87; S. Painter, "Western Europe on the Eve of the Crusades," in K.M. Setton, ed., *A History of the Crusades* (Madison: University of Wisconsin Press, 1969), I, 4-9; Henri Pirenne, *Medieval Cities* (Garden City: Doubleday, 1956), pp. 76-77; Ellis Rivkin, *The Shaping of Jewish History* (New York: Scribner, 1971), pp. 116, 138-39; J.W. Thompson, *Economic and Social History of the Middle Ages (300-1300)* (New York: Appleton-Century, 1928), pp. 392-95.

Halevi, born ca. 1075 probably in Tudela, a Muslim outpost, spent some years as a physician in Christian Toledo.³ He knew very well how troubled the world had become. He was surely aware of the pogrom which had overtaken the Jews of Granada a decade or so before his birth, and he is unlikely to have been astonished by the ugly Judeophobia which could infect the writings of a mid-eleventh century Muslim Granadan poet-jurist like Abu Ishaq, whose famous ode speaks of Jews as a "bastard brood," calls for them to be reduced "to the lowest of the low," to the level of "outcast dogs," and even urges the Emir of Granada to slaughter them.⁴ Halevi surely knew also of the Jewish blood shed in the Rhineland and in the East (and not least in >Erez Yiśra>el) during the closing years of the eleventh century as Seljuk incursions and the First Crusade took shape.⁵ He himself experienced the anti-Jewish violence which flared in Toledo during the early years of the twelfth century, violence which indeed convinced him to quit Christian Toledo for Muslim Cordova. Ultimately, we know, Halevi left Spain altogether, though, unlike Maimonides and his family later in the twelfth century, he appears not to have left Spain to escape persecution. The North African primitives had not yet begun threatening non-Muslims in al-Andalus, and what prompted Halevi's journey to the East was religious devotion – coupled apparently, if *The Kuzari* is any guide, with a feeling that his labors had gone unappreciated in Spain: "he deserves blame," his spokesman in *The Kuzari* says, "who does not look for visible reward for visible work."⁶ Halevi seems not to have been

---

³*Encyclopaedia Judaica*, X, 355; Haim Schirmann, ed., *Ha-Shirah Ha-<Ivrit Bis'farad u-ō'Provence* (Jerusalem: Mossad Bialik, 1954), I, 426. See also Yitzhak Baer, *A History of the Jews in Christian Spain* (Philadelphia: Jewish Publication Society, 1961), I, 67ff.,391; Julius Guttmann, *Philosophies of Judaism* (Philadelphia: Jewish Publication Society, 1964), pp. 120ff.; Isaac Husik, *A History of Medieval Jewish Philosophy* (Philadelphia· Jewish Publication Society, 1948), pp. 150 ff.; Israel Zinberg, *A History of Jewish Literature: The Arabic-Spanish Period* (Cleveland: Western Reserve University, 1972), pp. 83 ff.
⁴See Eliyahu Ashtor, *The Jews of Moslem Spain* (Philadelphia: Jewish Publication Society, 1979), II, 186-89; Bernard Lewis, *Islam in History* (London: Alcove, 1975), pp. 158 ff.; Norman A. Stillman, *The Jews of Arab Lands* (Philadelphia: Jewish Publication Society, 1979), pp. 60 ff. See also Yitzhak Baer, "Ha-Maẓav Ha-Politi shel Y'hudē S'farad B'doro shel Rabbi Yehuda Halevi," in *Ẓiyon* (Jerusalem), I (1935), 6ff.; Haim Schirmann, ed., *Yehuda Halevi: Shirim Niḇḥarim* (Jerusalem: Schocken, 1966), pp. ix-xii.
⁵Joshua Prawer, *The History of the Jews in the Latin Kingdom of Jerusalem* (Oxford: Clarendon Press, 1988), pp. 8-9.
⁶*Kuzari* V. 27 – Hirschfeld, pp. 294-95; Ibn Tibbon, p. 201. See also Schirman, *Yehuda Halevi*, p. xi, and *Ha-Shirah Ha-<Ivrit*, I, 425-27.

especially well known in his own time; Ibn Daud's *Sefer Ha-Qabalah* makes no mention of him.

Halevi's Spain, it is true, did not present the dismaying prospect of convulsion which one could discern elsewhere in contemporary Europe. Spain still had the ballast of Muslim economic development, but the intimations of mortality were abundant enough and, for a poet-scholar like Halevi, those intimations would have assumed a special intensity, though, pace Baer,[7] messianism is arguably not a keynote of *The Kuzari* or of Halevi's life.

Messianic ideas were certainly not absent from eleventh-century Spain, and Shlomo Ibn Gabirol earlier in the century had sung of the >*admoni*, the messianic *z'vi nehmad*, and asked how long "the stem of the Son of Jesse" would "remain buried."[8] But a systematic messianism had yet to awaken in Spain. Only later, 200 years later, when Spain had moved a good deal closer to the chaos of feudal decline which invested Europe beyond the Pyrenees, would a Spanish variant of mysticism, of Kabbalah, assert itself in the works of Abraham Abulafia and Moses de Leon.[9] So unmediated an approach to mysticism and messianism was not yet a significant Iberian option in Halevi's generation.[10] For Halevi, an appropriate response to the reality he was aware of is the pre-mystic tendency or proto-mysticism he champions in *The Kuzari*. It may indeed derive much from Neo-Platonism, but is more a mood than a commitment and virtually devoid of kabbalistic content.

When we understand something of Halevi's world, of the decline – though not yet the utter collapse – of a venerable civilization, and when we understand how that decline had already begun undercutting Jewish security everywhere in the Peninsula, we will find Halevi's effort in the *The Kuzari* far more meaningful. The very title Yehuda Ibn Tibbon's translation into Hebrew soon acquired for itself, that very title, *Sefer Ha-Kuzari*, then, has a resonant significance: its calling to mind of the

---

[7]Yitzhak Baer, *Galut* (New York: Schocken, 1947), pp. 29, 33.

[8]See T. Carmi, *The Penguin Book of Hebrew Verse* (New York: Viking, 1981), p. 314; Prawer, p. 10.

[9]See Baer, *A History of the Jews in Christian Spain*, I, 228, 260ff., 288; Moshe Idel, "Avraham Abulafia v'ha->Epifiyor," in *AJS Review*, VII-VIII (1982-83), and *The Mystical Experience in Abraham Abulafia* (Albany: State University of New York Press, 1988).

[10]Maimonides, of course, paid messianism some large attention in the late twelfth century, but the setting was not Spain; it was Egypt and the Eastern Mediterranean, and Maimonides' messianism is, in any case, notable for its utter want of a supernatural or metaphysical character: <*olam k'minhago noheg* – see *Mishneh Torah*, Book XIV (*Sefer Shof'tim*), Chs. 11-12. See also Joseph Gutmann, "The Messianic Temple in Spanish Medieval Hebrew Manscripts," in his *The Temple of Solomon* (Missoula: Scholars Press, 1976), pp. 129ff.

fabled Khazar kingdom where some centuries before in Central Asia Jews were reported to have become the ruling elite for an entire gentile nation.[11] That recollection betokened the very acme of Jewish success – and a far cry from the Jewish reality in the eleventh and twelfth centuries. No less suggestive is the title Halevi himself gave his work in Arabic: The Book of Argument and Proof in Defense of the Despised Faith. It was, to his mind at least, no proud, powerful Judaism that his generation had inherited, but what in Ibn Tibbon's Hebrew would be called *ha-dat ha-b'zuyah* – a religion which the world (i.e., Islam and Christendom alike) regarded with contempt and disdain.[12] Halevi would provide that *dat b'zuyah* with a defense, an apologia, which only a poet could offer. It would not be a systematic presentation of Yahadut but a clever, elegant polemic, now wry, now passionate – and now, for the modern reader, perhaps even a bit tedious – a polemic against the intellectual and religious perspectives he held responsible for Judaism's low estate.[13]

What Halevi is moved to do is strike out, on the one hand, against the Christianity and Islam which he sees as deformations of religion, of the biblical inheritance, and, on the other, against those who would have philosophical speculation, Aristotelian and Neo-Platonist thinking, usurp the place of religion. It cannot be said that Halevi provides a bracingly fair-minded picture of these rival systems, but one would not expect equability in a polemical enterprise: Halevi may very well be representing what popular reflection made of these challenges to rabbinic Judaism; here in particular he may exemplify Freud's notion that genius completes the "mental work" of a generation.

Philosophy is seen as a matter of respectable intellectual energy, intellectual capacity, but Halevi rejects its solutions as implausible and artificial; its doctrines are abstractions; it offers nothing a troubled spirit can rely on. The God of the philosophers, as Halevi represents him, "is above desire and intention." Moreover,

> He is, in the opinion of philosophers, above the knowledge of individuals, because the latter change with the times, whilst there is no change in God's knowledge. He, therefore, does not know

---

[11]The Warsaw 1929 edition of *The Kuzari* in Ibn Tibbon's translation contains the text of the correspondence between Hasdai Ibn Shaprut and the Khazar king Joseph, pp. 1-15. See also Ashtor, I, 194ff. Is the correspondence authentic? My friend Prof. Joseph Gutmann suggests that Ibn Shaprut "*fabricated* the Khazar correspondence to strengthen his own authority" (personal letter to me, 24 July 1989).
[12]See *Kuzari* I. 4,12 – Hirschfeld, pp. 40,44; Ibn Tibbon, pp. 22,25.
[13]See Meyer Waxman, *A History of Jewish Literature* (New York: Bloch, 1933), II, 532-33.

> thee, much less thy thoughts and actions, nor does He listen to thy prayers, or see thy movements. If philosophers say that He created thee, they only use a metaphor, because He is the Cause of causes in the creation of all creatures, but not because this was His intention from the beginning. He never created man. For the world is without beginning, and there never arose a man otherwise than through one who came into existence before him,... Everything is reduced to a Prime Cause; not to a Will proceeding from this, but an Emanation from which emanated a second, a third, and a fourth cause.[14]

The philosopher, the one in whom what Halevi calls the Active Intellect is manifest, is "without concern for the decay of his body or his organs, because ...[h]is soul... enjoys ... what is called allusively and approximately Pleasure of God [*r'ẓon >elohim,* Ibn Tibbon renders it]. Endeavor to reach it," Halevi adds,

> and the true knowledge of things, in order that thy intellect may become active, but not passive. Keep just ways as regards character and actions, because this will help thee to effect truth, to gain instruction, and to become similar to this Active Intellect [*ha-sekhel ha-po<el*: Ibn Tibbon]. The consequence of this will be contentment, humility, meekness, and every other praiseworthy inclination, accompanied by the veneration of the Prime Cause, not in order to receive favor from it, or to divert its wrath, but solely to become like the Active Intellect in finding the truth, in describing everything in a fitting manner, and in rightly recognizing its basis. These are the characteristics of the [Active] Intellect. If thou hast reached such disposition of belief, be not concerned about the forms of thy humility or religion or worship, or the word or language or actions thou employest.[15]

But philosophy cannot save souls, it cannot transcend its human limitations:

> ...One might expect the gift of prophecy [to be] quite common among philosophers, considering their deeds, their knowledge, their researches after truth, their exertions, and their close connexion with all things spiritual, also that wonders, miracles, and extraordinary things would be reported of them. Yet we find that true visions are granted to persons who do not devote themselves to study or to the purification of their souls, whereas the opposite is the case with those who strive after these things. ... ask the philosophers, and thou wilt find that they do not agree on one action or one principle, since some doctrines can be established by arguments, which are only partially satisfactory, and still much less capable of being proved.

---

[14]*Kuzari* I. 1 – Hirschfeld, p. 36; Ibn Tibbon, p. 19.
[15]*Kuzari* I. 1 – Hirschfeld, p. 38; Ibn Tibbon, p. 21.

Halevi does not suggest that the pursuit of philosophy is disreputable. He is even willing to concede that philosophy's emphasis on reason, *ha-śekhel,* deserves respect: "Heaven forbid that there should be anything in the Torah to contradict what is manifest or proved [by reason]."[16] And again: "Heaven forbid that I [a Jew] should assume what is against sense and reason."[17] Nature, the natural world, Halevi writes, is astonishing, but cannot be deemed intelligent. Natural powers and elements

> do not merit that wisdom should be ascribed to them... Forming, measuring, producing, ... and all that shows an intention, can only be ascribed to the All-wise and Almighty. There is no harm in calling the power which arranges matter by means of heat and cooling, "Nature," but all intelligence must be denied it.[18]

Halevi clearly knows a great deal about Christianity, too. Into the mouth of a Christian scholastic (*ḥakham mé-ḥakhmé >edom* is how Ibn Tibbon renders Halevi's Arabic) are put these assertions:

> I believe that all things are created, whilst the Creator is eternal; that He created the whole world in six days; that all mankind sprang from Adam, and after him from Noah, to whom they trace themselves back; that God takes care of the created beings, and keeps in touch with man; that He shows wrath, pleasure, and compassion; that He speaks, appears, and reveals Himself to His prophets and favored ones; That He dwells among those who please him. In short [I believe] in all that is written in the Torah and the records of the Children of Israel, which are undisputed, because they are generally known as lasting, and have been revealed before a vast multitude. Subsequently the divine essence [*ha->elohut:* Ibn Tibbon] became embodied in an embryo in the womb of a virgin taken from the noblest ranks of Israelitish women. She bore Him with the semblance of a human being, but covering a divinity, seemingly a prophet, but in reality a God sent forth. He is the Messiah, whom we call the son of God, and He is the Father, and the Son and the Holy Spirit. We condense His nature into one thing, although the Trinity appears on our tongues. We believe in Him and in His abode among the Children of Israel, granted to them as a distinction, because the divine influence [*ha-<inyan ha->elohi:* Ibn Tibbon[19]] never ceased to be attached to them, until the masses rebelled against this Messiah, and they crucified Him. Then divine wrath burdened them everlastingly, whilst the favor was confined to a few who followed the Messiah, and to those nations which followed these few. ... All nations are invited to this

---

[16]*Kuzari* I. 67 – Hirschfeld, p. 54; Ibn Tibbon, p. 32.
[17]*Kuzari*, I. 89 – Hirschfeld, p. 62; Ibn Tibbon, p. 37.
[18]*Kuzari* I. 76-77 – Hirschfeld, pp. 55-56; Ibn Tibbon, p. 33.
[19]David Neumark, *Jehuda Hallevi's Philosophy In Its Principles* (Cincinnati, 1908), p. 8, translates Halevi's Arabic *alamr alalahi* as "Divine Things."

religion, and charged to practice it, to adore the Messiah and the cross on which He was put, and the like. Our laws and regulations are derived from the Apostle Simon [Peter], and from ordinations [sic: ordinances?] taken from the Torah, which we study. Its truth is indisputable, as is also the fact that it came from God. It is also stated in the New Testament: I came not to destroy one of the laws of Moses, but I came to confirm and enlarge it.[20]

And Halevi is able to summarize Islam, too, with unabashed authority; he has a Muslim "Doctor" (ḥakham mé-ḥakhmé yishm<a>el) declare:

> We acknowledge the unity and eternity of God, and that all men are derived from Adam-Noah. We absolutely reject [the concept of God's] embodiment, and if any element of this appears in the Writ [the Quran], we explain it as a metaphor and allegory. At the same time we maintain that our Book is the Speech of God, being a miracle which we are bound to accept for its own sake, since no one is able to bring anything similar to it, or to one of its verses. Our prophet is the Seal of the prophets, who abrogated every previous law, and invited all nations to embrace Islam. The reward of the pious [Muslim] consists in the return of his spirit to his body in paradise and bliss, where he never ceases to enjoy eating, drinking, woman's love, and anything he may desire. The requital of the disobedient consists in being condemned to the fire of hell, and his punishment knows no end.[21]

Each of these faiths, Halevi is convinced, constitutes at best a deformation of true religion. Christianity is illogical; Islam partial, or unable to transcend Arabdom. Both he dismisses as derivative, and his dismissal is not unscornful.[22]

Only Judaism and the Jews represent or constitute something original: what he has his Khazar king recognize as "the evidence for the divine law on earth." The ḥavér, Halevi's rabbinical spokesman, has this to say:

> I believe in the God of Abraham, Isaac and Israel, who led the children of Israel out of Egypt with signs and miracles; who fed them in the desert and gave them the land, after having made them traverse the sea and the Jordan in a miraculous way; who sent Moses with His law, and subsequently thousands of prophets, who confirmed His law by promises to the observant, and threats to the disobedient. Our belief is comprised in the Torah – a very large domain.[23] ... God commenced His speech to the assembled people of Israel: "I am the God whom you worship, who has led you out of the land of Egypt," but He did *not* say [as philosophers would have

---

[20]*Kuzari* I. 4 – Hirschfeld, pp. 40-41; Ibn Tibbon, pp. 22-23.
[21]*Kuzari* I. 5 – Hirschfeld, pp. 42-43; Ibn Tibbon, p. 24.
[22]*Kuzari* I. 5-6, 170,114 – Hirschfeld, pp. 42-43, 77-78; Ibn Tibbon, pp. 23-24, 47-48.
[23]*Kuzari* I. 11 – Hirschfeld, p. 44; Ibn Tibbon, p. 25.

Yehuda Halevi: The Consolations of Utopia

it]: "I am the Creator of the world and your Creator." ...[God spoke] as was fitting, and is fitting for the whole of Israel who knew these things first from personal experience, and afterwards *through uninterrupted* tradition, which is equal to the former.[24]

Halevi, it seems unarguable, is here not a philosopher, not a systematic thinker. Husik's judgment that in Halevi "the poet got the better of the rationalist"[25] stands up very well; Halevi *is* an artist, a poet; faith and morals mean much more to him than reason and intellect. In this respect at least, *The Kuzari* might be compared to the Book of Job,[26] for it shares with the biblical Job more than a dialogue form; it shares with Job a sort of existential or even existentialist force – the God of *The Kuzari* and the God of Job are both arbitrary; both are inscrutable, utterly beyond rational expectation, even beyond justice, beyond ethical definition.

Halevi's God has embraced the Jews, and "uninterrupted tradition" (*ha-qabalah ha-nimshekhet*: Ibn Tibbon) affirms the divine embrace. The Jews are possessed of a special "good fortune"[27] (*ha-ṭovah >asher yétiv ha-bor>é >élénu*: Ibn Tibbon) which no gentile can appropriate for himself even on conversion to Judaism. Indeed, if Halevi had had any knowledge of genetics, he might very well have insisted that the special relationship between God and the Jews is a genetic inheritance and Jewish superiority a matter of the genes. As he has the *ḥaver* proclaim,

> ...any Gentile who joins us unconditionally shares our good fortune, without, however, being quite equal to us. If the Law were binding on us only because God created us, the white and the black man would be equal, since He created them all. But the Law was given to us because He led us out of Egypt, and remained attached to us, because we are [designated] *the pick of mankind*. [Ibn Tibbon renders it: *ha-s'gulah mi-b'né >adam*].[28]

Halevi has much more to say on this score:

> These conditions which render man fit to receive this divine influence [the *<inyan >elohi* which the Christian sage had mentioned? But Ibn Tibbon uses the term *ha-r'shamim... ha->elohi'im*] do not lie within him. It is impossible for him to gauge their quantity or quality, and even if their essence were known, yet neither their time, place, and connexion, nor suitability could be

---

[24]*Kuzari* I. 25 – Hirschfeld, pp. 46-47; Ibn Tibbon, p. 27.
[25]Husik, p. 150.
[26]Harry A. Wolfson said of *The Kuzari*: "it is less allied to Plato than to Job." See Wolfson, "Maimonides and Halevi," *Jewish Quarterly Review*, N.S., II (1911-12), 316-17. See also Heinrich Graetz, *History of the Jews* (Philadelphia: Jewish Publication Society, 1894), III, 327.
[27]*Kuzari* I. 27 – Hirschfeld, p. 47; Ibn Tibbon, p. 27.
[28]*Ibid.* (emphasis added).

discovered. For this, inspired and detailed instruction is necessary. He who has been thus inspired, and obeys the teaching in every respect with a pure mind, is a believer [in rabbinic Judaism].²⁹ ... We do not allow any one who embraces our religion theoretically by means of a word alone [which is the Christian and the Muslim practice] to take equal rank with ourselves, but demand actual self-sacrifice, purity, knowledge, circumcision, and numerous religious ceremonies. The convert must adopt our mode of life entirely. We must bear in mind that the rite of circumcision is a divine symbol ordained by God to indicate that our desires should be curbed, and discretion used, so that what we engender may be fitted to receive the divine Influence [*ha-<inyan ha->elohi*: Ibn Tibbon]. God allows him who treads this path, as well as his progeny, to approach Him very closely. Those, however, who become Jews do not take equal rank with born Israelites, who are specially privileged to attain to prophecy, whilst the former can only achieve something by learning from them, and can only become pious and learned, *but never prophets*.³⁰

At first – and maybe even second and third – glance Halevi must appear what our generation would term a "chauvinist" and a "racist." From our perspective, it is hard to imagine how such a charge can be avoided, though one might object of course that the "offense" would not have been deemed such in his generation. In Halevi's estimation, the Jews received the Torah not so much because God chose them as, to use terminology Halevi would not have known, because of a racial or genetic or biological strain which made them the *only ones who could* receive the Torah. Even wicked Jews, he stipulated, "remained, without doubt, of the [divine] essence inasmuch as they were part of it on account of their descent and nature, and begat children who were of the same stamp." ³¹ There is no philosophical appeal against this phenomenon, or this fate – for, after all, as Halevi says quite flatly: "In the service of God there is no arguing, reasoning, and debating. Had this been possible, philosophers with their wisdom and acumen would have achieved even more than Israel."³² No obscurantist *rebbe* could put it more flatly. The sophisticated Halevi, however, is not an obscurantist, and this stance of his must be especially troubling to us. Yet, Halevi seems quite unapologetic here: ritual, the ceremonial law, in his conception, is nothing rational or indeed rationalizable. It is, instead, an instrument whereby divine power and authority are manifested or projected – a manifestation or projection of something arbitrary, something which transcends, though it does not necessarily annihilate,

---

[29]*Kuzari* I. 79 – Hirschfeld, p. 56; Ibn Tibbon, p. 34.
[30]*Kuzari* I. 115 – Hirschfeld, p. 79; Ibn Tibbon, p. 48 (emphasis added).
[31]*Kuzari* I. 95 – Hirschfeld, p. 66; Ibn Tibbon, p. 40.
[32]*Kuzari* I. 99 – Hirschfeld, p. 72; Ibn Tibbon, p. 44.

Yehuda Halevi: The Consolations of Utopia 157

rational categories: "Religious ceremonies are, like the work of nature, entirely determined by God, but beyond the power of man."[33]

Consistency was not Halevi's forte – again the "artistic temperament"? Halevi, who must have been no mean linguist, valued Hebrew above all other languages: "To Hebrew... belongs the first place ... its original form is the noblest ...[Its] superiority... is manifest from the logical point of view if we consider the people who employed it for discourse ... at the time when prophecy was rife among them."[34] Yet, it is worth bearing in mind, this very same Halevi, the chauvinist racist and the lover of the Hebrew language, never hesitated to appropriate non-Jewish elements. He may have deplored the Jewish affection for Arabic – he has his *ḥavēr* denounce the use by Jews of Arabic prosody for Hebrew poetry: it was "because we [have] remained and [still] are froward" and have "corrupted the structure of our language, which is built on harmony"[35]; but he wrote his magnum opus in Arabic, not in Hebrew, and used a model, the philosophical dialogue, far better developed in Greek than in Jewish – biblical or talmudic – sources, to construct his defense of Judaism. Why it was Halevi preferred Arabic to Hebrew in composing *The Kuzari* is not especially perplexing. Obviously he was a highly gifted Hebraist (and would have appreciated the admirable Hebrew version Ibn Tibbon produced some thirty years later), but Arabic was a conscious choice: an Arabic book, he decided, would enable him to convey most effectively the message he wished to convey to the readership he had in mind, the upper-class Jewish businessmen and professionals who, whether in Spain or elsewhere in the Mediterranean world, read Arabic more readily than Hebrew, people who prayed comfortably enough in Hebrew, but whose quotidian, and intellectual, lives were lived in Arabic. For them – and perhaps also for urbane gentile intellectuals, who read or had read to them the squarish Hebrew letters in which Jews published Arabic texts – Halevi conceived his elaborate, yet stylistically forthright polemic.[36]

---

[33]*Kuzari* III. 53 – Hirschfeld, p. 181; Ibn Tibbon, p. 121.
[34]*Kuzari* II. 66-68 – Hirschfeld, pp. 124-25; Ibn Tibbon, p. 81.
[35]*Kuzari* II. 73-74 – Hirschfeld, pp. 126-27; Ibn Tibbon, pp. 82-83.
[36]*Encyclopaedia Judaica*, III, 239; S. D. Goitein, *Letters of Medieval Jewish Traders* (Princeton: Princeton University Press, 1973), pp. 5, 271, and *A Mediterranean Society* (Berkeley: University of California Press, 1971), II, 190, 207, 220, 341; Moritz Steinschneider, *Die Arabische Literatur der Juden* (Frankfurt a. M.: J. Kaufmann, 1902), p. 153. Bernard Lewis suggests that Halevi "composed poetry and Maimonides wrote on Jewish law in Hebrew, but when they wished to expound a philosophy both used Arabic, which possessed the necessary linguistic resources" (*The Jews of Islam* [Princeton: Princeton University Press, 1984], p. 76). More likely, it was a larger, more influential readership Arabic possessed.

It cannot be said of Halevi that he was antagonistic to philosophy – i.e., that he wanted to see philosophical speculation rooted out of Jewish life. He – like his contemporary Al-Ghazali where Islam was concerned – considered philosophy markedly inferior to revelation, but was willing to assume no rigidly anti-rationalist stand.[37] Indeed, to include Halevi in the canon of the so-called Golden Age of Spanish Jewry is to see what wide intellectual and esthetic range – from Halevi to Maimonides – the Spanish experience could accommodate. Halevi in this sense marvelously exemplifies a most extraordinary historical epoch.

The mythic pattern Halevi offers or manipulates in *The Kuzari* may appear static, but can actually, as he propounds it, be understood as a revolutionary theory of Judaism. The Judaism he depicts is one which, since in his presentation it is manifestly superior to Islam and Christianity and to philosophy as well, can achieve a political conquest – is not the Khazar conversion evidence of this? – and can ultimately hope to dominate human civilization.[38]

Is this no more than idle wish on Halevi's part? But perhaps it is something more. Perhaps it reflects an awareness on his part that the coming crisis holds promise, or at least possibility, as well as threat. The rulers of Khazaria adopted Judaism yesterday; why not the rulers of a bankrupt Christendom and Islam tomorrow? Halevi has seen territories long in thrall to Islam surrendered to Christian rule. He knows that the Greek Christian empire in the East has fallen prey to Latin Christian conquerors. Perhaps he also recognizes that North Africa and Syria were Christian before they became Muslim. Poems like "Y'didi Hashakhata" and "Yashén v'Libo <Er" can be read this way; also Halevi's famous ode to Zion, "Ziyon Hal>o Tish>ali."

"Halo> >az b'>ereẓ l>o z'ru<ah r'daftikha?" he asks in "Y'didi Hashakhata" – Have I not followed you [God] in a wilderness land? "V'>éch taḥaloq >atah k'v̄odi l'viladay?" How can you now award my glory to others? And in "Yashén v'Libo <Er": "Ẓé> na> v'hina<ér u-l'kha b'>or panay/Qumah ṣlaḥ u-r'khav̄! Darakh l'kha kokhav̄..." Go forth now awake and walk in the light of my face; up up and ride forth! A star has stepped forth for you..." And in the great ode to Zion: ">ashré m'ḥakeh v'yagi<a v'yir>eh <alot/>Orékh v'yibaq'<u <alav sh'ḥarayikh,/lir>ot b'ṭov̄at b'ḥirayikh, v'la<loz b'sim-/ḥatékh b'shuv̄ékh

---

[37] Rudolf Kayser, *The Life and Time of Jehudah Halevi* (New York: Philosophical Library, 1949), p. 139; *Encyclopaedia of Islam*, New Edition (Leiden: Brill, 1965), II, 1038ff.

[38] See Kayser, pp. 141,145. In myth, Roland Barthes observes, "history evaporates" (*Mythologies* [New York: Hill & Wang, 1972], p. 151). Neumark was certainly correct to question the view that, in *The Kuzari*, Halevi "presents *only a philosophy of history...*" (p.6).

Yehuda Halevi: The Consolations of Utopia 159

>*eli qadmat n'<urayikh!*" – Happy the one who is patient and arrives to see your [Zion's] light rising, your dawn breaking over him, to see the prosperity of your elect, and to share your joy in returning to the years of your youth![39]

What preoccupies Halevi in these poems? Has not Jewish history been filled with change? Are Jewish reverses beyond hope of amendment? When the Khazar king suggests that Jewish revival is unlikely, the *ḥavēr* reproves him for inferring "the extinction of our light from our degradation, poverty and dispersion" and for concluding "from the greatness of others, their conquests on earth and their power over us, that their light is still burning."[40] But it is not inevitably an other-worldly messianic figure Halevi means by *kokhav̄*, the redemptive star – can there be a hint here of an earlier "star," a political star *à la* Bar Kokhba? Might not the turmoil Halevi anticipates sweep away the gentile powers and leave Judaism ascendant? Is that not what God has in store for the Jews?

It is time to sum up: Halevi has weighed *kol ṭuv̄ S'farad*[41] – every advantage of life in Spain – and seems convinced of its transience. As he has the *ḥavēr* confess in *The Kuzari*: "I ...seek freedom from the service of those numerous people whose favor ...[e]ven if I could obtain it,... would not profit me."[42] Thus, everything he could gauge, every indication, seemed to point not in the direction of *kol ṭuv̄*, but in the direction of despair, unprecedented catastrophe, collapse into chaos. Muslim and Christian were pitted against each other in armed combat everywhere in the Mediterranean basin – with the Jew caught between them. The old world of S'farad, al-Andalus, once so notable a haven of security for Jews, was moving toward the abyss: Halevi was most probably well informed about unrest north of the Pyrenees and about the Latin Christian reduction of Byzantium and occupation of >Ereẓ Yiśra>el; no doubt he had some awareness even of Turks and Mongols bestirring themselves in Central Asia and penetrating the fragile defenses of Persia and Iraq.[43] It was clear enough to him that the Mediterranean world he had known was threatened with ruin – clear enough that Spain of the Caliphs and the Emirs would follow in the footsteps of Ummayyad Damascus and Abbassid Baghdad down into the

---

[39] I have used the Hebrew texts in Carmi, pp. 334,349, but see also Schirmann, *Ha-Shirah Ha-<Īvrit*, I, 466,483, 485ff.
[40] *Kuzari* IV. 20-21 – Hirschfeld, p. 225; Ibn Tibbon, pp. 152-53.
[41] "Libi-v̄'mizraḥ": see Carmi, p. 347; Schirmann, *Ha-Shirah Ha-<Īvrit*, I, 489.
[42] *Kuzari* V. 25 – Hirschfeld, p. 294; Ibn Tibbon, p. 201.
[43] See Lewis, *Islam in History*, pp. 187-88; George Holmes, ed., *The Oxford Illustrated History of Medieval Europe* (New York: Oxford, 1988), pp. 178-80.

abyss. Reality – the unfolding history – appeared too threatening. The rationalism, the rational expectations, Spanish life had fostered for so many generations under Muslim rule could provide no answer to the threat, no protection against what a learned, well furnished mind like Halevi's was bound to perceive as an irreversible decrepitude in the old order. Halevi seems to have seen it only too plainly; Al-Ghazali, too, among the Muslim scholars of Baghdad and Damascus. Survival evidently meant to both of them a repudiation of rational expectations, a reaching beyond philosophy and beyond history into another realm. Halevi was a harbinger, a pioneer if one will, of an intellectual and psychic orientation which would take some generations to ripen in the Peninsula[44] – and even the mighty Maimonides decades later would not be able to suspend that ripening.[45]

What might seem curious in a way is the want of messianic sentiment in Halevi. The rather intense interest in messianic beliefs to be found in the writings of an earlier philosopher-rabbi like Saadya,[46] for instance, finds few echoes in Halevi's work. Saadya, however, had been obliged in tenth-century Abbassid Baghdad to confront a rising tide of Karaite messianism, while messianic schismatics were remote from Halevi's experience, even though Karaism was not unfamiliar to him.[47] Jewish history – indeed, human history – he agreed, would have a messianic culmination. The messianic "day of the deliverance" would dawn; God would "arise and have mercy upon Zion, for the time to favor her... the set time is come,"[48] but Halevi was not minded to elaborate that certitude.[49]

---

[44]For Wolfson (p. 337), whereas Maimonides is now reduced to "a scholastic apology of religion," Halevi's thought "is old wine that is even now bursting new bottles. Contemporary thought ... may find its visions foreshadowed in Halevi's discussions": sic Wolfson ca. 1912.
[45]It is probably impossible to sever the mature Maimonides' faith in rationalism from his exposure to Saladin's relatively expansive Egypt. Had he been able to remain in his native Andalusia, he might have been or become less attached to a magisterial Aristotelian construction of reality. Ultimately, to be sure, "deconstruction" would be Maimonides' fate and Ayyubid Egypt's, too. See Goitein, *A Mediterranean Society*, III, 277; Rivkin, pp. 128ff.
[46]See Husik, p. 45.
[47]See, for instance, *Kuzari* III. 33-41, 65; V. 21 – Hirschfeld, pp. 166-73, 188, 292; Ibn Tibbon, pp. 111-16, 125, 200.
[48]See Psalm 102; *Kuzari* I. 115; V. 27 – Hirschfeld, pp. 79, 295; Ibn Tibbon, pp. 48, 202.
[49]Wolfson (p. 324) understood Halevi to use personal experience, "private religious experience," differently than did Al-Ghazali and other Muslim thinkers: Halevi "means personal experience as revelation or intuition. It is objectively perceptive and contains nothing 'mystical.'"

Yehuda Halevi: The Consolations of Utopia

The physician, it is likely, had become convinced that this ailment of social decrepitude, like so many others he had encountered, was incurable. In any case, he could not look on with dispassionate eyes, with the sang froid of a scientist or the fatalism of an oriental sage. The poet in him – the tragic poet – could not bear these forebodings. It was, finally, not philosophy as such he resisted or wanted to dispute so much as a rationalist spirit which dictated submission to the inevitable, the acceptance rationalism enjoined of what was beyond his power and beyond the power of his community to alter or avert.

The fruit of these broodings[50] – and let them be recognized as broodings more than speculations or philosophic inquiries – was an elegant, dazzling foray into the territory of myth (which, Roland Barthes reminds us, functions "to empty reality"[51]). In *The Kuzari*, of course, it is not historical Khazaria Halevi falls back on, it is a neverneverland of his own yearning spirit, which gathers its powers of poet and visionary to shape a metahistorical deliverance, the consolations of *Utopia*. The roster on which Halevi's name deserves an illustrious place is not that of philosophers; it is that of utopian writers. Not the thinker, not the architect of intellectual systems, rather the artist it is who has created *The Kuzari*. In this work, it may be, we have in the main another, though especially grand and memorable, example of what Isaac Bashevis Singer has designated as art: "a means of forgetting the human disaster for a while."[52] But *The Kuzari* cannot be left there. A question of self-esteem – what today we might call religio-ethnic pride – is surely involved in Halevi's book, a need to see in the Jewish condition a possibility of redemption which defies, though it will not condemn, rational measures. *The Kuzari*, then, is incontestably a denial of historical reality – that of course is the very nature of Utopia – but the denial here is no evidence of nihilism or apathy on its author's part. Halevi's denial, on the contrary, may be understood as his *gran rifiuto*[53]; a denial which aspires, however fallibly, to moral judgment.

My friend Prof. Norman Mirsky, after reading this essay in manuscript form, observed that Halevi, having noted the Christian belief that the messiah had already arrived, had a splendid opportunity to rebut the Christian view by stressing the contrary Jewish approach to messianism – and failed, or chose not, to do so: which, Prof. Mirsky suggested, only underscores Halevi's lack of messianic enthusiasm.

[50] Examples would be: *Kuzari* III. 1,7,73; IV. 3; V.2 – Hirschfeld, pp. 135, 141-42, 194, 201, 206-7, 248; Ibn Tibbon, pp. 91,95,129,137,140,172.

[51] Barthes, p. 143.

[52] I. B. Singer, *Lost in America* (Garden City: Doubleday, 1981), p. 250.

[53] The phrase is of course Dante's (*Inferno* III. 60), but I intend here no parallel between Halevi and Celestine V, the hermit pope who may have wished through abdication to spare himself an uncongenial political role.

12

Abortion and the Emergence of Human Life: Maimonides and the Judaic View *

By L. E. Goodman

Arguing for a biblical conception of creation, Maimonides draws an analogy between the Aristotelian view that excludes creation from the realm of possibility and a hyperbolically rationalistic view that would (if uncorrected by experience) declare impossible the entire process of human embryonic development:

> Everything that comes to be for the first time – even if it originates in matter that already exists and just sheds one form and puts on another – has a different nature after coming to be, once it is ready and settled, than it had while developing and emerging from potency to act – different, too, from its nature before starting out towards realization.
>
> The female seed, for instance, has a different nature as blood in the blood vessels than at conception, on meeting the male seed and starting to develop. And its nature is different at this stage from that of a maturing animal already born. There is no way of inferring from the nature of the stable, finished product to the condition of that same thing while it was developing, nor from the developmental state to what preceded the start of development. When you err in this way and try to infer from the nature of the thing that has reached completion to the prior potentiality, you are liable to fall into grave difficulties, mistaking necessities for delusions and impossibilities for necessities.

---

*An earlier and much abbreviated version of this paper was presented at the Constantinus Colloquy of the University of Exeter, March, 1988, and published in the proceedings. The author fondly recalls the memory of David Balme, the brilliant Aristotle scholar, who was present and commented fruitfully on that occasion. He extends his thanks to Professors David Novak and Menachem Kellner for their careful reading and helpful comments on the essay as it evolved.

Suppose, in our example, that a person of consummate ability were born and that his mother died after nursing him only a few months, leaving only men to finish raising him on an isolated island, so that he grew up and was educated and learned to reason without ever seeing a woman or any other female animal. Now he asks one of the men with whom he lives: "How did we come to be and in what manner did we develop?"

The other would answer: "Each of us developed entirely inside the belly of another of our kind, like us but 'female' – having such and such a form. Each had a tiny body that lived inside the womb, moving, taking nourishment, growing little by little, until reaching a certain size. Then a portal was opened for him on the underside of the body, from which he was extruded and came forth. He continued to grow until he came to be as you see us now."

The orphan then would have to ask: "This miniature of ourselves, when it was in the womb, living, moving and growing – did it eat and drink, and breathe through its mouth and nose? Did it defecate?"

"No," he would be told, and would doubtless lose no time in judging the entire account a lie and disprove all these facts, inferring their impossibility from the character of the mature and independent being.

He would argue: "Any one of us deprived of breath for even a few moments would die. All his movements would be stilled. How then is it conceivable that one of our number could exist enveloped in a heavy sac inside the body's cavity for months and yet remain alive and motile? If one of us swallowed a sparrow it would die as soon as it reached the stomach, let alone the abdomen! Every one of us who does not take food by mouth and drink water would perish in a few days, without a doubt, so how could a person stay alive for months without eating or drinking? Every one of us who takes in nourishment and does not defecate would die within a few days in dire pain. How then could *this* survive for months without evacuating? And if the belly of any one of us were pierced, he would die within days. So how can it be claimed that this 'foetus' is open at the navel? Or that it does not open its eyes or spread out its hands, or stretch out its feet, if all its limbs are sound and unimpaired, as you claim?"

In this way he would press the analogy, to show that a man cannot develop in the fashion described.[1]

The world for Maimonides, as for most medieval philosophers, is a macrocosm, a single, integrated organism, with limbs, soul, and living spirit.[2] For Maimonides, unlike strict Aristotelians, this organism has a

---

[1] *Dalâlat al-Ḥâirin (Guide to the Perplexed)*, II, 17, ed. S. Munk (Paris, 1856-1866; repr. Osnabrück: Zeller, 1964), 2.34b-35b.
[2] *Guide,* I, 72; 6-12. See my "Maimonidean Naturalism," in L. E. Goodman, ed., *Neoplatonism and Jewish Thought* (Albany: SUNY Press, 1992).

linear rather than cyclical history. It grew and developed, like a foetus in the womb, and had a different nature while developing from what we observe and study today. It was not subject before it began to develop – still less before it existed – to the laws and requirements that scientists now find to be settled and invariant. The foetus, then, is the type of the developing cosmos, as the man is the type of the cosmos we know today. Maimonides' interest, in the passage translated above, is the lack of parity between the embryo and the mature, free living adult: the world at large does not allow inferences like those made by philosophers of neo-Platonic/Aristotelian persuasion from the present, settled state of nature to its formative stages. But the illustration also casts light on Maimonides' idea of the foetus – in part because it resonates with echoes.

The notion of a perfect man growing up motherless on an isolated island harks back to Ibn Ṭufayl's classic story of Ḥayy ibn Yaqẓân,[3] although the naturally inquiring orphan philosopher of Maimonides' illustration is not quite as spectacularly brought into the world and reared as is the hero of Ibn Ṭufayl's philosophic romance. Both Maimonides' and Ibn Ṭufayl's figures of the natural human condition originate in ways that might seem incredible. Ḥayy ibn Yaqẓân develops (on the scientific account) by spontaneous generation; or (on a more mythic account) he is born in dramatic circumstances, concealed in a little ark and wafted by a providential current to the island where a doe nurses him. The scientists emphasize the proper preparedness of the matter that was to receive the human form; the fabulists stress the elements of pathos and particularity in their story. But both versions of the story find indispensable the divine afflatus which guides Ḥayy's fortunes or gives life to his clay.

Maimonides does not introduce any special appeal to the supernatural in his account of the foetus – quite the contrary. He sees God as acting through nature rather than despite it. But the spirited incredulity of his too purely rationalist young philosopher stumbles at the same issue that fascinates Ibn Ṭufayl: the emergence of one nature from another. This brings us to our second echo.

Arguing in behalf of prophecy, miracles and a kind of religious empiricism, al-Ghazâlî (1058-1111), the great Muslim theologian whose *Incoherence of the Philosophers* is an important backdrop to the work of both Maimonides and Ibn Ṭufayl, urges in his spiritual autobiography, *al-Munqidh min al-Ḍalâl* (Rescue from Error),[4] that without experience

---

[3]Tr. L. E. Goodman (Boston, 1972; repr. Los Angeles: Gee Tee Bee, 1983).
[4]Ed. F. Jabre (Beirut, 1959), pp. 50-51; cf. my "Three Meanings of the Idea of Creation" in D. Burrell and B. McGinn, eds., *God and Creation* (Notre Dame:

one would never admit that something no larger than a grain could devour an entire town and then itself. Yet fire has such a nature. Rationalist philosophers ascribe the effects of opium to its coldness and claim that earth and water are the cold elements. Yet pounds of water and earth have not the effect of a single dram of opium. Experience is the key to knowledge. Human reason has not the power to legislate the course of nature, but must await discovery of God's plan. As Maimonides puts it, man can learn the workings of a waterclock by taking it apart and following the sequence of its motions. But God, like the inventor of the clock, knows the workings of nature prior to its being. Indeed, God's knowledge is its cause.[5]

For al-Ghazâlî, as for Maimonides, the foetus is a central, paradigmatic case in understanding nature. In criticizing the rationalist philosophers' account of causality and defending the scriptural idea of miracles, al-Ghazâlî, as I have shown in my detailed studies of his arguments on this point,[6] is particularly concerned with the imparting of life and consciousness to dead matter. Here is a clear instance of the sort of transformation that aprioristic philosophers would deny.

Prior to al-Ghazâlî, Muslim theologians representing *kalâm*, or dialectical theology, addressed the problem of the imparting of life and consciousness to non-living matter rather frontally, almost by invoking the divine creative word. *Mutakallimûn* ("*loquentes*") of occasionalist persuasion devised a rather ad hoc but still powerful cosmological atomism, founded in turn upon a stringent logical atomism which enabled them to treat no fact in nature as dependent on any other[7] but required that all be dependent, without mediation, on God: this atom, given by God, exists here and now, not again or elsewhere unless God so pleases. This accident (it could be life or consciousness in an atom) is present because God so willed.[8] Consciousness and life, some argued,

---

Notre Dame University Press, 1990). See also *Galen on Medical Experience*, ed. and tr. R. Walzer (London, 1944), pp. 47, 122-3; the work was preserved intact only in the Arabic of Ḥubaysh ibn al-Ḥasan al-A'sam, who worked (in the 860's) from the Syriac rendering of the Greek made in about 850 by his celebrated uncle and teacher, Ḥunayn ibn Isḥaq; Walzer's translation is reprinted by Michael Frede in *Three Treatises on the Nature of Science* (Indianapolis: Hackett, 1985).
[5]*Guide*, III, 21.
[6]"Did al-Ghazâlî Deny Causality?" *Studia Islamica*, XLVII (1979), esp. 114-20; cf. "Ghazâlî's Argument from Creation," *International Journal of Middle East Studies*, II (1971), 67-85, 168-88.
[7]For a fuller discussion, see my "Ordinary and Extraordinary Language in Medieval Jewish and Islamic Philosophy," *Manuscrito*, XI (1988).
[8]See the critique of such thinking, ascribed to "Moses," in Galen, *De Usu Partium*, XI, and the discussion in R. Walzer, *Galen on Jews and Christians*

must be predicable of an atom, because no predicate is applicable to an aggregate unless applicable to its parts. Moreover, consciousness does not require the presence of life. Each thing, each accident, is what it is, and its presence does not require or entail the presence of any other. Thus there are no causal dispositions or capacities, but each thing or state of affairs is uniquely and directly created by God and re-created or allowed to vanish at His pleasure.

A straightforward argument from Aristotle, whose works were being translated when *kalâm* was in its heyday,[9] severely undercut this occasionalist line of thinking: if natural or voluntary agents lack the capacity to act, their action is impossible and will not take place.[10] Al-Ash'arî (d. 935), the great systematizer of *kalâm*, provides a careful response to this argument, which Aristotle used originally against the Megarians: things have capacities by which they act, but the capacities are not their own; they are imparted by God and compass no future event and no bivalency but only the immediate action which is at that very instant performed. Turning the tables on the Aristotelian reasoning, al-Ash'arî insists: if the requisite capacity is present and nothing is lacking for action, the action must take place.[11] No capacity governs the future. Al-Ash'arî preserves the force of the quranic dicta: "When you shot, it was not you who shot but God" (8:17); "There is no power but in God" (18:39).

Al-Ghazâlî went much further in his concessions to naturalism and thus offered a more sophisticated version of the idea of divinely imparted powers than had al-Ash'arî. His treatment creates a subtler gloss of the scriptural principle that all powers stem from God. Pressing the point that causal relations are not matters of logic (since "this is this and that is that" and there is no logical incongruity in affirming the one while denying the other),[12] Al-Ghazâlî concedes that in certain respects causal relations are matters of logic: one cannot simultaneously and univocally affirm and deny the same predicate of the same thing or affirm the particular while denying the general that it falls under. It

---

(London: Oxford University Press, 1949), p. 11; cf. J. Schacht and M. Meyerhof, "Maimonides against Galen on Philosophy and Cosmogony," *Bulletin of the Faculty of Arts of the University of Cairo,* V (1939), 82; tr. 70.
[9]See my chapter, "The Greek Impact on Arabic Literature," in *The Cambridge History of Arabic Literature,* I (1983).
[10]Aristotle, *Metaphysics,* Theta 3, esp. 1047a 10; cf. Delta 12, 1019b3.
[11]See *Kitâb al-Luma',* ed., R. McCarthy (Beirut: Catholic Press, 1953).
[12]*Tahâfut al-Falâsifa,* Discussion 17, ed. M. Bouyges (2nd ed.; Beirut: Catholic Press, 1962), p. 195 = Ibn Rushd *Tahâfut al-Tahâfut,* Discussion 17, ed. Bouyges (Beirut: Catholic Press, 1930), p. 517. The two works are cited below as *TF* and *TT*.

follows that one cannot ascribe consciousness, for example, to non-living matter. For conscious beings are a subclass of living ones, and the specific presupposes the generic. Even God cannot do the impossible.[13] Accordingly, there are natural prerequisites for natural changes and events. God performs miracles not by subverting the requirements of the natures of things, but by providing the necessary sequence of material and formal causes. The restriction is not a great one in al-Ghazâlî's eyes, "for matter can receive any form," and God can impart to bodies the form that He desires:

> Earth and the other elements can become a plant; the plant, when eaten by an animal, can become blood; the blood, sperm; and the sperm, implanted in the womb, can be formed into an animal. Familiarly this involves an extended temporal sequence. But our adversary cannot debar it from God's power for matter to cycle through these phases more rapidly than usual.[14]

Al-Ghazâlî quietly adopts the hylomorphism of "the Philosophers," and drops the atomism of the occasionalist *kalâm*. He allows the necessity, in any developmental transformation, of suitable matter and predisposing forms, exactly as required by the scientific mind, whose interest in the material conditions of change in nature Ibn Ṭufayl stresses. Al-Ghazâlî insists only that the necessary sequences of nature do not exclude the possibility of miracles, since God may initiate or accelerate all the relevant sequences. Similarly, al-Ghazâlî allows the bivalence of human volitional dispositions: men act voluntarily and at their discretion in the normal case. Indeed, the bivalency of human volition is the model al-Ghazâlî uses to establish the credibility of divine volition, on which hinges al-Ghazâlî's (and Maimonides') account of the credibility of creation.[15] But the key demand al-Ghazâlî makes is that God's volition can intervene in nature to produce motion in a corpse.[16] For, in a way, by al-Ghazâlî's account, that is just what God does in producing dispositions in us or any active "forms" in matter.

The image of the foetus and allied images related to the imparting of life, consciousness and ordered movement to what is in itself non-living, not conscious, not animate at all, recur repeatedly in al-Ghazâlî's analysis: the rod transformed into a serpent; the corpse that God causes to sit and write with an orderly movement; above all, the embryo emergent in the womb. For al-Ghazâlî's concern is not simply with "the

---

[13]*TF*, pp. 203-4 = *TT*, pp. 536.
[14]*TF*, pp. 200-1 = *TT*, pp. 533-34.
[15]*TF*, Discussion 1, pp. 57-58 = *TT*, Discussion 1, pp. 37-38. Cf. Aristotle, *Metaphysics*, Theta 2.
[16]*TF*, p. 204 = *TT*, p. 537.

Abortion and the Emergence of Human Life 169

miracles that disrupt the accustomed course of nature," but also with the more familiar but in a way even more mysterious miracles of birth, conception and development. He follows the lead of the Qur'ân in founding his conception of the miraculous upon his conception of the natural order. For in the Qur'ân God instructs Muḥammad to argue dialectically for the plausibility of resurrection from the established given of creation:

> Does not man see that We formed him from a drop of sperm?...He says: Who shall give life to these bones when they are rotted? Say: He will give them life who raised them up at the first. He knows the formation of every creature! The same who gave you fire from the green tree... Has not He who made heaven and earth power to create their like again? Indeed He has. He is the all-knowing Creator. When He commands a thing, He has only to tell it "BE" and it is.[17]

Saadiah too (882-942), Maimonides' great predecessor, links the rise of human life with the re-creation of man at the resurrection:

> Job's words "I am mindful, O Lord that Thou didst form me ...Didst Thou not pour me out like milk and curdle me like cheese? In skin and flesh dost Thou clothe me, and in bone and sinews dost Thou shelter me" allude to the three modes of generation by which God gives being to men at three different junctures: The first is His creation of Adam from dust... The second is procreation, by which God creates man through the mediation of two persons, as Job says, *Didst Thou not pour me out as milk?*, which is the second mode of generation, namely, from semen, which develops like a clot [cf. Qur'ân 22:5, 23:14]. The third is the resurrection... generation not, as in the first two cases, out of dust or semen, but beginning with flesh and bones, sinews and skin, as Ezekiel (37:8) says, *I looked, and lo there were sinews on them, and flesh and blood came upon them, and skin covered them over.*[18]

For al-Ghazâlî, as for Saadiah before him and for Maimonides after him, the sexual generation of a living human being is a paradigm case of a causally mediated miracle – the foundation conceptually of the more exceptional type of miracle which commonly exercises theologians. It is also the immediately present type of the initial, and consummatory, cosmic acts of creation and resurrection by which God originated and in the end will judge humanity. By al-Ghazâlî's account, even the most

---

[17]Qur'ân 36:77-82 and al-Ghazâlî's discussion in *Faḍâ'iḥ al-Bâtiniyya*, ed. A.-R. Badawi (Cairo: National Printing and Publishing House, 1964), p. 48.
[18]*The Book of Theodicy*, tr. L. E. Goodman (New Haven: Yale University Press, 1988), p. 231, *ad* Job 10:10. Cf. H. A. Wolfson, *Philo* (Cambridge: Harvard University Press, 1962), II, 200. I translate the text of Job here as in Saadiah's Arabic version.

dramatic miracles ascribed to the action or anticipation of scriptural prophets, those which seem to disrupt the course of nature, are no different in ultimate structure (but only in speed and outward appearance) from natural events. For in all natural events God acts through the provision of matter and forms. The development of the human embryo is the paradigm case. For the condition of the embryo is emblematic of the human condition at large.

From an archetype the embryo metamorphoses to an ideal. Al-Ghazâlî argues in the *Iḥyâ' 'Ulûm al-Dîn* (Reviving the Religious Sciences) that reliance upon God consists initially in simply trusting God's providence, but it reaches a higher state when one's relation toward God is like that of an infant toward its mother: "For the infant knows only her, turns only to her for support, and depends on none but her..." At its most sublime, reliance upon God means placing oneself in His hands "like the corpse in the hands of the washer."[19] Mediating these two images – the child at its mother's breast and the corpse in the hands of the washer – is the image of the foetus, not yet born, nor yet dead, wholly dependent on the sustenance it receives, as all things depend on matter and form, which stem ultimately from God.

Maimonides does not adopt foetus, infant, or corpse as an ideal. Nor does he share al-Ghazâlî's suspicion that reliance on the powers of natural or volitional causes is a subtle form of idolatry.[20] In fact, Maimonides criticizes fatalists, occasionalists, and predestinarians for making God's means unnecessary to His ends. Such thinkers in effect render God's acts futile or vain and ignore the subtlety of creation, which is not merely the attainment of God's ends but the attainment of those ends *by these means*, omitting no step from the natural sequence, each term of which serves a subtle purpose – as milk nourishes an infant and the womb shelters an embryo.[21] Maimonides argues even against Saadiah's claim that all things exist for man, and man, that he might worship God: to treat all things as means to human ends is to make the nobler serve the humbler and to ignore the fact that beings exist for their own sakes and not just for ours.

Maimonides is more comfortable than al-Ghazâlî is with the hybrid naturalism that al-Ghazâlî had initiated at the juncture between the views of the Aristotelian neo-Platonists and the scriptural idiom that

---

[19]*Iḥyâ'*, Book 35, pt. 2. (Cairo, 1967-1968), IV, 324-25.
[20]*Iḥyâ'*, Book 34, pt. 1. For Maimonides' treatment of natural and volitional causes, see my "Determinism, Freedom and Responsibility in Spinoza, Maimonides and Aristotle – A Retrospective Study," in F. Schoeman, ed., *Responsibility, Character and the Emotions* (Cambridge: at the University Press, 1987).
[21]*Guide*, III, 32, 13, 25; "Eight Chapters," 8.

ascribes all natural and human acts to God. But Maimonides' naturalism is, nonetheless, an adaptation and extension of the position pioneered by al-Ghazâlî, and the image of the foetus remains prominent in its exposition, as though to attest to the kinship. Arguing that biblical and Rabbinic angels are in fact natural forms and forces, Maimonides urges:

> If you told one of those men who purport to be the Sages of Israel that the Deity sends an angel who enters the womb of a woman and then forms the foetus, that would impress him and he would accept it as an expression of God's greatness and power and an instance of His wisdom – although still convinced that an angel is a body of flaming fire one third the size of the entire world – supposing that all this was perfectly possible for God. But if you told him that God placed a formative power in the semen, by which the limbs and organs are shaped and demarcated, and that this is the angel, or if you told him that the forms of all things are the work of the Active Intellect and that this is the angel constantly mentioned by the Sages as the magistrate of the world, he would bolt at such a view. For he does not understand the real meaning of greatness and power.[22]

The "Magistrate" (Šar) given charge over the world, the Active Intellect, imparts from itself the intelligent and intelligible forms of all things. It thus stands forth at all levels of nature in the spiritual aspect of reality. Its work is manifest in the forms imparted to elemental matter, which differentiate that matter and thus distinguish it from the mere "otherness" (and pure virtuality) of prime matter. Its work is manifest also in the living, conscious and choosing souls of rational beings, whose intellectuality, life and volition mirror the self-constituting, intellective and transcendent character of God.

As Maimonides analyzes the givens of our condition, there is really only one great problem of nature and grace – thus, ultimately, only one great miracle, of which all others are instances: the problem and the miracle of theophany, the manifestation on a finite scale of the infinite and transcendent God. Reverting to the words of the Sages of the Talmud, Maimonides meditates on the two mysteries which they withheld from common, public study: the scriptural account of creation (ma‹aseh b're›shit, the account of Genesis) and the account of theophany (ma‹aseh merkavah, the account of the chariot – Ezekiel's ecstatic vision of God in creaturely lineaments). These, Maimonides reasons, correspond, when considered as areas of inquiry, to the philosophical explorations of physics (that is, cosmology) and

---

[22]*Guide*, II, 6, Munk 2.17ab. For Maimonides' neo-Platonic approach to the naturalization of angels, see L. E. Goodman, "Maimonidean Naturalism," in Goodman, ed., *Neoplatonism and Jewish Thought* (Albany: SUNY Press, 1992).

metaphysics (first philosophy or theology, as Aristotle called it). Physics asks after the ultimate character and constitution of nature. For a scriptural monotheist, that means the principles of its creation. Metaphysics asks after reality at large – being as such – what, if anything, transcends the natural world; thus, after the existence and nature of God.

The two areas are linked by the metaphysical question which for centuries inflamed relations between philosopher theologians of the Aristotelian and neo-Platonic tradition on the one hand and those of the Mosaic tradition on the other: "Can the world have originated? How can a God that transcends time be manifest on a temporal scale?" But that question is readily seen to be no more than a special case of the larger question affecting all philosophical theists – creationists and eternalists alike – the question of the relation between the finite particularity of natural beings and God's infinity and transcendence. The great problem of theology was not so much how to reach God from our finite knowledge. For the contingency of being, the determinacy of things, the life and beauty – indeed, the existence – of the cosmos all argued the reality of a transcendent Cause. But how could a God who is infinite and absolute be related to this cosmos? The problem of creation, the problem of revelation, the related issues about physical resurrection and spiritual immortality, even the problem of evil, were all seen as special cases of this issue of divine condescension or contraction,[23] the emergence of the temporal and bounded from the Timeless and Boundless.

Maimonides' approach to a solution relies heavily on the philosophers' idea of emanation. He takes the philosophers to task only for their apparent loss of nerve in not following through on Plato's original conception. For by Plato's conception, matter would not be an independent (thus eternal) and radically recalcitrant (thus evil) Thing. Matter, Maimonides argues (and his point is paralleled by Ibn Ṭufayl), is not (like the natural forms and forces) a "son of God" but a mere principle of otherness and receptivity, itself given definitude (thus existence) by forms,[24] as Aristotle's metaphysics requires. The formation of a foetus, then, like the informing of a mind, is an achievement of order and organization. It is the imparting of form (conceived in Aristotelian terms as pattern and plan) under the guiding influence of the Active Intellect, which alone differentiates the virtuality

---

[23]Cf. David Novak, "Some Aspects of the Doctrine of the Self-Contraction of the Godhead in Kabbalistic Theology," in L. E. Goodman, ed., *Neoplatonism and Jewish Thought* (Albany: SUNY Press, 1991).
[24]*Guide*, III, 22, 3.46ab; Ibn Ṭufayl, tr. Goodman, pp. 114-27.

of matter (in itself non-existence – that is, without form) and thus imparts to it its character – its being as a member of its kind, which is, as Aristotle argued, all the being anything has.

That such imparting of being is a miracle is without a doubt, since it breaches the chasm that separates the finite from the Infinite. The vehicle of that breaching is intellectual; being is intellectual and so can be shared without division or loss. Form traverses the chasm between the finite and the infinite as light radiates from the sun – although (in Maimonides' view) not so mechanically and automatically, but rather volitionally and by grace. God imparts to each being its goal-directedness, and each pursues the Good by seeking the good defined for it by nature. It is in this sense that Maimonides interprets the dictum that God created all things for His glory as meaning that God created each thing and kind for its own sake.[25]

Commonly miracles are thought of as disruptions in the causal fabric. But it is clear that, in the "settled order of nature" established by Maimonidean naturalism, there will be little room for such miracles. Maimonides does leave the door ajar for them, citing the midrashic notion that ten miraculous objects were created in the twilight of the sixth day (See >Aᵥot 5:6 and Maimonides *ad loc.*) Even here, however, a Maimonidean-Ghazalian gloss is at work. For the Rambam argues that the midrashic reference to the ten things created in the twilight of the sixth day – the mouth of the earth that swallowed Korah (Numbers 16:32), the mouth of the well (that in legend accompanied the Israelites, as in Numbers 21:16), the mouth of Balaam's ass (Numbers 22:28), Noah's rainbow (Genesis 9:13), the manna (Exodus 16:14), Moses' rod (Exodus 4:17), the Shamir, that is, the worm that cleft the rocks for Solomon's Temple so as to form it with no iron tool (see Joshua 8:31), and the tablets, writing tool and script of the Ten Commandments – includes the script on the tablets in order to show "that the writing on the Tablets was like any other act of creation."[26]

---

[25] *Guide*, III, 13, 25.
[26] *Guide*, I, 66 *ad fin*. Maimonides argues in his Commentary on >Aᵥot that the ten things are named as paradigms of the miraculous in nature: the list is not intended to be exhaustive. Inclusion of the writing shows that it was part of nature. The general principle that the Sages were expressing in this midrash is that God does not "change His mind," i.e., does not alter the order of creation, does not interfere with the laws of nature embedded therein: the Sages "did not believe in temporal changes in God's will." They held, rather, "at the outset, in creating things, He set it in the nature of each thing that all that would be done with it could be done. Whether what would be done was commonplace and thus 'natural' or a novelty reserved for rare occasions and thus a portent, it was all the same," i.e., all was based on the natures established in things by God. Maimonides departs from al-Ghazâlî's response to the philosophers here only in

Just as the Rabbis (Genesis Rabah V: 5) picture God as stipulating at the creation that the sea must part to let the Israelites pass, the sun and moon stand still for Joshua, the ravens feed Elijah, the fire not harm Hananiah, Mishael and Azariah, the lions not maul Daniel, and the fish spew out Jonah (thus incorporating these miracles into the fabric of nature, rather than treating them as violations of the covenant of God with nature), so Maimonides can argue that the fish was moved by its own volition. For God does not literally speak to fish, making prophets of them.[27] Following al-Ghazâlî's adaptation of neo-Platonic emanationism, Maimonides can reason that God, at the creation, imparts to man the sort of matter that will make him capable of life and consciousness and (at the creation of the individual) even the particular material constitution that will make one person, say, incapable of prophecy, no matter how high his intellectual apprehensions may rise. For imagination is necessary to prophecy, and imagination depends on matter.[28]

The human embryo, on the Maimonidean model, then, is a natural miracle – the imparting of form to matter. Matter in general as we know it in nature is constituted as a particular receptivity by the initial creative imparting of form. But here matter is raised to a far higher pitch than customary, making possible the emergence of what is alive and conscious from what is in itself non-living and non-conscious – what is in itself, ultimately, nothing at all.

Having set out the ontic status of the human foetus in Maimonidean metaphysics, we are now perhaps in a position to make some determinations about the moral standing of the foetus. For matters of right and valuation, I would argue,[29] rest on the reality of the beings accorded one sort of treatment or another. That is, deserts are nothing distinct from the ontic claims made by each being in its own behalf, the claims which constitute its essence or *conatus*, duly qualified by the purtenant claims of others. Deserts belong to a human embryo as such, I argue, from the moment it makes entitative claims, in implantation for

---

restricting to the original creation the imparting of the necessary natures to things. He also, of course, gives a more positive emphasis to the fact (acknowledged by al-Ghazâlî) that man's nature includes the polyvalent capacity of volition. *Perush l'Masekhet >Aϑot*, ed. M. D. Rabinovitz (Jerusalem: Kuk Foundation, 1962), p. 182; tr. Arthur David as *Commentary to Mishnah Aboth* (New York: Bloch, 1968), pp. 100-1.
[27]See *Guide*, II, 48, for the fish; I, 67, for the finality of creation.
[28]*Guide*, II, 36-38. See my "Matter and Form as Attributes of God," in R.J. Long and C. Manekin, *A Straight Path: Essays in Honor of Arthur Hyman* (Washington: Catholic University Press, 1987).
[29]See my *On Justice* (New Haven: Yale University Press, 1991) and see Maimonides, *Guide*, III, 53, 3.131b.

example. Deserts grow *pari passu* with the growth of the embryo towards humanity.

II

Maimonides holds an interesting position in the history of Jewish jurisprudence on this matter, perhaps in part because of his role as a practicing physician, but no doubt also because of his philosophic stance. Biblically, abortion was dealt with as a tort, an assault upon a woman. The injury was not a manslaughter because the foetus was not yet born: "If men struggle together and one of them pushes a pregnant woman, causing a miscarriage, but no other harm ensues, he shall pay damages imposed by the woman's husband, according to the reckoning" (Exodus 21:22). Rashi, following the *M'khilta>*, explains that "no other harm" here means no fatal injury to the woman.[30] And the Rabbis gloss "according to the reckoning" as an allusion to the role of judicial authority in determining the damages, rather than leaving the matter to the discretion of the parties.[31]

But the Exodus text is rather elliptical. How do we know that "no other harm" refers only to mortal injury to the woman? The *M'khilta>* admits to having no direct evidence for the inference that only fatal harm is intended. But it offers a parallel use of the word for harm (>*ason*) in Genesis (2:38) to show that fatal injury is intended. It relies on the immediate sequel (Exodus 21:23) to show that the woman is the victim the law seeks to protect, since it treats this alternative as a case of homicide, and any lesser injuries had already been addressed as tort damages. The *M'khilta>* argues informatively: "Scripture comes to teach you about one who, aiming to kill his enemy, kills his friend."[32] Thus we have a clear division between homicide, which falls within the biblical law of persons, and aborticide, which is treated as a tort.

External evidence confirms the authoritative reading of the *M'khilta>*. For in the Code of Hammurabi compensation for an abortion of the type described in Exodus is dependent on the status of the parties, and the death of the woman is punished by the execution of the offender's *daughter*.[33] The egalitarian and moral thrust of the Mosaic law stands out vividly against this contrasting background. Here we see the

---

[30] See *M'khilta>*, Nezikin VIII *ad loc.*
[31] Cf. K'tuvot 3.2; Deuteronomy 32:31; I Samuel 2:25. For the "reckoning," see Maimonides, *Mishneh Torah*, XI, The Book of Torts, Laws of Wounding and Damaging, iv.
[32] See *Mekhilta de-Rabbi Ishmael*, ed. Jacob Lauterbach (Philadelphia: Jewish Publication Society, 1935), III, 63-69.
[33] See the Laws of Hammurabi, 209-14, in E. R. Driver and John C. Miles, eds., *The Babylonian Laws* (Oxford: Clarendon Press, 1955), II, 79.

expectant mother identified explicitly as the potential victim in the law's concern, and treatment of foeticide as a homicide emerges as precisely the kind of disproportion (see Genesis 4:23) that the biblical law seeks to correct (Exodus 21:20, 26, etc.) when it provides that damages shall be proportioned to the gravity of injuries sustained (Exodus 21:23-25), without regard for the status of the parties, that homicide belongs in a separate and restricted category of offence (Leviticus 24:17, Exodus 21:12-14), and above all, that "parents shall not be put to death for children, nor children for parents, but each individual for his own offense" (Deuteronomy 24:16; cf. Exodus 21:28, Leviticus 4:3, etc., Numbers 9:13, 12:11, 16:22).[34]

The Pentateuch does not directly consider the possibility of an intentionally induced abortion. As Stephen Ricks writes, "With the exception of the Middle Assyrian Laws (ca. 1600 B.C.), the earliest Near Eastern law codes do not deal with the willful destruction of the fetus with the consent of the mother."[35] The reason is not far to seek: it is beyond the moral horizon of the community the Law initially addresses to expect that a father or a mother might consider intentionally aborting a foetus. For in the moral environment where the law was first received, the memory of genocide and infanticide was still fresh (Exodus 1:16); every birth was precious; and, in keeping with the ideas of patriarchal times and the vision of national destiny which embodied those ideas, the loftiest and most sublime blessing to a patriarchal or matriarchal figure was God's promise: "I shall indeed bless thee, making thy seed as numerous as the stars of the heavens and as the sand on the shore of the sea" (Genesis 22:17; cf. the promise as to Hagar's descendants at Genesis 21:13). In this context the solitary and oblique reference to abortion in Exodus is all the more striking, since it shows us that aborticide, even through an assault, is not biblically deemed a homicide – although fatal injury to the expectant mother, as a result of the same incident, would be.

But in the Hellenistic period, contact of Jews with the ideas and practices of other nations regarding abortion and infanticide put the matter in a different light. As Tarn writes:

> The prevalence of infanticide in Greece has been strenuously asserted from the literary texts and as strenuously denied; but for the late third and second centuries (B.C.) the inscriptions are conclusive... Of some thousand families from Greece who received Milesian citizenship c. 228-220, details of 79, with their children

---

[34] See the discussion in my *Monotheism*, ch. 3, esp. pp. 93-97 and n. 17.
[35] Stephen Ricks, "Abortion in Antiquity," in *Anchor Bible Dictionary* (Garden City: Doubleday, 1992). Ricks also cites parallels from the Lipitishtar, Sumerian and Hittite laws.

remain; these brought 118 sons and 28 daughters, many being minors; no natural causes can account for these proportions... more than one daughter was practically never reared, bearing out Poseidippus' statement that "even a rich man always exposes a daughter." Of 600 families from Delphic inscriptions, second century, just 1 percent reared 2 daughters... The general conclusion from c.230 onwards seems certain: the one child family was commonest, but there was a certain desire for two sons (to allow for death in war); families of four or five were very rare; more than one daughter was very seldom reared; and infanticide on a considerable scale, particularly of girls, is not in doubt.[36]

In this environment, which in so many ways anticipates the commercialism and individualism of our own, the humanism of the Judaic ethos asserts itself in a fashion that the allied natalism of the same tradition had not found necessary. Thus the Septuagint renders the verse from Exodus:

> If two men strive and smite a woman with child, and her child issueth imperfectly formed, he [sc. the assailant who struck the blow] shall be forced a pay a penalty: as the woman's husband may lay upon him, he shall pay with a valuation. But if it be perfectly formed, he shall give life for life...[37]

Here the Greek glosses the Hebrew with a clear nisus towards finding an authority for the sanctity of human life, even before birth. It dissolves the mention of "other harm" into a disjunctive reference to the interests of the formed or unformed foetus, rather than the mother, whose interests it presumes to be already covered by the laws of assault, homicide and injury.[38]

Philo's exposition and paraphrase make clear what a Jewish reader in a Hellenistic milieu saw to be at stake in the Exodus passage,[39] and why the Septuagint translators brought to it the animus that they did: "If a man comes to blows with a pregnant woman," he writes, cutting

---

[36]W. W. Tarn, *Hellenistic Civilisation*, 3rd. ed. revised by the author and G. T. Griffith (London: Edward Arnold, 1952; repr., 1966), pp. 100-2, where further evidence is presented.
[37]Tr. Lancelot C. L. Brenton (London, 1851; repr. Zondervan, n.d.).
[38]Abraham Geiger inferred from the Septuagint passage that there must have been an ancient Jewish law which ruled as the LXX provides. See *Ha-Miqra> V'targumav*, pp. 280, 343. But the LXX does not need a legal authority if, as its authors believe, it *establishes* one in what the translators believe to be the correct interpretation of an elliptical phrase.
[39]Cf. the oath of Asaph in the seventh century and that of Amatus in the sixteenth, as expressions of the same abiding Jewish moral sensibility: F. Rosner and S. Muntner, *Annals of Internal Medicine*, LXIII (1965), 317-20; H. Friedenwald in *The Jews and Medicine* (Baltimore: Johns Hopkins, 1944), pp. 368-70.

away from the biblical *mise en scène,* where the assault is presumed incidental to a fight between two men, "and strikes her on the belly" (agreeing with the *M'khilta>,* here, that not just any blow is relevant), "and she miscarries, then, if the result of the miscarriage is unshaped and undeveloped, he must be fined, both for the outrage" of striking a pregnant woman upon the womb "and for obstructing the artist Nature in her creative work of bringing into life the fairest of living creatures." Here the values underlying natalism are made explicit.

> But, if the offspring is already shaped and all the limbs have their proper qualities and places in the system, he must die, for that which answers to this description is a human being, which he has destroyed in the workshop of nature, who judges that the hour has not yet come for bringing it out into the light, like a statue lying in a studio requiring nothing more than to be brought outside and released from confinement.[40]

The Septuagint knows nothing of Hammurabi, but is clearly alarmed by the indiscriminate practice of abortion and infanticide. By the time of the Roman empire the textual evidence Tarn referred to in the Hellenistic period has become categorical. The teacher of Epictetus and of Dio Chrysostom, Rufus Musonius, the first-century Stoic philosopher exiled by Nero, a pacifist moralist who bears the distinction of having condemned slavery, the sexual double standard, and concubinage even when legal, also condemned abortion. Nero's tutor, Seneca, later forced to commit suicide after being named a conspirator against the emperor, pays tribute to his mother, as Ricks remarks, for never "crushing the hope of the children nurtured in her body."[41] And Juvenal bitingly comments that giving birth seems to have become one of the toils of the lower classes.[42] Tacitus reveals the more widely held values of his day when he ascribes the Jewish prohibition of infanticide to Jewry's "passion for propagating their race" and desire to "provide for the increase in their numbers." What seemed humane to Jews seemed extreme to their pagan detractors and a good example of the "perversity" Tacitus found in Jewish institutions.[43] Against this

---

[40]*De Specialibus Legibus,* III, 108-9, tr. after F. H. Colson, *Philo* (London: Heinemann, 1958), VII, 545.
[41]*Ad Helviam, De Consolatione,* 16.3
[42]Juvenal, *Satires,* 2, 29-35.
[43]Tacitus writes: "Things sacred with us, with them have no sanctity, while they allow what with us is forbidden... all their customs, which are perverse and disgusting, owe their strength to their very badness." Tacitus betrays his penchant for disinformation by contradicting his own story about the image of an animal in the Temple of Jerusalem (*History,* 4.4 *vs* 5.9). He betrays his groundless hatred not only by ascribing the prohibition of infanticide to an unreasonable (in Jews!) desire to reproduce, but also in explaining *sh'miṭah* as

background, Philo, a contemporary of Caligula, explains the law he finds in the Septuagint:

> This ordinance carries with it the prohibition of something else more important, the exposure of infants, a sacrilegious practice which among many other nations, through their ingrained inhumanity, has come to be regarded with complacence. For if on behalf of the child not yet brought to birth by the appointed conclusion of the regular period thought has to be taken to save it from disaster at the hands of the evil-minded, surely still more true is this of the full-born.[44]

Philo's arguing *a fortiori* and his insistence that infanticide is a more important issue than abortion show that he does not confuse the two. But he does see a relationship in terms of the ethos that accepts either or both, an ethos that he characterizes in terms of what we would call narcissism. He describes it as hedonistic, cruel, selfish, and misanthropic. The foetus, like the infant, he argues, is innocent and helpless and, if fully formed, is no less human than an adult. Philo's intent, consistent with that of the Septuagint, is to set out a middle ground between the treatment of the foetus as a mere appanage of the mother's body and its treatment as a full legal person. By insisting on a sharp distinction between a formed and unformed foetus, as Philo makes clear, the Septuagint assimilates late abortion to infanticide, and thus brings the formed foetus within the scope of the Torah's protection of persons. For, as Philo argues, "the Law is not concerned with ages, but with a breach of faith to the race."[45] Yet Philo knows that in physiology, as schematized in his day, the foetus is deemed part of its mother, and that Jewish law, as systematized in his day, does not categorically prohibit abortion or even rhetorically equate it with murder.

The Mishnah recognizes that a woman may need to abort her foetus: "If a woman is in hard travail, the embryo is dismembered within her and brought out limb by limb. For her life takes precedence over its life. But once its greater part has emerged, it may not be touched, since we do not set aside one person's life for another" (>Ohalot 7:6). The full claims of humanity are acknowledged in the prohibition against

---

an extension of "the charm of indolence" from a weekly to a septennial cycle. Still, it is interesting that the historian's negativity about the fugitive (5.2) and disfigured (5.3-4) race of Jews, who hate and are hated by all the gods, although attracting converts and clients from the outcasts of other nations (5.5), should alight particularly upon the Jews' kindness and honesty to one another, avoidance of relations with foreign women, fearlessness in battle, and rejection of infanticide. See Moses Hadas, tr., *The Complete Works of Tacitus* (New York: Random House, 1942), pp. 657-66.

[44]*Spec. Leg.*, III, 110-11.
[45]*Ibid.*, 112-19; cf. Josephus, *Antiquities*, 4.278.

preferring the claims of one life to another, as spelled out in another context: "How," the Talmud asks, "do you know your blood is redder than his?" (Sanhedrin 45b). As Maimonides sums up the law (and his formulation still preserves the odor of the Roman Imperium): "If the heathen said to them, 'Give us one of your company and we shall kill him, otherwise we kill all of you,' let them all be killed but not deliver a single soul of Israel!" Only a specified criminal whose life was forfeit *de jure* could be given up – even to save many lives.[46]

The great exception to this rule is in the case of an aggressor, talmudically called a *rodef* (pursuer), where the demands of protection of the innocent and prevention of the gravest mortal sins (Sanhedrin 8:7) suspend the presumed inviolability of human lives. Maimonides explains the Sages' willingness to set aside the deserts of the human foetus as due to their treatment of the foetus itself as like a *rodef*.[47] He writes:

> It is a negative commandment (Deuteronomy 25:12) not to have pity for the life of an aggressor (*rodef*). That is why the Sages ruled that if a woman is in hard travail the embryo is removed, either by drugs or surgery: because it is regarded as one pursuing her and trying to kill her. But once its head has appeared, it must not be touched. For we may not set aside one person's life to save another, and what is happening is the course of nature.[48]

Later authorities are puzzled that Maimonides resorts to the law of hot pursuit to justify embryotomy, since the Mishnah seems to find sufficient warrant for its ruling in the precedence taken by a mother's life to that of her foetus – a precedent explained by Rabbi Israel Lipschutz on the grounds of the unestablished viability of the as yet unborn.[49] Indeed, in addressing the case of a woman condemned to death by a court unaware of her pregnant state, the Talmud remarks of the foetus: "of course, it is part of her body" (<Arakhin 7a).[50] The

---

[46]Maimonides, *Code, Hilkhot Y'sodé Ha-torah*, glossing I Samuel 20:4-22 and following Resh Lakish, T. Y. T'rumot 8:12.
[47]Maimonides, *Code, Ḥovel Umaziq*, 8, 15, with *Migdal <Oz, ad loc.*; cf. David Feldman, *Marital Relations, Birth Control and Abortion in Jewish Law* (New York: Schocken, 1975), p. 278. For the *rodef*, see Emanuel Rackman, "Violence and the Value of Life: The Halakhic View," in S. Baron, G. Wise, and L. E. Goodman, eds., *Violence and Self-Defense in the Jewish Experience* (Philadelphia: Jewish Publication Society, 1977), pp. 124-25, 129.
[48]Maimonides, *Code, Hilkhot Roẓeaḥ*, 1.9.
[49]See *M'khilta>* to Exodus 21:12-14; J. David Bleich, "Abortion in Halakhic Literature," in F. Rosner and J. D. Bleich, eds., *Jewish Bioethics* (New York: Hebrew Publishing Co., 1983), pp. 155-56.
[50]See also Ḥulin 58a, Giṭin 23b, Nazir 51a, Baba> Qama> 88b, T'murah 31a and the responsa cited by Rosner in "The Jewish Attitude toward Abortion," in M.

Jerusalem Talmud (Shabat 14) explains further: Once the babe has begun to emerge into the open air, we can no longer say who is a threat to whom. But prior to that event, as Rabbi David Novak phrases the mishnaic criterion, the mother's is clearly "the more proximate life."[51]

Rashi uses the reasoning of the Mishnah to draw a clear line between the foetus and the deserts of personhood. As he observes, when the Mishnah says that we do not set aside one person's life (*nefesh*) for another, it plainly does not consider the foetus a person (*nefesh*). Accordingly, Rashi states the normative view of the status of the foetus: "As long as it has not emerged into the air it is not a person" (*ad* Sanhedrin 72b). It is for that reason that there can be sufficient grounds to warrant some abortions.[52] The act is not regarded as a homicide in Jewish law. This the Sages warrant by the wording of the basic prohibition against homicide: "He that smiteth a man so that he dieth..." (Exodus 21:12): "a man," not a foetus (Sanhedrin 84b).

Why then does Maimonides have recourse to the negative commandment[53] to have no pity on a pursuer, an appeal normally used to obviate charges of homicide? Clearly the impact is to lay narrow grounds for the permission of abortion. What warrant has Maimonides to do so? To begin with, there is the situational context evoked by the mishnaic law itself: Without "hard travail," the foeticide would not be acceptable. But why not? What values is the Mishnah protecting? The Mishnah distinguishes abortion from homicide when it categorically prohibits harming the infant once born. And Maimonides agrees: we have seen that he is a cardinal exponent of the talmudic principle that we are not permitted to sacrifice one human life to save another. Yet, like the Mishnah, he does not extend this protection to the foetus.

Rabbi Isser Yehudah Unterman, the former Ashkenazi Chief Rabbi of Israel, explains the basis of the Rambam's stance: apart from the prohibition of homicide, there is an obligation to preserve fetal life.[54] Novak grounds this specific obligation upon the general prohibition of destructiveness (*bal tashḥit*), much as Philo points up the value in question by calling the human foetus the fairest of nature's artistic

---

Kellner, ed., *Contemporary Jewish Ethics* (New York: Sanhedrin, 1978), p. 267, n. 7.

[51] See David Novak, *Law and Theology in Judaism* (New York: Ktav, 1974), p. 118; cf. R. Moses Schick, Responsa Maharam Schick, Yoreh Deah, 155; R. David Hoffman, *Responsa Melamed Leho'il, Yoreh Deah,* 69.

[52] See *Tos'fot Yom Tov* on >Ohalot 7:6.

[53] The commandment is grounded in Leviticus 19:16 and Deuteronomy 25:11-12.

[54] *Sheveṭ mi-y'hudah*, pp. 26 ff; cf. R. Nahum Rabinovitch, *Ha-darom*, XXVIII (5729), 19 f., cited in Bleich, p. 148.

creations, thus giving it a special precedence among the things one is forbidden to destroy. It is this value that explains the classic ruling (Shabat 151b) which permits violation of the Sabbath to save a foetus or enhance its chances of survival[55]: the human embryo enters the penumbra of personhood, although it is not a person. One may not arbitrarily or wantonly destroy it. As Novak explains, "This is why Maimonides emphasized that the fetus is 'like' a pursuer"[56] – not that it literally *is* an aggressor, with the deserts of a person that may be set aside because of an intentional threat, but because it has material deserts of its own, which approach those of personhood and ultimately reach those of personhood at the point of birth.

The commandment against destructiveness places the foetus on a scale of deserts with other living beings whose claims to life advance with their claims to being.[57] Rashi's sharp line, then, is between the realm of such relative claims and the absolute deserts of personhood. Some authorities, like Rabbi Yair Ḥayyim Bacharach (1638-1701),[58] derive the prohibition against fetal destruction from the prohibition against wasting the male seed. But the argument is a weak one, since it assimilates abortion to the realm of birth control and was criticized powerfully on those grounds by Rabbi Unterman. Rabbi Bacharach, known for his general opposition to casuistry, struck closer to the Torah's theme when he related the law on foeticide to the biblical pro-natalism by citing Isaiah: "He created it not a waste but formed it to be inhabited" (45:18). Yet pro-natalism alone and the general commandment to be fruitful and multiply again are too weak to govern here. For it is not the case that one who has fulfilled his obligation to be fruitful may abort his offspring arbitrarily. Nor may one, say, conceive offspring and abort them for the purpose of using fetal brain tissue in the therapy of Parkinson's or Alzheimer's disease, or in any medical research, no matter how many lives might potentially be saved. Here the life of the foetus becomes "more proximate."

---

[55] Naḥmanides, *Torat Ha->Adam,* ed. B. Chavel, 2, 29; and on Nidah 44b.
[56] See R. Ezekiel Landau of Prague (1713-1973), *Nod<a biy'hudah,* II (Vilna, 1904), *Ḥoshen Mishpaṭ* 59 and Heller, *Tos'fot Yom Toṽ* to Nidah, as cited in Novak, *Law and Theology,* p. 119.
[57] Cf. Spinoza's language about the claims beings make upon existence, *Ethics* I, Prop 11, Scholium: "Nam cum posse existere potentia sit, sequitur, quo plus realitatis alicuius rei naturae competit, eo plus virium a se habere, ut existat": "For since it is a power to be able to exist, it follows that the more reality pertains to the nature of a thing, the more powers it has to exist of itself."
[58] *Ḥavot Ya>ir,* 31; cf. *Z'khuta> de>Aṽraham,* cited in *Ḥemdat Yiśra>el*; and *Responsa <Aṭeret Ḥakhamim, >Eṽen Ha-<ezer,* 1, R. Jacob Emden, *Responsa Sh'>elat Yaṽeẓ,* 1, 43.

We are brought back inexorably to the entitative claims of the foetus, spoken for by the command against wanton destruction, and to the recognition that fetal claims are ontically grounded, as are the more absolute claims of personhood. The claims of the foetus become increasingly more like the claims of personhood as the foetus matures. Thus Maimonides' reliance on the case-narrowing appeal to the *rodef*, for the foetus is like a *rodef* inasmuch as the foetus has entitative deserts that must be set aside before we can act against it even in defense of human life. Specifically, with a *rodef* we must scale our response to the imminence of the danger and block a blow or cut off a hand if we must and can, before we may place even an aggressor's life at risk (Sanhedrin 72b-73a). And if the danger is brought about unintentionally, say, if the *rodef* is a mere human missile or somnambulist, we may cause that person no harm, because we may not sacrifice one (innocent) person's life to save another. Symmetrically, the foetus which is like a *rodef* makes claims to life that are not yet absolute. So when it threatens maternal life its claims are overthrown. But only a grave threat could outweigh the entitative claim it does make – not because we seek to populate the earth but because a human life is precious, and a human foetus situates itself upon and advances along the continuum that divides human personhood from everything that it is not.

It follows that Philo, the Septuagint and the Mishnah are justified in assigning lesser deserts to the foetus in the early stages of pregnancy and progressively greater deserts in the later stages, based on the phases of the formation of the foetus and the occurrence of "quickening." Human deserts do emerge *pari passu* with the entitative claims of the foetus as an organism, and we can understand Philo's explanation of the rule he found in the Septuagint, that a perfectly formed foetus is not to be distinguished in principle from a newborn infant.[59] The Jewish norms do not ignore but seek to protect the human virtuality of the human foetus. In its characteristically fabular idiom, the Zohar vividly explicates what is at stake, in language that all but echoes Philo's: "One who kills the foetus in his wife's womb desecrates what was built by the Holy One and mars His craftsmanship." The ethos of Israel, the Zohar argues in effect, is to respect that craftsmanship, which is in fact the human image. When Pharaoh decreed, "everyone that is born shall ye cast into the Nile" (Exodus 1:22), "not a single Israelite was found who would kill the foetus in the womb – let alone the newborn after birth. It was through this merit," the Zohar urges, "that Israel went forth from

---

[59] See Shabat 135b, treating Numbers 18:16.

bondage."⁶⁰ Here >agadah underscores the values that ground the halakhah: at every stage of embryogenesis there are real deserts; we must dismiss the rhetorical claim that the foetus is just the exuviae of the mother with the same rigor that we must dismiss the equally rhetorical claim that abortion at any stage is tantamount to murder. The Talmud artfully grounds the virtuality to be protected in a midrashic glossing of the biblical text to yield the thesis that, while a foetus is not a man, it is a virtual man, "a man within a man."⁶¹

Maimonides accordingly sets his authority and the sentence of his Code behind a strict reading of the mishnaic permission – or rather, mandate, for the authorities are in clear agreement that, when a foetus threatens its mother's life, abortion is not optional but required; when there is no such threat, the requirement to preserve the foetus prohibits abortion. The subsequent authorities follow, differing only as to the seriousness of the threat that would justify a decision to abort. Rabbi Hayyim Soloveichik (d. 1918), for example, read the Mishnah as restricting abortion to cases of an imminent and direct threat to maternal life.⁶² Rabbi Israel Mizrahi in the nineteenth century, following Nahmanides' treatment of insanity as a threat to life, allows abortion to prevent mental illness.⁶³ Rabbi Joseph Trani (1568-1639) permits abortions to preserve maternal health, rather than only life itself.⁶⁴ Rabbi Jacob Emden (1697-1776) sanctions abortions even up to the onset of labor (fetal "disengagement") to end severe pain or (by the hand of the mother) to prevent the grave stigma of biblical bastardy resulting from adulterous or incestuous unions.⁶⁵ We can see an analogy here to the permissions widely discussed today for cases of rape and incest, although the analogy is not drawn by Rabbi Immanuel Jakobovits.⁶⁶

---

⁶⁰*Zohar*, Exodus (Warsaw), 3b.
⁶¹See Sanhedrin 57b, glossing Genesis 9:6; cf. *Sifra>* to Leviticus 12:3.
⁶²*Hidushé R. Hayyim Levi* (1936) to Maimonides, *Code, Hilkhot Rozeah*,1.9. See the discussion in Feldman, p. 279.
⁶³*Pri Ha->Arez*, III (1899), cited in Bleich, p. 158; Feldman, p. 286.
⁶⁴*T'shuvot Maharit*, 1, no 99. As Bleich points out (p. 153), Joseph Trani, the Maharit, regards abortion as a form of "wounding," therefore justifiable, like surgery, for the sake of maternal health. But fetal interests are still not overridden *ad libitum*.
⁶⁵*Sh'>elat Yavez* (New York, 1961), no. 43, and Bleich, pp. 152, 159. Rabbi Emden's rulings on these two points are widely disputed by other halakhists. Notably, he remarks *ad* Tosafot Nidah 44b: "Who is it that permits the killing of a foetus without reason?"
⁶⁶See *Jewish Monthly*, August-September, 1989, p. 21.

Rabbi Judah Ayash (d. 1760) and others even allow abortions to preserve the life of a nursing sib.[67] The background for this ruling: Rabbi Ḥisda (Y'vamot 69b), in a context not directly related to abortion, treats the human embryo up to forty days as "mere water"; and the Mishnah (Nidah 30a) does not discover the impurity of childbirth prior to that term. In specific, talmudically enumerated cases, Rabbi Meir Dan Plocki (1867-1927) allows a woman's use of an abortifacient pessary in the first forty days of pregnancy, for the Talmud (Y'vamot 12b) allows the use of a contraceptive pessary by pubescent wives, pregnant women and nursing mothers. If there is "mere water" for forty days after conception, Rabbi Plocki reasons, abortion during that period is not to be more restricted than contraception. He treats the two as equivalent – as was typical in the secular culture in recent years in descriptions of intrauterine devices for birth control. Rabbi Eliezer Yehudah Waldenberg extends the period of permission and broadens the acceptable grounds to include evidence that a deformed or abnormal child might be born, but few Orthodox rabbis concur with him.[68]

The highly conditional character of all these rulings and the varied but real gravity of the threats they address clearly reflect the impact of Maimonides' principle, which, as we have seen, is grounded in a biblical and Rabbinic reverence for the emergent life and imminent personhood of the human foetus. While there are disagreements among the authorities as to the exact conditions which may warrant abortion, these are in many ways matters of detail, comparable to the slight differences among the talmudic Rabbis as to whether the exact point at which the newborn emerges into the open air is when the head or the main body mass or any part breaches the birth canal.[69] The normative ethos and the judgment of the tradition are, thematically speaking, remarkably stable over the ages and remarkably consistent across the diverse shadings of opinion and constituency. Indeed, the issue of abortion is one on which we can see the roots of a genuine Judaic-

---

[67]*T'shuvot Bét Y'hudah* (Livorno, 1758); Rabbi Z. Uziel, *Responsa Mishp'ṭé Uziel*, p. 5. 3, 46-47; *Responsa Bét Y'hudah, >Even Ha-<Ezer, 13; Sh'e>lot Yiẓḥaq*, 69; *Ẓiẓ Eliezer*, IX, 51:3; see Bleich, p. 139, Rosner, p. 265.

[68]*Ẓiẓ Eliezer*, IX (1967), 236, 13 no. 102. That the permission involved a prospective Tay-Sachs birth indicates the gravity of the justifying fetal abnormality and the certitude of the prognosis required to move a rabbinic jurist on this point: Tay-Sachs disease can be detected *in utero* and is invariably and agonizingly fatal in infancy. For the problems of mass screening for Tay-Sachs carrier status, see M. J. Goodman and L. E. Goodman, "The Overselling of Genetic Anxiety," in *Hastings Center Report* (October, 1982), pp. 20-27, and F. Rosner, in Rosner and Bleich, pp. 177-90. For R. Plocki's decision, see his *Ḥemdat* Yiśra>el (Pietrokow, 1927).

[69]See Shabbat 14:4, <Avodah Zarah 2:2.

Christian[70] consensus or harmony of views. For one of the central issues on which ancient pagan authors criticized both Jews and Christians was their principled rejection of abortion and infanticide. Amongst the Rabbis, the Noahidic law against bloodshed was traditionally interpreted as prohibiting abortion and used in arguments *a fortiori* to show that abortion must be restricted for Jews as well, lest the Torah seem to permit what the universal laws of civilized humanity forbid.[71] Rabbi Bacharach argued explicitly that a common Judaeo-Christian morality can and should inform halakhic decisions in such areas as this,[72] and David Novak argues in our own days that the common moral commitment to humane and humanizing norms offers a valid starting place in common concerns for the ongoing dialogue between Christians and Jews.[73]

None of this settles the detailed and casuistical questions that bedevil today's abortion controversy. Any Solomonic resolution of such questions is rendered difficult by litigious behavior, ideological argument, and politicized debate. But the moral weight and moral concord of our tradition and the extent of its harmony with other moral and religious traditions should not be obscured by the insistent and increasingly shrill demands that surround the issue and tend to submerge both the niceties of bioethical detail and the broader issues of humane concern. As Novak remarks, fewer than one percent of the abortions performed in the United States today are for reasons of a direct threat to maternal life.[74] A high proportion are performed for convenience and on demand. Judaic values cry out against such excess: Rabbi David Feldman sums up their central theme: "Although it is warrantable under some circumstances, abortion... remains a last resort in the Jewish view... Potential life has the sanctity of its potential – casual abortion is accordingly abhorrent...abortion for reasons such as 'population control' is repugnant to the Jewish mind. Abortion for economic reasons is also not admissible."[75] Rabbi Laura Geller similarly collates the sources and the values they articulate:

---

[70]Among the key early Christian texts, *Didache,* 2:2, treats the prohibition of abortion as a corollary of "Love thy neighbor as thyself," and 5:2 speaks in Rabbinic style, of abortion as destroying the image of God; cf. Epistle of Barnabas 19:5, 20:2, *Apostolic Constitutions* 7.3.2.
[71]Sanhedrin 57b.
[72]*Havot Ya>ir* (Lemberg, 1869) 31; cf. Qidushin 12b, Soṭah 47b, Genesis Rabah, LI, 1.
[73]*Jewish-Christian Dialogue* (New York: Oxford University Press, 1989), pp. 9-11.
[74]*The Jewish-Lifecycle* (New York: Jewish Theological Seminary, forthcoming).
[75]David Feldman in *Jewish Monthly*, August-September, 1989, p. 23.

1. In the case of a conflict between maternal and fetal life, the mother's life must take precedence.
2. Abortion is not murder, but it is a serious loss.
3. There can be no casual use of abortion as implied by the rhetoric of "abortion on demand."
4. The notion that a woman has a right to control her own body is not acceptable; no one has the right to harm himself/herself or to commit suicide. Issues of life and death are in God's hands, not ours.[76]

In the same spirit, Rabbi David Novak reads the prohibition against destructiveness (*bal tashḥit*) in the light of its special case, the prohibition against self-mutilation – so that, even if the foetus is simply a part of the mother's body, no blanket permission of abortion is entailed.[77]

The entitative claims of the foetus are not diminished by its dependence on the mother. If that were possible, all human beings would be vulnerable in the same way, for we are all dependent on one another. The presumptive deserts of the foetus are powerful and positive. In the Judaic sources, as in nature, they are scaled[78] to its ontic standing, from "mere water" to the onset of labor, and are suspended, prior to birth, virtually never, unless the presence of the foetus represents a clear threat to maternal welfare. Formalizing the moral concerns, as is the function of law, halakhah draws a sharp line: Once the birth canal is breached, any threat must be ascribed to God – heaven is now the pursuer, as the Talmud (Sanhedrin 72b) expresses it. That is, as Maimonides explains, the danger confronted now is part of the course of nature, a risk that must be borne, since no human being has the right to place one human life before another.

The central impact of the Rambam's resort to the theory of pursuit, then, comes in the fact that the Law's treatment of the foetus as less than a full person does not set its deserts at nullity. If the claims of the foetus can be recognized without threat to the mother's life, those claims are to be met. Thus the nuance drawn from Maimonides' text by Rabbi Isaac Schorr (d. 1776): when Maimonides specifies that the threatening foetus may be eliminated by drugs or surgery, the indication is that phased measures are to be used, with preference given to the least violent and violative – the same phased approach that is applied in the case of a *rodef*: deadly force may not be used where lesser measures would suffice.

---

[76]Laura Geller in *Jewish Monthly*, August-September, 1989, p. 25.
[77]*The Jewish Lifecycle.*
[78]Cf. G. R. Dunstan, *The Artifice of Ethics* (London: SCM, 1974), p. 53.

Rabbi Ḥayyim Soloveichik caps the discussion by explaining that it is not the principle of saving human lives (for which the laws of the Torah may be set aside almost *en bloc*) that determines the Mishnah in favor of abortion to save a mother's life. For that principle (*piquaḥ nefesh*), he argues, might have been pleaded in behalf of the foetus. Rather, it is the fact that the foetus is the aggressor that renders its life forfeit.[79] Soloveichik here overstates the case somewhat, since the foetus is not literally a person (*nefesh*) in Jewish law and does not enjoy the full protections of a person. But the presumption in favor of the entitative deserts of the foetus and the need for a clear danger if those deserts are to be overthrown are the values that Soloveichik, like the Mishnah itself, underscores. One need not assign full personhood to the foetus to recognize the force of Soloveichik's argument. For a *rodef* need not be a person or a moral agent. Even excess baggage on a ship can pose the same threat. Property rights in a life-threatening emergency literally go by the board.[80] The same (entitative, conative) considerations that give a foetus deserts deny it those deserts when their fulfillment would destroy those of another. But it is not the case that the foetus has no deserts. It has the powerful deserts of its virtuality as a human being, undercut in rare cases by the threat it represents to its mother. Were it not human, its claims would be nugatory. Were it not a threat, they would be the near equal of any other human claims.

Throughout the Jewish discussion we see the signature of the Rambam in the assignment of narrow grounds for warranting abortion and in the recognition of constitutive deserts on the part of the developing foetus. Maimonides' ruling is informed by the recognition that sacred work is underway when lifeless matter is making its way toward the air in which it will have thought and life. But it is not the case that the Rambam simply "reads into" the ancient canonical texts the findings of the science of his day or the opinions of his philosophy. On the contrary, that science and the philosophy that interprets it only heighten his sensitivity to the values bespoken by the biblical and rabbinic texts. Rather than competing with the revealed law, these pronouncements of reason complement and inform it. They allow coherence to emerge from the dialectic of the sources and a single,

---

[79] Responsa *Koaḥ Shor,* no. 20, and *Ḥidushé R. Ḥayyim HaLevi* (1936) to Maimonides' *Code,* both discussed in Feldman, pp. 277, 279.
[80] See Maimonides, *Code, Ḥoẕel Umaziq,* 8.15, and *Migdal <Oz, ad loc.* Maimonides points out that the property damage in such a case is mandatory; cf. David Feldman, *Marital Relations, Birth Control and Abortion in Jewish Law* (New York: Schocken, 1975), p. 278, and for the *rodef,* Emanuel Rackman, "Violence and the Value of Life: the Halakhic View," in Baron et al., eds., *Violence and Self-Defense in the Jewish Experience,* pp. 124-25, 129.

powerful theme to stand forth as the underlying message of the canon and the ethical nerve of the culture it informs: the theme of the value and sanctity of all that pertains to human life, even the human virtuality.

The Rabbinic discussion of abortion does not hinge upon theories of ensoulment and so does not seek an instant where the biblical right to life springs from nullity to absoluteness. Rather, with the gradual emergence of form in the "shapeless mass" of which the psalmist speaks (139:16), the developing foetus moves toward the shores of life and gradually acquires heightened moral standing. *De facto*, full moral personhood is not acquired until well after birth. Some of us may never acquire it. But even prior to the emergence of a real moral person, the Law extends the dignity of humanity, out of deference to what will be, spreading its protections to life and limb ("it may not be touched") up to the portals of light and, even prior to that point, recognizing gradually emergent, distinctively human[81] deserts.

In recent years strong claims have been made in many quarters for an absolute maternal right of abortion. A. J. Ayer, who in other contexts denied the very meaning of such concepts as rights, urged that every pregnant woman has an inalienable right to an abortion. James Gustafson, eloquently pleading the case of a hypothetical victim of sexual abuse and social neglect, successfully extracts from many the concession that the social and psychic impact of an unwanted pregnancy may loom with such enormity that we must extend the permission of abortion beyond the realm of a direct threat to the mother's life.[82] Others have argued that a foetus (being dependent) is and remains an appendage, to be removed at the discretion of the mother, with no more compunction than a diseased body part or (some have said) one's own excrement – and no more legitimate sphere of social concern or legal intervention. In some quarters more passion is expended in behalf of animal entitlements, the life of trees, the inviolability of inanimate objects or artifacts, than is conceded to the deserts of the unborn. This imbalance is no mere anomaly but a symptom of the values and the ethos that claim allegiance and attention in our age and culture.

In the rhetoric surrounding the abortion controversy, which has not abated but continued since Roe vs. Wade (1973) and grown more fierce since Webster vs. Reproductive Health Services (1989), the notion of an

---

[81]Cf. Paul Ramsey, *The Ethics of Fetal Research* (New Haven: Yale University Press, 1975).
[82]In J. Noonan, ed., *The Morality of Abortion* (Cambridge: Harvard University Press, 1972), p. 107.

unwanted child has been conflated with that of an unplanned pregnancy, and the tragic but sometimes overpowering necessity of what is paradoxically called therapeutic abortion has been muddled with disease prevention, social disability prevention, and even infanticide.[83] The powerful claims that urge restraint in the area of abortion are met with rhetorical and dialectical arguments about one's body as one's property or about the hazards of unlawful abortions. Such arguments have been applied in political practice to justify literally millions of abortions of healthy but unplanned embryos, whose deserts, in these pragmatic arguments and in the laws and rulings they have fostered, are set at nil and in general unrepresented. There have been well over twenty-five million abortions in the United States since the Roe vs. Wade decision of 1973. Today in major cities the rate of abortions now exceeds the live birth rate.[84] Recollection of the ontic standing of the foetus and its placement – if not as a person, then as a miracle – is a clear desideratum.

---

[83]See L. E. Goodman and M. J. Goodman, "Prevention," in *Hastings Center Report* 16 (1986), esp. pp. 31-32.

[84]In 1985, the most recent year for which we have thorough statistics, there were some 1.6 million abortions in the United States, a typical number for recent years. Some 3 percent of the women of reproductive age annually have been obtaining abortions. Nearly 30 percent of the pregnancies that did not end with stillbirths or miscarriages were terminated artificially. In metropolitan areas there have been over 1,500 abortions per 1,000 live births annually since 1980. The annual number of abortions in metropolitan areas has exceeded that of live births since 1976. Note, however, that few abortions are performed in non-metropolitan areas, since most abortion services are metropolitan. See S.K. Henshaw et al., "Abortion Services in the United States, 1984 and 1985," in *Family Planning Perspectives*, XIX (March-April 1987), 63-70.

13

Flexibility in Halakhah: Jewish Authorities at Work – Former Days

By Edward Zipperstein

This article will focus upon the thought, approach, methodology and guidelines to halakhic issues of a few leading rabbinic authorities from the Middle Ages up to modern times. What is especially intriguing is the halakhic flexibility to be found in their rulings.

Jacob ben Meir, known as Rabbenu Tam (1100-1171), was a French tosafist, grandson of Rashi and brother of Samuel ben Meir (Rashbam). He was widely recognized as a great talmudic authority by the Jews of Western and Central Europe. Queries were directed to him from all countries in which Jews resided. His decisions were deemed binding and accepted as Jewish law. His home at Ramerupt was destroyed by Crusaders in 1147, and he was barely saved from death. Rabbenu Tam settled in Troyes, where in 1160 a conference of rabbis convened under his leadership. Other such synods assembled at which ordinances, Jewish law and *taqanot* were established under his authority. The leading rabbinic figure of twelfth-century Ashkenazic Jewry, he was a gifted intellectual who made use of logic and creative abilities. His decisions were lenient in issues of economics and in non-Jewish associations. He insisted on adhering to established custom in most instances.[1]

Rabbenu Tam also attempted to follow the decisions of the rabbinic authorities of prior generations. He understood well the essential need for continuity in Jewish law and tradition. He was confronted with various and diverse problems, many unique to his era. It must be noted that scholars may differ in methodology, in factors utilized, in

---

[1] Fred P. Kanarfogel, "R. Jacob Tam: The Man and His Activities in Light of Modern Historiography" (unpublished Master's thesis, Bernard Revel Graduate School, June 1977), p. 1.

conditions regarded, and may differ as to interpretation of source material. Another problem was errors existing in the available written texts; these errors required correction. The educational background of the particular scholar had a bearing upon his rendering a decision. The methodology of Talmud study altered during the period of the Crusades. The transmission of Jewish law, learning and tradition had heretofore been accomplished by oral and verbal means, in which memory was utilized to its utmost. Centers of Jewish learning were demolished by the Crusaders. This necessitated scholarship to seek texts and written data from prior times. Rashi, the grandfather of Rabbenu Tam, was the outstanding scholar of this period. Perhaps one of the elements of his success was his ability to take written notes meticulously from the lectures of his teachers.[2] Note taking may have been the secret of Rashi's success.

When talmudic law varied from actual practice, Rabbenu Tam would not accept the explanation that, since conditions had changed, so the law also changed. His approach was that the same law applied in the talmudic and medieval periods, and rather than initiating a new law, the case involved the concept of custom.[3] A case in point is dealing with non-Jews on their holidays. It had been the practice to prohibit conducting business with non-Jews for three days prior to their holidays (m. <Aᵛodah Zarah 1:1). The rationale was that the non-Jew would extend appreciation to his god, and the Jew involved in the transaction would be thereby accountable for idol worship. During the Amoraic age, Samuel had limited the prohibition to only one day, due to the difficulty in its enforcement. By the Middle Ages this law was no longer in force, since the non-Jews were not engaged in idol worship. Rabbenu Tam maintained that the prohibiting mishnah referred only to the selling of religious items to be used in idol worship.[4] Rabbenu Tam upheld a custom by which a non-Jew's touching of wine rendered it forbidden for the Jew to drink, yet the Jew was permitted to benefit from the wine. Economic loss or hardship was a viable rationale for customs since the growing of grapes, viticulture, was a prime source of income resulting from contact with non-Jews. Rabbenu Tam permitted a non-Jewish laborer to work on the Sabbath during the period of a contract and contended that his position was based on Talmud interpretation. The case involved a potentially severe monetary loss. Thus, social conditions and potential monetary loss were factors considered in the halahkah and in establishing customs. Rabbenu Tam maintained that

---

[2]*Ibid.*, p. 2.
[3]*Ibid.*, p. 13.
[4]*Ibid.*, p. 14.

talmudic law is not subject to change. The non-Jews of his era were not the idolaters in whose wine Jews of the talmudic period had been forbidden to trade, but his method was to reinterpret the basic text, the talmudic source material.

In addition to existing conditions, another factor in halakhic decisions is the secular law precedents, the recognized legal principles in non-Jewish courts. The halakhic authority is concerned with the needs of his generation. The Talmud prohibited commercial dealings during the intermediate days of a festival (ḥol ha-mo‹ed) unless the merchandise was perishable, resulting in a monetary loss. Rabbenu Tam ruled that moneylending was excluded from the prohibition. It appears that he was lenient in rendering decisions in which an economic loss was at stake.[5]

The noted rabbi, a leading tosafist, analyzed, commented, clarified and applied talmudic law. Similar to the Amoraim who analyzed the opinions of the Tannaim, so the tosafists were concerned with apparent contradictions and varying ideas in the Talmud. Their queries and replies were similar to those of the Amoraim, and their task was in essence a continuation of the talmudic method. It should be noted that the word continuity is a vital and most important concept in Jewish tradition and halakhah, which implies an unchangeable Jewish law from Sinai to the present day. This continuous process, not subject to change, requires clarification, elucidation, commentary and application. The tosafists confronted the Jewish legal issues of their era and submitted far reaching decisions which influenced Jewish life and institutions in the Middle Ages and up to our own times.

The following case is an example of leniency as ruled by Rabbenu Tam based upon interpretation. The Mishnah (Y'vamot 16:3) states that, to identify a corpse for the purpose of freeing an ‹agunah (a woman whose husband's death is suspected, but remains unproven and in consequence she is not permitted to remarry), the nose was needed even if there were other signs on the body that the corpse was the deceased husband. Rabbenu Tam ruled that the nose must be complete only if the head alone is found. However, if the body is otherwise intact, the nose is not needed.[6]

Rabbenu Tam was concerned lest a burden be inflicted on the community. He considered factors such as potential physical harm or damage, monetary loss, undue burden, hardship and economic stability. It was the scholar's task to safeguard the religious practice of the community and not to overburden the people with undue trifles and

---

[5]*Ibid.*, p. 17.
[6]*Ibid.*, p. 20.

ordinances, particularly if the community will not abide by the edict. It must be emphasized that not only Rabbenu Tam but all recognized rabbinic authorities in rendering decisions, lenient or otherwise, base such conclusions on legal principles and submit proofs and rational arguments for positions they advance. On occasion, other authorities may disagree and offer their own outlook, analysis and conclusion regarding a particular issue. The maintenance, welfare, peace and continuity of the Jewish community will be utmost factors in the deliberations, lengthy at times. Unique and special circumstances have been factors in deliberations as has hesitancy to alter heretofore accepted practice. However, when required, such practice has been revised and established custom has become law. An example is a prevalent custom during the time of Rabbenu Tam of including a minor in a prayer quorum (*minyan*) if he held a Bible in his hand. The rabbi considered such a custom absurd on the grounds that a Bible does not make a person. He contended that he never would change community order; where customs were contrary to Jewish law, he acted with deliberation and tact in amending them. He opposed widespread leniency and yet sought leniency within the text interpretation and application and considered possible loopholes. The authorities did not seek the negation of customs because other scholars valued and abided by them. There was no desire to divide a community on the issue of altering customs, which had a force similar to law. In any event, customs were not worth fighting over, and so they prevailed except in isolated pressing instances. Rabbenu Tam upheld custom on the rationale that it is a legacy of an earlier generation and part of Judaic tradition.[7]

Rabbenu Tam viewed the community not as an entity in and of itself, but a collectivity of individuals united for mutual benefit recognizing personal rights. Accordingly, he ruled that the members of the community should not be forced to donate charity. This position appears contrary to a talmudic statement which reports that Raba forced Rabbi Nathan to give charity (Baba> Batra> 8b), indicating that one can and should be forced to give charity. Rabbenu Tam interpreted the talmudic passage to mean that only verbal coercion was utilized. The talmudic statement would apply in a situation where the community agreed unanimously that the charity collector be endowed with the power to force individuals to contribute. A guiding principle was that the rights of the individual were to be protected, the

---

[7]*Ibid.*, p. 28.

individual's civil, property, monetary, religious, personal, domestic and legal rights.[8]

Rabbenu Tam possessed great intellectual ability, tremendous knowledge and learning and was endowed with a logical mind. These are attributes required for a rabbinic authority of note. Upon encountering two contradictory sources, or when a talmudic law was in conflict with custom, Rabbenu Tam hesitated to favor one over the other. He would rather, upon analysis, deliberation and logic, posit the two sources as compatible. His approach was to indicate that solutions to current issues were vested in earlier sources. He was a mentor to countless students in his generation and to scholars in succeeding periods who followed his methodology and logic. He is considered one of the great authorities of the halakhah.

Another outstanding European rabbinic scholar during the Middle Ages was Asher ben Yehiel, known as Rosh (1250-1327), a codifier and talmudist, who had been born in Germany and died in Toledo, Spain. His teacher was the noted Rabbi Meir of Rothenburg. The Rosh was one of the foremost leaders of German Jewry in his generation. In 1303, after experiencing riots and persecution, he left Germany and in 1305 assumed a rabbinical position in Toledo, where he established a widely known rabbinical academy. He was regarded as the most prominent rabbi in Spain after the death of Solomon ibn Adret of Barcelona. The Rosh, although he did not initiate it, agreed to a ban on secular studies below the age of twenty-five, a ban which subjected transgressors to ostracism. Jewish studies and study of medicine were permitted. The ban was focussed particularly on the study of philosophy. He did allow the pursuit of astronomy as an aid to talmudic understanding.

Joseph Caro, the famed author of the Shulḥan ῾Arukh, based his code upon three authorities: Alfasi, Maimonides, and the Rosh. The latter maintained that new opinions had to be based on the Talmud. Without a source in the Talmud, he contended, he may disagree with other authorities. He placed major emphasis upon the study of Talmud, primarily the halakhic aspects and only secondarily the aggadic portions.[9] The Rosh issued laws regarding civil and marriage matters and was concerned with the administration of justice. He was watchful that the rabbis refrain from overextending their authority for personal gain and power. The Jewish court, by virtue of Spanish law, was empowered to inflict fines and punishment.[10] The Rosh approved the

---

[8]*Ibid.*, p. 29.
[9]Richard H. Viener, "The Life and Works of Asher ben Yehiel" (unpublished Master's thesis, Bernard Revel Graduate School, June 1964), p. 28.
[10]*Ibid.*, p. 30.

death penalty for informers who placed Jewish communities in jeopardy, though it is doubtful whether such sentences were ever carried out. He was extremely careful in rendering legal decisions which were clear and lucid. All manner of problems and cases were directed to the Rosh from far off Jewish communities. He abolished the practice, prevailing among Spanish Jews, of placing a debtor in chains. In his era, the prevailing custom was to refrain from writing during the intermediary days of a festival. He, however, would reply immediately to queries received, and it has been reported that he would write during the intermediary days, so as to reply promptly.

It indeed was remarkable that the Rosh, born, raised, and educated in >Ashk'naz and an exponent of the Ashkenazic customs of Germany and France, should become the chief rabbi in Spain. Thus, even though the Rosh disagreed with many of the prevailing Sefardic customs, he refrained from opposing them outright, for the sake of maintaining peace, a most important concept in Jewish law.[11] However, in matters of absolute halakhah, in which a thorough knowledge of Talmud was essential and in which he was a recognized expert, his opinions would prevail. He maintained, and no doubt rightfully so, that the more learned rabbis were those from Germany in contrast to those of Spain. The Spanish rabbis who studied the Talmud were familiar with Alfasi and Maimonides, the two Sefardic scholars, but not with the voluminous writings of German and French scholars. The name of Rabbenu Gershom was practically unknown among Spanish Jews. Although the Rosh took issue with Maimonides for not stating sources, he would abide by the opinions of Maimonides. It was the custom in Spain to engage for synagogues a cantor with a pleasing voice rather that one noted for piety. The Rosh opposed this practice. He attempted to justify customs which were not completely acceptable on the rationale of preventing the community from erring. In one case, he approved a decision to have the face of a harlot disfigured, thus inflicting corporal punishment. The woman had had relations with a non-Jew, and the incident had brought shame to the community. The punishment was to serve as a warning and act as a deterring factor.[12] In his opposition to philosophy, the Rosh contended that it is based on critical research whereas religion rests on tradition and, as such, the two are not compatible. He wrote that none who go to philosophy may return, and so he feared and opposed its study.[13]

---

[11]*Ibid.*, p. 34.
[12]*Ibid.*, p. 31.
[13]*Ibid.*, p. 38.

In his greatness, the Rosh maintained that, if a law is not clearly stated in the Talmud, we need not follow the decisions of authorities, even those of the G'>onim. This should not be accepted as a lenient or liberal position. The burden is thrust upon the *poseq* to exert himself, his talents, his intellect, to deal with problems as they arise. The responsibility is that much greater. The Rosh migrated from Germany amidst an atmosphere which emphasized talmudic studies to the exclusion of secular studies. Spain, however, was a place of intellectual, scientific and secular pursuits, the land of Maimonides. The Rosh did not speak Arabic, the language of Spain, nor was he interested in learning the language. Yet, he brought talmudic methodology to Spain. His work has become so popular that it is included in most editions of the Talmud.

Rabbi Moses Isserles, known as Rama (ca.1530-1572), systematized the German-Polish halakhic decisions and customs. His *Mapah* (tablecloth) was included with the Shulḥan <Arukh of Joseph Caro, thus combining the Ashkenazic together with Caro's Sefardic portion in one complete code, which is and has been a source and authority of Jewish law. Isserles served as rabbi in Cracow, where he founded a yeshivah and became recognized as a *poseq* among the Jewish communities. He became a member of the important *bét din* of the city. Jews were at that time permitted to live according to their Judaic laws and teachings. The Rama attained a reputation as an expert scholar and was known as a man of humility, yet courageous amidst criticism for some of his decisions. In one case, Isserles performed a wedding ceremony on Friday evening after sunset, contrary to prevailing practice. His action brought criticism and resulted in a *taqanah* in Cracow prohibiting wedding ceremonies on Fridays. In the event it was determined necessary to perform the wedding on Friday, then the ceremony was to take place outside the gates of the city.[14] In another instance, he maintained a lenient position in a case regarding non-Jewish wine. He hesitated issuing prohibitions in new matters, not heretofore adjudicated. He also rendered a lenient decision as to the inspection of the lungs of a slaughtered animal, a decision which is not accepted by Sefardim. It appears that, to be lenient, one must be a highly recognized, courageous scholar and be able to disregard criticism. It is easy to render harsh decisions, whereas a lenient decision requires keen insight, intense scholarship, great erudition, logical analysis and application. It must not be assumed that Isserles was lenient in all instances. Each case was considered on its own merits. When firmness was required, he so ruled. The principle of monetary loss is a basic

---

[14]Asher Seiv, "The Rama," *Tradition*, II (Fall 1959), 135.

consideration; all items are to be evaluated. Proper respect for the Sabbath is another factor leading to lenient decisions. The Rama had deep feeling toward people and was minded to dispense kindness, concern and love toward humanity. The character and personality of the judge has a bearing upon the outcome of a particular case.[15]

Isserles insisted that *minhag*, custom, be followed and considered it equal to halakhah, even lacking a halakhic source. He also accepted custom as having precedent over halakhah. In some instances where the custom was based on error, he still maintained that he did not possess the authority to abrogate it. Most of the customs he followed were initiated among Ashkenazic Jews. Opposition to him arose based upon the following reasons: one compiling a Jewish code of laws is obliged to decide by the majority rule. It was contended by the Rama's opponents that he tended to adopt a lenient view of the *Ri>shonim* (the earlier authorities) over the harsher view held by the *>Aḥaronim* (the later authorities). His customs, opponents complained, were those of Polish Jewry, but he ignored the customs of German Jewry. His opponents also argued that codes are harmful in that they result in neglect of the study of the basic source, the Talmud. The codes will be considered the authority and the public will not heed the rabbis. Since Isserles took issue with Caro, why should others not disagree with Isserles? Why should German Jewry follow Isserles since he did not give effect to their customs? It was charged that the code of Isserles is his own without association or consultation with other authorities. Other objections to Isserles have been enumerated. Notwithstanding the opposition, his pronouncements and rulings were and still are widely accepted as binding on Ashkenazic Jewry.

The Rama was also devoted to Qabbalah and wrote books on this topic. Many of the rabbinic scholars studied only halakhah and Judaic subjects. However, there were those, including the Rama, who pursued secular topics; he in particular studied and was well versed in history, mathematics, astronomy and philosophy. It was contended that the knowledge of such subjects was essential in arriving at a proper halakhic decision in some cases. Isserles was both a rationalist and a mystic and a zealous follower of the Rambam. He, the Rama, indeed, is one of the great figures in halakhah.[16]

Another rabbinic leader, a contemporary of Rabbi Moses Isserles, was Solomon ben Yehiel Luria (1510-1573), known as Maharshal. He was a scholar of note and as such was greatly respected, though his independent thinking and views created opposition. Luria (to be

---

[15]*Ibid.*
[16]*Ibid.*, p. 137.

distinguished from the like-named "Ari" of Safed) was a talmudic, halakhic authority and codifier. He took issue with the Shulḥan <Arukh, which was based on the works of codifiers, rather than utilizing the Talmud as the source for halakhah. He served as rabbi in Lithuanian and Polish communities. His method was one of logic and rationality and determining the correct meaning of the text. He, like all scholars, would devote the same due and proper attention to all cases, minor and major, more important and less important. In his analytic and critical approach to halakhah, the Maharshal would examine and scrutinize the halakhic material available, past and present, and the applicable talmudic sources. Luria dealt with cases of all types and from various countries, including Poland, Lithuania, Germany, Russia, Italy and Turkey. His main correspondent was his contemporary, Moses Isserles.

The Talmud has been and still is accepted as the basic authority of Jewish law. This principle was of prime concern to Luria, since in his era the authority of the Talmud had weakened. From the completion of the Talmud to Luria's own day the work had been constantly studied, taught, interpreted and applied. The vast majority of scholars were sincere, honest, dedicated and devoted to their task, but there were a few self-centered, unscrupulous scholars who misrendered the text for personal egotistic reasons. This must be differentiated from the process of honest rabbinic variances in analysis, application and interpretation, which may conclude with opposing results. The Maharshal undertook the task of taking issue with those scholars who distorted the talmudic texts for their own purposes. An earlier authority cannot prevail over a later one if, in fact, the earlier scholar is in error. This is what Luria confronted in his undertaking to reestablish the Talmud as an ultimate halakhic authority for scholars of all generations, including the Ri>shonim and the >Aḥaronim.

In addition to the above perplexing condition, the problem of errors by the hands of the scribes and errors accompanying the invention of the printing press were to be rectified. The proper and authentic text had to be determined. Luria's purpose was to correct the inaccurate texts, to establish the exact law and to bring stability to Jewish life by ascertaining the truth. This truth in essence is divine truth, which accounts for the urgency and necessity of such a pursuit. He opposed the scholars who deemed old manuscripts genuine and correct without proper authentication.[17] Luria accepted the authority of the Talmud; its laws were not subject to question. As to the G'>onim, Luria regarded

---

[17]Simon Hurwitz, *The Responsa of Solomon Luria (Maharshal)* (New York: Bloch Publishing Company, 1938), p. 6.

them on a high level of authority whose decisions were not to be questioned, but on a lower level than the talmudic Rabbis. He took issue with and questioned the authority or the veracity of many of the later rabbis. Legal opinions and rabbinic decisions lacking proper documentation as to sources utilized were criticized by Luria. Similarly, he opposed rendering decisions without legal argumentation.[18]

Luria praised Maimonides, the codifier of Jewish law and author of *Mishneh Torah*, as an outstanding rabbinic scholar, though he did not accept the code completely. One of the basic criticisms of the code is that it fails to specify sources. The Maharshal also contended that the Maimonidean code was not entirely correct and that it contained several errors in Jewish law. Luria also finds fault with and errors in the code of Joseph Caro, and detects errors in decisions of other recognized scholars. He deems it his duty to assert himself and to declare the truth in halakhah when and where the occasion arises. He does not maintain a status quo or precedent and will not hesitate to disagree with opinions of other contemporary or earlier rabbis in instances which are based on false or faulty interpretations or misreadings of talmudic texts. He was always available, ready and willing to acknowledge error on his own part, should the opposition prove fallacious reasoning or positions not in accord with the Talmud or with the early G'>onim. He articulates disparaging remarks regarding the halakhic decisors of his era, and charges them with lack of Judaic scholastic knowledge and learning. The state of affairs was such that the unscrupulous practicing rabbis were concerned only with their personal, egotistic self-interest and pursued procedures which would tend to maximize their fees.[19] Such a condition must not be tolerated, exceptionable as it may be in Jewish history. It is anticipated, and rightfully so, that the halakhic scholar, the *poseq*, will devote himself completely to study of the law. Attention must be devoted to his welfare and that of his family, yet not on a primary basis. He is not to be involved in amassing material resources or to pursue to excess worldly gratifications. In Luria's day, many rabbis were ordained, but only a few were learned and deserving of ordination. For due compensation those ordained committed all types of unethical practices. Under such circumstances, Luria abolished the prevailing Jewish law requiring the payment of a fine of a gold pound by one who insults a scholar. In the rare cases in which the fine was paid, rather than going to the rabbi who was presumably wronged, the gold pound was disbursed to the needy. It was Luria's resolve to rectify the deplorable conditions.

---

[18]*Ibid.*, p. 9.
[19]*Ibid.*, p. 15.

The Maharshal was antagonistic not only to many of the rabbis of his day but also to the practices of the people, the laity. The youth would attend dancing events on the Sabbath and on Jewish holidays, which would lead to moral offenses. Luria opposed the prevailing practice among some wealthy German Jews of drinking Gentile wine or eating fish prepared in Gentile pots and pans. Yet, these very people regarded as of prime import Judaic practices which in reality are not of a grave character, such as head attire. The importance of *kashrut* or of sabbath observance far exceeds that of covering the head. It is no surprise to learn that a rabbi like Luria, outspoken in his critical comments, may not win friends, but on the contrary may experience antagonism and acquire many enemies. Such was the case and Luria was forced to leave his rabbinic position.

During his generation, the *pilpul* was the prevalent method of studying the Talmud. Disputes, logic, argumentation and deductions were means of elucidating the Talmud. Such a methodology, leading to a positive concrete halakhic conclusion, was acceptable to Luria. However, he opposed such methods when carried to extremes without logical termination. He did not oppose *pilpul* as such, but viewed *pilpul* as of value when it entailed practical results. Here, too, Luria experienced harsh opposition. He urged that the *pilpul* method, if not limited and controlled, could result in mistakes and make for confusion in arriving at a correct position in the halakhah.[20] Luria's methodology of study was objective, logical and scientific. He would undertake a detailed search of all source material and gather data on the topic at hand from the scholars and trace the issue to the initial sources. All aspects of the law were considered and scrutinized, and an opinion was formulated which, in turn, was a subject of discussion among students and scholars. It can readily be determined that to arrive at a point of halakhah is not a simple matter. It involves an intensive pursuit and endless research. Luria failed to find value in the study of philosophy and differed from the position of Maimonides that philosophy is the entrance to wisdom, perfection and eternity. Nor had he any regard for Greek philosophy. He did embrace the Qabbalah, but urged that its study be restricted only to scholars. Luria was a superb authority on the Talmud and the halakhah and was widely acclaimed as such.[21]

The leader of Lithuanian Jewry in the eighteenth century was the famous Elijah Ga>on of Vilna (Rabbi Eliyahu ben Solomon Zalman, 1720-1797). In his day he was the foremost rabbinic authority and wrote several commentaries on the Torah and Talmud. Vilna at the

---

[20]*Ibid.*, pp. 20-21.
[21]*Ibid.*, pp. 22-23.

time was the center of talmudic studies in Eastern Europe. The Ga>on was knowledgeable not only in halakhah but also in Qabbalah, mathematics, geography, astronomy, geometry and algebra. He maintained that the sciences could only benefit Judaism and would inflict no harm on religion. He urged his students to acquire a liberal education and become well versed in secular subjects. The Ga>on contended that, if one fails to comprehend an item in the secular sciences, he will fail to understand one hundred items in Judaic law. The secular subjects were required to understand portions of Talmud.[22] The Ga>on was considered liberal in his views. He maintained that, technically, not wearing a head covering was not a sin even during prayer, but since well established custom requires a head covering, it should be done and custom must prevail. He encouraged the translation of books pertaining to natural sciences and Hebrew, but opposed the study of philosophy. He also opposed the *Haskalah* movement, and viewed it as a threat to Judaism. He is well known for his intense opposition to the Ḥasidic movement.[23] Yet, he was modern in encouraging the study of secular sciences. It was his opinion that all knowledge is necessary since it is all included in the Torah or Talmud. He urged that females must have some knowledge of the Bible, contrary to the then existing practice.[24]

Rabbi Isaac Elḥanan Spektor (1817-1896), of Kovno, was perhaps the most outstanding rabbi of his era, similar to Rabbi Eliyahu of Vilna in his day. Rabbi Isaac Elḥanan was a world-renowned halakhic expert, perhaps the foremost in his generation, and served the Kovno Jewish community as rabbi for some thirty years. He and all rabbinic authorities who expound Jewish law exhibit steadfast adherence to Torah in their decisions, yet practice leniency when special circumstances so require, within the area of proper halakhah. In a divorce case, where the specific and exact name of the woman being divorced is required, the instrument stated the name of Hasya, where the correct name was Hasha. The woman had remarried, and so the issue was whether or not halakhah required that the woman be divorced from her second husband.[25] Rabbi Isaac Elḥanan ruled that, considering the facts in this case the names of the husband and of his father are correctly stated, and since there is no woman by the name of Hasya in the community, it is well understood that the woman in

---

[22]"Elijah ben Solomon Zalman," *Encyclopaedia Judaica*, VI, 651.
[23]*Ibid.*, col. 652.
[24]*Ibid.*, col. 653.
[25]Ephraim Shimoff, *Rabbi Isaac Elchanan Spektor: Life and Letters* (Jerusalem and New York: Sura Institute for Research, Yeshiva University, 1969), p. 37.

question is the one being divorced. Thus, according to biblical law the initial divorce is proper, though Rabbinic law would require a divorce from the second husband.[26] Rabbi Isaac Elḥanan, however, decreed in this case that the woman should remain married to her second husband. The decision was based upon the rationale that to decide otherwise would cause suffering, anguish and pain to the innocent woman and her family. The error was that of the rabbi who dealt with the initial divorce; it was not the woman's fault and so a lenient view was pursued, though contrary to the position of some former authorities.[27] Thus, the deciding rabbi in the case at hand considered special circumstances and pursued a lenient conclusion, yet within the limits of proper, correct and accepted halakhah. It is more permissible to be lenient in matters of Rabbinic law than biblical law.

It should be noted that many (if not most) deans and heads of *y'shivot* do not participate in rendering halakhic decisions. They are devoted to and are masters of the study of Talmud. Their attention is directed to its study in depth, to its interpretation and penetration. Study of the earlier authorities is also pursued, but dwelling on the works of later rabbis is not the concern of many rabbinic scholars who do not engage in halakhic decisions. Authorities also differ on the nature of submitting responsa. Some may be brief, concise, without indicating rationale or sources upon which their decision is based. Others may render a detailed report of all aspects of the case, citing references, sources and authorities. As to the methodology of Rabbi Isaac Elḥanan, he utilized later authorities. He would determine if the particular issue at hand had been confronted by any of the halakhic experts. The Talmud, of course, remained the primary source of research; he was thoroughly familiar with its contents and the commentaries thereon. His responses were characterized by length, detail, analytic depth, logic, citation of source data and argumentation of all facets of the issue. He pursued novel talmudic interpretations and brought realistic considerations to bear on the issue. The classroom academy, the yeshivah, may be the locale for theoretical exposition and expounding of the Talmud. However, he never occupied the position of dean of a talmudic academy in the academic field. The problems he faced were practical, and as such he would dwell only upon matters pertinent to the case, would stress clarity and lucidity and would shy away from irrelevant data.[28]

---

[26]*Ibid.*
[27]*Ibid.*
[28]*Ibid.*, pp. 87-90.

Rabbi Isaac Elḥanan once rendered an interesting lenient brief decision which he desired to be kept private. In one particular case he allowed a woman whose life might be endangered by pregnancy to use contraceptives. Perhaps he did not wish to have this case of special circumstances utilized as a source justifying a general principle of permissiveness for such a practice.[29] A case arose regarding a man married for some ten years, without children, who desired to divorce his wife. She, however, refused to accept the divorce. The issue was whether or not the husband would be permitted to marry if he procured the consent of one hundred rabbis, in accord with halakhah. The decision rendered was in favor of the husband. The rationale was that the prohibition of polygamy instituted by Rabbi Gershom (960-1040) around the year 1000 was only for a definite period of time, whereas the requirement that a wife must give her consent to a divorce is not limited as to a specific time. Another reason submitted is that the rule against polygamy was not accepted by all Jewry, whereas the rule that consent of the wife is needed in a divorce action was widely accepted. So Rabbi Isaac Elḥanan ruled that the husband may marry another woman upon procuring permission from one hundred rabbis.[30]

Rabbi Isaac Elḥanan was deeply concerned with the <agunah, a serious and perplexing problem for halakhic experts. The rabbi, a person of concern for humanity in general, maintained an intense regard for the plight of the <agunah and attempted to alleviate her condition by rendering a liberal decision in her favor, while always remaining loyal to halakhic principles. He would pursue all avenues of approach to assist that unfortunate woman.[31] In one <agunah case, he permitted her to remarry, but insisted that two other competent rabbis, after reviewing the facts and all pertinent material, consent to his decision. Extenuating circumstances are factors to be reckoned with in arriving at a halakhic decision.

Rabbi Isaac Elḥanan also pursued lenient conclusions in issues of law regarding ritual matters. He also tended to be lenient in cases pertaining to Passover.[32] It must be understood that a rabbinic authority proceeds in his analysis of the issues in question with complete honesty and impartiality. It has been contended, and perhaps rightfully so, that it is easy to be strict in a case. However, to arrive at a lenient conclusion requires great scholarship, knowledge, investment of time, effort and talents of intellect with abilities in logical

---

[29]*Ibid.*, p. 92.
[30]*Ibid.*, pp. 92-93.
[31]*Ibid.*, pp. 93-95.
[32]*Ibid.*, p. 96.

analysis. It must not be concluded that Rabbi Isaac Elḥanan rendered only lenient opinions. Many are the cases in which stringent positions are self-evident. For example, he forbade non-Jews to be required to perform work on the Sabbath which is not biblically permitted, even though such work may be required for the fulfillment of a *miẓvah*. Similarly, in a case where non-Jews milked the cows, the issue was whether or not such milk may be used in making cheese. Even though some authorities permitted the practice, Rabbi Isaac Elḥanan prohibited it because of the possibility of mixing the milk with that of non-kosher animals.[33] As lenient as he was in <*agunah* cases, he did not admit missing teeth of a deceased man as proper evidence of death and insisted that only missing limbs be admitted as acceptable evidence.[34] No doubt contemporary technology would require the contrary decision today, and missing teeth, with available dental records, would be deemed sufficient evidence of death.

---

[33]*Ibid.*, p. 98.
[34]*Ibid.*, p. 99.

Part Three
THE MODERN WORLD

14

Translation and the Project of Culture: On Transferring Western Literature into Hebrew, 1893–1930 *

By William Cutter

This tribute to Professor Samson Levey is about the project of translation in >Ereẓ Yiśra>el. It deals with the role of Western literature in building the Jewish nation from its pre-settlement period in 1893 until 1930 when the literary culture matured. It is a subject well suited to the interests of Samson Levey, who has devoted so much of his academic career to interpretation and translation.

Professor Levey notes in his book on the Ezekiel Targum that philological problems in a text are solved only through an understanding of the historical context and its intellectual milieu, while the sensitive translator must understand as well the audience which the translated text is designed to address.

The titles of the sections of Professor Levey's introductions demonstrate that he attended to those major issues of translation. He understood the "task of the translator" in his treatment of the translation of a book deemed itself the translation of God's word. His sections on "framework" and "tradition" address the literary and historical context; his section "Son of Adam" is a philological statement clarifying the eighty-seven times God addresses the prophet; The Targum's "theology" is treated in a section of that title; and the section entitled "Impact and Influence of the Targum Ezekiel" includes,

---

*I am grateful to the staff of the William Andrews Clark Library in Los Angeles for access to works of English literature, research apparatus, and especially the Clark Library's fine collection of nineteenth-century essays, poetry and fiction.

I acknowledge as well a travel grant from the National Endowment of the Humanities.

broadly, what we today call "reception" – or the audience for whom the translation was intended. It is this "audience" aspect of thinking about translation that attaches itself to another of Levey's passions: the liberal agenda in the transmission of tradition. These areas occupy the attention of any student of translation today: language, ideology, history and reception. My essay, dedicated to a master of translation, is about translation at another pole of Jewish history: the time of the *Yishuv* and its struggle to rebuild culture for a new-old nation. The messianic overtones of that activity shared the messianism of much of the Ezekiel Targum. Is this a coincidence entirely? Or is it an inevitable consequence for those who believed they were translating God's word – however liberally we interpret the meaning of that phrase and however politically grounded were the participants in the activity? These were the very issues that occupied the pioneers of modern Israel – the rebuilders of the nation who were occupied with creating a new language as well as linking different historical times and dissolving geographical boundaries in that new language.

Translations have always been important, if problematic, literature for the Jewish people, and so it is fitting that a tribute to Samson Levey should include a modern manifestation of the translation phenomenon. Although my work here will be less technical than Samson Levey's scholarship, it remains within a tradition for which he has reverence and which he, in fact, helped establish. Yet that tradition contains an interesting twist: while a targumist was preserving a sacred literature which was already part of a canon; and while Samson Levey has helped make the work of the targumist a part of a slightly larger scholarly canon; the modern literary problem has been what to put into a newly developing canon. What should the new Jew be reading?

Translations have been a part of the Hebrew canon for as long as there has been a modern Hebrew literature. Israelis today may recall with near native pride Hebrew translations they read of Tolstoy, Dostoevski or Flaubert, Hamsun or Björnson; and if they are especially diligent, they may even speak of their translators by name. Some are able to compare the development between an early translation (for example, Shlonsky's Shakespeare) and a later one (for example, Carmi's texts, or a stage adaptation of Shakespeare by David Avidan or Nissim Aloni). But while the industry of translation has been unabated since the time it began in earnest, the 10's and 20's of this century, the precise meaning of translation within the history of Hebrew literature is still being refined. Was translation subversive of Hebrew culture, or did it foster it? What part did translation play in what Zohar Shavit calls "the literary life of >Ereẓ Yiśra>el"?¹

The various translation projects of the *Yishuv̄* were a source of considerable anxiety among writers and intellectuals during the Second and Third <*Aliyot*, with different shades of anxiety at different times. Both the anxieties and the enthusiasms about translation are chronicled and explained by Zohar and Yaakov Shavit in their essay of 1977 "To Fill the Land With Books."² It is the most complete statement of the translation phenomenon in the *Yishuv̄* from a statistical, bibliographic and historical point of view. Others, from the Tel Aviv School of poetics, have added immeasurably to understanding the more theoretical aspects of the translation phenomenon. Their contributions have been, shall we say, more international in scope, and attention to their work has been more global. But the work of Gideon Toury, Itamar Ewen-Zohar and Zivah Porat has expanded our understanding of the particular national phenomenon even as it has added to the theoretical literature.³

Certainly the study of translation within >Ereẓ Yiśra>el must be centered within the contemporary Israeli academic communities, where professional resources and bibliographic materials exist within a rich environment of archival and personal memory. But the possibility of Diaspora scholars adding a dimension to the study is extremely tantalizing, with regard to this topic especially. Just as Israeli scholars have drawn so heavily on the particular localized experience of Hebrew Language development within a particular time and place for their international theoretical understandings, so the concerns of scholars in the Diaspora ought now to be added to the particular and localized issues within Israel. The distance between contemporary American and

---

¹Zohar Shavit, *Ha-ḥayim Ha-sifruti'im b'>Ereẓ Yiśra>el* (The Literary Life in the Land of Israel) *1910-33* (Tel Aviv: Ha-qibuz Ha-m'>uhad, 1982).
²Zohar Shavit and Yaakov Shavit, "To Fill the Land with Books" (Hebrew), *Ha-sifrut*, No. 25 (October, 1977), pp. 46-67. The reader is urged to refer to the numerous inventories within the article. For a wider backdrop to the literature of the first migrations to Ereẓ Yiśrael, see Gershon Shaked, *Ha-Siporet Ha<Iv̄rit 1880-1980* (Hebrew Fiction between 1880-1980) (Jerusalem: Keter Publishing, 1983).
³Itamar Ewen-Zohar, "The Place of Translated Literature Within the Literary Polysystem" (Hebrew), *Ha-sifrut*, No. 25 (October, 1977): first delivered as a lecture at the 1976 conference on translation, Leuven, Belgium; Zivah Ben Porat, "Yefet's Appearance within the Tents of Shem" (Hebrew), *Ha-sifrut*, No. 29 (December, 1979); Gideon Toury, *Normot shel Tirgum* (Norms of Translation, Literary Translation to Hebrew Between 1930 and 1945) (Tel Aviv: Mif<alim >Univ̄ersiṭi'im L'hoẓa>ah La>or, 1977): Toury's book best captures my suggestion about using the immediate setting for universal extrapolations.

Israeli cultures may be helpful and may invite the special sensitivities of a foreigner whose perspective is removed and whose familiarity with world literature is unencumbered by the intensity of cultural transfer which has already taken place within the Hebrew-speaking community. Those living within the literary community of the West may be able to ask new questions. More attention to the problems of translation by Diaspora scholars will be welcome at this time in the history of modern literary scholarship, especially with increased communication and the inclusion of numerous theoreticians of world literature into the Israeli discourse. My original interest in this project actually came from Arnold Band's efforts as an American critic to grasp the poetics of Bialik's language essays as poetry.[4] It was furthered by European and American explorations of hermeneutics and tropes. What made original research possible was the presence of a relatively large collection of translated works within the library of the Hebrew Union College-Jewish Institute of Religion in New York. Thus the research problem can itself be an instance of the nuance presented by translation study: the role a foreign culture will play in building a native culture can be mirrored in the scholarly activity which sets out to understand it. (In the case of Samson Levey, a similar distance was helpful – in his case: the passage of time.) Only time will tell whether study by Americans and Europeans will have added unique features to the examination of this aspect of the history of Hebrew literature.

My paper is divided into two parts: some general reflections on attitudes towards translations in >Ereẓ Yiśra>el, along with the historical and cultural aspects of the translation culture of the *Yishuv̄*; and a review of specific justifications for translation of certain Western literature into Hebrew during the period 1893 to 1930.

Early in the 1920's, in *Ha-t'qufah*, Ya'akov Fichman wrote two lengthy essays on translation, which are contained in the more contemporary collection of his writings.[5] Fichman understood then that translation represented a rich advantage for an emerging national culture which had not yet established the necessary bases for a native literature.

> Indeed, translation serves principally as the stimulus to new development. Had we had good translations of Shakespeare and

---

[4]Arnold Band, "The Revealment in Concealment, The Function of Metaphor in Bialik's Essays" (Hebrew), *Meḥqaré Yerushalayim BeSifrut Ivrit*, volumes 10/11, 1988, Pp. 189-200. First delivered as a working paper, Los Angeles, Spring 1986.
[5]Yaakov Fichman, "On Translations" (Hebrew), Parts I and II in *Kol Kit'v̄é Yaakov̄ Fichman* (Tel Aviv: D'v̄ir, 1960): Part I appeared in *Ha-t'qufah*, XVI (1922), pp. 413-25; Part II, in *ibid.*, XIX (1923), 405-18.

Goethe thirty years ago, there is no doubt that we would have had by now original creations like them. A good translation gives security. It educates, it excites and it encourages.

Whether or not this early enthusiasm was shared universally, many writers agreed that Hebrew literature itself had not produced the literary tradition that was desired. Brenner's famous plea in 1911 ("The >Erez̧ Yiśra>el Genre") is well-known for its attitude to the inadequacy and naïveté of the contemporaneous literature and the immaturity of its environment.⁶ Thus translation served a double function: not only did it help influence the development of new literature, but it actually provided reading material which, some said, was absent in Hebrew itself. Translation projects did not abate between 1922 when Fichman's earliest translation essay appeared, and the early thirties, by which time, as the Shavits note, Fichman was already becoming antagonistic to the enterprise.⁷

It seems, indeed, that publishers in the 1920's may have privileged translation for commercial reasons as well as for the idealistic purpose of supplying Western literature for the national renascence. So, in spite of Fichman's enthusiasm of 1922, his concerns in 1930 that translation might replace original writing were realistic. By that time the amount of significant "original" literature was greater, and thus the commercial motive may have replaced some of the ideological motives.

Any depiction of the tension between the need for translation and the threat which translation presents to native literary development continues to stimulate our imaginations and our research. In a less critical and perhaps more banal way, Israeli intellectuals still must struggle against translations – in spite of the apparent amplitude of markets for both translated and original literature. Young Israeli readers might yet prefer the American or English mystery story translated into Hebrew to a serious novel by one of Israel's contemporary or classic writers. The implications of this preference are serious, but they are of a different order. They have more to do with a public suspension of serious print culture in favor of popular culture; and they are more closely related to the global concerns of an E. D. Hirsch than to the promotion of an ethnos through literary patriotism and cultural messianism. But, though different in its makeup, the translation phenomenon is always present to force us to think about cultural exchange.

---

⁶Y. H. Brenner, "The >Erez̧ Yiśra>el Genre and its Aspects" (Hebrew), *Kol Kit'v̄é Brenner*, II (Tel Aviv: D'v̄ir, 1960).
⁷Z. and Y. Shavit, *op.cit.*, p. 46.

The tables of the Shavits' article signify an astounding involvement in translation during the *Yishuv* period. Some of the most startling statistics come from the early years of the second decade of the twentieth century, where one sees that a handful of readers absorbed scores of translated works. In one extraordinary instance we can see an example of the strength of the issue: in a five-year period, 1909-1913, ninety-nine works of natural science were produced in the *Yishuv*.[8]

This surprising number and the success of translation in spite of all the cautions against it are indications of what makes study of this problem so complex. Cultural history is always an elusive subject, since it depends on taste and subjective definitions as much as upon data. Zohar Shavit's book on the development of a literary life in Tel Aviv is certainly emblematic of the nuanced nature of this subject. As she herself has said in a brief interview in *Modern Hebrew Literature*: "unfortunately the socio-historical study of literature has not yet succeeded in setting up a model sufficiently sophisticated to deal with the literary life."[9] But the aspect of cultural history that attempts descriptions of native canon and of translation which suits the canon is

---

[8]*Ibid.*, p. 52. The chart includes nearly 2,000 books published between 1908 and 1928:

Year	Original Belles Lettres	Belles Lettres Translated	Natural Science	Religious Books	Textbooks	Misc.
1908	5	4	5	5	2	-
1909	7	4	10	21	1	1
1910	8	4	18	1	2	3
1911	5	3	16	6	-	4
1912	7	3	25	12	7	6
1913	10	4	30	3	4	7
1914	14	2	11	-	3	5
1915	7	4	5	-	2	5
1916	22	4	3	-	7	3
1917	8	2	5	-	5	-
1918	7	2	1	2	1	10
1919	22	9	24	7	7	42
1920	6	12	8	7	6	9
1921	18	4	13	3	5	13
1922	19	10	13	-	7	14
1923	20	16	15	6	4	14
1924	32	11	27	28	10	43
1925	40	15	32	16	3	45
1926	61	26	42	36	24	65
1927	88	43	51	31	26	77
1928	<u>87</u>	<u>65</u>	<u>47</u>	<u>21</u>	<u>16</u>	<u>85</u>
	493	247	401	205	142	451

[9]"Talking to Zohar Shavit," in *Modern Hebrew Literature*, VIII (Summer 1983).

perhaps the most elusive part of that difficult enterprise. Not only are there linguistic issues, market considerations and elements of reception theory, but the critic must face the question of indeterminate factors. It may happen that a writer will wish to translate a given work out of personal enthusiasm; or an editor may have a personal relationship with another editor or publisher who has encouraged a project. Even the private passions of intellectuals play a part in this selection, as we might see suggested at the conclusion of this article. What is common to all of these considerations, the random subjective preferences as well as the more normative systematic triage,[10] is the opportunity to study how culture develops and how a specific culture grows through its alliances and its battles with cultures foreign to it. This article is part of the research and speculation taking place in the last several years regarding the cultural interface between Hebrew and the languages of Europe.

My work begins with the appearance of George Eliot's *Daniel Deronda* in Poland in David Frishman's translation. It concludes more or less with the emergence of new translation vigor and the work of Shlonsky and the expanded translation output of the 1930's, as well as the emergence of what is known as the *K'tuvim* group. By this time translation is no longer quite so controversial, the issues within the >Erez Yisra>el settlement move from concern with fostering writers as against translations, to larger literary questions of genre, academic life, and literary theory. Another <Aliyah had enriched Hebrew culture beyond anyone's wildest imagination. By the mid-1930's, Walter Benjamin's more metaphysical comment had come to have comfortable meaning within the cultural milieu of >Erez Yisra>el: "All works," Benjamin said in 1924, "wait to be translated."[11] Benjamin's dense essay announced the coming of age of a sense of universalism about language, while nationalisms were beginning to strengthen again and perform their narrowest tasks. The Third <Aliyah, the experience of the cultural life of the *Yishuv* itself, expanding world horizons, and the presence of major translators whose personal literary output was blended with their translation output, seem to have created a far more hospitable climate. But just prior to the 1930's the struggle was reflected in another element of the problem: the foreign languages which continued to be spoken within the Palestinian environment. At this time Hebrew literature was struggling for position against the literatures

---

[10]See Z. and Y. Shavit, p. 46. Here they use another foreign loan word, "tirage," to characterize the purchasing intensity of translated works in the *Yishuv*. My note is simply to remark on the convenience of foreign words to discuss the problem of foreign literature – and words that look alike at that!
[11]Walter Benjamin, "The Task of the Translator" (German), *Illuminations* (New York: Schocken, 1969).

of English, German, French and Russian for at least three reasons: either because of the nature of the readership, because of the presumed lack of Hebrew authors, or because of the complex cultural need of new immigrants to have native pride in the cultures of their original homelands. There was no doubt that the four major foreign literatures were destined to be assimilated into Hebrew culture in one way or another.

Two essays are especially illuminating in this regard: Yaakov Steinberg's more general remarks in *Safot* and Asher Barash's attention to more concrete problems in >*Aḥénu Ha-m'dabrim Bilshonot Nékhar* (1929).[12] Steinberg noted that language as such was always easy for Jews in the various lands of dispersion. Even where they were treated badly, Jews held on to languages such as German, Russian and English. Although Steinberg shared with Barash the sense of urgency about developing Hebrew, he had a global sense that, in moments of practical stress, use of languages like German or Russian would emerge spontaneously. After all, the languages of origin were nothing to be ashamed of – either in terms of the cultures that produced them, or in terms of their semantic adequacy. So, while German, Russian and Polish recalled events and attitudes that needed to be erased, the *Yishuv* had to live with its linguistic realities. Barash, on the other hand, reflected a more "institutional" urgency. As editor of the Miẓpeh Publishing House, he was at the center of this discussion about linguistic and literary canon. The problem for Barash was whether the cultures of "foreign nations" were to become part of Hebrew national life in Hebrew, or were to remain a foreign element within a nation blemished by guest cultures that resisted assimilation.

Sometimes the anxieties about the future of Hebrew culture seem, with our hindsight, to have been exaggerated. But the Shavits' review of attitudes and some of Dan Miron's essays make a convincing case that the anxieties were realistic. These essays review a particularly tenuous period of thirty years, in which a literature that may appear quite rich with the perspective of sixty years must have seemed lean indeed and created a deep concern among the intellectuals of the time.[13] Cordova and Herzog note correctly that the *Yishuv*, at least until 1935, could not claim an intellectual prestige equal to that of Warsaw. The translation

---

[12]Yaakov Steinberg, "Languages" (Hebrew), *Kol Kit'vé Yaakov Steinberg* (Tel Aviv: D'vir, 1959), p. 301; Asher Barash, "Our Brethren Who Speak in Foreign Tongues" (Hebrew), *Kol Kit'vé Barash*, III (Tel Aviv: D'vir, 1961).
[13]Dan Miron, "The Background to the Perplexity in Hebrew Literature at the Beginning of the Twentieth Century"(Hebrew), in *Halkin Jubilee Volume* (Jerusalem: Magnes Press, 1975).

program of the 10's and 20's gained strength from the awareness of that lack, resolving one anxiety as it promoted another.¹⁴

The anxiety about translation, the enthusiasm for translation projects, and the preoccupation with language and cultural transfer can be seen within an even more complete context, which includes numerous essays written before 1920 on language in general and on Hebrew language in particular,¹⁵ and some pieces in the 20's. No less a figure than Gershom Scholem addressed his dialectical concerns about the apocalyptic qualities in the Hebrew language as late as 1926, following on the heels of several influential essays noted above. Scholem added the dimension of concern that Hebrew's strength in ancient sources might undermine its contemporary utility.¹⁶

In every essay, whether the subject was translation or language in general, two questions drew attention, in addition to the propriety of translation at all: the restrictions within the Hebrew language itself, and the needs of the audience. The word commonly used in the 1920's for translation: *l'hariq* – "to empty" – captures both aspects of the question. Each aspect of translation inquiry implies that the cups from which and into which each language is poured are of different shape and may even be of different size. Brenner's metaphor for the language aspect of the question was: "Can one empty the beauty of Yefet into the little canisters of Jacob?"¹⁷ But as is often the case with Brenner's metaphors, the canisters signify two components in the exchange: both the language and the people who will read the language; the rhetorical and linguistic questions and the aspects of reception. The canisters, in other words, could also be viewed as the audience. An instance of the

---

¹⁴Abraham Cordova and Hanna Herzog, "The Cultural Endeavor of the Labor Movement in Palestine: A Study of the Relationship Between Intelligentsia and Intellectuals,"in *YIVO Annual of Jewish Social Science*, XVIII, 238-59.
¹⁵See, for example, essays by Brenner, Berdichevski and Bialik written 1908-1920: Bialik, "Revealment and Concealment Language," "Birth Pangs of Language," and "Our New Poetry," *Kol Kit'vé Bialik* (Tel Aviv: D'vir, 1961); Y. H. Brenner, "Reflections of a Writer," "Birthpangs of Expression," and "The >Erez Yisra>el Genre and Its Aspects," in *Kol Kit'vé Brenner*, II (Tel Aviv: D'vir, 1960); M.Y. Berdichevski (Bin Gurion), "Language Matters," and "Hebrew and Aramaic," in *Kol Ma>amaré Bin Gurion* (Tel Aviv: D'vir, 1960) (all in Hebrew).
¹⁶See my "Ghostly Language, Ghastly Speech: Scholem to Rosenzweig, 1926," *Prooftexts*, X, No. 3 (1990).
¹⁷See Brenner's "Yefet," and also his "Birthpangs of Expression" (1914), *supra*. The Yefet title evokes the dichotomy of Shem and Yefet and almost always refers to languages of Christendom in the language discourse of the period. It was also the name of a prominent translation project in the early teens of this century. (Volumes of the Yefet project are often bound together and available in the National and University Library at Jerusalem and other libraries with strong collections of translated literature.)

tension between these two poles of concern will tantalize contemporary audiences with our rich sensitivity to the interplay between audience and language in regard to textual indeterminacy. In an instance where the rhetorical limits of the language may mirror sociological boundaries, David Frishman wrote in 1893 of the problems of audience in his introduction to *Daniel Deronda*.

> Because the first portion of the story does not speak about Jewish matters, but rather about the lives of people in general and the lives of noblemen ....So the Hebrew translator had this in mind when he came to placing his translation before you, and thus I have written this little introduction. Indeed, the first portion of the book is wonderful, and contains great scenes, and even sets out the character motivations and the plot, and any sophisticated person will appreciate it; yet in respect for the reader who is reading this because he is a Jew, the translator has abbreviated and changed this first portion where possible without losing its essence.

What can a Jew know about horse racing or roulette? Frishman asked,[18] and although Frishman may have been ironic because of his own fascination with British society, his concern about the ability of Eastern European Jews to absorb direct translation of the culture was justified. Similar sociological boundaries are suggested by Rabinowitz's resistance to Dostoevski's Christian icons and ideas in 1913, when he translated *Notes from the Death House* for the Yefet project.[19] The difference was that Frishman seems to have been chastising his audience for their parochialism, while Rabinowitz fostered it.

But the problem is not only one of sociology. The modest vocabulary of Hebrew has been a well-chronicled problem, and throughout the decades of change it has been addressed in a variety of ways: from Bialik's notion of *Milon M'khanes* (a dictionary that grows organically) to articles by Howard Marblestone and Naomi Zohar on the ability of Hebrew to deal with the literature of classical antiquity.[20]

---

[18] David Frishman, Introduction to *Daniel Deronda* by George Eliot (Warsaw: >Aḥi>asaf, 1893).

[19] Brenner discusses this change scornfully in his article "Yefet." Rabinowitz's introduction renders a lengthy justification for his deletions: "How did the artist create such beautiful pictures out of material that is so ugly?" asked Rabinowitz in his introduction, where he justifies excluding the Gospel material on Jesus' suffering and death and the alleged Jewish responsibility for them. Rabinowitz retained the material on Christian holidays and folk observances and saw some analogies between Russian folk experience and the Jewish folk experience. The point, once again, is that the translation is seen as important for its relationship to the social needs of the emerging Hebrew-speaking society rather than for more purely aesthetic considerations.

[20] Howard Marblestone, "Greek Literature in Hebrew Clothing" (Hebrew), unpublished paper for the annual meeting of the National Association of

Translation and the Project of Culture 219

Efforts to translate Shakespeare into Hebrew demonstrate that one strategy for compensation may be the use of biblical and Rabbinic allusion,[21] and in the 1930's Yaakov Steinberg demonstrated the power of construct forms (*s'mikhut*) to expand Hebrew vocabulary.[22] Bialik tried to deny the inherent leanness of Hebrew through his thinking about language in general, but the reality has not supported his perspective.[23]

It is the focus on audience which will occupy us in the remainder of this paper. That area of literary criticism remains the newest and perhaps the most promising for an understanding of the development of canon. When all the more technical issues of language, rhetoric and philology are described, there remain the questions of epistemology and the public assessment of quality and social importance. Frishman's attention to the audience for *Daniel Deronda*, therefore, becomes the hallmark of the question and – as readers will see – was the central issue for the translators of Western fiction into Hebrew. A comment by F. R. Leavis in *The Great Tradition* of 1954 gives us the other side of the *Daniel Deronda* discussion:

> As for the bad part of *Daniel Deronda*, there is nothing to do but cut it away....If, having entertained such a purpose, George Eliot had justified it, *Daniel Deronda* would have been a very great novel indeed. As things are, there is, lost under that damning title, an actual great novel to be extricated ... It will be best to get the bad half out of the way first. This can be quickly done, since the weakness doesn't require any sustained attention, being of a kind that has already been thoroughly discussed. It is represented by Deronda himself, and by what may be called in general the Zionist inspiration.[24]

The question of audience relationship to material, then, assumes many forms and in some of them even has to do with assumptions about what is quality. Even among sophisticated readers, private passions and personal interest may enhance our sense of quality. In the battle between Frishman and Leavis, at least, Frishman is generous – granting

---

Professors of Hebrew, June, 1987; Naomi Zohar, "Between Shem and Yefet, on One Example of Translation in the Literature of the Haskalah" (Hebrew), *Mo>znayim* (April, 1988).
[21]William Cutter, "Hamlet in Hebrew," on the allusive figures in Carmi's translation of Shakespeare. For the annual meeting of the National Association of Professors of Hebrew, June, 1990. See T. Carmi, *Hamlet* (Tel Aviv: D'vir, 1981).
[22]Steinberg, "Hebrew" (Hebrew), *supra*.
[23]Bialik, "Birth Pangs of Language," *op. cit.*
[24]See F. R. Leavis, *The Great Tradition* (Garden City: Doubleday, 1954), p. 150. My thanks to Prof. H. Daleski for this turnabout.

that the part that might be cut out is still of high quality (since he prefers it to the audience he privileges). This form of the audience question is fairly straightforward; other forms are more subtle. In 1914, Brenner asked how Tolstoy or Dostoevski would have sounded in Hebrew had they written in Hebrew.[25] That is the ultimate reception question; since to reverse the question: "How close can we make our Hebrew to the original Russian" relates more to philological precision.[26] Each generation, then, needs new translations, because it is the nature of cultures to keep growing. The farther one gets from the original translation, the freer one might be to think in audience terms. But to expunge from a translation may reflect a lack of historical sensibility in all cases.

It is in terms of this audience problem, I believe, that the early translators did most of their thinking. Brenner, himself a translator, had an uncanny sense of the place of audience in the discussions on literature within an historical period. He (and the narrators in his novels) understood the problem of distance, of course, but masked another kind of sophistication behind ostensibly innocent questions about given time and place. His question about audience for a certain kind of story is really a question about an audience for all kinds of literature – translated or written in the original.

In the frame opening of *Sh'khol V'khishalon*, for example,[27] Brenner's narrator ruminates on the fate of novels of introspection during "these tumultuous times." It is a theme of some of his other introductions as well, but it is carried through with special intensity in this, his final novel. Brenner's tense question about his audience is a trope for our question: "What shall be translated?" And it is also

---

[25] Y. H. Brenner, "Yefet" and also "Birth Pangs of Expression."

[26] This debate seems not to have been carried out explicitly, but one does find several points of view about the function of translation: How would Russian sound in contemporary Hebrew? How would contemporary Hebrew sound in the Russian of the period in which something was written? What is the relative weight of linguistic accuracy vs. audience comfort with language? What are the strategies for compensating for inadequate vocabulary? How realistic is Bialik's belief that the living language will slowly compensate for what is missing from the lexicon? And more.

[27] Brenner in his introduction to *Sh'khol V'khishalon*:
...however one looks at it, and until this very day, and in spite of all my hesitations about the form, which hasn't ceased and probably won't, certainly, I have decided, finally, to cast this "story" among readers! ...I can skip over in one step my hesitation with regard to one issue, which isn't really essential, but which nonetheless arouses doubt, namely with regard to the time of publication, a time which doesn't cause and isn't even suited to reading stories like this... (My translation).

exemplary of the general anxiety in this period about the destiny of good literature. During the Mandate Period, the literary questions were as much a part of the political tumult as the Balfour Declaration or the establishment of workers' collectives, and Miron has demonstrated that perplexity about the destiny of literature created as much ill ease as the perplexity about malaria and typhus. Who wants to read which literature is another version of the question: "What kind of literature does this audience need?"[28]

Part of that cultural tumult was the problem of translation: it forced people to define where there was a qualitative difference between translated literature and literature created in Hebrew, and it may have caused people to ask whether European literature was too preoccupied with the private lives of individuals for a new nation which had to think about community. The classic problem in Hebrew literature was about the place of history in the making of the new secular nation; naturally, placing foreign literature within that history was fraught with ideological issues.

To be sure, the question of Brenner's narrator: "can a novel of introspection and personal destiny find an audience?" may also be asked about the "reception" for translation. Who was the audience, let us say, for a Hebrew translation of a French Socialist novel of amours and inward rumination about those loves?[29] Or who wanted to read a British aesthete's extended confession from jail about his soul imprisoned in a troubled body (Oscar Wilde)? What did a klatch of literary exiles like Keats and Shelley or Byron have to do with the *Shivat Ẓiyon*? Was there any literature that really captured the native feelings of a Jew settling in Palestine? Were these the motives for translation? And were the shifts away from positivism (Ahad Ha-Amists opposing translation), reflected in the translation enterprise?

The comprehensive study which must be undertaken eventually involves even more than audience and more than textual and language questions. It includes another level of discourse on which resides the notion that translation creates language, and addresses that great problem which Bialik inaugurated early in this epoch (1915): whether a language grows from within or through the scientific development of corresponding words.[30]

As part of that concern I have elsewhere discussed the figurative language which appears in the essays on language and translation during

---

[28]Miron, "Background of Perplexity," *op. cit.*
[29]Magdaleine Marx, >*Ishah* (*Femme*), translated by Rachel Neuman (Tel Aviv: Mizpeh, 1928).
[30]Bialik, "Birthpangs," *op. cit.*

this era of vigorous conversation about language.³¹ The coherence between language development in general and translation in particular is an important problematic, because it suggests that developing language at all is itself a form of translation. But this paper is more limited, designed to lay out the problems of a larger empirical study which must continue.

At this stage my attention will turn to an examination of some of the introductions to translated works of this period. My sample includes nearly one hundred works translated between 1893 and 1930, only a portion of the inventory in the Shavits' listing. But it is a convenient sample collected as a unit by the Klau Library of the Hebrew Union College-Jewish Institute of Religion in New York.³² The existence of this collection in one setting in America is itself instructive and a kind of "symbol" for what translation signifies and what the study of translation promises. It is, on one hand, the result of one librarian's concentrated effort; and, on the other, represents the Zionist enthusiasm of the New York School of the College-Institute. Here, too, personal taste combined with institutional policy to create a cultural phenomenon.

These introductions will serve for the time being as a representative sample, enabling us to make some summary comments about the reasons the works were translated and the effects they were expected to have on their readership. By being selected for translation, the novels, essays, and poems became part of the "polysystem" of Israeli literature. The earliest version of that polysystem was grounded in Berlin, Warsaw and Odessa until it was transferred to >Erez̧ Yiśra>el.

The introductions to the various works are of uneven seriousness. They include long essays or short pithy notes. Sometimes they are brief biographies of authors, and sometimes books included no introduction at all. For the most part, they reflect surprisingly little engagement in

---

[31] William Cutter, "Language on Language," on the figurative language used to describe the development of language in the modern Hebrew essay: Association of Jewish Studies, December, 1988.

[32] My thanks here to the librarian of Hebrew Union College-Jewish Institute of Religion in New York, Philip Miller; to Harvey Horowitz, the College's librarian in Los Angeles, and to the Director of Libraries at the College-Institute, Dr. Herbert Zafren in Cincinnati. Yaffa Weissman, of the Los Angeles campus Library, was especially helpful, as was Henry Resnick, in New York. I am grateful to the librarian of the National and University Library in Jerusalem, Malachi Bet Arie, for enabling me to pursue work on these translations under a grant from the National Endowment for the Humanities. David Cohen and Philip Nadel rendered valuable assistance and judgment, and Ezra Spicehandler's unpublished essay "Americanism in American Hebrew Literature" prompted much discussion with its author and added the particular element of translations from English published in English speaking lands.

the larger theoretical linguistic issues of the period. They are written with little attention to questions of metaphor, calquing, expressionism and romantic theory and make little reference to the questions which appeared in the essays of Bialik, Brenner, Berdichevski, Barash, Fichman and Yaakov Steinberg. They focus almost exclusively on the suitability of a given "content" for the audience: the themes and values generally acknowledged as central within the works, and the public which seemed appropriate for a consumption of those themes and values. From reading all of these introductions, it would be difficult to believe that this epoch in Hebrew literature was a time of rich linguistic speculation and interest in emerging theories of people like de Saussure, Frege, Wittgenstein and Heidegger, Benjamin and Scholem. The question of "translatability," noted by Brenner as a literary value, is dealt with rarely: in Bialik's lengthy discussion of *Don Quixote* and Salkinson's comments about *Romeo and Juliet* (though its 1870's date precedes the period under discussion).[33] One is tempted to explain this lack by the likely circumstance that introductions were composed for the popular readership that takes the books in hand, and that they were carefully monitored by publishers with an eye on the marketplace and not on an intellectual posterity. Yet that hardly seems an adequate explanation, given the importance of the introduction in Hebrew literature in general and the rich Hebrew literary tradition of the feuilleton and essay.

Most of the introductions do attempt to justify the need for the translation. These justifications range from considerations of the social values and morality of virtuous character types (as in the translations of Jack London and Björnstjerne Björnson by Lamdan and Kimchi)[34] to an effort to understand the way nations develop (as in the translation into <*Iqar Ha-l'>umim* of Zangwill's *Principle of Nations*).[35] Tschernichowski insisted that his primary reason for translating *Anacreon* was the need for such an epic in the Hebrew language (Uri Zvi Greenberg's epic *Anacreon on the Pole of Sadness* was to come later).[36]

A modest attention to language problems is reflected in only two of the introductions. A. L. Mintz in 1929 discusses his decision to render Heine into prose as the only way to preserve the beauty of Heine's

---

[33]Bialik, Introduction to Cervantes" *Don Quixote* (Odessa: Turgeman, 1912); "Ram V'Ya>el," translated by Y.A. Salkinson (Vienna: Spitzer, 1871).
[34]Jack London, *Three Stories from the South Seas*, Lamdan, trans. (Tel Aviv: Mizpeh, 1926); Björnson, *Arneh – The Story of a Village*, Kimchi, trans. (Tel Aviv: Mizpeh, 1926).
[35]Israel Zangwill, *Principle of Nations*, A.S. Orlans, trans. (New York: Qadimah, 1918).
[36]*Shiré Anakreon*, Tschernichowski, trans. (Warsaw: A.J. Stybel, 1920).

language, but one could hardly expect such a decision to pass unremarked. Jabotinsky discusses his own translation of Poe's delicate sensitivity to language in an introduction to "The Raven" (his famous change of an earlier translation of the signature line "quoth the raven never more" is one of the fine examples of the suppleness of Hebrew, where "*l'neẓaḥ lo*" becomes ">*el <ad >én dor.*")[37] Such technical and textural issues merit extensive analysis of the material itself, and I plan to include that in future studies.

Most of the introductions concentrate on relatively simple issues relating a piece of literature to a public. The public lacks characters from *<edot ha-mizraḥ*, so translation brings the public a figure like *Joseph Peretz*,[38] the levantine hero of a story by Avraham Elimelech. Between generalities about heroic virtue, social values and the sparse rhetorical questions, the introductions do contain an occasional reference to the question of narration. In the instance of *Dr. Jekyll and Mr. Hyde*, by Robert Louis Stevenson, Barash deals fleetingly with point of view and tries to describe why Stevenson is considered the storyteller par excellence[39]; Stendhal and Anatole France are identified with the naturalistic tradition and its emphasis on "the slice of life" and the genre portrait.[40] Even Halkin's more sophisticated concerns about the importance of Shelley's "Defence of Poetry" are composed in social terms.[41] Two interesting comments emerging more from anthropology than from literature as such are Lachower's suggestion that Carlyle's notion about great men would serve to counter distortions of the superman idea, and Tschernichowski's view that "Hiawatha" should be an important part of the new Hebrew culture because it takes one back to *b'r>eshit*, a purer time and place.[42] But many of the concerns were, at best, parochial and were partial justifications for translation as filling a vacuum suffered by the native Hebrew culture.

The standard of these essays was not high, and no format of any level was established. Indeed, many of the most significant translations were not accompanied by an introduction. Most surprising of all,

---

[37] A.L. Mintz, *Selections from Heine's Poetry* (Berlin: S'guliyot, 1929); Jabotinsky, *Ha-<areṽ* (Berlin: Hasefer, 1924).
[38] Avraham Elimelech, Introduction to *Joseph Peretz*, Elimelech, trans. (Jerusalem: Solel, 1926).
[39] Barash, Introduction to *Dr. Jekyell and Mr. Hyde* (Tel Aviv: Miẓpeh, 1927).
[40] Anatole France, *Thirsty Gods*, Barash, trans. (Tel Aviv: Miẓpeh, 1927); Stendhal, *Le Rouge et Le Noir*, Kabak, trans. (Tel Aviv: Miẓpeh, n.d.).
[41] Halkin, Introduction to Shelley's "In Defence of Poetry" (Tel Aviv: Hédim, 1928).
[42] Lachower, Introduction to *Heroes* by Carlyle, A. Einhorn, trans. (Warsaw: Stybel, 1919); Tschernichowski, Introduction to "Hiawatha," by Henry Wadsworth Longfellow (Berlin and Jerusalem: Moriah, 1922).

perhaps, is the absence of discussion about the place of classical Hebrew forms or *m'liẓah* in the modern translations. Occasionally one finds a glossary of terms, which suggests awareness of earlier translation solutions. The problem of the place of the classical language in the modern vessels is so basic that it might have lent itself quite naturally to the content of even a popular introduction.

Finally, there is little self-consciousness that the introductions are being read. The introductions exclude more than they contain, although one sees in them a deep concern for serving national needs at the time and for forwarding at least one of the programs of modern Zionism. In a sense these introductions represent responses to some of the critiques of translation activity which agitated the essays discussed by the Shavits in "To Fill the Land with Books" and the essays of Fichman, Barash and Jabotinsky in their time. They represent an address to the consumer side – the concerns which Cordova and Herzog claim belonged to the publishing houses and the more political (as opposed to literary) types of people.

One could contend, then, that much of the argument in the introductions supports the one over-arching theoretical and historical issue of the period: the problems of the new society needed to be addressed and its accompanying inadequacies needed to be remedied in the Hebrew language, even if it meant borrowing solutions from cultures where the problems had reached a more fully developed expression. But at least so far as the introductions are concerned, one finds discussed more of content and its social value than of aesthetics or new literary forms. Those issues seem to have been concentrated in the essays devoted exclusively to those problems. The readership of periodicals was certainly distinct from the readership of the translations.

No issue brings this out more than a question which occupied Brenner and which is an undercurrent in the introductions to stories and biographies of his fictive narrators: what is the relationship of the individual to the collective? How does literature attend to the poles of preoccupation with self, on the one hand, and concern with communal norms, on the other? This tension is represented in the very selection of materials to be translated. Frishman's affinity for the character type of a Cain, or his fascination with people like Oscar Wilde,[43] represents a dramatic counterpoint to the public attachment to characters of national destiny or to ideal moral types. Shofman's interest in the erotic sides of Altenberg's characters may have been shared by other readers,

---

[43] Frishman, Introduction to Byron's *Cain* (Warsaw: Tushiyah, 1900); Introduction to Oscar Wilde's *De Profundis* (Warsaw: Stybel, 1920).

but it clashes with models of community building,⁴⁴ just as Barash's affinity for the personal freedom of a Don Carlos is in some opposition to his belief that the nation aborning needs specific kinds of literary figures with particular moral standards.⁴⁵ These abrasions help us define current and countercurrent; but a discussion of these currents and countercurrents is rarely seen within the introductions themselves. Obviously it is from what might not seem to fit into a young culture that we may learn something about the newest steps which that culture is about to take. Whether translation is an avant-garde or a conserving activity, is its own kind of issue.⁴⁶

The most vivid instance of this abrasion is the appearance in the mid-1920's of *Femme* by the French Communist and feminist, Magdaleine Marx. Writing in the July 4, 1920, issue of the *New York Times*, the anonymous reviewer comments about Adele Szold Seltzer's translation into English of *Woman*:

> The free love tenet of Socialism, which some Socialists deny, here comes boldly forth. And another of its teachings is sanctioned also in what M. Henri Barbusse describes as her crying out with magnificent, impressive sincerity against the fallacy of the maternal instinct. Without any doubt Miss Marx's book will be much read and discussed in certain "advanced" circles.⁴⁷

Surely the reviewer would not have included the *Yishuṽ* in these "certain advanced circles," even if we took into account some of the non-conformist behavior within certain enclaves in >Ereẓ Yiśra>el.⁴⁸ And the book does not appear to have been "much discussed" either in America or within the *Yishuṽ* (there are two Hebrew reviews of the novel: one in *K'tuṽim* in 1928 and the other in *Do>ar Ha-yom* in 1927). We know much, of course, about the interest in sexual freedom in the 20's from all kinds of chronicles, and from the essays on women's rights in *Ha-po<el Ha-ẓa<ir*.⁴⁹ And American readers must be especially interested in the loop connecting >Ereẓ Yiśra>el to the young daughter of the Szold family, who married the publisher Thomas Seltzer who, in

---

⁴⁴Shofman, Introduction to Altenberg's *Selected Writings* (Warsaw: Stybel, 1921).
⁴⁵Barash, Introduction to Schiller's *Don Carlos* (Tel Aviv: Miẓpeh, 1923).
⁴⁶See Ewen-Zohar, *supra*.
⁴⁷Unsigned review in *New York Times*, July 4, 1920.
⁴⁸*Q'hiliyaténu*, with commentary by Muki Tzur (Jerusalem: Ben Ẓvi Institute, 1988).
⁴⁹*Pirqé Ha-po<el Ha-ẓa<ir* (Selections from *Ha-po<el Ha-ẓa<ir*) (Tel Aviv: Twerski, 1933); Devorah Bernstein, *>Ishah b'>Ereẓ Yiśra>el* (Women in >Ereẓ Yiśra>el, The Search for Equality During the Period of Settlement) (Tel Aviv: Ha-qibuẓ Ha-m'>uḥad, 1987).

turn, became one of the American patrons of D.H. Lawrence. But it is still difficult to trace the reasons for translating this work. We have to assume that the translation of *Femme* into Hebrew had something more to do with the society than simply responding to the whims of the wife of Miẓpeh's publisher, Mordechai Newman. Certainly one would want to continue tracking Devorah Baron's influence on the literary canon of the time, and her "feminist" perspective may have had some influence on this selection.[50] Perhaps someone from the *Yishuṽ* had a liaison with someone in Paris; or perhaps Stefan Zweig's German translation of the book gave it a temporary momentum which simply faded. Yet *Femme*'s urban erotic setting in which women could ruminate about many loves, mock cultural continuity, and challenge the idea of family raising, is at odds with the more normative ethics of enriching the new society with the safely canonical literature of the West; or of presenting the literary or communal models that were needed. Neither of Mme. Marx's major novels (*Femme* and *Toi*) could be justified on purely literary grounds. And, no matter how haphazard the process of building a translation canon, a quantity of readers is necessary beyond the enthusiasm of a small coterie.

For our purposes here, the appearance of >*Ishah-Femme* in Hebrew, along with other isolated and eccentric works, demonstrates that the struggle to enrich the Jewish nation through translation took many forms. The struggle introduced us to distance between cultures as wide as Daniel Deronda's gaming tables were from the Friday night dinner tables of Eastern European *y'shiṽot*; and as clumsy as the attempt to bring erotic rhythms to physical efforts of a workers' collective. The rustic phrase for a romantic (or illicit) tryst in the *Yishuṽ*, "four feet in a bed," hardly captures the register of Mme. Marx's descriptions of amorous nights. The struggle of an individual against the law in Oscar Wilde's England simply isn't the same struggle against norms and authority which is part of the legend of the Third <*Aliyah*. The links fit as neatly or as awkwardly as the ties between a new Hebrew language and its French antecedents in the pages of a long forgotten French novel; between a modern scholar of Targum and the object of his study; or between *M'dinat Yiśra>el* and a collection of books found in 1988 on a shelf in a library built by American Reform Jews in Greenwich Village.[51]

---

[50]Nurit Govrin, *Devorah Baron, Parshiyot Muqdamot* (Early Events in the Life of Devorah Baron) (Jerusalem: Mosad Bialik, 1988). My personal thanks to Dr. Govrin and to Mrs. Barash-Kohen for much assistance and personal reminiscence.

[51] Muki Tzur et al., eds., *Ka>n <Al P'né Ha->adamah* (Here on the Soil) (Tel Aviv: Ha-qibuẓ Ha-m'>uḥad, 1981).

15

A Note on Peter Berger's "Charisma and Religious Innovation: The Social Location of Israelite Prophecy"

By David H. Ellenson

An individual well versed in one field of academic inquiry steps into another area of intellectual endeavor only with the greatest trepidation, for the fear is always present that the expert will criticize the non-expert for his sweeping, ill-conceived use of the expert's data. Nevertheless, it is also true that the non-expert, by bringing a different point of view to bear upon certain facts, may shed new and interesting light upon them. Furthermore, the non-expert, by utilizing facts gathered in another area for his own use, may bring separate areas of inquiry into closer contact and often can illuminate his own area of expertise. All this said, it is my aim in this brief note to comment upon a sociological controversy between Peter Berger and Max Weber in light of an article written by the eminent biblical scholar Harry Orlinsky.[1] In so doing, I dedicate this paper to my teacher and colleague, Samson Levey, whose own catholicity and range of interests encompass and encourage the interdisciplinary approach that this paper strives to embody.

As is well known, Weber's notion of charisma has been characterized as possessing "inherent antinomian and anti-institutional pre-dispositions." Furthermore, as Berger has pointed out, and as every reader of Weber's *Ancient Judaism* knows, Weber based this aspect of his theory of charisma largely upon his interpretation of Israelite

---

[1] See Peter L. Berger, "Charisma And Religious Innovation: The Social Location Of Israelite Prophecy," *American Sociological Review*, XXVIII: 940-50; Harry M. Orlinsky, "The Seer-Priest and the Prophet in Ancient Israel," in his *Essays in Biblical Culture and Bible Translation* (New York: Ktav, 1974).

prophecy.² Basically, Weber claimed that the classical Israelite prophets, men such as Amos and Jeremiah, were individuals who stood apart from the social institutions of their day and enunciated messages in virtue of their personal sense of vocation. Significantly, they were able to create and foster new values, thus, in effect, promoting social change, precisely because they were socially detached from the cultic framework of the dominant Israelite institutions of their time. As Weber wrote, "The pathos of solitude overshadows the mode of the prophets."³

Yet, Peter Berger claims that this characterization of the prophets as solitary individuals standing apart from the established institutions of their day is based upon outmoded scholarship and has to be modified in light of recent scholarly developments which hold that the classical Israelite prophets operated within an institutional, cultic framework. That is to say, Berger relies upon those scholars who claim that the classical prophets were court prophets associated with already existing guilds, sanctuaries, and cultic functions. Thus, even though he does not fault Weber for relying upon the scholarship of his day, he states that, by virtue of this new knowledge available to us about the social location of Israelite prophecy, we need to revise Weber's theory of charisma insofar as it is based upon a notion of the prophets as individuals who operated outside of the established institutional frameworks of their day. Berger therefore concludes, "The prophet emerges from a traditionally defined office, exercising his charismatic activity in terms of this office, but carried far beyond its traditional definition by his religious message."⁴

This last statement of Berger's is crucial, for it establishes precisely the parameters of his dispute with Weber. Berger is not disputing Weber's claim that charisma, in at least one of its aspects, can be innovative and promote social change. Rather, Berger is arguing that "charismatic innovation" does "not necessarily originate in social marginality."⁵ Indeed, based upon his interpretation of modern biblical scholarship, Berger is saying that Weber's theory of charisma must be modified so as to admit the likelihood that charismatic forms of innovation are as apt to emerge from within an institutional framework as they are to arise from an exterior challenge.

However, is this the case? Should Weber's theory of charisma be modified on account of Berger's claim that modern scholarship holds the

---

²S.M. Eisenstadt, *Weber On Charisma and Institution Building* (Chicago: University of Chicago Press, 1968), p. xix; Berger, p. 940; Max Weber, *Ancient Judaism* (New York: Free Press, 1952).
³Weber, p. 292.
⁴Berger, p. 950.
⁵*Ibid.*

prophets to be bearers of a cultic office? In short, I do not intend to discuss whether Weber's view regarding the socially marginal nature of the original bearers of a charismatic message is right or wrong. This is surely debatable. I do claim, on the basis of Orlinsky's work, that the scholars upon whom Berger relies must be questioned. Consequently, a modification of Weber's theory of charisma founded upon the evidence Berger presents is, in this instance, dubious at best.

Orlinsky, in his "The Seer-Priest and the Prophet in Ancient Israel," shows that the phenomenon of "classical prophecy" should be viewed against the background of pre-existent "prophecy," that form connected with figures Orlinsky calls "seer-priests." Orlinsky admits that these "seer-priests" had much in common with the classical prophets. Both received communications from God, asserted God's authority, and were associated with scribal activity.

Nevertheless, the seer-priest held membership in a guild with masters and apprentices, associated with a sanctuary. The classical prophet, on the other hand, was a lone individual. While the office of the seer-priest was apparently hereditary, the classical prophet received a call. Financial reward was given the seer-priest, but the classical prophet went unrewarded. The seer-priest was a craftsman who offered sacrifices, presided over the sanctuary, and engaged in dream interpretation and magical activity. By contrast, the prophet was a man of words. He reasoned, argued, and exhorted.

Moreover, it is crucial to note that the seer-priests were integral members of Israelite society and had, in effect, a religious monopoly as heads of religious shrines. They were, then, a religious elite and, as such, an essentially conservative group. This is underscored by the fact that the seer-priests maintained their monopolistic control of oracles, sacrifices, and the Yahweh cult in spite of monarchic attempts to gain control over them. They were thus an integral part of the old guard power structure in ancient Israel and had very little, if anything, to gain from social innovation. They could hardly, then, have been the bearers of charismatic innovation in the Weberian sense.

The classical prophets, however, men such as Amos, Hosea, and Jeremiah, were isolated individuals who enunciated messages on behalf of non-established elements, though not necessarily poor ones, in ancient Israelite society. More importantly, they did not receive remuneration and they were "individualistic: there is no record of a prophet having learned prophecy in association with or under another prophet, or of having acquired his calling by enrolling in a guild of prophets."[6] While Orlinsky's scholarship is, of course, far more

---

[6]Orlinsky, p. 44.

sophisticated than that of his predecessors of almost a century ago, it is important to note that, at least in respect to the non-establishment framework within which he sees the classical prophets operating, he supports the work of Weber. Indeed, it would seem from Orlinsky's work that the biblical scholars upon whom Berger relies have failed to draw the distinction Orlinsky draws between the seer-priest and the classical prophet. Consequently, they have failed to see the uniqueness of the classical prophet and have improperly viewed him as emerging from a cultic office.

Any attempt, then, to claim that the social location of classical Israelite prophecy was within the cult would seem, on the basis of Orlinsky's paper, to be radically wrong. Indeed, Orlinsky's view may be said to support the sociological thesis of Max Weber, for it would appear that these classical prophets were individuals who emerged outside of the established institutional framework of ancient Israel. From this bit of historical evidence, then, Berger's modification of Weber's theory of charisma on the basis of the scholarship he cites would appear to be wrong and any sociologist who would construct a theory of charisma as being as likely to emerge from within established institutional structures as from without should look elsewhere for historical evidence to support this thesis.

16

The Use of Reason in Maimonides – An Evaluation by Ahad Ha-Am *

By Alfred Gottschalk

The medieval Jewish philosopher, Rabbi Moshe ben Maimon (Maimonides, the Rambam), was held in special regard by Ahad Ha-Am, who considered him his guide and teacher.[1] Among the Sadigura ḥasidim, with whom Ahad Ha-Am was reared, studying Maimonides was anathema, yet it was to Maimonides that the rebellious young Ahad Ha-Am was drawn and whose thought epitomized for him *shilṭon ha-śekhel*, "the supremacy of reason."[2] It was his exposure to Maimonides that finally changed him from a *mitnaged* to a *maśkil*.[3] Ahad Ha-Am paid supreme tribute to the Rambam for having brought him out of the deep

---

*The original version of this paper was delivered at the Fifth World Congress of Jewish Studies. I am proud to have it included here in tribute to my esteemed friend and teacher Samson Levey.

[1] *Kol Kit'vé Aḥad Ha-Am* (Tel Aviv: D'vir, 1956), p. 487. In his discussion of the influence of Jewish religious philosophy upon him, Ahad Ha-Am wrote: "Naturally, in the area of religious philosophy, the *Moreh N'vukhim* led the list." Further references to Maimonides' influence on Ahad Ha-Am can be discerned on pp. 487, 493.

[2] *Ibid.*, p. 493. "*Shilṭon Ha-Śekhel*" ("The Supremacy of Reason") is the title of the study Ahad Ha-Am made of Maimonides' philosophy and opens the fourth volume of the <*Al Parashat D'rakhim*, published in 1913. *Kol Kit'vé*, pp. 355-69.

[3] "Particularly dear to me was the philosophic literature from the Rambam to Ranak [Rabbi Nahman Krochmal]. I 'contemplated it day and night' until through its impact the gates of general literature were opened to me": *ibid.*, p. 495. That his opposition to Hasidism was a way-station to subscribing to the Enlightenment, is attested to by his own words: *T'qufat ha-hitnagdut sheli lo> >arkhah harbeh. >Aḥaré z'man qaẓar hayiti l'maśkil* ("My period of opposition [to Hasidism] did not last long. A short while thereafter I became a *maskil*"): *ibid.*, p. 480.

religiosity in which he had been steeped from his youth onward.[4] The *Moreh (Guide)*, Maimonides' philosophical magnum opus, awakened in Ahad Ha-Am, it appears, that great inquisitive spirit which was his natural gift and which brought him renown in the intellectual milieu of his time.

Throughout his life Ahad Ha-Am venerated Maimonides, for he saw him as the creator of the doctrine of the "supremacy of reason" developed to its most radical formulation.[5] Attempting to render religion meaningful through reason, as far as Ahad Ha-Am was concerned, was a fruitless effort. Ahad Ha-Am never found any satisfaction in a religious philosophy which was built upon metaphysical principles. Religion for Ahad Ha-Am was not a question of belief but of the heart,[6] and therefore it seems anomalous that it was Maimonides, the supreme exponent of reason, who led Ahad Ha-Am out of his ḥasidic piety and awakened his mind to the fruits of speculative thought. If religion is a matter of feeling,[7] then that feeling would hardly have been changed by Maimonides' rational method, or, for that matter, anyone's rational methods.

One can appreciate how Ahad Ha-Am, whose mind was always alive to new ideas, would have taken to Maimonides so avidly. In Maimonides one can find all the subtleties of philosophic thought as he wrestles with the obvious anthropomorphic and anthropopathic passages of the Bible, as well as his controversial discussions on whether the universe was created *ex nihilo* by a creator-God or has existed from eternity. Relative to Yehudah Halevi's arguments in *The Kuzari*, Maimonides appears to be providing the intellectual case to make it possible for Jews to entertain the notion of the eternity of matter and the universe. After amassing the evidence, particularly from Aristotle's philosophy, which leads to the conclusion of a non-created universe, Maimonides brings his reasoning to an abrupt halt and casts doubt upon the evidence which he had so brilliantly propounded. He suddenly embraces the position that one

---

[4] Ahad Ha-Am to Simon Dubnow, Vilna, January 13, 1905: he speaks of Maimonides as "the one to whom I am indebted for leading me out of the forty-nine gates of 'holiness' in which I was immersed in the beginning of my youth": Ahad Ha-Am, *Ig'rot* (Tel Aviv: D'vir, 1956), III, 334.

[5] It is because of his feeling of indebtedness to Maimonides that Ahad Ha-Am in mature years felt obliged to write a major exposition on Maimonides' contribution to Jewish thought: *ibid.*, pp. 334-35, n. 1.

[6] Ahad Ha-Am to M.K. (Moses Kalisher?), April 12, 1899: in *Ig'rot Aḥad Ha-Am*, revised and enlarged edition, ed. by Aryeh (Leon) Simon (Tel Aviv: D'vir, 1956), II, 275.

[7] Aryeh Simon and Joseph Heller, *Aḥad Ha-Am, Ha-\>ish, Po\<alo V'torato* (Jerusalem: Hebrew University Press, 1955), p. 183.

cannot conclusively prove Aristotle's contention,[8] and since Jews have a tradition of creation, the latter is to be accepted as binding upon the believer.[9]

For Ahad Ha-Am and other readers of the *Guide*, even more important than this particular conclusion at which Maimonides arrives are the arguments which he formulates in readily understandable modes of Jewish philosophical expression. Although Maimonides' conclusion is a traditional one, his method for arriving at that conclusion must be studied on its own terms. It is possible to see how, if one understands Maimonides correctly, massive doubt about traditional Jewish beliefs and dogmas could be generated, notwithstanding that Maimonides posits the thirteen principles of dogmatic Judaism as a credo of faith. Ahad Ha-Am was fully cognizant that Maimonides had introduced a new dimension to Jewish religious thought, a dimension that was not indigenous to it. This may be gleaned from his reference to Maimonides when he states: "The people has not opposed those of its sages who have filled its cask with new wine from foreign vintages, [sages] such as

---

[8]In his Introduction to the second part of the *Moreh N'vukhim*, Maimonides states:
> The premises needed for establishing the existence of deity, may He be exalted, and for the demonstration that He is neither a body nor a force in a body, and that He, may His name be sublime, is one, are twenty-five – all of which are demonstrated without there being a doubt as to any point concerning them. For Aristotle and the Peripatetics after him have come forward with a demonstration for every one of them. There is one premise that we will grant them, for through it the objects of our quest will be demonstrated, as I shall make clear; this premise is the eternity of the world.

See Moses Maimonides, *The Guide of the Perplexed*, trans. Shlomo Pines (Chicago: University of Chicago Press, 1963), p. 235. The twenty-sixth premise, "that Aristotle constantly wishes to establish as true," is opposed by every *Mutakallim* and affirmed as "necessary" by every commentator of Aristotle. Maimonides maintained that his premise in Aristotle's opinion was "the most fitting and probable." As to its "necessity," Maimonides says, "To me it seems that the premise in question is possible – that is, neither necessary . . . nor impossible": *ibid.*, pp. 240-41.

[9]*Ibid.*, pp. 329-33. Maimonides does not leave at rest the traditional Jewish concept of creation. He sets forth his own, "by means of arguments that come close to being a demonstration, that what exists indicates to us of necessity that it exists in the virtue of the purpose of One who purposed": *ibid.*, p. 303. Maimonides does not presume to call his premise "a demonstration." Since it is counterbalanced by Aristotle's premise, it is the tradition which ultimately tips the scale in favor of creation. Cf. Zvi Diesendruck, "The Philosophy of Maimonides," *Central Conference of American Rabbis Yearbook*, XLV (1935), 8-13.

the Rambam and his school, neither have they withheld reverence nor honor from them."[10]

The seventh centenary of the death of Maimonides (datable to December, 1204) occasioned essays of tribute in his memory from major Jewish thinkers throughout the world. Ahad Ha-Am took this occasion to repay a long felt debt to one whom he considered his guide and who, more than any other Jewish thinker, had led to his intellectual emancipation. The tribute to Maimonides was originally an address delivered in Russian to the Jewish Club of Odessa. Ahad Ha-Am developed the nucleus of this address into the Hebrew essay which appeared in Ḥa-shiloah under the title, "The Supremacy of Reason."[11] The article reappeared in the fourth volume of <Al Parashat D'rakhim in 1913. The noted scholar Dr. Israel Friedlaender responded, joining issue with some of Ahad Ha-Am's comments on Maimonides but dealing with Ahad Ha-Am's treatment of the subject as one expert to another.[12]

"The Supremacy of Reason," a thorough if not completely balanced presentation of Maimonides' thought, contains material germane to our present discussion. Ahad Ha-Am begins the essay by noting the different climate in the intellectual world of his day compared to what had existed previously. In the past, it would have been impossible for an educated Jew to have a single day go by without Maimonides being called to mind. Whichever way such a person would have turned, whether to religious and philosophical speculation, or to legal studies, or to problems relating to ethics, he would have had to confront Maimonides and recognize his great authority, the high place of honor and deep respect in which he was held, even by those who differed with him. Even the non-scholar met him daily when he sealed his morning prayers with the >Ani Ma>amin, the Thirteen Principles of Faith. How was it possible to forget the man who established the "principles" of Israel's faith? Today, however, if a Jew from those times were to rise from his grave and we wanted to show how far removed from our forefathers we are, it would be sufficient to tell him that now it is

---

[10]Kol Kit'vé, p. 74.
[11]Leon Simon, Ahad Ha-Am, A Biography (Philadelphia: Jewish Publication Society, 1960), p. 207.
[12]Letter to Dr. I. Friedlaender, London, June 3, 1913, Ig'rot, V, 136-41. A sober estimate of Ahad Ha-Am's mode of thought as being thoroughly Jewish while modern is made by Israel Friedlaender, Past and Present (Cincinnati: Ark Publishing Co., 1919), p. 401. Max Gruenewald, while critical of Ahad Ha-Am's sundering of the religious and the national aspect of Maimonides' thought, nevertheless concludes: "Trotz dieses Einwands ist das, was Achad Haam über das Verhältnis M.s zum Volke ausführt, bedeutsam." See Gruenewald, "Die Stellung Achad Haam's zu Maimonides," Monatsschrift für Geschichte und Wissenschaft des Judentums, LXXIX (1935), 180.

possible for a man to read Hebrew works extensively without encountering a reference to Maimonides. This is not because we have satisfactory answers to all the spiritual questions that vexed our forebears and therefore no longer need to turn to the ancient philosophy of Maimonides. It is rather because the questions themselves have been blotted out from our daily agenda and thoughts. Spiritual matters seem to be pushed aside by modern civilized men, and earthly concerns seem to hold sway. It is as if we are ashamed of spirituality in a way comparable with Aristotle's belief that the sense of touch is something of which we ought to be ashamed.[13]

In Ahad Ha-Am's estimation, Maimonides cannot be regarded as the originator of a new system. He was persuaded that Maimonides had borrowed extensively from the philosophy of Aristotle, as it was available to him through the Arab philosophers. The basic guidelines were of Aristotelian thought with an admixture of neo-Platonic doctrine, again as this had been absorbed and transmitted by the Arab philosophers.[14] What was unique in Maimonides was that he brought to their logical conclusions the ethical consequences of the assumptions borrowed from the Greeks and Arabs. Further, he developed them into something new and previously unstated, though they were implied in the fundamental principles from which he deduced these consequences.

Ahad Ha-Am gives us a clue to his own methodological reconstruction of Maimonides' thought by stating that the various sources which he is setting in logical sequential order are scattered throughout Maimonides' work. Thus, Ahad Ha-Am uses portions of the *Mishneh Torah* (Maimonides' code, his *Foundations of the Law*), Chapters i-iv, and all parts of the *Guide*.[15]

Ahad Ha-Am's thesis in this particular essay is that Maimonides subsumed all of the beliefs current in his age under the aspect of reason. In the beginning of Part II of the *Moreh*, Ahad Ha-Am underscores that Maimonides would not have evaded asserting the principle of the eternity of the universe if he had found conclusive proof to that effect, even if this meant rejecting the contrary teachings of Scripture. One would have expected, then, if Ahad Ha-Am is correct about Maimonides, that he proffer some reason for believing in the principle of creation other than that it has "the authority of prophecy." It is in this way,

---

[13] *Kol Kit'vé*, p. 355.
[14] *Ibid.*, p. 356.
[15] He also utilizes a number of secondary sources, such as Munk's *Le Guide des Égarés*, I; Scheyer's *Das Psychologische System des Maimonides* (Frankfurt, 1845); Joël's *Die Religionsphilosophie des Mose ben Maimon* (Breslau, 1876); R. Shem-Tob's *Commentary on the Guide*; and D. Rosin, *Die Ethik des Maimonides* (1876). See *Kol Kit'vé*, pp. 356 ff.

however, as Ahad Ha-Am notes, that Maimonides left room for belief in the existence of a revealed religion. Thus, Ahad Ha-Am concludes, "If the belief in the creation of the world is possible, every difficulty with regard to this question is removed."[16]

Why has God given of his prophecy to one and not to another? Why did He give his Torah to one nation in particular and not to another, and why *then*, not before or after? These were serious problems, but such troublesome questions can be resolved, according to Ahad Ha-Am, by resorting to the answer that it was God's will or wisdom which determined these happenings.[17] One may ask, however, of what relevance and use is the divine Torah? Divine religion cannot lead to man's supreme goal which, as posited by Maimonides, is the development of his intellect from the stage of potentiality to that of actuality. This is a goal achievable only by the activity of the intellect through a long process of contemplation and rational thought. Divine religion cannot lead to this goal as it is not able to elevate its followers to the level of the "actual" man, but is confined to being operative, rather, in his potential state. It must, therefore, be assumed that religion is the interim instrument required to prepare for the sought after goals.[18]

Society is the necessary environment for the realization of the actual from the potential state. The aim of religion, then, is to "regulate the soul and the body" of society so that it may produce the largest number of "actual" men possible.[19] To accomplish this, it is necessary for religion to be popular, for its teachings and ordinances to be directed not only to the select few who strive for ultimate perfection, but to all the people. Society must furnish both "true opinions," in a form acceptable to the understanding of the masses, and true moral teachings, personal and communal, providing for the welfare of society and the well-being of its members. These must be furnished through a code of religious observance whose purpose is to educate the people by reminding them constantly of the "true opinions" and their ethical obligations. Through the development of such a society, religion makes it possible for a greater number of men to develop to an "actual" state.[20]

Maimonides' presuppositions regarding the Torah of Moses are: (1) on its theoretical side it reflects "true opinions"[21] in popular form; and, (2) from a practical point of view, it is a moral doctrine geared to the individual and society which emanates from the "true opinions"

---

[16]*Kol Kit'vé*, p. 260.
[17]*Ibid.*, referring to the *Guide*, Chapter xxv. Cf. Pines trans., pp. 327-30.
[18]*Kol Kit'vé*, p. 360.
[19]*Ibid.*
[20]*Ibid.*, pp. 360 f.
[21]"*ha-de<ot ha->amitiot.*"

postulated and which, together with them, educates men and society both in right opinions and morality.[22] It is because of Maimonides' presuppositions about Torah that the Torah itself presented him with formidable problems of interpretation. The beliefs expounded in the Torah seem to be at opposite poles from the philosophical points of view characteristic of Maimonides' system. He had a clear choice to make. Either the words of the Torah as they are written mean what they say and therefore are binding, subordinating the philosophic principles, or the Torah is to be subordinated to the philosophic principles as enunciated by Maimonides. Since Maimonides, in Ahad Ha-Am's viewpoint, was convinced that he had "true opinions," necessity compelled him to subordinate religion absolutely to philosophy; he had to explain the words of the Torah so as to make them compatible with his philosophic principles and have the Torah fulfill a role which philosophical requirements imposed upon it. The methodology of homonyms reduced anthropomorphisms and anthropopathisms to rational principles, and, because of his great skill in finding support for his interpretations from other portions of Scripture and the Talmud, the Rambam succeeded in bending religion to the needs of his philosophy.[23]

Ahad Ha-Am does not explain Maimonides' method of exegesis in detail, considering it only a "memorial" that stands as a reminder of the weakness of the written word in the face of a living force[24] which converted "yes" to "no" and "no" to "yes." Ahad Ha-Am identifies this living force as a spiritual force which led Maimonides to turn the "living God" of the Torah of Moses into an abstract philosophic idea, empty of all content except the summary of various negations.[25]

Ahad Ha-Am treats Maimonides' view of divine revelation in a footnote, calling to mind Part II, Chapters xxxii-xxxviii, of the *Guide*, and Chapter vii of the *Mishneh Torah*. He disposed of these two sources in a sentence or two. The prophet, as far as Maimonides is concerned, is the most perfect ("actual") man who receives divine revelation through the "active intellect," which is charged with the guidance of the world and with bringing from potentiality to actuality all forms, including the soul.[26]

---

[22]*Kol Kit'vé*, p. 360.
[23]*Ibid.*, p. 361. Part I of the *Guide* is by and large devoted to this effort. The *Guide* is a very complex work, constructed for the double purpose of public teaching and to impart secret lore to the elite few. Of particular interest on the structure of the *Guide* is Leo Strauss' "Introduction" in Pines trans., pp. xi-lvi.
[24]"*koaḥ ḥai ba-nefesh.*"
[25]*Kol Kit'vé*, p. 361.
[26]*Ibid.*, p. 360. n. 3.

It is Ahad Ha-Am's decided point of view that Maimonides' assertion of the "supremacy of reason" effected a tremendous and fundamental revolution in the history of Jewish thought. Others before Maimonides had tried to make faith compatible with reason – but, in the last analysis, reason was subordinated to the written word. This was the case with Saadia and Yehuda Halevi. The latter gave preeminence to religion, and Ahad Ha-Am cites in a footnote a quotation from Halevi which reads: "Whosoever accepts the Torah completely without investigating it with his reason is better off than the one who investigates and researches it."[27] Saadia[28] and Halevi chose philosophical views which confirmed their religious faith. Not so Maimonides, for whom religious faith was subordinate to reason.[29]

Ahad Ha-Am ascribes to Maimonides, as the motive for postulating the "supremacy of reason," his cognition that much in Judaism could stand restructuring. It was not fulfilling its role as a "divine religion" in the way that Maimonides envisaged that role. In Maimonides' commentary on the Mishnah, he tried to give a clear statement of the "true opinions" of the Torah as well as the practical commandments through which these were to be realized. The commentary clearly concerned itself with the latter aspect, and Maimonides provides the answers from the G'mara> whenever the Mishnah leaves a point in doubt.[30] In Ahad Ha-Am's opinion, Maimonides' commentary did not make a great impression nor bring about the revolution of popular thought for which he had intended it. Later in life, with greater clarity he composed the *Mishneh Torah* ("The Second Law"), in which he set forth both practical laws on religion and morality and all the "true opinions" in language understandable to the masses. It is a masterpiece of systematic and logical arrangement in which only the decisions are cited, without supporting proofs. This time Maimonides succeeded, in Ahad Ha-Am's opinion, in teaching philosophical truths to the masses in the guise of revealed truth, which required no demonstration or proof.[31]

Maimonides next wrote the *Guide of the Perplexed*. The *Guide*, Ahad Ha-Am notes, was composed for those chosen few for whom it was necessary to show, through reason, the philosophic truth that underpinned the religious form. The few were "perplexed," torn

---

[27]*Ibid.*, p. 363; the reference is to the *Kuzari*, II, chapter xxvi.
[28]*Kol Kit'vé*, p. 363.
[29]It was the role of religion, since it could not directly raise up the "actual" from the "potential" man, to prepare the context which would make this possible. Religion was "to regulate the soul and the body" of society so as to make it yield the largest number of "actual men": *ibid.*, p. 360.
[30]*Ibid.*, p. 365.
[31]*Ibid.*

between the demands of reason and the doctrine of the divine revelation of the Torah. The *Mishneh Torah* had filled this need for the masses. The *Guide* was written for the philosopher who was also trained to believe in the truth of the Torah. Such a person would necessarily always be "in a state of perplexity and anxiety." If he were solely guided by reason, he would have to reject the fundamental beliefs of the Torah. If he chose, however, to abandon reason and adhere to the literal meaning of the Torah, he would still be in a constant state of perplexity, since his abandonment of reason would leave him with only a fundamentalist approach to the Torah resulting in fear, anxiety, and even greater perplexity.[32] Ahad Ha-Am summarizes the teaching of the *Guide* as the admonition by Maimonides to his readers to follow reason, and reason only and to interpret religion in conformity with reason. Reason is the purpose of human life. Religion remains only a means to that end.[33]

Ahad Ha-Am sees a master plan of intellectual enterprise in Maimonides' life, for he notes that Maimonides took care to establish himself first as the greatest living exponent of Judaism. Had the *Guide* been published before the *Mishneh Torah,* he certainly would have been accused of heresy by his opponents. In any case, they did precisely that after his death.[34] Having shown Maimonides' great spirit in emancipating reason from all authority, Ahad Ha-Am adds a postscript in which he, in Maimonidean style, attempts to posit the supremacy of the national sentiment. Ingeniously, Ahad Ha-Am attempts to supply an escape from the problems that confronted Maimonides. Those elements of Jewish thought and life whose intrinsic value was not readily discernible and whose rational bases were in question, were subjugated to reason by Maimonides. These elements, Ahad Ha-Am maintains, could have been rescued had Maimonides paid sufficient attention to national sentiment.[35] Maimonides could have discovered thereby that many religious statements, so troublesome to him, had no purpose other than to strengthen the feeling of national unity. He would not have had to state, for example, that the purpose of the Festivals was "their use in the establishment of friendship which is necessary among people living in political societies."[36] In dealing with the future redemption, he would not have had to say that "the wise men and the prophets longed for the day of the Messiah so that they might be free to study the Torah and its

---

[32]*Ibid.*
[33]*Ibid.*, p. 366.
[34]*Ibid.*
[35]"*ha-regesh ha-l'>umi.*"
[36]*Kol Kit'v̄é*, p. 367; with reference to the *Guide*, III, Chapter xxxxiii, Pines trans., p. 571.

wisdom without pressures so as to merit the eternal life of the world to come."[37] Statements such as the above, as well as the tenor of his teaching, indicated to Ahad Ha-Am that Maimonides did not recognize the value of the national aspect of Jewish life and did not stress it in his exposition of Judaism.

In the last part of his study on the Rambam, Ahad Ha-Am openly deals with the question of the intensity of the Rambam's national feeling. Reluctantly, Ahad Ha-Am concluded that, in the Rambam, national sentiment or feeling was not supreme. Reason was supreme. But the national sentiment was present as an unconscious instinct sometimes playing havoc with the logic of reason. By applying the criteria of national sentiment as the basic frame of reference for the appreciation of the Rambam's contribution to Jewish thought, Ahad Ha-Am has explicitly revealed his major presupposition. Reason must be yoked to *ha-regesh ha-l'>umi*.[38] For Ahad Ha-Am this national feeling, or "sentiment," whose powers are elaborately depicted in the balance of his essays, shaped Jewish consciousness and subordinated all creative powers to its will. Whereas the attainment of the active intellect is the ultimate objective for the Rambam, it is merely a means to an end in the speculations of Ahad Ha-Am. It is apparent that even the Rambam, great guide and emancipator that he was, served as an imperfect model for the perplexed of Ahad Ha-Am's time. The Rambam's thought was a point of departure rather than a program for the future.

The last lines with which Ahad Ha-Am concludes his *Shilṭon ha-Sekhel* ascribe to Maimonides an unconscious goal of supplying for the nation a system of thought upon which it could mature and grow during its dark exile. Ahad Ha-Am singles out the Rambam from his predecessors by reaffirming that, while they placed Judaism above reason, he identified Judaism with reason. Truly this was a new beginning in the evolution of Jewish thought. Ahad Ha-Am, ever the eclectic, took from the Rambam's thought elements which he later recombined into his own system as he attempted to become the *moreh n'ṽukhim* – the guide to the perplexed – for the Jews of his time in their attempt to find a solution for the Problem of Jewish Culture.

---

[37]*Ibid.*; reference to the *Mishneh Torah*, *Sefer Ha-mada<*, "Hilkhot T'shuṽah," 9:2.
[38]*Ibid.* See particularly Baruch Kurzweil's critique of Ahad Ha-Am in his "Ha-Yahadut K'giluy R'ẓon Ha-ḥayim Ha-l'>umi Ha-biologi," *Luaḥ Ha->areẓ* (Tel Aviv, 1943), and a rejoinder by Mordecai M. Kaplan, "Anti-Maimunism in Modern Dress," *Judaism*, IV, No. 4, (Fall 1955), 303-12.

17

Freud, Moses, and the Law

By Norman B. Mirsky

Professor Samson Levey's strength as a scholar, an intellectual and a human being is that he not only knows the lines, he knows how to read between the lines. He combines what appears to be total control of his sources with a fearless use of his powerful imagination. What Sigmund Freud wrote of himself, "I have often felt as though I had inherited all the defiance and all the passions with which our ancestors defended their temple,"[1] can be said of Levey. Along with Freud, Levey has all the defiance and passion of those greats who have the courage to withstand the pressures of what Freud called "the compact majority."[2] It is because Samson Levey has these virtues, particularly the virtue of imagination, that I have found the courage to write this essay in his honor.

As students of Freud know, Freud, in addition to being a man of compassion, was also a man of obsession. Though he was remarkably willing to reexamine and restructure theories and techniques in which he had invested enormous energy and many years of work, he was unwilling and unable to let go of certain objects and ideas to which his passion was wedded. In the realm of objects, two spring readily to mind. He would not or could not abandon his cigars, though they may have caused and certainly exacerbated the cancer of the jaw which led to his painful death. A less dramatic example of Freud's obsessive side is found in his passion for collecting archaeological artifacts. While his admirers have judged this passion to be a charming departure from his concern for words, ideas and the welfare of others, he himself found the need to collect these objects beyond his control, particularly since he

---

[1] Sigmund Freud, *An Autobiographical Study* (London: Hogarth Press, 1923), p. 1.
[2] *Ibid.*

had expensive tastes and was continually in financial straits. A responsible and devoted family man, he purchased these artifacts with the family treasury and had to expand his caseload to ease his self-induced financial burden. And Freud's obsession extended into another area not unrelated to his passion for archaeological artifacts: he was obsessed with the biblical Moses.

Much has been written of Freud's identification with Moses.[3] Peter Gay reminds us that "the figure of Moses," as Freud himself told Lou Andreas-Salome in 1935,

> had haunted him all his life. All one's life is a long time, but a quarter century before, in 1909, he had indeed compared Jung to a Joshua who would take possession of the promised land of psychiatry while he, Freud, the Moses was destined to glimpse it only from afar.[4]

Most students of Freud know that the bombastic *Moses and Monotheism*, published in 1938, was his last sustained work. Peculiarly structured and even for Freud remarkably tendentious, ambivalent and ambiguous, *Moses and Monotheism* had something in it designed to offend everyone. Freud was hardly unaware of the book's peculiarities and seemed rather proud of its potential to offend – as though he were acting out yet again his self-comparison to those of his ancestors who had fought to the last defending the Second Temple.[5] Terminally ill and in pain so agonizing that his attending physician, Max Schur, could barely endure witnessing it, Freud remained with the book and did not call for the lethal injection of morphine that ended his suffering until *Moses and Monotheism* appeared in print.[6]

Though my effort here is intended to add to the weight of evidence that supports Freud's identification with Moses and though it is possible and challenging to interpret *Moses and Monotheism* as an autobiographical text, nevertheless I will to some degree accept this as a given. Instead, it is my intent to concentrate on Freud's earliest ruminations on the subject of Moses, his essay entitled "The Moses of Michelangelo," which is to be found in Volume IV of *The Collected*

---

[3] See especially Peter Gay's *Freud: A Life for Our Time* (New York: W.W. Norton, 1988), and Paul Roazen, *Freud and His Followers* (New York: Knopf, 1975).
[4] Gay, *Freud*, p. 605.
[5] *Ibid.*, p. 604; Roazen, p. 23.
[6] Max Schur, *Freud: Living and Dying* (New York: International Universities Press, 1972). For a detailed discussion of Freud's illness and its relation to the publication of *Moses and Monotheism*, see pp. 454-75 and 511-29.

Papers, edited by Freud's official biographer, Ernest Jones.[7] The essay had originally appeared anonymously in the 1914 volume of *Imago* where it was prefaced by an editorial note:

> Although this paper does not strictly speaking conform to the conditions under which contributions are accepted for publication in this journal, the editors have decided to print it since the author who is personally known to them belongs to psychoanalytical circles and his mode of thought has in point of fact a certain resemblance to the methodology of psychoanalysis.[8]

Again, those familiar with Freud will recognize the intentional irony in this note. In 1912, in association with Hans Sachs, Otto Rank had founded the periodical *Imago*, "specializing, as its masthead proclaimed, in the application of psychoanalysis to the cultural sciences."[9]

When the paper on Michelangelo's Moses was published in 1914, it was printed as being "by ******." Freud had assisted in the founding of *Imago*, and at least two of Freud's associates, Karl Abraham and Ernest Jones, were aware of its authorship.[10] Abraham questioned the anonymity and wrote to Freud, "Don't you think that one will recognize the lion's claw?"[11] Certainly, Rank and Sachs recognized Freud's style (if indeed they had not actually been told that he was the author of the paper). It is impossible to surmise that, among *Imago*'s subscribers (fewer than 500), most of them familiar with Freud's interests and his writing style, some did not know that the paper had been written by Freud.[12] Freud, nevertheless, referred to the paper as his "love child" and did not acknowledge his paternity for ten years.[13]

Though the footnote to the essay is sardonic in tone, Freud's reluctance or psychological inability to put his name to the essay is too consistent with other behavior, where Moses is concerned, to allow either irony or shyness to explain the initial insistence on anonymity. *Moses and Monotheism* offers a comparable indirection. According to Gay, Freud began work on this last opus in the summer of 1934, but kept it "a fairly closely held secret."[14] "Who this Moses was and how he

---

[7] Sigmund Freud, *Collected Papers* [*CP*] (New York: Basic Books, 1953), IV, 257-87.
[8] Ibid., p. 257.
[9] Gay, *Freud*, p. 311.
[10] *Ibid*, p. 314.
[11] *Ibid*.
[12] *Ibid*.
[13] *Ibid*.
[14] *Ibid*., p. 605.

had worked his way with the Jews," Freud would answer "in a kind of historical novel."[15]

If this is not sufficient evidence to convince the reader that Freud had some difficulty in acknowledging his "Moses situation," there are the fainting spells. Twice in the presence of Jung, Freud fainted. One spell took place in 1909, at Bremen, as the two set sail for the United States. The second, more dramatic and more relevant to the Moses theme, took place at Munich in 1912. Freud and Jung had been discussing Karl Abraham's recent paper on the ancient Egyptian Pharaoh Amenhotep IV (Ikhnaton). Years later, in *Moses and Monotheism*, Freud would ascribe to the pharoah's teachings both Moses' monotheism and most of the ethical and legal strictures which Moses imposed on the Hebrews and for which, Freud supposed, he was killed by them; he thus stamped his character on the Hebrews through residual guilt. Moses, Freud speculated, was an Egyptian and a follower of Ikhnaton.[16] Paul Roazen quotes Jung:

> the point was made that as a result of his negative attitude to his father [the pharoah] had destroyed his father's cartouches on the steles and that at the back of his great creation of a monotheistic religion there lurked a father complex. This sort of thing irritated me, and I attempted to argue that [Ikhnaton] had been a creative and profoundly religious person whose acts could not be explained by personal resistances toward his father. On the contrary, I said, he had held the memory of his father in honor, and his zeal for destruction had been directed only against the name of the god, Amon... at that moment Freud slid off his chair in a faint.[17]

As Roazen correctly concludes, the question of the origins of the Jewish religion and, one may add, its derivatives, Christianity and psychoanalysis, along with the fate of their founding fathers, was of no small concern to Freud.

Freud's essay on the Moses of Michelangelo includes all the elements discussed above: his obsession with Moses, his need for anonymity or the "cover of the historical" when writing about the lawgiver, his hostile relationship with Jews, the nature of the constituency with whom Moses was dealing – these are all touched upon in the 1914 *Imago* article. My paper will ultimately rest its case on Freud's acceptance of all but one theory put forward by art historians. "It was to be only a fragment of the gigantic tomb which the artist was to have erected for the powerful Julius II." Freud wrote:

---

[15]*Ibid*.
[16]Freud, *Moses and Monotheism* (New York: Vintage Books, 1955), p. 21.
[17]Roazen, pp. 247-48; Freud, *CP*, IV, 259-60.

> It always delights me to read appreciative sentences about this statue such as that it is "the crown of modern sculpture" (Herman Grimm), for no piece of statuary has ever made a stronger impression on me that this. How often have I mounted the steep steps of the unlovely Corso Cavour to the lonely place where the deserted church stands, and have essayed to support the *angry* scorn of the hero's glance! Sometimes I have crept cautiously out of the half gloom of the interior as though I myself belonged to the mob upon whom his eye is turned, to the mob which can hold fast no conviction, which has neither faith nor patience and which rejoices when it has regained its illusory idols.[18]

Because Moses was to be one of five figures enthroned at the papal tomb, Moses too is seated. Whether or not his visage is one of anger or sadness is not self-evident. Nor is it self-evident that Moses is looking toward a "mob" or avoiding their glance. There is no mob in sight. It is not clear whether Moses intends to remain seated, is forcing himself to remain seated, or is about to stand up, nor is it abundantly clear what Moses intends to do with the tablets of the law. Is he about to rise and smash them in a rage? Is he trying desperately to hold onto them and his famous temper? Perhaps these are even the second set of tablets that a more sanguine Moses has received. None of this is self-evident. The last possibility is not even suggested. What is argued is that Freud, anonymity and modesty aside, feels that he is uniquely qualified to divulge Michelangelo's intent in carving the statue as it appears. Freud writes:

> I do not mean that connoisseurs and lovers of art find no words with which to praise such objects to us. They are eloquent enough it seems to me. But usually in the presence of a great work of art each sees something different from the other: and none of them says anything that solves the problem for the unpretending admirer. In my opinion, it can only be the artist's intention, in so far as he has succeeded in expressing it in work and conveying it to us that grips us so powerfully. I realize that it cannot be merely of intellectual comprehension. What he aims at is to awaken in us the same emotional attitude, the same mental constellation as that which in him produced the impetus to create. But why should the artist's intention not be capable of being communicated and comprehended in words like any other fact of mental life? Perhaps where great works of art are concerned this *would never be possible without the application of psychoanalysis.*[19]

Here let us disregard the fact that a particular work of art is the object of psychoanalytic interpretation. Rather let us read the above as a declaration of the unique qualification of the psychoanalyst. Lovers

---

[18]Freud, *CP*, IV, 254-60 (my emphasis).
[19]*Ibid.*, p. 258 (my emphasis).

and connoisseurs, those who claim to know a person or his products either through emotional bonding or trained expertise in objective judgment, are only capable of saying something endearing about the product in question.

What both the lover and the expert connoisseur lack is the method necessary to draw forth and interpret the latent intent of both the artist and the work. Only a psychoanalyst has the right to claim such ability. If in place of Michelangelo's Moses we substitute the anorexia of Anna O. or the fantasies of the "Rat Man," or less dramatically, the everyday repetition-compulsion of the hand-washer or the ordinary dreamer of dreams, we have in Freud's statement quoted above as concise and as arrogant a justification of the need for psychoanalysis and psychoanalysts as we are likely to find anywhere. Everybody interprets. It is how we human beings survive. We are presented with the data of everyday life and consciously or unconsciously we interpret them, we categorize them and rightly or wrongly, destructively or healthily, all of us deal with those data. Temporarily, we must set Freud's genius aside and concentrate on the exclusivity of his claim of truth for psychoanalysis and its practitioners.

Furthermore, to underscore the possible validity of my essay I propose to set aside an even more obvious fact. Whatever the claims of psychoanalysts and their methodology, it must be said that in most instances they are dealing with living patients – with individuals – who can testify in some way to the validity of an analyst's claim and to the correctness of the interpretation. Where the datum is an inanimate object like Michelangelo's sculpture of Moses, its creator has been dead for over three hundred years. How is it possible to venture anything more than a creative tendentious conjecture as to the intent of the artist and his work? And if the question is relevant to art and artifacts, how much more relevant is it to the mental reconstruction of the origins of the entire enterprise which we call culture?

The answer is that it does take a great deal of confidence in one's methodology to attempt such a feat. But what Freud does in employing psychoanalysis is in reality no different from what anthropologists and historians do as their daily work. They move with impunity from the known (artifacts, documents) to the unknown (motives, intents). It can be said for Freud that, where his works on Moses are concerned, he was uncommonly reticent: in the instance of Michelangelo's Moses, Freud employed anonymity and, in the case of *Moses and Monotheism*, he was originally going to call the book an historical novel. Even so, the criticisms raised with regard to the audacity of one who interprets art with what can at best be called "informed imagination" can be levelled against Freud no more than against the most reputable anthropologists and historians. Thus *it is impossible* for me not to feel a certain unease as I attempt to do to Freud what he did to others – namely, attempt to read into Freud's reading of Michelangelo's Moses more about Freud than about Michelangelo.

What gives Freud *carte blanche* to speculate on what Michelangelo intended in carving the great sculpture is both the ambiguity of the sculpture and the lack of information as to Michelangelo's psychological intent. The same cannot be said of Freud – who indeed has left much evidence of his intentions with regard to psychoanalysis, his proprietary feelings toward the psychoanalytic method, and his own inner conflicts. Furthermore, Peter Gay to the contrary[20] notwithstanding, throughout his life and throughout his work Freud manifests a powerful ambivalence, not only towards the situation of being Jewish in the nineteenth and twentieth centuries, but towards the Jewish *religion*. It is easy to see Freud as the debunker or the patronizing interpreter of the need for religion. It is also easy to surmise that Freud's description of religion as an obsessive-compulsive neurosis for the masses could have emerged from his familiarity with traditional Judaism with its heavy emphasis on salvation attained through the performance or avoidance of behaviors believed to have been revealed as divine law. If, however, we concentrate on Freud's "Moses fixation," it is just as easy to claim the powerful tug of Freud's ancestors. As has been noted before, for a man who had so little use for religion in general or Judaism in particular, Freud certainly had a great deal to say about both religion and Judaism.

But let us limit the scope of this essay to Freud's Moses – or should one say Freud's many Moseses? The Freudian Moses is presented as a complex and contradictory figure, but above all as a Moses who had a grandeur about him. It is not necessary to delve too deeply into the Moses of the Torah. It is merely sufficient to acknowledge the grandeur of the Mosaic personality as well as the contradictions within the text.[21] As recently as Janson's *History of Art* in the mid-1980's,[22] various interpretations of Michelangelo's intent are still being argued. We are thus left with the entire complex of Freud's relation to Moses, the mythic, ambiguous figure manifest in Freud's *projections* onto the *statue* and later amplified in Freud's extended *projection*, his book *Moses and Monotheism*.

It is my contention that a careful reading of *Moses and Monotheism* yields an inner autobiography of the father of psychoanalysis. Freud's

---

[20] See Peter Gay *A Godless Jew: Freud, Atheism, and the Making of Psychoanalysis* (Cincinnati: Hebrew Union College Press, 1987).
[21] Freud, *CP*, IV, 279.
[22] H.W. Janson, *History of Art* (New York: Harry Abrams, 1986), pp. 423-28.

cancer of the jaw and his need for a foreign spokesman in the person of his "brother" Aaron have been adduced to substantiate the claim that the stuttering Moses served as a screen for the projection of a Freud who needed a non-Jewish articulator or the claim that the stuttering Moses was a reflection of Freud's own physical pain after his surgery. Both have led to the interpretation of Freud's identification with a tongue-tied Moses.

Furthermore, a first reading of *Moses and Monotheism* would obviously lead one to conclude that Freud saw himself as both accepted and rejected by the Jews. He was personally well liked by many Jews, both intellectuals and those less intellectual, but Freud threatened the new position of Jews struggling to overcome what Cuddihy has called the "ordeal of civility." Freud had dredged from the unconscious of humankind the very material that the new middle classes had driven underground, both consciously and unconsciously. If ever the term "dirty Jew" could apply to anyone, it could be and has been applied to Sigmund Freud. Freud himself, of course, maintained that psychoanalysis was a science and that science transcended all national boundaries.

A reading of *Moses and Monotheism* discloses, in addition, Freud's distaste for Christianity, his feeling of physical and intellectual insecurity under the Roman Catholic Church and his notion that Judaism, despite its neurotic solution to the obsessive compulsive syndrome, was superior to the God-devouring rituals and beliefs of Christianity. Though, to some, Freud appears personally ambivalent about being Jewish (indifferent is the word Peter Gay uses) and, to others, defiantly proud of his Jewishness (Paul Roazen), it is quite evident to me that Freud never denied his Jewishness and, beyond that, in *Moses and Monotheism* even made an outright assertion that Judaism with its devotion to abstract ethical behavior had produced a morally and ethically superior people, no matter how tortuous the road to that achievement was.

Freud's feelings about Judaism and his own Jewishness are clearly manifest as is his desire for acceptance by the emancipated Jewish elite. In this sense, he stands somewhere between Spinoza and Maimonides. The opinion of Jews meant a great deal to Freud, though their religious beliefs were not his own and his "creation," psychoanalysis, was antireligious. Nevertheless, as has been repeatedly asserted, Freud was not immune to the opinions of Jews or to a concern for their destiny. His wish was to replace Judaism with the superior "revelation" of science and especially his contribution to it, psychoanalysis. These and other variables made the connection between Freud and the Jews problematic. Still, if Freud regarded the Jewish mind as superior at attaining an elevated ethical level due to whatever cause (even the killing of the Egyptian lawgiver, Moses), then it is reasonable to assume that Freud regarded Jews as a kind of chosen people.[23]

In Freud's originally anonymous essay on Michelangelo's Moses sculpture, another aspect of Freud's cathexis to Moses emerges, this time in a "mechanism of defense" projection. The ego (the reality principle) mediates between the stern edicts of the superego and the lustful wishes of the id. The ego protects itself by projecting onto others whatever inappropriate impulses it itself possesses. Aggression in the form of hostility is one of those impulses. For the ego to protect itself from feelings damaging to its self-esteem (in this instance, hostility), it needs to project those very feelings onto the object of the arouser of those feelings.[24]

We have seen that Freud had an obsession with Moses the statue and with Moses the man. I have strongly hinted that Freud regarded himself as a latter-day Moses. What remains to be demonstrated in this essay is that Freud, at least as far back as 1914, but probably as early as the very inception of the psychoanalytic technique, developed a relationship with his patients that he unconsciously felt was similar to Moses' relationship to the masses Moses had liberated from slavery.

Among Freud's truly innovative techniques was that of free association – a technique in which the patient was encouraged to let the unconscious roam free, expressing not only its fears, but its most socially inappropriate fantasies, including of course those which violated not only the "Mosaic" code but the strictures of "Victorian" (i.e., bourgeois) society as well. Freud himself was no libertine. He was by all accounts as proper in his public and (it is likely) in his private behavior as any bourgeois gentleman could be. Yet, his "law," his talking cure, was based on one fundamental "dictum": "Thou shalt listen without apparent judgment, hear whatsoever a patient divulges by way of action through his wishes!" Without this method, psychoanalysis is but another cure. We can only imagine what Freud the healer, Freud the innovator, Freud the Viennese bourgeois, Freud the Jew felt about what he heard. We do know – as Freud knew – that, without the *Law of Freedom of Association as Technique*, psychoanalysis would not have been unique.

Here is the primal scene! Freud, an educated, semi-assimilated moralist, is bound by law (his own!) to be privy to all the physical and psychological acting out of his patients. Without free association, psychoanalysis has no claim to uniqueness. Without *it*, the employment

---

[23] Freud, *Moses and Monotheism*, p. 150.
[24] Gay, *Freud*, p. 281.

of the psychoanalytic method is deprived of its most innovative, most curative element. Therefore, Freud the moralist binds himself to a law – the law of listening unjudgmentally to the free association of others (the message?), while the lawgiver himself is restrained, forbidden by laws he himself has laid down to impose punishment upon the "guilty."

In other words, the role of analyst and patient are reversed. It is the analyst who dares not deviate from the law. It is the patient who is liberated (as part of the cure) to roam freely among the libidinally charged objects of desire! From a psychotherapeutic point of view, this is innovative, curative, and unique. From the first analyst's perspective, it must have been a severe strain. The analyst has bound himself to "the law." The patient has been told to express in effect all the impulses connected with the Golden Calf scene – every violation of Mosaic prohibitions. Here is the paradox and my suggestion as to Freud's reaction to the Moses of Michelangelo.

We cannot say how far back Freud's identification with Moses goes. We do know that, in *Moses and Monotheism*, the relationship between Freud and Moses appears to be highly complex. What I am proposing in this paper is the following: Freud, a genius, an innovator, but also a bourgeois, had discovered, or invented, or "revealed" a law through which the quality of human life could be elevated. Most of his contemporaries, elitist or common, found this law threatening, while those who accepted it out of desperation, fear or need were bound by its strictures. This "law" encouraged the masses (the patients) to liberate themselves from "the law" of bourgeois constraints. The patients' cure lay in the verbal confession of their wish to run amuck or in admitting that they had indeed "sinned."

Who, then, was bound by "the law"? To some degree it was the patient. But to a far greater degree it was the analyst. For, if truth be told, no matter the secret proclivities of leaders, they are bound in public by the rules they are empowered to defend! If a leader wishes to remain a leader, he has to appear to defend the rules by which he leads. The leader is, in theory, more constrained by "the rules" than are the led. Freud was the founder of psychoanalysis. He was both its God and its Moses. He was creator and revealer and enforcer of the law. The law included the "commandment" that it is the analyst's obligation to remain nearly impassive as the patient struggles to free himself of his symptoms through verbal liberation from the laws of civilized society.

How tempting it must have been for the first psychoanalyst to leap up and shriek to the patient, "that's disgusting, that's foolish, that's immoral" – yet, for Freud to express himself so would have destroyed not only the patient but the method. It would have broken the *law*! In fact, the patient, having spewed forth his deeds and his wishes could have left the office and never returned. If the patient found the "law" too taxing, he could go on leading his life as he had before. The analyst, on the other hand, has no such freedom. Is it too far fetched, therefore, to see in Freud's obsession with and his reaction to Michelangelo's statue a projection of the analyst's own ambivalence?

Almost alone among the various interpretations of the statue is Freud's. He sees Moses struggling to remain seated. He sees the lawgiver stroking his beard with one hand while clinging to the tablets with the other. He does not see Moses as about to get up and smash the tablets. Indeed, Freud's interpretation is the exact opposite. It is my opinion that the Moses of Michelangelo represents to Freud's unconscious his own situation. Bound by the law he has given, Freud the analyst-lawgiver to his people (disciples, patients, the enlightened world) unconsciously sees in the enigmatic, seated Moses of Michelangelo – himself.

Freud is the liberator of those enslaved to guilt, yet at the same time he is the collector of antiquities (idols). Freud is the giver of the law of pure tolerance, first to himself, then as lawgiver to his followers. Freud as creator, revealer, defender of the law is bound to observe it. If he breaks the law, he discredits it. In short, Sigmund Freud is the enthroned Moses of Michelangelo. He is seated but not as judge and not in judgment. Sitting among the great (at the tomb of Pope Julius II), he is bound by that which makes him great. He dare not break the law, for it is the law which he has given which makes him great. Yet it is also the same law that constrains human instincts (on the part of the analyst). To break the law is to lose one's place in history. For Freud, a place in history was his self-promised land!

18

The Good Life

By J. Wesley Robb

Rarely does one find a teacher who embodies what he teaches, but Samson H. Levey is an exception. First and foremost, Professor Levey is a rabbi, a teacher in the most profound meaning of that term. His impeccable scholarship has made a lasting contribution to scholars throughout the world. He is an exemplar of the best within his own tradition and within the larger framework of the humanistic community. His scholarly interests are boundless; his vision reaches out to all mankind; his personal warmth knows no stranger; his counsel to his students is wise; his ethical and moral concerns are expressed through a deep commitment to universal human well-being; and his stature as a man of integrity and moral courage is an inspiration to us all.

When I was asked to contribute to this volume, I was greatly honored, but I pointed out to the editors that I am not a talmudist and wondered what contribution I might make to the Festschrift in his honor. When Professor Levey heard of my quandary, he suggested that he would like me to adapt the address I gave at the Baccalaureate Service at the University of Southern California in May, 1988. My immediate response was my concern for the appropriateness of such an address for a scholarly volume. However, since the address is about the good life, based upon the prophet Micah's understanding of what the good life entails, and since Professor Levey has made dramatically clear, in his own life, what constitutes the good life, I am pleased to include this statement as my contribution. Perhaps the affiliate relationship that the Hebrew Union College-Jewish Institute of Religion and the University of Southern California enjoy, and the fact that Professor Levey was very influential in establishing this union, makes this essay even more fitting.

When the early settlers of the American colonies planned for the future, they thought of the importance of higher education and the close tie that religious values should play in the education of the future leadership of our country. These common values were expressed in the purposes for which the colleges were established: (1) to prepare young men and women for responsible leadership roles in the society; (2) to educate future teachers who would instill in young people religious values; (3) to assure an educated clergy – in other words, to prepare all of their students for the good life.

As a focus for our remarks, I call your attention to two statements, one from Jewish sources and the other from the founders of the University of Southern California.

First, from the eighth-century B.C.E. prophet Micah:

> He has shown you...what is good; and what does the Lord require of you, but to do justice, and to love kindness and to walk humbly with your God.[1]

And, as the Babylonian Talmud adumbrates it,

> ... and what the Lord doth require of thee: (i) only to do justly, (i.e., maintaining justice), and (ii) to love mercy, (i.e., rendering every kind office), and (iii) to walk humbly before God (i.e., walking with modesty as in a funeral and bridal procession).[2]

The second statement is from an inscription at the entrance to the campus written by the founders of the University:

> The University of Southern California established here July 29, 1879 to the glory of God and to the preservation of the Republic. An institution of higher learning dedicated to the search for and the dissemination of the truth, to freedom of thought and discussion. To intelligent, unbiased analysis of the forces that have shaped the past and will mold the future, to the development of manhood and womanhood for ... service and for loyal citizenship.

You will note that neither of these statements mention power, success, longevity, wealth, leisure, financial security or even happiness as essential values. Rather, the emphasis is upon honor, responsibility, love, justice, honest inquiry, and humility in the search for truth – the formula for the good life.

The word good is an ethical or moral term. We speak of a good person as possessing a quality of life that we admire. He or she may have little social status or power and may not be successful in the common understanding of that term, but that person is an individual of integrity and trustworthiness who expresses generosity of spirit, human warmth and understanding. Doubtless, as you read these words, you are

---

[1] Micah 6:8.
[2] T.B. Makot 24a: I am indebted to Professor Arnold Dunn for this reference.

thinking of some special individual, that rare and authentic human being, who has made an unforgettable impact upon your life. In all probability, the life of that individual was characterized by what the prophet believed was our highest duty: to do justice, to love mercy (lovingkindness), and to walk with dignity and modesty before God. Therefore, I would like to propose the rather bold and, in our time, the somewhat novel notion that the good life is inseparable from the moral life.

Often we meet such persons in the formative years of our lives, and they make a lasting impression upon us. In my own childhood, I knew such a man. He was a member of my father's parish and made his living repairing automobile radiators in the days of the Model A Ford, the Essex and the Studebaker – cars that always seemed to have leaky radiators. I would frequently ride my bicycle down to his shop in an old barn and watch him work. I can still smell the solder and the acid and see the little torch he used to seal the holes in the tubes of the radiator. Why was I so enchanted? It was not because of what he did for a living, though I found that interesting, but because he talked about life and ideas and those values he cherished. Though he had never sat in a college classroom, the loft of his shop was filled with hundred of books and magazines that nourished his mind and soul; indeed, he embodied those values that gave stability and meaning to life – a concern that others be treated justly, caring for their wellbeing combined with a deep faith. For him the good life was the moral life.

As an outline for this reflection, I want to look briefly at the prophet Micah's formula for the good life.

Justice
The Just Person in a Just Society

I am fully aware of the difficulty in defining justice. It has been the topic for scholarly deliberation from ancient times to the present. It has been the subject for college courses, and its implementation has been and will continue to be a source of political, legal and legislative debate. For our purposes, however, may I suggest that in a very fundamental and elementary sense the notion of justice means that we treat other persons with a sense of fairness and equity and respect for their dignity as human beings with rights that correspond to what we expect for ourselves. Certainly these principles were in the mind of the prophet and assuredly these ideas marked the commitment of our nation's Founding Fathers when they proclaimed equality and justice for all.

The plea for justice by the eighth-century prophets was based upon the prevailing practices of the time in which the powerful disregarded the rights of the poor and the disenfranchised within society. Their preachments were unambiguous:

> *Amos*: [You] sell the righteous for silver, and the needy for a pair of shoes...[you] trample the head of the poor into the dust of the earth, and turn aside the afflicted...you who afflict the righteous, who take a bribe, and turn aside the needy at the gate.[3]
>
> *Hosea*: There is no faithfulness or kindness and no knowledge of God in the land; there is swearing, lying, killing, stealing ...you break all bounds and murder follows murder.[4]
>
> *Micah*: Woe to those who devise wickedness and work evil upon their beds! When the morning dawns, they perform it, because it is in the power of their hand. They covet fields, and seize them and houses, and take them away; they oppress a man and his house, a man and his inheritance. [And finally] is it not for you to know justice? ...you who hate the good and love the evil.[5]

Parallels to conditions in our own time are not difficult to find. The plight of the homeless, the poor, including the working poor, those who are victims of exploitation and greed, human beings – in the language of our religious tradition, "children of God" – whose right to be treated justly is the same as that we demand for ourselves.

Shortly after World War II, Edward R. Murrow, celebrated war correspondent, was asked, "What was the most impressive thing you saw during the war?" He replied, "When London was under siege, Parliament spent the good part of a day debating the rights of the prisoners of war they had captured." One would have expected him to mention some dramatic incident in battle in which soldiers showed great courage in defending themselves against great odds. No, Murrow chose an event that illustrated the very essence of what it means to be a civilized society, a society that respects human rights and justice.

We have made great strides within the past generation. The Civil Rights Act of 1964 and the Voting Rights Act of 1965 were landmark events in our history. But there is still work to do, and that is the challenge for all of us. In April, 1988, a group of religious and civil rights leaders stood in front of homeless people in downtown Los Angeles, as a memorial to the death of Martin Luther King, Jr., and proclaimed once again the demand for a "society of justice, peace and mutual respect."

Anthony M. Kennedy, recently appointed to the United States Supreme Court, addressed the faculty of law at the University of Virginia. He talked about the three R's that he believed to be essential

---

[3] See Amos 2:6-7; 5:12.
[4] Hosea 4:1-2.
[5] Micah 2:1-2; 3:1-20.

to a legal education, and one of them was "reverence for justice." He said he chose the word "reverence" rather than "respect" because he found it more compelling. It places a concern for justice within the context of a frame of mind that recognizes it as an ultimate value in contrast to a socially contrived standard or convention.

Freedom is an ally of justice. When men and women are denied justice, they want to be free from tyranny and oppression. The cry for freedom is not limited to one area of the globe, but typifies conditions in all parts of our world where people are denied their human rights. This longing for liberation from the forces of oppression and evil is expressed from the Western Hemisphere to South Africa and beyond. In the late 1950's Voznesensky, the Soviet poet, was denied permission to leave the Soviet Union to read his poetry at a literary festival in New York City. He wrote a letter to *Pravda* and said, "I am a Soviet writer, a human being made of flesh and blood, not a puppet to be pulled on a string."

The desire for freedom and justice seems innate within the human species regardless of those social forces that would endeavor to condition us to accept slavery and bondage. In *Notes from the Underground*, Dostoevski speaks of the innate desire on the part of humankind to be more than "keys of a piano," or "stops on an organ." He points out that no matter what man's lot in life might be, he would have "to prove to himself...that men are still men... And this is not all," he adds:

> even if man were really nothing but a piano key, even if this were proved to him by natural science and mathematics, even then he would not become reasonable, but would purposely do something perverse out of simple ingratitude, simply to gain his point.[6]

Yes, the just person in a just society makes the good life possible.

Lovingkindness
The Loving Person in a Caring Society

Love and justice are integrally related. Unfortunately, altruism is often expressed in condescending ways demeaning to the person we are trying to help. Frequently, acts of assistance are performed out of duty without empathetic identification with the person who is in need. But if I really care for your wellbeing, I will not only try to understand your plight, but I will also work within society to remedy those conditions

---

[6]Fyodor Dostoevski, *Notes from the Underground*, in *Three Short Novels of Dostoevsky*, trans. by Constance Garnett (Garden City: Doubleday, 1960), p. 206.

that have brought about your suffering, or if I cannot do that, I will do everything that is within my power to be of assistance to you.

Some time ago the Simon Wiesenthal Center in Los Angeles paid special homage to Father Joseph Gorajek, a Polish priest who saved dozens of Jews from the Nazi invaders by hiding them in his parish at great risk to himself and others. What made this ceremony so moving was that it brought together Father Gorajek and Eugene Winnik, a Southern California resident, whose life had been spared as a child by the lovingkindness of this priest. Mr. Winnik said that he was coached by the priest to pretend to be Catholic by observing Catholic rites, but "at no time," reported Mr. Winnik, "did this courageous priest, who risked so much, ever encourage me to leave my faith or my people." In my view, this is what authentic lovingkindness means and links a concern for justice and love with action. I think this awareness that love and justice are inseparably linked was in the minds of the United States Roman Catholic Bishops' Pastoral Letter on Catholic Social Teaching and the American Economy. Their concerns not only focussed on the social problems we face as a nation, but upon the global community that, in their view, must be based upon dignity, solidarity and justice. They were unequivocal in their affirmation that "human dignity, realized in community with others, is the primary criterion for evaluating every social institution."

In more specific terms, a caring community places high on its agenda of concern the plight of the unemployed, the infirm, the hungry, and the inadequately clothed and sheltered. It is estimated that there are thirty-three million Americans who live below the poverty level and another twenty to thirty million who are needy, and the alarming fact is that the largest single group among the poor are children who, through no fault of their own, are caught in circumstances over which they have no control. In the field of health care alone, it is estimated that at least thirty-five million Americans have no provision for health care, either public or private. Here the challenge is to translate love and caring into action.

On the very personal level, love and caring are perhaps two of the most important ingredients of a good life. I have asked my students over the years in my courses in human values to list the most important values that they believe would bring fulfillment and meaning to their lives and invariably it was to love and be loved. Perhaps more books about love are currently published than ever before; yet, authentic love is so elusive. We idealize and fantasize about it, but so infrequently experience love's depth and richness of meaning. I think that one of the reasons why so many people are disillusioned about love is that it is often divorced from its ethical and moral underpinnings. We ask, what will I get from the relationship, not what can I give to the relationship. Erich Fromm, humanistic psychologist, whose writings I have used as a reference source in my teaching, states well the ethical components that give love substance and meaning:

> Love is the productive form of relatedness to others and to oneself. It implies responsibility, care, respect and knowledge, and the wish for the other person to grow and develop. It is the expression of intimacy between two human beings under the condition of the preservation of each other's integrity.[7]

Note the ethical elements: responsibility, respect, and the preservation of the integrity of both individuals in the relationship. This understanding runs counter to the prevailing image of love that permeates the television airwaves and slick magazines on our newsstands.

For most of us, the quality of love that Fromm describes is discovered through deep and abiding relationships of family and close friendships. These are the ties that give meaning and direction to our lives; for many of us, they have profound religious significance. Martin Buber, venerated Jewish philosopher, saw this clearly as he wrote about the divine and the sacred emerging within the context of human understanding and love. Likewise, Gabriel Marcel, noted Roman Catholic philosopher, saw human love as expressive of divine love in which all persons bear within themselves the divine image and thus should be seen as persons and not as objects to be exploited or used for one's own selfish ends.

Marcel visited the University of Southern California campus a number of years ago and gave a most impressive lecture. He pointed out that most people are only valuable to us as they have a service to perform that we need. For example, the plumbing in our home stops up and the plumber becomes the most important person in the world because of our immediate need. He comes and performs his service and soon passes into oblivion as an individual until we need his services again. Marcel's point was that in an increasingly complex urban society, people become objects, impersonal agents whose identity becomes synonymous with their function in society. These nameless faces, often torn with pain and sorrow, haunt my memory as I think of the waiter, the maid in the hotel, the taxi driver, the porter, and many others who have personal problems as we do, but live behind the mask of their social roles. Marcel's point is well taken, and although we cannot provide equal caring and attention to every person we meet, we

---

[7]Erich Fromm, *Man for Himself* (New York: Rinehart, 1947), p. 110.

can express a basic courtesy and respect that all human beings deserve as children of God.

I believe Marcel points the way to a more profound understanding of what love means when he suggests that, when true love is manifested, there is a *presence* that is felt and experienced and is grounded in a *divine presence* or God. One of Marcel's commentators summarizes this notion of the relationship between love and the experience of the Divine as follows:

> The more I love you the surer I am of your eternity: the more I grow in authentic love for you, the deeper becomes my trust and faith in the Being which founds your being. There is no question of loving God or the creature, since the more I really love the creature the more I am turned on to the Presence which love makes bare.[8]

Whatever your theology or lack of it might be, a loving person in a caring society nourishes the good life.

Modesty and Dignity in the Presence of God and Truth
The Modest Person In a Reverent Society

Although our coins bear the inscription, "In God we trust," and our pledge of allegiance affirms "one nation under God," modesty and humility are not two of the most prominent traits of the American temper either individually or collectively. In fact, our society tends to reward those who are self-assured, aggressive and even arrogant. Our achievements in the fields of science and technology, particularly, often cast upon us the illusion that we are invulnerable and self-sufficient. The reality, however, is that we exist not only within a fragile framework of global interdependence, but also within a cosmic context of an Ultimate Reality upon which we are dependent and to which we belong – call it God, Nature, the Absolute, the Tao, or whatever name you might want to ascribe to it. We are mortal, finite creatures who exist, if we are fortunate, for only a few years beyond fourscore.

I am reminded of the psychiatrist who asked his patient to tell him the first thing that came to his mind, and the patient replied, "In the beginning I created the heavens and the earth." Both Jesus and the prophets realized humankind's ultimate dependence upon God. At one point in the Gospels Jesus talks about the seed growing in itself.[9] We nurture it, but we do not give it life (Recombinant DNA

---

[8] Kenneth T. Gallagher, *The Philosophy of Gabriel Marcel* (New York: Fordham University Press, 1962), p. 80.
[9] Mark 4:26-32.

The Good Life

notwithstanding). Rather, the potential for life is a given within the nature of the seed itself. The monotheistic religions emphasize that we, as human beings, are creatures, not creators; we bring into new relationships only what is already given. It was St. Augustine who reminded us that only God creates out of nothing. And here the prophet Micah links our highest ethical duties, justice and lovingkindness, with piety.

When the founders of my University dedicated the institution to the Glory of God, the search for truth and the development of men and women for service, they saw no conflict between these goals and excellence in higher education. And why should they have? It was their conviction, and one I share, that if God is the source of truth, we have no fear in pursuing truth courageously and fearlessly as long as we are open to the many dimensions of human experience that inform our understanding of what truth might be. Openness of mind and spirit, in contrast to a narrowness of vision that affirms there is only one methodology or one approach to truth, is essential to spiritual growth and understanding. The founders of the University saw faith as complementing learning because they viewed scholarly pursuit as a sacred process.

Ralph Tyler Flewelling, Director of the School of Philosophy for many years and one of the leading American exponents of the philosophy of Personalism, founded a philosophy honorary society, Pi Epsilon Theta, "Through Philosophy to God," a phrase taken, as I recall, from Boethius, the sixth-century C.E. Roman philosopher. This affirmation is based upon the assumption that honest inquiry in the pursuit of truth will lead to an Ultimate Ground of Reality. Nothing is more inspiring than to push back the barriers that separate us from the unknown in God's world. This can be a sacred process in which every new breakthrough in knowledge opens new doors and vistas to greater realms of mystery.

Albert Einstein was not known as a theologian, but his insights about the relationship between the spirit of true science and authentic religion are provocative. He often wrote and spoke about the mystical element in a scientific understanding of the universe that elicited the responses of awe, wonder and humility. Shortly before Einstein's death in 1955, William Miller, one of *Life* Magazine's editors, took his son, a Harvard undergraduate, to visit him. The young man was beginning to doubt if human endeavor had any significance at all in this kind of universe. In the course of the discussion, he asked Einstein, "Is there anything in which one could believe?" The greatest scientist of our time replied:

> Certainly there are things worth believing. I believe in the brotherhood of man and the uniqueness of the individual. But if you ask me to prove what I believe, I can't. You know them to be true but you could spend a whole lifetime without being able to prove them. The mind can proceed only so far upon what it knows and can prove. There comes a point when the mind takes a leap – call it intuition or what you will – and comes out on a higher plane of knowledge...All great discoveries have involved such a leap...One cannot help but be in awe when he contemplates the mysteries of eternity, of life, of the marvelous structure of reality...Never lose a holy curiosity. Try not to become a man of success but rather to become a man of value.[10]

Although Einstein put it in secular terms, I think he captured the essence of Micah's admonition for humility and modesty in life's journey.

Dear readers of these words, I wish for each of you the good life that will be characterized by justice, lovingkindness, and a life of modesty and humility as you walk with your God.

---

[10]William Miller, "Death of a Genius" (Memoir), *Life*, May 2, 1955, p. 64.

19

The Stranger in Our Mirror

By Harold M. Schulweis

Why is so much of the Jewish agenda centered around the convert? Why is so much Jewish energy spent on outreach programs, on Jews by Choice, on the proposals and arguments dealing with patrilineal descent, on the legitimacy of proselytizing agencies and procedures, on the intermarried and the mixed married? Why is the major issue shaking the foundation of Jewish solidarity focussed on the Amendment to the Law of Return – a matter that has now appeared before the Israeli Knesset forty-three times – and which again focusses on the convert?

Why the convert? Why the *ger*? And why now? It is a symptom of an internal cultural and religious crisis, of a *Kulturkampf* within our people. Our concern with the *ger* is not simply a matter for Reform Judaism – though Reform remains on the cutting edge of that issue. The controversies over the Law of Return are not simply manifestations of political power plays among religious factions within Israel or between Israel and the Diaspora. On the surface, the attitude towards the *ger* is only a concern about the drop in Jewish numbers or the protection of the status of proselytes who make <*aliyah*.

But the depth of feeling expressed by world Jewry on the "Who Is A Jew" issue evidenced an intuitive folk awareness that something deeper than definitions and demography is involved. Consider that even the appeal to the Holocaust, that ultimate argument for Jewish unity, failed to keep the lid on the seething cauldron of Jewish disputation. This time the glue failed to keep in check the angers and threats to Jewish unity. It was perhaps the first sign of the exhaustion of the Holocaust as the unifying memory.

We are concentrated on the *ger*, the stranger in our midst, because the *ger* has become a litmus test for the character and destiny of Judaism. How we see the *ger*, how we relate to the stranger in our midst, reflects the way we relate Judaism to the world around us. The *ger* who stands on the threshold of our home is a metaphor for our relationship to Western civilization. The attention focused on the proselyte is a paradigm of the emerging cultural struggle. Hermann Cohen wrote: "in the stranger, man discovered the idea of Judaism." I would add that, in the stranger, Jews discover the moral ideal of Judaism.

Towards the *ger* there is an ambivalence within our tradition. In the words of Aaron Lichtenstein, the *ro>sh y'shivah* of Har Etzion, there is "encouragement on the one hand and repulsion on the other; some esteemed the *ger* while others approached him with cautious apprehension."[1]

I identify two dominant strains in Judaism towards the *ger*, two fundamental attitudes towards the proselyte, that express two basic philosophies of Judaism. At one end of the spectrum is "the Ezra strain," named after the biblical Scribe who, returning from Babylonia, sees calamity in the intermingling of the "holy seed" with the foreign wives whose assimilated children spoke "half in the speech of Ashdod and could not speak the Jew's language." For Ezra there is no conversionary solution for this tragic entanglement. The presumption is that there is in the *ger* a primordial foreignness that cannot be Jewishly assimilated. The unique purity of the people can be restored only by excluding the alienating partner. "Make confession unto the Lord God of your fathers...separate yourselves from the people of the land and from the strange foreign women" (Ezra 10:11).

On the other end of the spectrum is "the Ruth strain," which stands genealogical conceit on its head and transforms alleged genetic flaws into providential virtue. The ancestry of Davidic royalty and messianic status is doubly flawed, audaciously traced back to incestuous unions with biblically forbidden peoples. On his mother's side, David stems from Ruth, a Moabite – the representative of a people who, according to Deuteronomy, "shall not enter the assembly of the Lord" and whose eponymous ancestor, Moab, is child of an incestuous union between Lot and his daughter. On his father's side, David's lineage is derived from Peretz, a product of the incestuous union of father-in-law and daughter-in-law, Judah and Tamar (Ruth 4:12). The Ruth strain contradicts with a vengeance the genealogical purity of the Ezra strain. The convert is as the new-born: "Whoever brings another person under the wings of *Sh'khinah* is considered as having created him, shaped him and brought him into the world" (t. Horayot 2:7). "A *ger* is like a new-born babe" (T.B. Y'vamot 22a).

---

[1] "On Conversion," *Tradition* (Winter, 1988).

The Body Revealed

The Book of Ezra and the Book of Ruth are both canonized biblical texts. Each approach has its own *gilgulim*, its transformations. The Ezra strain is evident in the thinking of Yehudah Halevi, the Maharal of Prague, and the School of Ḥabad. Its most contemporary resurrection is found in Professor Michael Wyschograd's book *The Body of Faith* (1983). A graduate of Yeshiva University and a teacher of philosophy at Baruch College of the City of New York and one of the principal Jewish spokesmen in the international Jewish-Christian dialogue, Wyschograd boldly articulates the Ezra strain. Judaism is a carnal election. God chose the route of election through a biological principle. The *b'rit* of God with Israel is not an ideological, spiritual, disembodied covenant. Israel's election is transmitted through the body. God chose to elect "a biological people that remains elect even when it sins." The Jew is corporeally chosen, chosen in the flesh, regardless of his spiritual or moral merit. The frontispiece of Wyschograd's book carries a statement from the Sifra>, "Even though they [the Jews] are unclean, the Divine Presence is among them."

Those non-elected, those not born Jewish, will of course be hurt for they are not of the seed of Abraham whom God loves above all others. But election has nothing to do with the virtues of the person or people. Wyschograd argues a theology of the Jewish body, a metaphysical sociobiology down to the putatively Jewish facial physiognomy and culinary predilections.

> There are those for whom their Jewishness means gefilte fish, bagels with lox and cream cheese, or the smell of chicken simmering in broth. Those who think of those things with derision do not understand Jewish existence as embodied existence. Just as the gait and face of a person is that person, at least in part, so the physiognomy of the Jewish people is, at least in part, the people.[2]

"Anatomy is destiny," Freud observed. I have heard such arguments, not from philosophers, but from Jews for whom the unassimilability of the proselyte is alimentary. *De gustibus non disputandum est.* The People of the Book includes an Ashkcnazic menu.

Following the Ezra strain, Judaism is not essentially a matter of faith, or ethics, or ideology; it is a matter of mysteriously inherited traits. The *Tanya>*, the hasidic classic authored by the founder of Ḥabad, Shneur Zalman, is the sacred text studied daily by the Lubavitchers. Its metaphysical biologism runs throughout the text,

---

[2]Michael Wyschograd, *The Body of Faith* (New York: Seabury Press, 1983), p. 26.

distinguishing Jewish souls from the souls of the nations of the world which emanate from unclean husks devoid of any good whatever.

All the good that the nations do is done only from selfish motives: "From the lower grades of the *Qlipot*, altogether unclean and evil, flow the souls of all the nations of the world and the existence of their bodies, and also the souls of all living creatures that are unclean and unfit for human consumption" (Chapter 6). Within the Ezra strain, pure, impure, clean, contaminating, are the critical categories that divide the souls of God's creation.

Still there is a felt embarrassment in the Ezra strain. If Jews inherit character, how can someone not born of that people acquire those congenital virtues by a sheer act of will? And yet there is the unambiguous legal possibility of conversion. Here the Ezra strain feels compelled to put some limits on the elevation of the proselyte. For Yehudah Halevi (*Kuzari* I. 115), it is clear that "those who become Jews do not assume equal rank with born Israelites who are specially privileged to attain prophecy." No other nation besides Israel knows the true meaning of the Tetragrammaton, no other people has the connection with God. For the *Zohar*, while the proselyte receives a new soul from heaven, it is not of the same calibre as the souls of Jews by birth.[3]

The Attractions of the Ezra Strain

If I dwell on the Ezra strain and barely mention the Rabbinic traditions endorsing the Ruth strain, it is because liberal Jews are not exposed to the Ezra tradition. The books we read, the traditions we select, the rabbis we hear have filtered out the Ezra view of Judaism. But if we are to understand the implications of our outreach program for Judaism itself, we must understand the Ezra strain because it is more alive than we may think, and its presuppositions and implications are very much a part of the contemporary *Kulturkampf*.

The arguments I hear mostly contend that "Jews by choice" are hopelessly deaf to the ethnic strains of Jewishness. This is, I suspect, a more polite way of saying that Jewishness is an ascriptive not an acquired character, something one is born with, or as a patient congregant put it, "Jewishness, dear rabbi, comes with the mother's milk." Indeed, it seems to me that the less practicing and believing the Jew, the more insistent the contention that Jewishness is something born into. The weaker the Jew, the more powerful the attraction to make Jewishness a genetic affair.

---

[3]Jacob Katz, *Exclusiveness and Tolerance* (New York: Schocken, 1962), Chapter XII.

We Ruth followers must understand the heart of Ezra. Ezra cannot be simply dismissed as bigoted or xenophobic. Ezra has no trust in the viability of a community of choice. Choice is too fragile to assure the Jewishness of his grandchildren. He seeks something independent of choice, a covenant in the flesh, a circumcision in blood. *B'damayikh ḥayi* – "In thy blood shalt thou live" – is recited at the *b'rit*. The Ezra strain seeks a genetic transmission of loyalty as certain as a transfusion of blood.

There is something reassuring in the genetic fixity applied to Judaism. So the sociologist Nathan Glazer argues:

> the converted may be better Jews than those born within the fold and indeed often are, but it seems undeniable that their children have alternatives before them that the children of families in which both parents were born Jewish do not – they have legitimate alternative identities.[4]

Choice is chancy. Jews by choice chose. But he who chooses for Judaism one day may opt to choose out of Judaism another day or else his child may. In halakhic terms, the infant of a Jewish womb, whatever he or she may later choose, is irrevocably Jewish – *yiśra>el >af <al pi she-ḥaṭa> yiśra>el hu>;* no theological or ritual text is called for. But a non-Jewish infant converted before his or her majority can protest this conversion. The biological Jewish infant is safe. Such an individual cannot protest and cannot revert.

Choice and Heresy

There is in tradition a greater confidence in being chosen than in choosing, in choosing because one is commanded rather than choosing out of one's autonomous decision. The election of Israel (<Aṽodah Zarah 2b) took place without consultation with Israel. God overwhelmed Israel. He suspended a mountain over Israel like an upside down vault and declared, "If you accept the Torah, it will be well with you and if not there you will find your grave." It is God's choice, not Israel's choosing, that assures the irrevocable election and singularity of the Jew.

But it is precisely here that the *ger* in our times comes to challenge the presuppositions of the traditional society. The very title "Jews by choice" challenges the genetic understanding of Judaism and the preference of biological fate over chosen faith. It raises root questions that touch the nature of our identity and the character of our education.

---

[4]Nathan Glazer, *New Perspectives in American Jewish Sociology* (New York: American Jewish Committee, 1987).

Is Judaism essentially a biological affair, a congenital matter determined by the ovum, or is Judaism an ideological, spiritual matter of faith to be chosen? While formally these alternatives are not contradictory – for Israel is a community both of birth and of choice – *de facto* the Ezra and Ruth strains pull at either end oppositionally. And there are pragmatic advantages for the Jewish community to retain elements of both, i.e., to accept a Jew by birth without any theological or ritual tests and to accept one born a non-Jew as a Jew by religious and cultural decisions. There are powerful theoretical and pragmatic arguments to reject the extremes of the Ezra strain that border on metaphysical racism.

Outreach to the proselyte affects our self-understanding of Judaism. In the conversion of the *ger*, the native-born is forced to confront himself. The *ger* of adoption places greater weight on choice, will, faith, ideology. The contemporary calls for greater Jewish "spirituality," the growing emphasis on theological clarification within the religious movements, the disenchantment with mere belonging – all reflect the shifting of the pendulum from destiny to decision, from being chosen by an external fate to freely choosing by inner conviction.[5]

"Heresy" comes from a Greek word *hairein*, which means "to choose." In the closed society of a pre-modern world, choice was heretical. In the open society, choice has become the nobler spiritual imperative. "Modern consciousness," Peter Berger summarizes, "entails a movement from fate to choice." In modernity, the pendulum shifts from Ezra to Ruth. The *ger* challenges the presuppositions which value biological fate over faith, make of Judaism a theology of the inherited body-soul and ignore the willful attachment to faith, the longing for spirituality. All this affects the consciousness of the native-born. The Jewish attitude towards the *ger* presents in concentrated form a clue to the Jewish relationship to Western civilization which lies at the heart of the contemporary *Kulturkampf*. The *ger* is the microcosm of the world outside us.

We are shaped by those we shape. The artist is revealed in his art. The *ger* comes to us from the outside and leads us to look inside. In the process of *giyur*, conversion, the native Jew is enlarged. The *ger*, who

---

[5]The rulings of the Israeli Supreme Court gave greater weight to the subjective elements of identification than to the objective, legal genetic factors. Whereas the halakhic tradition could regard the converted Brother Daniel as a Jew by virtue of his birth, the Israeli judgment placed greater weight on Brother Daniel's choice to convert to Christianity, which detracted from his Jewishness (1962). In the Shalit affair (1988), Justice Zussman for the majority's opinion stated that "determining a person's affiliation to a certain religion and a certain nationality derives essentially from the subjective feeling of the particular person in question."

enters a new covenant with God and with us, transforms us, reminds us of the genius of Jewish universalism. The *ger* who brings *bikurim*, the first fruits, to the Temple is entitled to declare that God has sworn to his fathers to give them the Land, for when God spoke to Abraham he said, "I have made you a father unto the multitude of nations" (Genesis 17:8). In this sense, Abraham is transformed. For, as the Yerushalmi Bikurim has it, while in the past Abraham was only the father of Aram, through the acceptance of the *ger*, he has become "father of all those in the world who ever become Jewish." Through the *ger*, the view of Judaism is enlarged. A universal community of faith is added to the particular community of birth. When the *K'neset Yiśra>el* turns away from the *ger*, the *K'neset Yiśra>el* turns away from the world; turning towards the *ger*, the *K'neset Yiśra>el* enters the wider world. The *Kurturkampf*, the struggle over our posture towards the *ger*, entails a struggle over our attitude towards Western civilization.

The Cave

A critical talmudic episode evidences the depth of our burgeoning *Kulturkampf*. The Talmud (Shabat 33b) records a conversation among a group of Rabbis which took place about the year 130 C.E., when Palestine was under Roman rule. Rabbi Yehudah ben Ilai observed, "How fine are the works of these people," the Romans. "They have made roads possible, built bridges and markets, and erected bath-houses." Rabbi Jose remained silent, but Rabbi Simeon ben Yoḥai noted caustically, "All these edifices and structures they make for themselves [alone]. The marketplaces are to put harlots into them, the bridges are to levy tolls for themselves, the bath-houses are to pamper their bodies."

The Roman government issued a death decree to punish Simeon ben Yoḥai's blasphemies. He and his son Eleazer escaped to a cave and remained there, praying and studying, for twelve years. When it was rumored that the decree had been annulled, the two left the cave and went out into the world. They were aghast at the activities they saw. Men were ploughing and sowing the fields, and the pair condemned them: "People forsake life eternal for the business of temporal life." Whatever they looked at was immediately burned up. Thereupon, a heavenly voice cried out: "Have you come to destroy My world? Get back to the cave!" Chastised, they returned to the cave, there to pray and to study another twelve years – then heard again the heavenly echo cry out, "Go forth from your cave." It was on the eve of the Sabbath when the Rabbis emerged and saw an old man holding two bundles of myrtle. They asked him, "What are the myrtles for?" He answered,

"They are for the honor of the Sabbath." "And why two myrtles?" "One is in honor of the commandment to 'observe the Sabbath.' And the other in honor of the commandment to 'remember the Sabbath.'" The minds of Simeon ben Yoḥai and his son Eleazer were set at ease. The myrtles are not in the cave. They are in the world among the thorns and thistles.

The retreat of Simeon ben Yoḥai from the world, his contempt for the culture and civilization of his day, is echoed these days in many circles – not all fundamentalist.[6] It is a critical aspect of the contemporary *Kulturkampf*. Particularly after the profound disillusionment of the Holocaust era, the cave looms large as an attractive option. For the cave mind-set, there is no good in Western civilization, and associating with it entails the risk of a contamination that will poison Jewish identity and continuity. Democracy, pluralism, humanism, science, tolerance, conscience, the Enlightenment – those are the seductions of foreign wives that eat away at the unique holiness of Israel. The *Tanya>* (Chapter 8) warns against those who occupy themselves "with the sciences of the world, for the uncleanness of the science of nations is greater than that of profane speech."

In the cave there are no foreign elements to intrude. Out there in the world at large is an innate irreconcilable conflict between "them" and "us" in the very womb of Rebekkah. Rabbi Elie Munk in his commentary *The Call of the Torah* explains that the hostility between Esau and Jacob is "pre-natal," a "providential factor in history which escapes the control of the will." The intra-uterine hostility between Esau and Jacob projected in talmudic and medieval times onto Rome and the Christian world is not to be explained in natural terms, on economic, political, or psychological grounds. Jewish and non-Jewish hostility is an "apriori fact," something born in conception. "Two nations are in your womb and two kingdoms will separate from your entrails. One kingdom will be stronger than the other and the elder will serve the younger."

The long and wicked history of anti-semitism aggravates the Ezra strain and gives it credibility beyond its historical context. The impotence of the victim seeks compensation in the malediction that characterizes the oppressor as evil to the core. "If someone is cruel and does not show mercy," Maimonides writes in *Matnat <Aniyim*, "there are sufficient grounds to suspect his lineage, since cruelty is found only among the other nations." The angers and resentments of the persecuted must be understood, but the indiscriminate curses extending

---

[6]For more on Simeon ben Yoḥai's position, see T.B. B'rakhot 35b.

beyond historical context and appropriate target hurl dangerous boomerangs against us.

In the reports from Israel today, there are signs of a reversion to medieval and talmudic categorizations of non-Jews as <akum, idolators. Such atavistic definition of the non-Jews as <akum further separates Jews and non-Jews. Yeshivah communities are still being taught that the biblical terms of "brother" and "neighbor" exclude non-Jews and that the obligations towards the well-being of my brother or the love of my neighbor mean only to include Jews, and perhaps only observant Jews. "Who is thy neighbor?" refers to b'né <amekha – only Jewish kinsfolk. They are to be loved "as thyself." But who is "as thyself" but those Jews who think and pray and behave as thyself? The creeping exclusionary definition begins by separating non-Jews from Jews, but ends by dividing Jews from Jews.

Responsa from contemporary Israeli rabbis uphold a prohibition of selling or renting an apartment to non-Jews in Jerusalem. Rabbi Eliezer Waldenberg would on halakhic grounds expel all non-Jews from Jerusalem, and the Sefardi Chief Rabbi Mordecai Eliahu forbids Jews to sell apartments or flats "even to one Gentile." It is as if the talmudists Menahem Ha-Meiri of the fourteenth century and Moshe Rivkes of the seventeenth century had never lived – as if their landmark judgments distinguishing idolators from "nations governed by the ways of religion and committed to godliness" had never taken place.

The conclusion of the Simeon ben Yoḥai >agadah repudiates his *contemptus mundi*, the xenophobia that cremates the products of civilization. The heavenly voice teaches that there is no safety in the cave, only the smothering self-incarceration of the Jewish spirit. For the Ezra mind-set there is no foreignness in the cave, there are no *gerim*, no synthesis, no challenge from civilization. But to turn away from the world and its civilization is to turn against God's gift to us of opportunity. Our task is not to escape civilization, but to refine it. Civilization is not divine and it must not be indiscriminately embraced. But neither is it the work of Satan. The land must be sowed and ploughed. The two myrtles in honor of the Sabbath of creation and recreation are reminders of a society that is yet to be. The Rabbis would not dismiss Roman civilization in the time of Simeon ben Yoḥai. What, then, should be our attitude towards a democratic Western civilization which has enriched Judaism and elevated the lot of our people?

The Ezra advocates of Jewish isolation are fond of citing the verse from Deuteronomy 33:28: "Israel dwelleth in safety alone." But they ignore the talmudic passage (Makot 24a) that rejects the questionable values of Jewish insularity. In the Rabbinic interpretation, Amos the prophet arose to challenge Moses' benediction. "How shall Jacob stand alone?" The Talmud continues: "The Lord repented concerning Moses' acclamation. This also shall not be, saith the Lord God" (Amos 7:5-6).

Ruth, Naomi, and Boaz in Our Times

Much of the conflict between the followers of Ezra and of Ruth lies beneath the surface of the *Kulturkampf*. But for Jews for whom Ezra is outmoded and irrelevant, the Ruth strain presents its own challenges. Who is the Ruth of our times? The Ruth of our era who approaches us is not the Ruth of pagan times nor even of the height of Christian dominance. The Ruth of modernity is less likely than before to come to us with church dogmas from alien theologies. She comes from a highly secularized culture, a neutral society. She seeks in Judaism the warmth of a family attached to the rootedness of tradition, the joys of festival celebration and commemoration, the sense of superordinate purpose that can overcome the shrivelled culture of secular neutrality. She seeks songs to be sung, stories to be told, choreography to be danced, memories to be relived, wisdoms to be enacted, faiths to be revered. She seeks a family of spiritual literacy and refinement.

The Ruth of modernity comes to us with great expectations. She has felt the shiver of history. She has immersed herself in *miqvah* and study. She comes to the promised Sabbath table of her beloved and to the Sabbath table of her betrothed's Jewish family. The table is beautifully set, but the evening is graceless and without benediction. The conversations are pedestrian, banal, materialistic, hedonistic, indistinguishable from any non-Jewish middle-class family. The native-born family is Jewishly mute. They are pseudo-universalists like those who would, as Santayana put it, "speak in general without using any language in particular." Ruth seeks the particular language of Judaism. But there is in her adopted Jewish family no ethnicity of song or narration, no Jewish poetry or ritual choreography or theology. Ruth is prepared to pledge to her beloved: "Thy people shall be my people, thy God, my God." But where is the God and where the people in the native-born husband and in-laws? The Jewish native-born family are neither/nor Jews, "Do you believe in God?" "No." "Are you an atheist?" "No." "Are you a Zionist?" "No." "Are you an anti-Zionist?" "No." "Do you observe the Sabbath?" "No." "Are you opposed to observing the Sabbath?" "No." We deal with born Jews of double negation.

Philip Roth confesses his childhood memories. "What a Jewish child inherited was no body of law, no body of learning, no language and finally no Lord." Ruth's Jewish family are in most things neutral souls, living spiritually in the naked square. They are the modern descendants of Disraeli, who, when asked by Queen Victoria which Bible he used, answered, "I am, alas, dear Queen, the blank page between the Old and New Testaments."

The question is not whether Ruth, the stranger, can be integrated into the Jewish family, but whether the estrangement of the Jewish family from Judaism can be overcome. It is the foreignness, the alienation, of the Jewish family, not the purported foreignness of the proselyte, that haunts us. The Ruth of modernity is not the Ruth of the tradition, neither are the Boaz and Naomi of our times those of the Scriptures. The *ger* challenges us to think deeply of our noblest intent to reach out. Reach out – with whom? Reach out – with what? And after touching the *ger*, bring her or him home – where?

There can be no outreach without inreach. Outreach without inreach is not only premature, it results in frustration, embarrassment and disillusionment. Outreach must be doubly targeted. It must be simultaneously directed towards the alienation within as much as towards the stranger without. Emerson said it so well: "That only which we have within can we see without. If there are no gods, it is because we harbor none."

You cannot reach the *ger* except through the native-born. And especially in Judaism, whose substructure is the family, it is in the private home, not in the public institution, that the Jewishness of belonging, believing and behaving is most effectively transmitted and lived. Outreach to the stranger must be coupled with the Jewish empowerment of the host family.

The *ger* cannot be converted to Judaism as a theological abstraction. The *ger,* like the native-born, cannot thrive in the megastructure of Jewish society. The *ger* needs a sustaining, personal environment. Jews need Jews to be Jewish. The *ger* needs Jews to be Jewish. The *ger* needs a Jewish home. To support that home must be the primary task of Jewish public institutions. I propose for their consideration that each synagogue, each temple, each center encourage the formation of *m'ḥankhé mishpaḥah*, lay and professional family educators resolved to enter the private domain, the *r'shut ha-yaḥid*, for the purpose of enhancing the Jewish home. The education of the *ger* cannot be isolated from the education of the native-born. Both need to cultivate Jewish talents, competencies, and sensibilities. And that is the twin goal, the dual task of a lay and professional teaching collegiality. One law and one pedagogy for the homeborn and for the stranger that dwells among you.

The *ger* is our mirror. We have only to look at it to discover that the stranger is us. Not to fear: it is a shock of recognition that holds in promise the renewal of the Jewish spirit. As we pray on the evening of Return, on Kol Nid'ré: "And the congregation of Israel shall be forgiven as well as the stranger that dwells in their midst."

20

Judaism as Interpretation: Text and Spirit *

By Michael A. Signer

The two hundred years since the French Revolution and the Enlightenment tradition have left an indelible impact on the nature of Jewish thought and religious practice. The steady faith in progress and rational thought which characterized Jewish thought in modernity has been seriously eroded since the *Sho>ah*. Concepts such as ethical monotheism, the mission of Israel, and autonomy or choice no longer have the clear endorsement of the liberal Jewish community. In their place the spectre of pietism and spirituality seems attractive. Yet, the rise of fundamentalist attitudes among some Jews suggests that spirituality may be a form of escapism from the complexity of our current dilemmas within the Jewish and non-Jewish community.

It seems that as modern Jews we are in the unenviable paradox of moving toward the vocabulary of spirituality within our tradition, while modern life moves us away from the integrity constituting the environment in which our tradition mandates that we live. Are these two activities of spiritual aspiration and fragmentation necessarily in conflict with each other? Is it possible that the search for a more profound emotional and spiritual grounding is really complementary to our desire to live in and care for the world we share with others?

The fundamental question at stake in this dilemma is how Jewish religious thinking can constitute and preserve Jewish life. Is it to be preserved exclusively through performance of the commandments, through action divinely mandated? Or, can it be preserved exclusively

---

*This article is dedicated with affection and esteem to my teacher, Rabbi Samson Levey, who infuses the texts of tradition with the spirit of modernity. Portions of this article were presented as the Rabbi David Polish Lecture to Temple Beth Emet, the Free Synagogue of Evanston, Illinois..

by adopting appropriate attitudes which provide the framework and context for our actions? A survey of our traditions would indicate that Jewish life continues because of actions taken within the appropriate frame of intention. Is it then possible to reframe the opposition between action and intention and propose that action and spirituality exist in a complementary relationship? Arthur Green appears to find this possible when he defines Jewish spirituality as "life in the presence of God – the cultivation of a life in the ordinary world bearing the holiness once associated with sacred space and time."[1]

I would suggest that there is yet a more fundamental question relating to spirituality, the question of hermeneutics or interpretation. What are our attitudes toward interpreting the written texts of our tradition?[2] Our hermeneutical presuppositions provide a context for both action and attitude. To explore our personal link to our God, our tradition, and our world, we require texts to measure ourselves. We are a textual community: which means that "wherever there are texts that are read aloud or silently there are groups of listeners that can potentially profit from them. The people who enter the group" of listeners and readers "are not precisely the same as those who go out."[3] Jewish life is, therefore, lived most authentically when Jews read, interpret, and act on texts.

Our prayerbook provides a fine example of the relationship of life, attitude and text. In the morning blessings it quotes the Talmud:

> These are the obligations without measure, whose reward, too, is without measure: to honor father and mother, to perform acts of love and kindness, to attend the house of study daily, to welcome the stranger, to visit the sick, to rejoice with bride and groom, to console the bereaved, to pray with sincerity, to make peace where

---

[1] Arthur Green, ed., *Jewish Spirituality: From the Bible Through the Middle Ages* (New York: Crossroad, 1986), p. xiii.
[2] Hermeneutics as a discipline has been associated more with Christian theology than Jewish religious thought. However, the writings of David Tracy, *The Analogical Imagination* (New York: Crossroad, 1985), have suggested some methods which might prove useful for Jewish thinkers in structuring their conceptualizations of Judaism. For efforts toward creating a hermeneutical approach to Jewish theology, one might consult: David Blumenthal, *God at the Center* (San Francisco: Harper & Row, 1987); M. Fishbane, *The Garments of Torah: Essays in Biblical Hermeneutics* (Bloomington: Indiana University Press, 1989); J. Faur, *Golden Doves with Silver Dots: Semiotics and Textuality in Rabbinic Tradition* (Bloomington: Indiana University Press, 1986). It is possible to argue that these books may be narrowly interpreted to be analyses of classical texts, but the authors themselves acknowledge that their purpose is to push forward the dialogue with the Jewish tradition.
[3] Brian Stock, *Listening for the Text: On the Uses of the Past* (Baltimore: Johns Hopkins University Press, 1990), p. 150.

there is strife, and the study of Torah [*talmud torah*] is equal to them all because it leads to them all.[4]

The sequence of action is clear. Priority is accorded to the study of Torah; it is the *a priori* to all the actions which constitute Jewish life.

Most people assume that our reverence for Torah implies that it is a set text with a single meaning. It would follow, then, that the purpose of studying Torah is to acquire the single meaning which the author intended when the text was set into writing. Once the meaning has been mastered, it must be put into immediate action. If the learning does not lead to immediate action and repetition of action, then it loses all its value.

This set of common assumptions sets up a series of barriers between us and our relationship to Torah. We may immediately feel alienated or estranged from a document whose language escapes us. If Torah has a single meaning then it is a document divorced from life, for no life experience may be reduced adequately to one meaning. If the purpose of study is only to recover a single meaning from the text, then it is not study at all but a rote activity. Repetition of the same patterns of behavior could never account for four thousand years of Jewish survival. *Talmud torah,* then, must describe a more encompassing process.[5]

The concept of *talmud torah* is not an academic debate, but it is at the heart of the modern Jewish dilemma. The debate about the unity of the Jewish people is, at its very heart, an argument about the nature of a text and its community of readers who measure their thoughts and actions by the text.[6] Does Torah have a univocal, a single, meaning which is the possession of an elite group whose purpose of *talmud*, of study, is to recover that single meaning? Or, are there alternate approaches to both text and study which can provide a focus for the entire Jewish community?[7]

---

[4]See T.B. Shabat 127a. The translation here is from *Gates of Prayer* (New York: Central Conference of American Rabbis, 1975), pp. 52-53.
[5]On the role of theologians as re-presenters of a religious tradition, one should consult David Tracy, *The Analogical Imagination, op. cit.* For discussions of the relationship between literature, life, and imagination in Judaism, see Arthur A. Cohen, "Myths and Riddles: Some Observations about Literature and Theology," *Prooftexts*, VII (May, 1987), 107-22; Geoffrey H. Hartmann, "On the Jewish Imagination," *Prooftexts*, V (September, 1985), 201-20.
[6]The centrality of hermeneutics to the public discussion about the unity of the Jewish people is to be found in the articles by David Ellenson, "The Integrity of Reform within *Kelal Yisrael*," and Walter S. Wurzburger, "*Kelal Yisrael:* Challenge and Opportunity," *Central Conference of American Rabbis Yearbook,* XCVI (1986), 21-39.
[7]Susan A. Handelman, *The Slayers of Moses: The Emergence of Rabbinic Interpretation in Modern Literary Theory* (Albany: State University of New York

The word *torah* derives from the same root which yields the Hebrew terms for "teacher" and "parent." From parents and teachers one derives instruction. Instruction, however, need not be a uni-directional and rigid set of rules. Ideally, instruction should provide an environment in which the learner can put diverse elements together and find meaning. It is an interactive process.[8] If we look at the part of the Bible which we call Torah, it is clear that many elements combine to constitute that document. Gunther Plaut refers to the Torah as the "record of the Jewish people's experience with its God."[9] Torah is not identical with those experiences, but is the residue, the seeds which can then be nurtured into life by those who turn to it. The experience of the Jewish people as it is reflected in the text is, as we know, not linear or straightforward. Rather, it is circular, ambling, wandering. They find their way to the Promised Land, to lose it and then to regain it again. Torah, in its essence, is more than legal categories, it is a web of narratives together with laws. It is not a single literary statement, but a thesaurus, a treasure house of written discourses of many types.

Torah is linked to *talmud* – to study. The process of study may be understood as a contemplative act. Out of curiosity we come to the text in order to know. For many, such a contemplative form of study is a human act held in the highest esteem. They maintain that, if God is thought thinking itself, then it is only when the human being abandons everything but abstraction that the imitation of God is a reality. *Talmud torah*, however, ought never remain exclusively contemplative and divorced from the world. In *talmud torah* we do not begin, like the philosopher, with a reflection on human experience, but in the relationship of human experience to the text. This, too, is *imitatio dei*. A careful reading of the Bible indicates that God is constantly in relationships. Images of the divine in texts of the Jewish tradition illuminate the mutual longing between God and the world, God and the people Israel, and God and human beings. The act of creation which forms the initial narrative in the Torah is not the impetus of an uncaring

---

Press, 1982), provides a guide into the possibilities of multiple meaning in Jewish texts. Appropriate cautions about her description of classical Rabbinic texts are to be found in David Stern, "Moses-cide: Midrash and Contemporary Literary Criticism," *Prooftexts*, VI (May, 1984), 193-203.

[8]Thomas H. Groome provides a description of an educational philosophy which promotes the interdependence of text, tradition, and the individual in *Christian Religious Education: Sharing Our Story and Vision* (San Francisco: Harper & Row, 1980).

[9]Plaut, *The Torah: A Modern Commentary* (New York: Union of American Hebrew Congregations, 1981), pp. xviii-xxv.

deity, but of a divinity which evaluates the creative act as either ṭov, good, or ṭov m'>od, very good.

If we no longer understand *talmud torah* as an act of recovery of a single meaning, we are required to reshape our thinking about Jewish learning. The common denominator of both Torah and learning is life and its experience. This means that text and commentary are no longer in a hierarchy where commentary is subordinate to the text.[10] Rather, text and commentary shape each other. Both have value and are interdependent. What is most significant is that we the students become a vital part of the process of shaping Jewish life.[11]

What permits this new vision of our relationship to the texts of tradition is a new insight into the nature of written texts.[12] The text is a "situated use of language marked by a tense interaction between mutually implicated yet at times contestatory tendencies."[13] This definition implies that there is a dynamism of words on a page. At times they may contradict one another; at times they appear to be in perfect harmony with one another. These contradictory tendencies become more severe because the very nature of a written text divides the act of writing and the act of reading into two sides between which there is no communication. The reader is absent from the act of writing. The text thus produces a double eclipse of reader and writer. It thereby replaces the relation of dialogue which directly connects the voice of one to the hearing of the other.[14] We are, then, directed to move into the text as

---

[10] David Stern, "Midrash and Indeterminacy," *Critical Inquiry* (Autumn 1988), 132-61, demonstrates that Midrash cannot simply be reduced to theory, but also is an attempt to "recapture the fullness of divine presence."

[11] Jacob Katz has demonstrated that medieval Jewish legal texts often represent the interaction between social change and literary tradition: see his *Exclusiveness and Tolerance: Jewish-Gentile Relations in Medieval and Modern Times* (New York: Schocken, 1962).

[12] One of the clearest presentations of the ambiguity inherent in the word "text" is to be found in Stanley Fish's title essay in his *Is There a Text in This Class: The Authority of Interpretive Communities* (Cambridge: Harvard University Press, 1980), pp. 303-21. The intersection between post-modern literary theory and theology is grounded in new views of what constitutes a text. Many of these theories of textuality and their relationship to classical Jewish literature are presented in Geoffrey H. Hartman and Sanford Budick, *Midrash and Literature* (New Haven: Yale University Press, 1986). Lawrence Hoffman, *Beyond the Text: A Holistic Approach to Liturgy* (Bloomington Indiana University Press, 1987), demonstrates how insights from cultural anthropology and language philosophy expand our traditional notion of texts.

[13] Dominic LaCapra, "Rethinking Intellectual History and Reading Texts," in *Rethinking Intellectual History* (Ithaca: Cornell University Press, 1984), p. 26.

[14] Paul Ricoeur, "What is a Text?" in *Hermeneutics and the Human Sciences* (Cambridge: Cambridge University Press, 1981), pp. 146-47.

an entity within itself rather than being impelled into the search for the author and his or her intended meaning.

What appears to be an eclipse or an estrangement may provide a stimulus. The texts of our tradition allow a broader context in space and time for our own life experiences. It is this search for a larger context which brings us to our connection with the text. We are "readers" and as a result of reflection upon our reading we can become interpreters. In reading and interpretation, text and spirit are fused. In reading we fulfill the destiny of the text as it communicates its life into our own.

To be an authentic reader and interpreter of the Jewish tradition does not mean that one must secure rabbinical credentials. That would move us to a discussion of "product," the final result, and my concern here is for "process," how we live out Jewish life. The type of reading in *talmud torah* is different than our entertainment or recreational reading. It should be. There is much more at stake: the survival of the Jewish people and its covenant.

Let me suggest that the way in which we read religious texts may have some parallels with categories which have recently been described by scholars in the field of religious education as the "faith development" of the individual.[15] The categories generated by this model derive from developmental psychology, and have no direct correlation with chronological age or academic acumen. There are adults who engage in childish behaviors and children who conduct themselves in a mature manner. Our development and sophistication as religious readers may begin at any stage of our chronological lives.

At the earliest stages of religious development we tend to view the world as filled with ourselves. The images of the divine and the religious community tend to become parental or authority figures. When they disappoint us, we reject them and turn away to establish our autonomy. Often this autonomy is expressed by a total leavetaking of the religious community and its vocabulary. The act of reading which parallels this early stage might be called "pre-critical."[16] In pre-critical reading the

---

[15]The literature on faith development has advanced since I first wrote this paper. My explication and use of the model here are entirely idiosyncratic. Thanks are due to Rev. Kenneth Stokes, who shared his insights with me at earlier stages of his work. For some examples of faith development in the adult life cycle, one should consult: James D. Fowler, *Stages of Faith: The Psychology of Human Development and the Quest for Meaning* (San Francisco: Harper & Row, 1981); Kenneth Stokes, ed., *Faith Development in the Adult Life Cycle* (New York: Sadlier, 1982).

[16]The terms "pre-critical," "critical," and "post-critical" originated for me in the classes I taught with Rev. Phil van Linden, C.M., at St. John's Seminary in

texts are perceived as authority figures demanding obedience. As our faculties of reasoning mature, we note the dissonance between the presentation of reality in our religious texts and the way we organize reality in our lives. Our relationship to these texts as pre-critical readers is highly individualized. The questions we put to them reveal little patience or empathy for the texts to speak in their unique vocabulary. When the pre-critical reader asks, "Is it true that God spoke to Abraham?" it is not a question about the nature of divine communication, but about the process of that dialogue. The reader is acquainted with several technologies of communication, and if one of them does not suit the biblical text, then the investigation ceases. Pre-critical reading imposes our immediate experience on the text.

My favorite example of pre-critical reading occurred after I had taught a lesson in a church on the twenty-third chapter of Matthew where the text states: "Call no man father, for you have only one father who is in heaven" (23:9). One student eagerly proposed, "That means the Catholics are disobeying Jesus when they call their priests 'father'." In speaking out of her Protestant heritage, the student imposed her reality upon the text without regard for the independent context of the matthean gospel.

If the pre-critical stage of reading and religious development imposes the self on the text, the next level, the "critical," allows for the texts and modern commentaries to impose themselves upon the reader. Life experience is totally subordinated to the "historical" background of the text or what the modern scholar has said in print about the text. In religious development, the critical phase is the period when the "myths" of the early stage are shattered and an analytic or fragmented view of the tradition holds sway. There is a tendency to denigrate religious practice or community folk-ways as superstition. In both cases, reading or religious development, life experience is devalued in favor of the scholarly opinion on the singular meaning of the text. When we view texts of our tradition as archives of previous civilizations, we risk an alienation from them which is no different than that of the pre-critical reader. This estrangement occurs because, as bearers of modern culture, we erroneously consider our culture superior to the culture of ages past. Part of the difficulty for those within the religious community who subject every text exclusively to the criterion of

---

Camarillo, Ca. For the literature which utilizes this system, one might consult J. Jeremias, *The Problem of the Historical Jesus* (Philadelphia: Fortress Press, 1964); Charles E. Curran and Richard A. McCormick, eds., *The Use of Scripture in Moral Theology* (New York: Paulist Press, 1984); Raymond Brown, "Hermeneutics," in R.E. Brown, comp., *Jerome Biblical Commentary* (Englewood Cliffs: Prentice Hall, 1968).

scholarly writing is that they are isolated both from the living community and from the texts themselves. This double alienation makes good critical readers, but also creates a group which devalues the living experience underlying the text. Though they may be open to contesting opinions *about* the text, there is very little effort to *encounter* the text. The voices from behind the text are as alienating as the voice heard by the pre-critical reader, a voice which speaks only from the front of the text. In either case there is little opportunity for dialogue between text and reader.[17]

Both pre-critical and critical methods of reading are necessary preparation for the final stage, post-critical reflection. Scholars who have investigated the religious development of individuals call this the "mature" or "integrated" stage. The integrated religious person will have the insights which were developed both in the early and middle parts of the religious journey. Self-knowledge plus critical reasoning and study will enable this individual to have a sense of balance which permits re-engagement. Religious texts which seem dissonant with experience might occasion opportunities for insights into the basic structures of life. Scholarly discoveries from history, philosophy, or physics provide new questions and new solutions. Literary text and life experience become complementary and not contradictory. There is an opportunity to approach questions which previously appeared alien or foolish with a sense of empathy and tolerance. When the same biblical passage of "God spoke to Abraham" reappears at this level of reading, it is no longer an exercise in frustration, because the questions have shifted to the message communicated in the divine speech rather than the mechanics of communication. Legal practices which seemed to be superstition may be approached as efforts to promote social cohesion under the communal sense of the divine.[18] For the post-critical reader, the message is not in front of the text in immediate experience, nor does it lie behind the text in striving to recreate the world of the author.

---

[17]As part of the broader post-modern cultural critique of the Enlightenment, Jewish scholars are seriously evaluating the assumptions and results of critical biblical studies: see Jon D. Levenson, "The Hebrew Bible, The Old Testament, and Historical Criticism," and Alan Cooper, "On Reading the Bible Critically and Otherwise," in Richard Elliott Friedman and H.G.M. Williamson, eds., *The Future of Biblical Studies: The Hebrew Scriptures* (Atlanta: Scholars Press, 1987), pp. 19-80. James A. Sanders, *Canon and Community* (Philadelphia: Fortress Press, 1984), writes eloquently about the alienation between biblical scholars and lay persons in Protestant communities.

[18]Robert Goldenberg demonstrates the spiritual context of the Sabbath laws in "Law and Spirit in the Jewish Tradition," in Arthur Green, *op. cit.*, pp. 232-52.

Rather, it emerges from the individual and the text in encounter – both text and reader are changed in that moment of insight.

The question, "What does the text mean to me?" is different for each reader. The pre-critical reader overemphasizes "me." The critical reader eliminates "me" and emphasizes only "the text." The post-critical reader is able to appreciate both text and self. Such readers will have reflected on their life experience and articulated the basic insights which result from the encounter with the text. They will also listen to the text, appreciating its complexity before attempting to arrive at their own resolution of its meaning.

The post-critical Jewish reader will recognize another crucial dimension about our tradition: it is a community of texts which speak to one another. In Scripture itself we can trace the development from oral communities to textual communities: from "God spoke to Moses" to the prophetic proclamation, "Thus saith the Lord," to the reading and interpretation of "the book of the law of God" which Ezra reads and the priests expound to the people.[19] This textualizing is repeated in the post-biblical tradition which defined itself as a continuation of the biblical community, as *torah she-b'<al peh* (oral Torah) – an oral torah which, ironically, we know only in its written form.[20] The implication of this textual tradition for modern Jews is that insight into a biblical text alone is *not* a religiously mature insight. We need to correlate our understanding of the biblical tradition with what other texts have said. At times our interpretations will be unique, more often they will be confirmed within the tradition. In the very work of reading the texts which adduced it, our original idea will be broadened, modified, or enriched. Put another way, "the interpretation of a text culminates in the self-interpretation of a subject who thenceforth understands himself better, understands himself differently, or simply begins to understand himself."[21]

The well-known story of Hillel's recitation of the essence of the Jewish tradition, "That which is hateful unto you, do not unto your neighbor," concludes with the statement, "The rest is commentary, now go forth and learn."[22] It seems that too much emphasis has been put on the first part of the statement, rather than understanding that the final

---

[19]Tamara Cohn Eskenazi, *In an Age of Prose: a Literary Approach to Ezra-Nehemiah* (Atlanta: Scholars Press, 1988); Paul Hanson, *The People Called: the Growth of Community in the Bible* (San Francisco: Harper & Row, 1987).
[20]Michael Fishbane, "Inner Biblical Exegesis: Types and Strategies of Interpretation in Ancient Israel," and James L. Kugel, "Two Introductions to Midrash," in Hartman and Budick, *op. cit.*, pp. 19-40 and 77-104.
[21]Ricoeur, *op. cit.*, p. 150.
[22]T.B. Shabat 31a.

words convey at least as much meaning. Furthermore, Hillel's conclusion in Aramaic is *zil g'mar*. The word *g'mar* in that context probably meant "learning" in the Rabbinic tradition of interpretation. A single insight into the biblical text required correlation with a broader context.

Is the work of reading only the task of a religious elite? Is post-critical reading a possibility for non-scholars? I would hope that this is the case. Liberal Jews cannot demand autonomy in religious life and abdicate their responsibility to develop into serious post-critical readers of the Jewish textual tradition. At present both clergy and laity vacillate between the pre-critical stage of identifying their individual and immediate experience with the entire Jewish tradition, and the critical stage in which they either dismiss the tradition as superstition or abdicate to the experts their responsibility for critical synthesis. I believe this dichotomy occurs because liberal Jews have been more focussed on the nature of religious experience than on the process of their religious development. The more we focus on Judaism as a series of categories or doctrines, the more alienated we become because we reduce everything to behaviors or attitudes. By emphasizing products rather than process we tend to exclude people for whom those products are not meaningful. Let me illustrate this process of exclusion. In the Skirball Museum of the Hebrew Union College in Los Angeles we have a painting by the famous German artist Oppenheim. The painting depicts a *Shabat* afternoon at home: the family is seated around the table; the father is discussing the weekly Torah portion with his son; the daughters are engaged with their mother. For me, this painting depicts an ideal *Shabat* afternoon. However no *Shabat* that I have spent with my family resembles the painting: the children are not well-behaved; they resist discussing the weekly portion; they are not exclusively male. Does the dissonance between the image of *Shabat* in the painting and my actual *Shabat* invalidate my experience? The answer is, not if I note that my own life experience of *Shabat* has validity and not if I have other images of *Shabat* which are drawn from other times and places.

What becomes significant in this process is that reading and interpretation become the primary acts of Jewish life. The page of text becomes a metaphor for community. We may be looking at different parts of a page; we may emphasize different words; we may even punctuate the sentences differently. However, the text supplies us with a series of words which are common ground for discussion. Some of us may have broader experience with some phrases than others. Many will find in the text analogies to their life experiences, and their lives will be enriched by discussing the individual experience within the context of a caring and empathic community. Reading together becomes a process of re-experiencing the page. Our own experience is filtered through the process of text. Each word may be a lens which provides a new perspective on our lives. The reciprocity of life and text, individual and community, merge to create deeper experience for all.

If we can put the texts of our tradition at the center of our Jewish experiences, then we can become part of the community that cares for and nurtures those texts. We will, however, not be readers who concede absolute authority to any text, because our premise is that *talmud torah* precludes a single meaning. Since we read the texts together in communities, we will be less likely to privatize our interpretation.

The understanding of Judaism as interpretation will reshape much of what we do with our time together in Jewish celebration and living. It will put a process at the center of Jewish life. Our focus will be on questions rather than on answers. As a result, we will have a greater sense of possessing the tools for forging a Jewish life for ourselves and our children.[23]

---

[23] Lawrence Hoffman, *The Art of Public Prayer: Not for Clergy Only* (Washington: Pastoral Press, 1988), proposes a model for community self-transformation based on insights from anthropology and philosophy.

21

Segregation or Unity in Diversity: The Controversy Between Samson Raphael Hirsch and Seligmann Bär Bamberger and Its Significance

By Leo Trepp

On July 28, 1876, Samson Raphael Hirsch saw the realization of a long pursued goal. On that day the Prussian Diet passed a law permitting Jews, for reasons of conscience, to resign from their communities without at the same time resigning from Judaism.[1] Hirsch and his congregation, the Israelitische Religionsgesellschaft at Frankfurt, immediately severed all organizational bonds with the existing "city congregation," the *Gemeinde*. It was a separation which had significant social, religious and halakhic consequences that reverberate to this day both in Israel and in the Diaspora. For Hirsch, the secession was the culmination of his life, the crowning consequence in the progression of his thoughts and actions.

Background

Up to the passage of the law, every Jew had to belong to the local *Gemeinde* or, in effect, resign from Judaism. These congregations were established by the Prussian and other German States and authorized to impose on their members taxes to be collected by the State.

The State authorities were greatly interested in the assimilation of the Jews to modern culture and favored far reaching reforms in Jewish worship and practice. The Jews eagerly responded for two reasons.

---

[1]See Samson Raphael Hirsch, *Gesammelte Schriften* (Frankfurt: J. Kaufmann, 1922), IV, 250 ff., for Hirsch's Appeal to the Prussian Diet; pp. 267 ff. contain the text of the legislation.

They wished to be recognized as equal citizens, and that meant accepting the norms and formalities of the environment, especially in worship. They realized also that their youth could not be kept within the fold, especially as the temptation to convert to Christianity was powerful among those who looked for careers in civil or university service closed to them as Jews. A modernized Judaism, it was hoped, might open these gates to them. Acculturation was inescapable. Hirsch himself was committed to it.

Hirsch's Background – His Life at Oldenburg and His Theology

Hirsch had been born at Hamburg in 1808. From early childhood on and through his formative years, he witnessed the clash between Orthodoxy and the new *Tempel* movement. His father was a leader of the militant Orthodoxy spearheaded by Rabbi Isaac Bernays. A man of competence in both Jewish and secular disciplines, Bernays had studied for some time at a German university and deemed it permissible to engage in secular studies and to blend Torah with a limited measure of secular wisdom.

Hirsch studied for several semesters at the University of Bonn. On the strength of his university studies, he became State Rabbi of the Grand Duchy of Oldenburg in 1830.[2] The state authorities, reluctant to appoint him due to his aggressive Orthodoxy, accepted him on the strong recommendation of his predecessor, Dr. Nathan Adler. It was hoped that, "having been admitted to study at the University of Bonn, [Hirsch] would be able to combine the more tolerant attitudes prevailing there with those of Orthodoxy."[3] But first he had to pass an examination given him by the State Superintendent of Churches. To the question on the purpose of man, he answered, "faith in the revealed law."[4] The word "faith" is important. By using it, Hirsch excluded any contrary conclusions of *jüdische Wissenschaft*, the Science of Judaism. He had learned that exposure to secular education was the admission ticket to society, even for a rabbi, but he claimed to have made no concessions in his own traditionalism.

---

[2]Leo Trepp, *Die Oldenburger Judenschaft* (Oldenburg: H. Holzberg, 1973), pp. 119ff. Hirsch held this position until 1841 without ever receiving a salary increase from a hostile government, then moved, forced by physical want, to nearby Emden, where he remained as rabbi until 1845, subsequently to Nikolsburg, where he served as Chief Rabbi of Bohemia and Moravia until 1851, when the founders of the Orthodox congregation at Frankfurt called him to be their rabbi.
[3]Trepp, p. 122.
[4]For the transcript of the examination, see Trepp, p. 123.

Hirsch understood that a Judaism separated from the mainstream of general culture cannot survive. He found his justification in the statement of Rabban Gamaliel ben Rabbi Yehudah, the Prince: *Yafeh talmud torah <im derekh >ereẓ* – study of Torah combined with a secular occupation is proper, for labor in the two of them makes sin forgotten (>Aṿot 2:2). This had long been understood to mean that, joined together, they keep the Jew honest and upright in his worldly pursuits, as he is then guided by the word of Torah.[5] Hirsch, however, gave it a wholly new meaning: "It is proper that Torah be combined with secular *culture*."

Henceforth, Hirsch wore the robe prescribed for the clergy, preached in German, introduced a choir, and gave the liturgical song of the synagogue a German character. He was even concerned with the pronunciation of Hebrew. Acknowledging that neglect had disfigured it, he clearly shared the distaste Yiddish-Hebrew inspired in his enlightened contemporaries.[6] On the other hand, he did not wish to introduce the Sefardic pronunciation, perhaps because he sought to distance himself from general scholarship, which had adopted it, and above all from Reform, since the Hamburg *Tempel* used it in its worship. The result was a typically German pronunciation, soft, melodic and "romantic."

On the orders of his State superiors in Oldenburg, Hirsch developed a school system, including general education, a system he eventually transferred to Frankfurt. In contrast to the pre-modernist traditional rabbis, who concentrated on the Talmud, he emphasized the study of the Hebrew Bible and wrote commentaries on it – which later on brought him into conflict with his congregants during his tenure as Chief Rabbi of Bohemia and Moravia (1846-1851). Chidingly, they said of him: *"er lernt Tillim und sogt Gemore"* – he studies Psalms, and merely recites Talmud, though traditionally, of course, *"man sogt Tillim und lernt Gemore"* – one recites Psalms and studies Talmud. Hirsch had placed himself in opposition to "old-time" Jewish ways, "amulet-bunk in defense against physical ills or for the construction of mystical worlds."[7] At the same time, his position regarding halakhah remained uncompromisingly Orthodox. His only link with organized Judaism was, therefore, with its Orthodox element. This may in part explain his detailed halakhic exposition of the stand he ultimately took on

---

[5]*Machsor Vitry* (Berlin, 1893), p. 494.
[6]Ismar Schorsch, "The Myth of Sephardic Supremacy," in *Leo Baeck Institute Year Book*, XXXIV (London, 1989), 53 ff.
[7]Hirsch, *Neunzehn Briefe über Judentum* (Berlin: Welt-Verlag, 1919), Third and Seventeenth letters.

separatism (we shall discuss this briefly further on). He had to demonstrate to an "old-time" Rabbi Seligmann Bamberger that his erudition in Talmud and codes was as profound as that of his contestant.

Hirsch's superiors in the Ministry of Religion were greatly displeased. Hirsch, they thought, was not meeting his obligations of acculturating and transforming the Jews into loyal subjects of the State. In 1831, the Ministry recommended to the Grand Duke that Hirsch be dismissed.[8] This was not done, but Hirsch was subjected to severe restrictions and the threat of dismissal, which were to hang over him as a sword of Damocles for the rest of his tenure at Oldenburg. Eventually, he was forced to leave. In 1836, shortly after his discharge had been barely avoided, Hirsch published his first book, *Nineteen Letters about Judaism*. We may regard it as an *apologia pro vita sua*, addressing not only Jews but his superiors as well.

The *Nineteen Letters* was essentially a demonstration that Orthodoxy was the only true way to citizenship, because Torah commanded that the Jew bind himself wholeheartedly to the State. The commandments of Torah, which Hirsch outlined, were the means of acculturation and the safeguards of abiding loyalty. He attacked the Reform movement as destructive of Judaism. We may conclude that Hirsch, implicitly, may also have wished to convey that the patriotism of the non-Orthodox Jew was flawed; he may have persuaded himself that loyalty to the State required separation from non-Orthodox Jews.

Hirsch's principle was that Judaism would develop the "Israel-Man," the *Jissroel-Mensch*, who would serve his "non-Jewish brethren [with] love in your heart... by counsel and action... as your Torah commands you."[9] A tombstone inscription he prepared eulogized the departed for having "promoted the welfare of non-Jews."[10] Basing himself on Jeremiah 29:5-7, Hirsch insisted that the Jew was commanded by Torah to submerge himself totally in the State and never "regard his own welfare as distinct from that of the State."[11] The Jew, then, was forbidden to work for a return to the Land of Israel, an event that would occur miraculously at the end of days. He was, however, obligated to pray for this time.

Hirsch's *Nineteen Letters* reveals that, at this stage, he had already acquired his militancy against Reform, seen the necessity of blending secular culture with Judaism, recognized the power of the secular state to help or hinder him in the pursuit of his goals, and developed a

---

[8]Trepp, pp. 126 ff.; Hirsch, *Neunzehn Briefe*, Fifteenth Letter.
[9]Hirsch, Fifteenth Letter.
[10]Trepp, pp. 202 f.; picture facing p. 80.
[11]Hirsch, Sixteenth Letter.

profound confidence in himself. He gloried in being a loner in defiance of the world around him. "I have travelled the road toward a reconstruction of Judaism virtually alone..."[12] He could not endure opposition, as he had experienced none among the Jews of Oldenburg whose absolute governor he was by State law. These character traits found their full expression in his ultimate secession from the Frankfurt *Gemeinde* – with the help of the State – and in his controversy with Bamberger. Hirsch "germanized" Orthodoxy and was able to do so, due to a radical Orthodox position that placed him beyond any suspicion of halakhic compromises with the non-Jewish world. At the same time, ideas such as his postponement to an eschatological future of the *shivat Ziyon* aspiration, accompanied by the prohibition against working for it, and the external forms of synagogue worship he introduced approximate those of Reform.

Liberal Rabbis and Liberal Congregations

Many of Hirsch's rabbinical colleagues did not share his views. Some, like Geiger and Holdheim, favored radical Reform. Others, guided by Zacharias Frankel and the historian Heinrich Graetz, a disciple of Hirsch, inaugurated a "positive-historical" trend that was the ideological forerunner of what we would today call "Conservative Judaism." It became the prevailing "denomination" in German Judaism. For Hirsch, they all constituted "Reform" and had to be put under ban. Hirsch never attended any of the rabbinical synods.

Congregational Reforms

Initially, the rabbis and lay leaders in many communities were of radical bent. These men, filled with great enthusiasm, set themselves the task of assimilating Judaism to their new environment. For them the messianic age had arrived with the Emancipation, and Germany was now to be deemed the homeland. Prayers for *shivat Ziyon*, a return to the Land of Israel, and for coming of the Messiah and the renewal of the Temple with its sacrificial service were to be abolished. Halakhah was to be radically revised.

The Plight of Orthodox Jews

Orthodox Jews found themselves disenfranchised. If they wished to have an Orthodox synagogue and Orthodox institutions, such as *miqvah*, *sh'ḥiṭah*, etc., they had to establish these as private societies at their own expense while, at the same time, being forced to pay their

---

[12]Hirsch, Nineteenth Letter.

synagogue taxes to the *Gemeinde*. They were harassed. When the Orthodox Jews at Mainz organized such a society, their rabbi, Dr. Markus Lehmann, was, at the request of the "Grand Ducal Chief Rabbi" Aub of the main congregation, prohibited from calling himself "Rabbi." He was at best "Preacher *in* the Society."[13]

At Frankfurt a private *Religionsgesellschaft*, organized under Hirsch's leadership in 1851, built a synagogue with a thousand seats, opened a soon to be accredited high school with an enrollment of 470 students and provided for all the needs of Orthodox Jews.[14] Chafing under the compulsion to pay taxes to the State-sponsored *Gemeinde*, Hirsch lobbied for the law permitting separation and got it. His call was no less than a demand for freedom of conscience for all.[15] This separation was thus of lasting benefit to German Jewry and to Jewry as a whole. It forced the official communities to consider the needs of their Orthodox members if they wished to retain them. The prevalence of a traditionalist Judaism in Germany may well have been one of its results.

The First Results of the Separation and the Conflict with Bamberger

Now, owing to the law of 1876, the Orthodox Jews of Frankfurt were able to secede from the *G e m e i n d e* and join Hirsch's *Religionsgesellschaft*. The leaders of the *Gemeinde*, afraid of losing a large number of distinguished and wealthy Jews, were now willing to make far reaching concessions. The Orthodox group was given a binding pledge that it would be granted all the institutions it needed and that these would be placed under the exclusive leadership and supervision of an Orthodox rabbi and board, though they would be wholly financed by the *Gemeinde*. Jewish unity would be maintained in an *Einheitsgemeinde*. Hirsch, in flaming words, rendered his official ruling as *mara> d'>atra>*, rabbi of his *Religionsgesellschaft*, that halakhah forbade any affiliation with the community even under these conditions. A number of distinguished members in Hirsch's congregation, however, proved unwilling to secede and create a breach within the Jewish people; these now resolved to maintain membership in both congregations, which was a blow to Hirsch. To convince them of the halakhic necessity for secession, several of Hirsch's close friends, possibly inspired by Hirsch himself, went to Würzburg to persuade Rabbi Seligmann Bär Bamberger to come to Frankfurt, investigate the situation, and then render a halakhic ruling.

---

[13]Paul Arnsberg, *Die Jüdischen Gemeinden in Hessen* (Frankfurt: Societäts-Verlag, 1971), pp. 22ff.
[14]Hirsch, "Der Austritt aus der Gemeinde," *Gesammelte Schriften*, IV, 317.
[15]Hirsch, "Das Prinzip der Gewissensfreiheit," *Gesammelte Schriften*, IV, 267ff.

Seligmann Bär Bamberger[16]

Bamberger (1807-1878) was the leading talmudic authority in Germany. A scholar of the "old school," he nevertheless was very much in touch with the world. In 1836, he had defended the interests of the "Torah-true" element at a conference of notables called by the king of Bavaria, and in 1840 he was elected rabbi of Würzburg over the opposition of the liberal element in the community. Obviously he was able to get along with them, which called for diplomacy. The Würzburg *Gemeinde* remained Orthodox to its end. Bamberger established a Jewish elementary school in his city and, later on, founded a Jewish normal school for the education of State-certified elementary teachers who were at the same time strictly Orthodox and capable of leading communities as *ḥazanim* and *shoḥaṭim*.

Bamberger in 1872 had signed an opinion issued by 390 rabbis in response to a request by Rabbi Solomon Spitzer, of Vienna. It was required of an Orthodox Jew, the opinion stated, to resign from a *Gemeinde* if it introduced reforms such as the elimination of the hopes for the Jews' return to the Holy Land, for the coming of a personal messiah, and for the restoration of the sacrificial service. Such reforms would constitute apostasy.[17] Hirsch's friends were certain, therefore, that Bamberger would endorse Hirsch's ruling.[18] His opinion would carry weight.

The "Würzburger Rov," initially very reluctant to undertake the assignment, eventually yielded, came to Frankfurt, conferred with numerous Orthodox Jews and finally rendered a decision that was devastating for Hirsch. Bamberger ruled that, in view of the binding pledges given the Orthodox members by the leadership of the Frankfurt *Gemeinde*, it was halakhically unnecessary for them to resign.

The Consequences of Bamberger's Ruling

Bamberger's decision preserved the unity of the Jewish people. In larger cities, unified communities, *Einheitsgemeinden*, were established. Interaction between the constituent groups was inevitable. While the liberal wing was held back from radicalism, the Orthodox wing remained closely linked to general culture. The Orthodox rabbinate, as a rule, became strict in rendering halakhic decisions that separated the two groups.

The Orthodox wing of the Frankfurt community came to be led by outstanding men and *talmidé ḥakhamim*: Rabbi Marcus Horowitz,

---

[16]*Encyclopaedia Judaica* (Berlin, 1929), III, 1016-17.
[17]Gutachten, reprinted in Hirsch, *Gesammelte Schriften*, IV, 359f.
[18]Hirsch, *Gesammelte Schriften*, IV, 340f.

Rabbi Anton Nehemiah Nobel, and Rabbi Jacob Hoffmann. Hirsch's congregation flourished, and some communities followed his example. The Adass Yisroel Congregation in Berlin was one of them, but the Rabbinerseminar, an offspring of the congregation founded by its distinguished rabbi, Ezriel Hildesheimer, permitted its graduates to accept pulpits in the Orthodox branches of *Einheitsgemeinden*.

The significance of Hirsch's secession cannot be overestimated. Only through Hirsch's success did the liberal leadership feel inclined to meet the needs of Orthodox Jews. Had the Orthodox element been forced to remain within the main *Gemeinde*, it might have withered away.

The Controversy with Bamberger

Hirsch's Initial Argument[19]

Hirsch distinguishes between institutions and individuals. Regarding institutions, any compromise is forbidden by Torah, but individuals need not be shunned.

Prooftexts

Hirsch bases his position on the principle of *minut v'>epiqorsut*, "heresy and apostasy." A community that eliminates the hope for the coming of the messiah, the ingathering of the exiles and the restoration of the sacrificial service and propagates the idea that the *miẓvot* of the Torah are antiquated practices is guilty of *minut*. Of such a community, it is commanded: *harḥeq mé\<aleha dark'kha* ("keep your distance from [that community]") and *kol ba>eha lo> y'shuvun* ("all who come to it [associate themselves with it] shall not return [to the true Judaism]").

1. He cites Rabbi Tarphon: "Even if someone chases after him to kill him, or a snake pursues him to bite him he may take flight to their [the heathens'] houses [of worship], but not enter *their* houses [namely, of the *minim*]. For these [apostates] know God and deny him, while the others [the heathens] do not know God and [therefore] deny him" (T. B. Shabat 116a).

2. Rabbi Ishmael would not permit his nephew, who had been bitten by a snake, to be healed by an apostate and preferred to have him die, although he would have permitted him to be healed by an idolator, "for

---

[19]Hirsch, "Offener Brief an Sr. Ehrwürden Herrn Distrikts-Rabbiner S.B. Bamberger," in *Gesammelte Schriften*, IV, 331-58.

heresy is seductive and one can be enticed by it" (T. B. ʿAvodah Zarah 27b).

3. Every appearance of approving <aʿodah zarah is to be scrupulously avoided. The Shulḥan ʿArukh therefore rules: "A Jew may not partake of a dinner given by an idolator, even when the Jew brings his own kosher food and has his own servant to attend him" (Yoreh Deʿah 152:1). "He may not declare himself to be an idolator, even if this may cost him his life, and [he] may give the impression of being [an idolator] only if his life is actually in danger" (Yoreh Deʿah 157:2).

Hirsch's Comment

An idolator's sanctuary does not change its character even if a mezuzah is affixed to its door. King Ahab's misdeeds were not alleviated by the fact that he did not remove God's altar from the Temple and "merely" built an heathen altar next to it (II Kings 16).

Hirsch translates >éleh >elohekha yiśra>el (Exodus 32:4), "you have several forms of worship serving God, distinct in their principles, but with either of them you fulfill your duties toward your God." This is absurd: the existence of an Orthodox synagogue next to a liberal one is as absurd to Hirsch as the coexistence of the Ten Commandments with the golden calf. The majority of the members of the official *Gemeinde* might constitute an <ir nidaḥat (Deuteronomy 13:13ff.), a community subverted by scoundrels that deserves total extermination. Such a community would not lose this character even if it tolerated an Orthodox synagogue and *bét ha-midrash* for the minority.

Regarding Individuals Compromise Is Possible

While any contact with "Reform" is forbidden, this does not apply to Jews who follow it. We are taught, *nokhrim she-ba-ḥuẓ la>areẓ la>v <oṽ'dé <aʿodah zarah ninhu* ("gentiles outside the Land of Israel are not deemed idolators") and *>én minin ba>umot* ("there are no heretics among the gentiles"), since they do no more than follow the ways of their parents. The same applies to the second and third generation of contemporary non-Orthodox Jews. Hirsch cites Maimonides as proof:

> The children and grandchildren of those that have gone astray, whose parents have misled them and brought up them as Karaites..., can be regarded as being under duress... it is appropriate that we bring them to repentance and draw them near with words of peace until they return to the foundation of Torah (*Hilkhot Mamrim* 3:2).

Bamberger's Opinion[20]

Bamberger condemns the changes in the Reform prayerbook as *minut v'>epiqorsut* provided that they have resulted *not* from ignorance but from deliberation, *l'hakh<is*. In actual life, the difference can be easily ascertained. If a community has the means of doing justice to its Orthodox members by establishing the institutions needed by them, but denies Torah and deliberately deprives them of these institutions, it falls into the category of *minut v'>epiqorsut*. If, however, it offers binding guarantees that it will establish and maintain out of the *Gemeinde* budget all the institutions needed by its Orthodox members and place them under the jurisdiction of their own Orthodox rabbi and board, then it cannot be accused of *minut*. Such a *Gemeinde* recognizes the claims of Torah upon these members as existing by right and is even prepared to support them. In this manner it removes from itself the taint of being a deliberate negator of Torah truth. Bamberger appears to indicate that from the Orthodox point of view reforms are based on a different, although mistaken, understanding of *pos'qim* and *>agadah*, but the claim of Torah is nevertheless recognized. This makes separation of Orthodox Jews no longer required.

Proofs

1.) As proof he cites the controversy between Maimonides and his successors. To Maimonides, a Jew who ascribes a body to God is a *min* (Hilkhot T'shuv̄ah 3:7). This, however, was challenged by Rabbi Abraham ben David of Posquières, "Rabad," who had argued that many of the great masters held this belief (i.e., ascribing a body to God). Such an error resulting from a faulty understanding of *pos'qim* or *div̄'ré >agadot* does not make a person into a *min* (see Rabad's glosses to Maimonides). Joseph Caro, commenting in *Kesef Mishneh*, repeated Rabad's view, adding that even Maimonides, correctly read, could be so understood. Bamberger gives as further proof the T'shuv̄ot Maharil to Kelim 17:16. A person who violates Torah not from denial but out of misunderstanding acts reprehensibly, but is not a heretic, and one is not required to separate from him.

Against Hirsch's Prooftexts

Rabbi Tarphon's statement (Shabat 116a) refers not to Jews who follow unauthorized ways within Judaism, but to those who had converted to idolatry and thus were Jews no longer. As Rashi explained,

---

[20] "Offene Antwort des Distrikts-Rabbiners Seligmann Bär Bamberger zu Würzburg auf den an ihn gerichteten offenen Brief Sr. Ehrwürden des Herrn S.R. Hirsch," in Hirsch, *Gesammelte Schriften*, IV (Anhang), 539-67.

Segregation or Unity in Diversity

they had made revised copies of the Tanakh, supposedly confirming their claims, in order to attract Jews to their ideology. They were to be shunned more completely than heathens.[21]

Rabbi Ishmael's case (<Avodah Zarah 27b) refers to the same type of person, as is clearly evident from Rashi's explanation and also from Ramban, Ritvah and Ṭur Shulḥan <Arukh 155. The Rabbi prevented his nephew from seeking out a physician who had abandoned Judaism for another faith, lest it be believed that he had healed him by the power of his new religion. As Rashi holds, the term *min* applies only to an apostate Jew who endeavors to convert a Jew to a foreign religion.[22] Such passages do not apply to Reform Jews, but refer to Jewish Christians, though Bamberger is very careful not to mention the early Christians since he expects his open letter to be published in the general press.

The ruling of the Shulḥan <Arukh forbidding a Jew to give the impression of being in agreement with idolaters is inapplicable, first of all, because Reform Jews are not idolaters. Additionally, Orthodox Jews who remain in the official community under the condition that they have their own institutions make it manifest that they oppose and detest Reform and that their affiliation serves the purpose of maintaining the unity of the Jewish people and of bringing their non-Orthodox friends back to the ways of traditional Judaism. This is in the spirit of

---

[21] Actually, Rashi does not give this explanation, but the G'mara>, later on this same page, tells us in this context that Rav would never go *l'vé niẓ'fé*, by which is meant the House of the Nazarenes, i.e., the Jewish Christians, and Rabbi Meir called the Gospel of St. Matthew >*evēn gilayon* – a stumbling stone of paper, while Rabbi Jochanan called it <*avon gilayon* – sin papers. This text is not found in the regular, censored editions of the Talmud, but is given in translation by Lazarus Goldschmidt, based on the Bomberg edition and various manuscripts. Hirsch and Bamberger may not have known it.

[22] The physician who offered to heal the young man is called Jacob of Kfar Hananiah, namely the Apostle James (T.B. <Avodah Zarah 27a). The Jewish Christians engaged in many disputations with the Rabbis: "Rabbi Eliezer stated, Once I went to the upper market of Sepphoris and there met one *of the disciples of Jesus the Nazarene*, whose name was Jacob of Kfar Hananiah" (<Avodah Zarah 17a). According to Rashi, "This was the same person mentioned below on page 27a." Rabbi Eliezer engaged in a discussion with him and, later on during the time of the persecution of the Christians, was arrested as a Christian. He saw in his ordeal a punishment for his association. The words in italics, above, are censored out in most Talmud editions, but appear in the Goldschmidt translation: *Der Babylonische Talmud* (Berlin: Verlag Biblion, 1934), <Avodah Zarah, pp. 483-84 and notes 350, 518, and 113. While neither Bamberger nor Hirsch may have known this passage, it reinforces Bamberger's view that the Talmud speaks of Jews who formally converted to Christianity and were actively engaged in missionary work. We cannot draw any conclusions from it in regard to Reform Jews.

Maimonides. "Separation is, therefore, not demanded nor can non-separatists be regarded as being mischievous."

Hirsch's Rebuttal

Taking up the prooftexts, Hirsch affirms that they confirm his position. He states that *min* is merely a higher degree of *mumar* and the terms *min* and *>epiqoros* are so ill defined that they are interchangeable. This allows him to use any source that mentions either of them. These terms apply only to Jews, which means that the prooftexts merit application to Reform Jews. The case of Rabbi Eliezer reinforces this. Rabbi Eliezer stated, "Once I went to the upper market of Sepphoris and there met one whose name was Jacob of Kfar Hananiah" (<Aīodah Zarah 17a). Rashi explains, "This was the same person who is mentioned below on page 27a." Rabbi Eliezer engaged in a discussion with him and was later on arrested. He saw in his ordeal a punishment for this association.

It is irrelevant whether or not a Jew has officially converted to another faith. Under Jewish law he remains a Jew. Actually these terms can be applied only to Jews. And these Jews are outside the fold: "A Jew who has embraced idolatry has repudiated the entire Torah, and so it is with the apostates among the Jews. Such an individual is not to be deemed as belonging to Israel" (Mishneh Torah, <Aīodah Zarah 2:5); "anyone who does not affirm the [divine origin of the] Oral Law.... and any who say the Torah does not come from Heaven... and the idolators; all of these are excluded from the Jewish community" (Mishneh Torah, Mamrim 3:1-2).

According to Hirsch, there exists no difference between a *mumar la<aīodah zarah*, a Jew who has embraced idolatry, and a *mumar l'ḥilul shabat*, a Sabbath violator, even *l'te>aīon*, for personal gain or "appetite" (rather than for ideological reasons), and clearly when this is done *l'hakh<is*, spitefully. Reform Jews have deliberately adopted heresies. This to Hirsch is witnessed by their prayerbooks, their sermons, etc. Their education propagates desertion from traditional Judaism. They are, therefore, identical with those who commit idolatry, and actually even worse. Every contact with them is to be shunned: "And the apostates (*>epiqorsim*)... go astray after the foolish desires of their heart, as we have said, until they end up by spitefully [or deliberately] transgressing the ordinances of the Torah and [even] claim, 'There's no transgression in the [denial of Torah].' And it is forbidden to speak with or respond to them in any way" (Mishneh Torah, <Aīodah Zarah 2:5).

Hirsch's argument that Reform Jews are to be deemed equal to apostates who carry out active missionary propaganda for another faith among Jews, is arbitrary. Otherwise, his argument is well reasoned and more compelling than Bamberger's, especially when we consider that Bamberger, too, condemns the changes in the Reform prayerbook as heretical if they resulted not from ignorance but from deliberation (*l'hakh<is*).

We must assume that Bamberger was motivated by a concern for the unity of Israel and a love for the people. He did not wish to create a breach. He was, after all, the rabbi of a unified *Gemeinde*, albeit an Orthodox one with numerous non-Orthodox members, for whom he had to care. Hirsch, in contrast, had to defend his decision and, more importantly, the survival of his own separatist congregation. Hirsch's apprehensions are evident in his admission that secession would occur only rarely in a smaller community, whose Orthodox minority lacked the means of maintaining all required institutions.[23] On the basis of his argument and conclusions, he had no justification for permitting Orthodox Jews anywhere to remain within a community that had a liberal wing. If their affiliation was with "idolators," then these Jews simply would have to move, as Maimonides in his letter advised the Jews of Yemen to do.[24] Knowing they would not do that if they had all their needs met by the official *Gemeinde*, he struck this compromise that casts doubt on his entire argument. The same considerations may have been in Bamberger's mind, and then his decision becomes logical and compassionate. He preferred the Jews in small communities to remain within their local *Gemeinde* with rabbinical approval rather than with qualms of conscience.

The Principle of Torah <im Derekh >Ereẓ

Hirsch expressed doubt that Bamberger favored the principle of *Torah <im Derekh >Ereẓ* and, therefore, pointed out to him that this was "the only principle that would lead to truth and peace and bring healing to all the sickness and religious confusions of the present time."[25] He gave an outline of the work done by his congregation, emphasizing his school system that gave the young strong Jewish convictions and, at the same time, a human-civic education – a *Bildung* second to none in everything that was true and good. These young people, he pointed out, were "exemplary in their enthusiasm for the

---

[23]Hirsch, "Prinzip," *op. cit.,* p. 291.
[24]"Epistle to Yemen": see Isadore Twersky, *A Maimonides Reader* (New York: Behrman House, 1972), pp. 448 f.
[25]Hirsch, "Offener Brief," *op. cit.*, p. 354.

renewal and a true affirmation of the ancient and eternal Judaism within all currents of the time."²⁶

It is difficult to understand why Hirsch included a long statement in his halakhic analysis. He may have done so to bring his congregational institutions to the attention of the public. After all, his letter was published in a general newspaper. But why did he accuse Bamberger of "not favoring" the idea of *Torah <im Derekh >Ereẓ*? What connection did it have with Bamberger's ruling?

Hirsch may have believed that Bamberger did not favor the idea of *Torah<im Derekh>Ereẓ* as a function of an Orthodox congregation, but saw the need for it, which would then be met by the official *Gemeinde*. If this is the case, it reinforces Hirsch's conviction that Orthodox Judaism could not survive unless integrated into the culture of the world. Mindful of his sad experiences as Chief Rabbi of Bohemia and Moravia, Hirsch may perhaps also have believed that Bamberger was antagonistic to his new ideas and wished to undermine their realization in an Orthodox congregation. Bamberger replied that he did, in fact, favor the principle and pointed to the success of the normal school for Jewish elementary school teachers he had founded. Teachers of religion and rabbis very much needed a good secular education; Jewish schools were to be founded and were to develop scholarly and scientific disciplines – but none of this at the expense of a thorough cultivation of Jewish learning. Bamberger and Hirsch are, therefore, at one in emphasizing the need for a secular education of rabbis, teachers and Jews in general to safeguard the survival of Judaism.

The Authority of the Local Rabbi

Bamberger had assumed his function as arbitrator with great reluctance. He had consulted with Jews of great learning, who had given him their reasons and supportive arguments for wishing to remain in the State-sponsored *Gemeinde*. He had suggested that Hirsch follow a Jewish tradition going back to the time of the G'>onim, and invite three rabbis to hear the matter and issue a ruling binding on all parties. Hirsch rejected this proposal, insisted on his right as *mara> d'>atra>* and raised the issue which Ḥulin 44 states this way: "What a Sage rules to forbid, his colleague is not free to permit" – unless he can prove that the decisor has committed errors in Mishnah, codes, or his logical deductions: *ta<ut bid'ʋar mishnah pos'qim >o b'shiqul ha-da<at* (Shulḥan <Arukh, Yoreh De<ah 242:31). No rabbi may overrule a colleague. Especially as an outside rabbi, then, Bamberger had no right to declare permissible what Hirsch had declared forbidden.

---

²⁶*Ibid.*, p. 353.

Bamberger's Reply

Bamberger for his part argued:

1. The Ḥulin ruling was nowhere to be found in Maimonides' code. On the principle that the Rambam had included every halakhah found in the Talmud, its absence from the Mishneh Torah means that the Talmud itself did not hold it. It was not found in Bet Yosef or the Shulḥan <Arukh (Yoreh De<ah 242:31). Therefore, it does not belong to the canon of basic halakhah. Since Rabbi Isserles includes it in his glosses, it has to be seriously considered, but Isserles also ruled that in controversies between rabbis the principle obtains: "A prohibition based on the Torah is to be decided stringently; one based upon the Rabbis [i.e., upon Rabbinic sources] is to be decided leniently" (Ḥoshen Mishpaṭ 25:1). Clearly the issue of rabbinical authority rests on a Rabbinical rather than a biblical ordinance. (*Safqa> d'rabanan l'qula>*: see T. B. Shabbat 34a; <Eruvin 45b; Ṭohorot 4:11).

2. Additionally, the principle held only when both decisors were of equal rabbinical capacity; if, however, one of them held higher qualifications, he was not required to defer to the ruling of the other. *V'yesh >om'rim she->afilu ha-sheni gadol mimenu b'ḥokhmah uv-'minyan >éno yakhol l'hatir v'yesh matirim b'gadol mimenu* – "Some hold that, even if the second authority outstrips the first in wisdom or experience, he cannot hand down a lenient ruling, while others do accept the right of the greater [i.e., more distinguished] authority to render a lenient ruling" (Ḥoshen Mishpaṭ 25:1; Šifté Kohen 50:3). According to the ruling of Rabbi Moses Isserles, mentioned above, the decision is to be *l'qula>* i.e., according to *v'yesh matirim b'gadol mimenu*.

3. A further requirement is stated in the codes: *ḥakham she->asar v'ḥalah hora>ato v'nitpash'ṭah* – "a sage who forbade [something] and whose ruling was accepted and [widely] disseminated" (Šifté Kohen Qiẓur, *>isur v'heter*). This is interpreted by Bamberger to mean that the ruling must have found general acceptance and circulation. This was not the case, especially as recognized *talmidé ḥakhamim* at Frankfurt had opposed it from the beginning: Bamberger mentions Rabbi Mosheh Mainz, whom he regarded as a halakhist no less competent than Hirsch. Mainz had rejected Hirsch's ruling and desired to remain within the main *Gemeinde*. Hirsch's decision is, therefore, analogous to the principle *sh'néhem hayu b'vét ha-midrash* ("the two of them were in the house of study"): i.e., as long as a matter is still being discussed in the *bét midrash*, in an academic setting as it were, everyone is permitted to overrule his fellow (Šifté Kohen, notes 52 and

55). Additionally, it falls under the principle of *lo> nitpash'ṭah*: lack of circulation.

4. Furthermore, Rabbi Isaak ben Joseph of Corbeil, one of the Tossafists, taught in his *Sefer Miẓvot Qaṭan* (S'mak, Par. 111) that a Torah authority was bound to give a ruling to anyone who turned to him for advice.

5. Finally the authority of the *mara> d'>atra>* rests, according to the Talmud and the codices, not on a law, *din*, but on custom, even though it is not common – *la>v >oraḥ >ar<a>* – to challenge his authority. It was, therefore, not necessary for Bamberger to show proof that Hirsch had made an error in Mishnah, codices or his own logical deductions – in which case his right to overrule Hirsch was beyond dispute (*loc. cit.* R'ma, Baer Heṭev Note 34, etc.). Bamberger, having been asked for one, was both entitled and required to render a decision – though his proofs are weak, suggesting that he had adjusted his proofs to a decision already made. This we shall recognize in Hirsch's rebuttal.

Hirsch's Rebuttal

Hirsch opens with a sharp attack against Bamberger's claim to be superior in wisdom and learning. Bamberger had, indeed, meant to point it out, although he had ascribed this wisdom to Rabbi Mainz. Hirsch cites a *baraita>*, "Since flattery has become powerfully entrenched ... no one may say to his friend, 'my works are better than yours'" (b. Soṭah 41b – Hirsch leaves out the middle part: "justice came to be perverted and works corrupted." He could know that Bamberger was familiar with the whole section and would get the gist). It leads to self-deception. Perception becomes *ḥarifut shel ḥavel*; lack of expert knowledge of the situation turns it to *ḥarifut she-bishta>*, the rabbi becomes *talmid ḥakham she->én bo de<ah*. For himself, so Hirsch stated, he makes no claim to greatness. He praises "those" who prefer controversy to flattering recognition, who may not be brilliant in "tournaments of cleverness," but who know "how to select the tradition appropriate to the halakhah," and, like young David, to choose the right stone for the right throw.

1. Regarding Bamberger's advice to call three rabbis for a binding decision, Hirsch points to the opinion of the "400" rabbis that had already settled the matter in their opinion rendered in the case of Rabbi Spitzer; he accuses Bamberger of arrogance in considering himself another Eliezer ben Horkenos, whose opinion outweighs all the others (>Avot 2:12).

2. Hirsch points out that the statement Bamberger had cited from Ḥoshen Mishpaṭ (25:1) and Šifté Kohen (50:3) has to be understood as

merely a summary of the various decisions given in the preceding text and not an independent ruling: one decision holds that the principle rests *not* on the recognition of the honor of the first rabbi, who had ruled to forbid, but on the fact that at the moment of his decision the object in question had forever become forbidden; therefore, the second rabbi, though more learned, has no power to reverse this fact. The second decision does, indeed, consider the honor of the first rabbi. This honor is not affected if another rabbi of recognized superiority rules against him. The ruling of the second rabbi may then prevail.

Bamberger had followed the second decision on the basis of >*isur d'>orayta> l'humra>, >isur d'rabanan l'qula>*. Hirsch raises the question whether we are indeed dealing with >*isur d'rabanan*. He points to a ruling in Yoreh De<ah (1:12). A *shohet*, in the presence of witnesses, has slaughtered an animal. A Jew comes and wishes to buy some meat, but the *shohet* declares, "you cannot buy it because I have not performed the *sh'hitah* on it"; then, because the *shohet* is not regarded as trustworthy, the purchaser may buy the meat and eat it. The *shohet* himself, however, may not eat it: *shvéh >anafshéh hatikhah d'>isura>*. This is *mid'>orayta>*, scriptural, and constitutes the foundation of *nidré >isur* in general, which *is mid'>orayta>*. Any person who goes to a rabbi with a question accepts his decision as binding. This applies even more so when a congregation has in its statutes that its rabbi is to be the exclusive authority in all communal and private cases that call for halakhic rulings.

Hirsch refers to the principle of the Talmud: *ha-nish>al lehakham v'tima> lo> yish>al lehakham vitaher lehakham v'>asar lo> yish>al lehakham v'yatir*: "If a Sage has declared something unclean, the questioner may not go to another Sage and ask him to declare it clean; if one [Sage] has forbidden it, he may not go to another [to request] that he permit it" (<Avodah Zarah 7).[27] The same principle, Hirsch points out, is invoked in other places: Nidah 20b, Hulin 44a and 49a, etc. In all these cases, the decision of the first rabbi becomes final, even if the questioner had not accepted it, as he has shown by going to a second rabbi. Furthermore, we cannot say that the validity of a decision depends on its being widely accepted, since all these cases are individual ones.

---

[27]Hirsch omits the continuation of the passage: "This applies only when both [of them], he who declares it unclean and he who declares it clean, the one who forbids it and the one who permits it, are equal. If, however, one of them is greater in wisdom or age, we follow him; otherwise, we follow the one who is more strict."

In the cases of which the Talmud speaks, both rabbis lived in the same town. The decision of the first was immediately brought to the second, who regarded the ruling of his colleague as erroneous. Nevertheless, he was not permitted to overthrow it. The learned Jew at Frankfurt, therefore, had no right to overturn Hirsch's decision. The only case when this may be done is when both rabbis are in the *bét midrash* and the discussion is still in progress, then either has the right to voice his opinion.

3. Ḥakham she->asar v'ḥalah hora>ato v'nitpash'ṭah does not mean, "the decision must have found general acceptance and circulation." *Ḥalah hora>ato* simply means, the decision has taken effect, the prohibition has been pronounced. *V'nitpash'ṭah* simply means that the matter has gone beyond the confines of the *bét midrash* and is no longer under discussion by the scholars there. Additionally, we do not find *v'nitpash'ṭah* in the commentary of the Šifté Kohen.

Bamberger was guilty of violating talmudic law, even more since he did not even reside in the same town. Hirsch is greatly concerned with the issue of the authority of the local rabbi, the *mara> d'>atra>*. This is understandable. He had reason to be afraid that his congregants might turn to another rabbi in significant cases and especially if another Orthodox rabbi were appointed as *mara> d'>atra>* in a halakhically legitimate congregation at Frankfurt, as indeed did happen. By temperament he was additionally incapable of tolerating other authority.

4. On the issue of *derekh >ereẓ* Hirsch opens his argument with an homiletic argument on *la>v >oraḥ >ar<a>*. Leviticus Rabah 9 has it that twenty-six generations of humanity, living before the giving of Torah, were preserved by God because they had *derekh >ereẓ;* it is the foundation of all human relations and even more so among scholars. Hirsch cites the opinion, "No *talmid ḥakham* has the right to render a decision in the community of another, as this is not *>oraḥ d'>ar'<a> (derekh >ereẓ,* "courtesy"). Although it is not forbidden, we put him under the ban, and for that reason one does not permit him to do so since the community has its appointed rabbi" (*K'neset Ha-g'dolah* to Yoreh De<ah 242:10). What Hirsch omits is that this injunction applies only if the overriding decision is handed down without detailed explanation of the reasons; in this latter case, it would be permitted. This was the reason Rav̄ did not receive ordination to render decisions on firstborn animals (T.B. Sanhedrin 5a), because he was so well versed that he rendered them without explanation (Šifté Kohen, note 17). Hirsch equally omits the variety of different opinions (*loc. cit.*).

From a discussion in Ḥulin 18b, he shows that the rule of the local practice is to be applied, even when it differs from other localities, which he interprets: "in a locality where a rabbi introduces a halakhah into practice, one has to follow this decision, even if the practice in other communities is different" (Shilṭé Giborim). Even when both live in the *same* community, the disagreeing rabbi, who believes that his colleague has erred in matters of Mishnah, has the duty to go to him and discuss the matter. If it is evident that the deciding rabbi has not so erred, but, interpreting the correct sources, has come to a different conclusion, then the other must concede that, though he is of a different opinion, he will not override his colleague's decision (*Rosh* to <Avodah Zarah 100).

With these and similar arguments he proves, not only to Bamberger but to the readers of his letter in the press, that Bamberger had no authority whatsoever, that his ruling would be void, even were he a local rabbi, and *a fortiori* is void coming from an out-of-town rabbi, who could not know the local conditions. At the same time Hirsch has covered himself against opposing decisions that take effect elsewhere. They have no bearing on Frankfurt.

The Consistency of Bamberger's Point of View

Hirsch's arguments are stronger and more solidly argued than Bamberger's. Both, naturally, offered those prooftexts which reinforced their respective propositions. Hirsch harped on one question: how could Bamberger, co-signer of the opinion of "400" rabbis in response to the rabbi of Vienna, categorically declare that it was the duty of an Orthodox Jew to secede from the community, if it introduced basic changes, and later on permit this Jew to retain his membership in a Frankfurt *Gemeinde* which did exactly the same?

Hirsch overlooked the differences in the two situations. Vienna had one congregation. If it changed its religious practices, an Orthodox Jew had no choice but to secede. Otherwise he would have no spiritual home. The Frankfurt community was prepared to provide that home. In Vienna the changes had not yet taken place. There was hope that a strong message by a large number of rabbis would prevent them. In Frankfurt they had taken place, and now there was a movement among the leaders to reverse themselves and acknowledge the right of the Orthodox to have their own institutions at communal expense. This was indeed a form of *t'shuvah,* irrespective of its motives, and should be encouraged. Finally, Bamberger on his visit to Frankfurt may have realized that numerous Jews, including men of great talmudic scholarship, simply would not leave the main community and create a rift in Jewry. Bamberger regarded it as desirable to give these Jews a *heter* and not burden their consciences.

The Consistency of Hirsch's Outlook

Hirsch in his *Nineteen Letters*, had already asserted the principle that Israel, since its expulsion from the Land, "has no other unifying bond but God and his vocation – indestructible, because [it is] spirit."[28] On this Hegelian premise he saw his own ideology as the synthesis, with pre-Mendelssohnian Judaism as thesis and Reform as antithesis. For Jewry as a whole the scales were still swinging freely. He felt certain they would descend in his favor: "Were they checked, our grandchildren would be at an impasse, as we are."[29] The union of Orthodoxy and Reform under one roof now checked the swing of the scales. It had to be opposed.

Hirsch, a violent opponent of organized Reform, had never attended any of the synods. With the establishment of a unified community, Orthodoxy was recognized, but so was Reform. Hirsch may also have regarded Reform Jews as deficient in patriotism. He always acted first and found the reasons afterwards. "The answer to the immediate call of life is afterwards to be proven by the scholars in scholarship and as scholarship. This is the road I intend to travel."[30] In this case it was through halakhah.

The call of life rested not merely on Hirsch's principles but also on his anxiety. Would his congregation survive if another Orthodox one were to be established and legitimized? While it was conducted along halakhic lines, the roots of the controversy were sociological and psychological. They embodied the life experiences of both men.

Some Conclusions

Both Hirsch and Bamberger call for a Judaism that is fully integrated into the culture of the world. Hirsch had recognized this need throughout his entire life and his theology was based on it. Bamberger had accepted it for pragmatic reasons. Neither Bamberger nor Hirsch, however, approved of non-Orthodox Judaism as a way of life. Both men saw the serious danger facing Judaism from unchallenged absolutism. The absolutism of the nineteenth-century Reform movement, with its desire to disenfranchise Orthodox Jews and deprive them of their vital institutions thereby weaning its generations away from sacred tradition, was a serious danger to the Jewish people. Bamberger agreed that Hirsch had done right in obtaining the law of 1876 and in establishing his own independent congregation as a challenge to the official *Gemeinde*. Hirsch's own absolutism, however, casting out non-

---

[28] Hirsch, Ninth Letter.
[29] Hirsch, Eighteenth Letter.
[30] Hirsch, Nineteenth Letter.

Orthodox Judaism, may have appeared to Bamberger as equally dangerous to the future of the Jewish people. He himself had been able to appease all elements in his congregation.

A compromise of lasting importance was found by Bamberger: a Reform Judaism that recognizes the right of the Orthodox to their way of life as true and to provide for their need is not to be banished. It follows its own way as a result of interpretations that are faulty and, in endorsing Orthodox rights, acknowledges the legitimacy of interpreting Judaism differently. Orthodox Jews, by having some organizational ties with non-Orthodox institutions, may maintain the unity of the Jewish people and may succeed in bringing some of their non-Orthodox brothers and sisters into the fold of traditional Judaism.

The authority of the local rabbi can be challenged. *Derekh >ereẓ* between discussants and competing schools of thought is the foundation of communal life, as Hirsch had correctly stated. To the detriment of the cause of Judaism, it is often violated in practice as the exchange between Bamberger and Hirsch reveals.

Additionally, we see that halakhah is malleable. Had the Jewish communities been independent and free of State control, State legislation and supervision, had rabbis not been appointed by the government, the whole evolution of Jewish life in Germany during the nineteenth century might have taken a different direction. It might have unfolded existentially, pragmatically, and without acrimony.

Developments

It was precisely the *Einheitsgemeinde* at Frankfurt that extended its help to all. The Lehrhaus grew on its soil and contributed materially to the revival of Judaism in Germany and the return of many to its fold. Rabbi Anton Nehemiah Nobel drew personalities like Franz Rosenzweig and Ernst Simon and guided them on their way back to the core of Judaism. Nobel influenced men like Martin Buber and Erich Fromm.

Hirsch's congregation eventually found itself on the way toward Eastern European piety and learning, evidenced by its yeshivah, which followed the methods of pilpulistic analysis, and by appointing a rabbi who held high prestige as a talmudic scholar, but was in limited touch with the German language and culture. The tragedy of the Holocaust led to its end and does not allow us to follow its possible evolution.

Hirsch's vision failed – his vision of an integrated Jewry, honored and respected by the world as a paragon of ethics ("unfold the whole noble fullness of your *Jissroeltum* and [what non-Jew] could possibly not respect and love you?"[31]). His halakhic ruling has stood. A post-

---

[31] Hirsch, Fifteenth Letter.

Holocaust Israeli rabbinate rejects contact with secular culture. There is logic in it, considering the crimes this world perpetrated on the Jews. It forgets, however, that Judaism resides within the world. Like Hirsch, the Israeli rabbinate insists on radical separation from non-Orthodox Jewry. It devalues the importance of ethical commitment toward non-Jews.

Bamberger's pragmatic approach has stood the test of time. Jews need to remain in touch with each other. Judaism needs to remain in touch with the world. In our time, we find non-Orthodox Jewry returning to principles it had once rejected, above all the accent on *k'lal Yiśra>el,* the belief in the return to the Land, a recognition of the validity of Orthodoxy, a renewed emphasis on Hebrew, on the study of Torah, on traditional forms in worship and life. The concern with ethics has remained. Bamberger's hopes, albeit imperfectly realized according to his ideas, have borne fruit.

Afterword

With a slight change of vocalization, I subscribe to the observation of Judah ben Tema (>Aṽot 5:21): *ben sh'monim la-g'ṽurah* – for one to reach the age of eighty requires a miracle of the Almighty. *Todah l'>el <elyon* – thanks to the Most High God!

Thanks, too, to my colleagues and associates who have contributed to this Festschrift in my honor. The various essays cover a broad spectrum of learning with which I have been associated over the years. Each of these provides innovative insight into a specific area of research.

As I studied the manuscript, I was impressed with its range and beauty, and I was left with a pleasant, sweet taste, like the taste of honey to which Torah is compared (Genesis Rabah 71:8; Song of Songs Rabah 1:3, commenting on Psalm 19:11). I feel that the Festschrift contains *nofet ẓufim,* bits of honey which will delight the heart and excite the mind.

I express my gratitude to President Alfred Gottschalk, Executive Vice-President Uri D. Herscher, and Dean Lee Bycel for their sustaining support, as well as their excellent essays; to Stanley Chyet and David Ellenson for their superb work in editing the manuscript and for their own literary contributions to the volume.

Kol ha-kaṽod l'>ishti Raḥel: I share this great honor with my beloved wife Rosalind, who worships at the shrine of learning.

B'<ezrat ha-shem!

Samson H. Levey
Hebrew Union College – Jewish Institute of Religion
Los Angeles, California

A Note on the Contributors

Lewis M. Barth is Professor of Midrash and Related Literature at Hebrew Union College-Jewish Institute of Religion in Los Angeles.

Lee T. Bycel is Dean of Hebrew Union College-Jewish Institute of Religion, Los Angeles campus.

Stanley F. Chyet is Professor of American Jewish History at Hebrew Union College-Jewish Institute of Religion in Los Angeles.

William Cutter is Professor of Education and Hebrew Language and Literature at Hebrew Union College-Jewish Institute of Religion in Los Angeles.

David H. Ellenson is the Anna Grancell Professor of Jewish Religious Thought at Hebrew Union College-Jewish Institute of Religion in Los Angeles.

Lenn E. Goodman is Professor of Philosophy at the University of Hawaii at Manoa.

Alfred Gottschalk is President of Hebrew Union College-Jewish Institute of Religion and Professor of Bible and Jewish Thought.

Uri D. Herscher is Executive Vice President of Hebrew Union College-Jewish Institute of Religion and Professor of American Jewish History.

Michael L. Klein is Dean of Hebrew Union College-Jewish Institute of Religion, Jerusalem campus, and Professor of Bible and Targumic Literature.

Jacob Milgrom is Professor of Near Eastern Studies at the University of California at Berkeley.

Norman B. Mirsky is Professor of Contemporary Jewish Studies and Sociology at Hebrew Union College-Jewish Institute of Religion in Los Angeles.

Jacob Neusner is Graduate Research Professor of Religious Studies at the University of South Florida in Tampa.

Gary G. Porton is Professor of Religious Studies at the University of Illinois at Urbana-Champaign.

J. Wesley Robb is Professor Emeritus of Religion at the University of Southern California in Los Angeles.

Melvin S. Sands, retired Rabbi, lives in Claremont, California.

Harold Schulweis is Rabbi of Congregation Valley Beth Shalom in Encino, California.

Michael A. Signer, long Professor of Jewish History at Hebrew Union College- Jewish Institute of Religion in Los Angeles, now holds the Abrams Chair in Jewish Thought and Culture at the University of Notre Dame in Indiana.

Lou H. Silberman is Adjunct Professor of Judaic Studies at the University of Arizona in Tucson.

Leo Trepp is Professor of Jewish Studies at the Johannes Gutenberg University in Mainz, Germany.

Ben Zion Wacholder is the Solomon B. Freehof Professor of Jewish Law and Practice and Professor of Talmud and Rabbinics at Hebrew Union College-Jewish Institute of Religion in Cincinnati.

Edward Zipperstein, Rabbi and Certified Public Accountant, lives in Los Angeles.

Index: Persons and Places

Aaron (biblical), 60-61, 250
Abba Sikra, 27, 29, 40-41
Abbassids, 159-60
Abed-nego (biblical), 116
Abraham (biblical), 4, 7-23, 32, 51, 133, 154, 267, 271
Abraham ben David, 298
Abraham, Karl, 245-46
Abu Ishaq, 149
Abulafia, Abraham, 150
Adam (biblical), 125, 153-54, 169
Adass Yisroel Congregation, Berlin, 296
Adkins, A.W.H., 72
Adler, Nathan, 290
Aha (talmudic), 124
Ahab (biblical), 297
Ahad Ha-Am, 221, 233-42
Akiba (talmudic), 33, 127
Al-Ash'arî, 167
Albeck, Chanoch, 22
Albright, William F., 115
Alexandria, 133
Alfasi, Isaac, 195-96
Al-Ghazali, 158, 160, 165-71, 173-74
Allan, D.J., 74, 76-78
Allon, Gedaliah, 31, 41

Altenberg, Peter, 225
Aloni, Nissim, 210
Amenhotep IV; see Ikhnaton
Amos (biblical), 230-31, 258, 273-74
Amram (Ga>on), 142, 144
Andalusia, 149, 159
Andersen, Francis I., 117
Andreas-Salome, Lou, 244
<Aravah, 132
Aristotle, 65-69, 71-84, 86-88, 90, 151, 163-65, 167, 170, 172, 234-35, 237
Armstrong, A.H., 83-84, 89-90
Asher ben Yehiel, 195, 307
Assyria, 176
Aub, Joseph, 294
Augustine (Saint), 263
Austria, 225, 251, 295, 307
Avidan, David, 210
Babcock, Barbara, 109
Babylonia, 40, 59, 116-17, 132-33, 266; see also Iraq
Bacharach, Yair Ḥayyim, 182, 186
Bacher, Wilhelm, 44-45
Baer, Yitzhak, 150
Baghdad, 159-60
Balaam (biblical), 173

Bamberger, Seligmann Bär, 292-310
Band, Arnold, 212
Barash, Asher, 216, 223-26
Barbusse, Henri, 226
Barcelona, 195
Bar Kokhba, 96, 98, 159
Baron, Devorah, 227
Barthes, Roland, 161
Baruch College, 267
Bavaria, 295; see also Munich, Würzburg
Benjamin, Walter, 215, 223
Berdichev; see Levi Yizḥaq
Berdichevski, M.J., 223
Berechya, 15-16, 125
Berger, Peter, 229-32, 270
Berlin, 222, 296
Bernays, Isaac, 290
Berreman, Gerald, 110
Bialik, Ḥayim Naḥman, 212, 218-19, 221, 223
Bibi bar Abba, 6-8, 11, 13-16, 19, 22
Björnson, Björnstjerne, 210, 223
Boaz (biblical), 275
Boethius, 263
Bohemia, 267, 291, 302
Bokser, Baruch, 105
Braude, William G., 125
Braudel, Fernand, 148
Bréhier, Émile, 80-81, 84-87
Bremen, 246

Brenner, Yosef Ḥayim, 213, 217, 220-21, 223, 225
Brook of Egypt, 132, 134
Buber, Martin, 261, 309; Solomon, 126-27
Byron, 221, 225
Byzantine empire, 158-59
Caligula, 179
Canaan, 115-17
Carlyle, Thomas, 224
Carmi, T., 210
Caro, Joseph, 195, 197-98, 200, 298
Central Asia, 151, 159
Central Europe, 191, 195; see also Austria, Bohemia, Germany, Moravia
Cohen, Hermann, 266
Cordova, 147, 149
Cordova, Abraham, 216, 225
Cracow, 197
Cuddihy, J.M., 250
Damascus, 159-60
Daniel (biblical), 174
Dead Sea, 132, 136-37
Devereux, George, 95, 100
De Vos, George, 110
Dimant, Devorah, 131
Diodorus Siculus, 119
Disraeli, Benjamin, 275
Dostoevski, 210, 218, 220, 259
Douglas, Mary, 61
Dubnow, Simon, 29

Eastern Europe, 197, 218, 309; see also Lithuania, Poland, Russia
Eden, 136-38
Egypt, 47, 51, 97, 104, 119, 133, 142-44, 154-55, 183, 246, 251
Einstein, Albert, 263-64
Eleazar ben Arak, 31-34, 37, 41
Eleazer ben Simeon ben Yoḥai, 271-72
Eliahu, Mordecai, 273
Eliezer (Rabbinic), 127, 300
Eliezer ben Hyrkanus, 34-36, 304
Elijah (biblical), 47, 174
Elijah Ga>on, 201-2
Elimelech, Avraham, 224
Eliot, George; see Evans, Mary Ann
Emden, Jacob, 184
Emerson, R.W., 275
En Eglaim, 132, 137-38
En Feshkha, 137
En Gedi, 132, 137-38
Esau (biblical), 272
Euphrates river, 132, 134
Evans, Mary Ann, 215; see also Daniel Deronda
Ewen-Zohar, Itamar, 211
Ezekiel (biblical), 113-19, 131-38, 169, 171, 209
Ezra (biblical), 131, 266-70, 272, 274, 285
Farmer, William R., 137
Feldman, David, 186

Fichman, Ya'akov, 212-13, 223, 225
Finkelstein, Louis, 116-17
Flaubert, Gustave, 210
Flewelling, Ralph Tyler, 263
France, 191, 196, 227, 277
France, Anatole, 224
Frankfurt, 289, 291, 293-95, 303, 306-7, 309
Fredman, Ruth, 144
Freedman, David Noel, 117
Frege, Gottlob, 223
Freud, Sigmund, 147, 151, 243-53, 267
Friedlaender, Israel, 236
Frishman, David, 215, 218-20, 225
Fromm, Erich, 261, 309
Galilee, 67, 70, 96, 129, 132
Gamaliel ben Yehudah, 291
Gamliel II, 144
Gay, Peter, 244-45, 249
Geller, Laura, 186-87
Germany, 149, 195-99, 222, 246, 286, 289-310; see also Frankfurt, Nazis
Gershom (medieval rabbi), 196, 204
Gilat, Y.D., 34-35
Ginzberg, Louis, 118, 129
Glazer, Nathan, 269
Goethe, 213
Gomorrah, 136
Gorajek, Joseph, 260
Gordis, Robert, 113

Granada, 52, 149
Great Britain, 218, 221, 227, 258, 275; see also American colonies, English literature
Greece, 176-77
Green, Arthur, 278
Greenberg, Uri Zvi, 223
Grimm, Herman, 247
Gunkel, Herman, 5
Gustafson, James, 189
Hagar (biblical), 176
Haggai (biblical), 43, 48
Halkin, Simon, 224
Hamburg, 290
Ha-Meiri, Menahem, 273
Hamsun, Knut, 210
Hananiah (biblical), 174
Har Etzion Yeshivah, 266
Hebrew Union College, 255, 286; see also Jewish Institute of Religion
Hegel, 308
Heidegger, Martin, 223
Heine, 223-24
Herzog, Hanna, 216, 225
Hezekiah (biblical), 38-39
Hildesheimer, Ezriel, 296
Hillel, 28, 30, 34, 44, 49, 285
Hiram (biblical), 125
Hirsch, E.D., 213
Hirsch, Samson Raphael, 289-310
Ḥisda (talmudic), 185
Hiyya (Rabbinic), 125
Hoffman, Jacob, 296

Holdheim, Samuel, 293
Horowitz, Marcus, 295
Hosea (biblical), 121-22, 231, 258
Huna (Rabbinic), 126
Hunt, Chester, 110
Hurwitz, S., 45
Husik, Isaac, 155
Ibn Daud, 150
Ibn Gabirol, Shlomo, 150
Ibn Tibbon, Yehuda, 150-53, 155-57
Ibn Ṭufayl, 165, 172
Ikhnaton, 246
Iraq, 159
Isaac (biblical), 7-23, 51, 133, 154
Isaak ben Joseph, 304
Ishmael (Rabbinic), 33, 296-97, 299
Israelitische Religionsgesellschaft, Frankfurt, 289, 294, 296
Israel, Land of, 4, 6, 35, 43, 45, 47, 63, 93-102, 109, 132, 134, 136-38, 142, 149, 154, 158-59, 209-27, 271, 280, 292-93, 295, 308, 310; see also Galilee, Jerusalem, Judaea, Restoration, Samaria
Israel (state), 25, 181, 211, 213, 222, 227, 265, 273, 289, 310
Isserles, Moses, 197-99, 303
Italy, 199, 247
Jabotinsky, Vladimir, 224-25

Index: Persons and Places

Jacob (biblical), 51, 111, 132-33, 154, 272, 274
Jacob ben Meir, 191-95
Jakobovits, Immanuel, 184
Janson, H.W., 249
Jastrow, M., 126
Jeremiah (biblical), 131-32, 230-31
Jerusalem, 5, 19, 25-29, 35, 37, 40-41, 93-94, 106, 118, 131-36, 273
Jesus, 89-90, 153, 262, 283
Jethro (biblical), 142
Jewish Institute of Religion Library, New York, 212, 222
Job (biblical), 155, 169
Johanan; see Yohanan
Jonah (biblical), 125-29, 174
Jonathan ben Uzziel; *see* Yonatan ben Uzziel
Jones, Ernest, 245
Jordan river, 96, 117, 132-33, 154
Jose (talmudic), 271
Jose HaKohen, 33-34
Josephus, 31, 106
Joshua (biblical), 48, 132, 174, 244
Joshua ben Levi, 130
Joshua ben Hananiah, 33-34, 37
Judaea, 26, 29-42, 111
Judah (biblical personality), 266
Julius II, 246, 253
Jung, Carl Gustav, 244, 246

Justin Martyr, 39
Juvenal, 178
Kahle, Paul, 22
Klapstein, Israel J., 125
Keats, 221
Kennedy, Anthony M., 258
Keyes, Charles F., 110
Khazaria, 151, 154, 158-59, 161
Kimchi, Dov, 223
Kimḥi, David, 114-15
King, Martin Luther, Jr., 258
Klein, Michael, 4
Kohut, A., 127
Korah (biblical), 173
Kovno, 202
Lachower, Fishel, 224
Lagarde, P. de, 45
Lamdan, Yiẓḥaq, 223
Lawrence, D.H., 227
Lazar (Rabbinic), 127
Leach, E. 61
Leavis, F.R., 219
Lehmann, Markus, 294
Lehrhaus, Frankfurt, 309
Leon, Moses de, 150
Levey, Rosalind, 311; Samson H., x, 144-45, 209, 227
Levi Yiẓḥaq of Berdichev, 143-44
Levy, Jacob, 126-27
Lichtenstein, Aaron, 266
Lieberman, Saul, 127, 129
Lipschutz, Israel, 180

Lithuania, 199, 201-5
Loew, Judah, 267
London, 258
London, Jack, 223
Longfellow, H W., 224
Lonzono, Moses, 127
Los Angeles, 258, 260, 286
Lot (biblical), 266
Luria, Solomon ben Yehiel, 198-201
Maccabees, 93, 142-43
Maharal; see Loew, Judah
Maharil; see Mollin, Jacob
Maharshal; see Luria, Solomon
Maimonides, Moses, 118, 149, 158, 160, 163-66, 168-75, 180-81, 183-85, 187-88, 195-98, 200-1, 233-42, 250, 272, 297-98, 300, 303
Mainz, 294
Mainz, Mosheh, 303-4
Malachi (biblical), 43, 48
Mandelbaum, B., 126
Marblestone, Howard, 218
Marcel, Gabriel, 261-62
Marmorstein, A., 126
Marx, Magdaleine, 226-27
Massada, 93
Mediterreanean, 132-33, 157, 159; see also Greece, Spain
Meir of Rothenburg, 195
Mendelssohn, Moses, 308
Micah (biblical), 255-58, 263-64
Michelangelo, 244-49, 251-53
Milik, J.T., 134

Miller, William, 263
Minio-Paluello, Lorenzo, 73
Mintz, A.L., 223
Miron, Dan, 216, 221
Mishael (biblical), 174
Mizrahi, Israel, 184
Moab, 117, 266
Mollin, Jacob, 143, 298
Moravia, 291, 302
Moriah, Mount, 12, 133
Morris, H.S., 110
Moses (biblical), 51, 60, 91, 131, 154, 172-73, 175, 238-39, 244-53, 274
Muḥammad, 169
Muilenberg, James, 116
Munich, 246
Munk, Elie, 272
Murrow, Edward R., 258
Nahmanides, 184, 299
Nakdimon ben Gurion, 27-28
Naomi (biblical), 275
Nathan (talmudic), 194
Nebuchadnezzar, 40
Needham, Rodney, 94-95, 100
Neo-Ezekiel, 131
Nero, 178
Neusner, Jacob, 39
Newman, Mordechai, 227
Newsom, Carole, 133
New York, 212, 222, 227, 259, 267
Nimrod (biblical), 39
Nineveh (biblical), 122, 125-29
Noah (biblical), 153-54, 173

Index: Persons and Places

Nobel, Anton Nehemiah, 296, 309
North Africa, 149, 158; see also Egypt
Novak, David, 181-82, 186-87
Odessa, 222, 236
Oldenburg, 290-93
Oppenheim, Moritz, 286
Orlinsky, Harry M., 229, 231-32
Ottoman empire, 199
Owens, Joseph, 77
Palestine; see Israel, Land of
Paris, 227
Parker, G.F., 75
Parthia; see Persia
Peor, 117-18
Persia, 93, 159
Phidias, 75
Philo, 177-79, 181, 183
Phoenicia; see Canaan
Plato, 66, 71-73, 80, 82, 84, 86, 90, 172
Plaut, Gunther, 280
Pliny, 137
Plocki, Meir Dan, 185
Plotinus, 71-72, 80-88, 90
Poe, Edgar Allan, 224
Poland, 197-99, 215-16, 222, 260
Porat, Zivah, 211
Poseidippus, 177
Prague, 267
Prussia, 289; see also Berlin, Frankfurt, Hamburg

Pseudo-Ezekiel, 131, 136
Pyrenees, 150, 159
Qumran, 27, 93, 131-38
Raba (talmudic), 194
Rabad; see Abraham ben David
Rabbenu Gershom; see Gershom
Rabbenu Tam; see Jacob ben Meir
Rabbinerseminar, Berlin, 296
Rabinowitz, Alexander Ziskind, 218
Rad, Gerhard von, 5
Rama; see Isserles
Ramban; see Naḥmanides
Rank, Otto, 245
Rashbam; see Samuel ben Meir
Rashi, 43-44, 114, 175, 181-82, 191-92, 298-300
Rav, 306
Rav Amram; see Amram
Rebekkah (biblical), 272
Resh Lakish; see Simeon ben Lakish
Rhineland, 149
Ricks, Stephen, 176, 178
Ritvah; see Yomtov ben Avraham
Rivkes, Moshe, 273
Roazen, Paul, 246
Roman empire, 26-31, 36-42, 70, 93-94, 178, 180, 271-72
Rome, 247
Rosenzweig, Franz, 309
Rosh; see Asher ben Yehiel

Roth, Cecil, 27; Philip, 274

Rufus Musonius, 178

Russia, 199, 222, 236; see also Soviet Union

Ruth (biblical), 266-70, 274-75

Saadya (Ga>on), 160, 169-70, 240

Sachs, Hans, 245

Salkinson, Y.A., 223

Samaria, 121-22

Samuel (>amora>), 192

Samuel bar Naḥman, 121

Samuel ben Meir, 191

Samuel (unidentified), 51

Santayana, George, 274

Saussure, Ferdinand de, 223

Schiller, 226

Scholem, Gershom 217, 223

Schorr, Isaac, 187

Schur, Max, 244

Seltzer, Adele Szold, 226; Thomas, 226-27

Seneca, 178

Shabbethai Ha-Kohen, 303-4

Shakespeare, 210, 212, 219, 223

Shammai, 35

Shavit, Yaakov and Zohar, 211, 213-14, 216, 222, 225

Shelley, 221, 224

Shimon ben Netanel, 33

Shlonsky, Avraham, 210, 215

Shmuel Hanagid, 52

Shneur Zalman, 267

Shofman, Gershom, 225

Silver, Abba Hillel, 38

Simeon ben Halafta, 126-28

Simeon ben Lakish, 122, 124-29

Simeon ben Yoḥai, 271-73

Simon, Ernst, 309

Simon Peter (New Testament), 154

Sinai, Mount, 51, 91, 99, 131, 193

Singer, Isaac B., 161

Sodom, 136

Solomon (biblical), 173

Solomon ibn Adret, 195

Soloveichik, Ḥayyim, 184, 188

Soviet Union, 259

Spain, 52, 147-61, 195-97, 223

Speiser, E.A., 4-5

Spektor, Isaac Elḥanan, 202-5

Spinoza, Baruch, 250

Spitzer, Solomon, 295, 304, 307

Stein, Menahem, 30

Steinberg, Yaakov, 216, 219, 223

Stendhal, 224

Stevenson, Robert Louis, 224

Strugnell, John, 131

Sumeria, 116

Syria, 35, 116, 158-59

Szold family, 226

Tacitus, 178

Tamar (biblical), 266

Tarn, W.W., 176-78

Tarphon (talmudic), 296, 298

Index: Persons and Places

Tel Aviv, 211, 214
Temple (Jerusalem), 5, 18-21, 26-29, 35, 37, 51, 59-60, 93-94, 96, 100-1, 105-6, 108, 118-19, 131-36, 173, 243-44, 271, 293
Titus, 26
Toledo, 149, 195
Tolstoy, 210, 220
Toury, Gideon, 211
Trani, Joseph, 184
Troyes, 191
Tschernichowski, Saul, 223-24
Tudela, 149
Turner, V., 57-58
United States, 186, 190, 211, 222, 226-27, 246, 256-60, 262; *see also* American colonies, American Jews, American literature, Los Angeles, New York
University of Bonn, 290
University of Southern California, 255-56, 261, 263
University of Virginia, 258
Unterman, Isser Yehudah, 181-82
van Gennep, Arnold, 57
van den Berghe, Pierre L., 111
Van Seters, John, 4
Vespasian, 26, 41
Victoria (queen), 275
Vienna, 251, 295, 307
Vilna, 201

Voznesensky, Andrey, 259
Waldenberg, Eliezer, 273; Yehudah, 185
Walker, Lewis, 110
Warsaw, 216, 222
Weber, Max, 229-32
Western Europe, 191; *see also* France, Great Britain
Wilde, Oscar, 221, 225, 227
Winnik, Eugene, 260
Wittgenstein, Ludwig, 223
Würzburg, 294-95
Wyschogrod, Michael, 267
Yadin, Yigael, 131, 134
Yavneh, 29-31, 36-37, 40-41
Yehudah ben Ilai, 271
Yehuda Halevi, 147-61, 234, 240, 267-68
Yemen, 301
Yeshiva University, 267
Yetman, Norman R., 109
Yohanan (3rd Cent. C.E.), 6-8, 11, 13-16, 19, 22, 124-25, 128-29, 142
Yohanan ben Zakkai, 25-42, 44
Yomtov ben Avraham, 299
Yonatan ben Uzziel, 34, 43-56
Zadok, Sons of, 133, 135
Zangwill, Israel, 223
Zechariah (biblical), 43, 48
Zohar, Naomi, 218
Zunz, Leopold, 44
Zweig, Stefan, 227

Index: Subjects

Abortion, 175-90

Acculturation, 157, 201-2, 209-27, 236, 266, 270, 289-93, 296; see also Western civilization

Adultery, 184

Adults, 282

African peoples, 58-60

Agriculture, 35, 99, 101-3, 108, 115, 132, 138, 148, 192, 205, 271

‹Agunah, 193, 204-5

‹Aliyot; see Immigration

Alphabet, 116-17

American colonies, 255

American Jews, 227, 265-76

American literature, 223-24, 274-275

Amusements, 201, 218, 227, 261

Ancestry, 9, 13, 16, 21-22, 110-11, 155-56, 243-44, 249, 265-72

Anthropology, 60-61, 224, 248

Anti-Semitism; see Judeophobia

Apocalypse of John, 136

Apostasy, 117-18, 290, 295-96, 299-300; see also Dejudaization

Arabic (as literary model), 157

Arabs, 147, 154, 159, 237; see also Islam

Aramaic, 43-56, 286; see also Targums

Archaeology, 243-44, 253

Architecture, 135

Art; see Archaeology, Music, Novels, Painting, Poetry, Sculpture

Ashkenazim, 198, 267; see also Central Europe, Eastern Europe, Western Europe

Assimilation; see Dejudaization

Atomism, 166-68

Atonement, 9, 15-17, 37, 276

Audience; see Readership

Authority; see Rulers

Autobiography, 165, 244, 249, 274

Baal, 117-19

Balfour Declaration, 221

Bêt Din; see Courts

Bible, 5-6, 9, 12, 15, 17-18, 22, 35, 37, 41, 43-45, 47-49, 51-52, 59-60, 63, 68-70, 89-91, 97, 101, 103-4, 113-19, 122, 125-28, 131-38, 141-44, 153-57, 163, 169, 171, 173, 175-83, 188-89, 194, 201, 203, 205, 219, 229-32,

234, 238-39, 244, 252, 266-75, 279-87, 291-92, 297; see also Moses, New Testament, Prophets, Targums

Biographies, 222, 225, 245

Birth, 169, 176, 178, 182, 185, 187, 190, 269-70; control, 182, 185, 204

Blessings, 141-45, 176, 278

Body, 267, 270, 298

Bourgeoisie, 250-51

British Mandate (Palestine), 221

Cain (poem), 225

Caliphs, 147, 159

Cantors, 196, 295

Capital punishment, 175, 178, 180, 196, 271

Charisma, 229-32

Children, 176-78, 257, 260, 263, 266, 269, 271, 282, 286, 290

Chosen, Jews as, 99-100, 155-56, 251, 267-69

Christianity, 36, 39, 89-91, 93, 144-45, 148-49, 151, 153-54, 156, 158-59, 186, 192, 218, 246-47, 250, 260-63, 272, 274, 283, 290, 299; see also Crusades, Judaic-Christian morality

Ciphers, 116-17

Circumcision, 156, 269

City of the Sanctuary, 134-36

Civility, 250, 306, 309

Civil Rights Act, 258

Classification, 61, 64-77, 80-81, 84, 86, 89-91, 95

Clerical garb, 291

Codes (law), 175-76, 178, 184, 195, 197-200, 237, 239-41, 251, 297, 299, 302-6

Commentary; see Exegesis, Hermeneutics

Commerce, 97, 99, 108-9, 177, 213, 223, 225

Communal norms, 30, 36-37, 39-40, 42, 225, 230, 238, 240-41, 249, 262, 270, 274-75, 277-79, 293-310; see also Customs, Orthodoxy

Concubinage, 178

Consciousness, 167-68, 171, 174, 270

Consecration ceremonies, 58-61

Conservatism (Judaism), 293

Contraception; see Birth (control)

Converts to Judaism, 133, 135, 151, 155-57, 265-76

Corporal punishment, 196

Cosmos, 89-90, 164-65, 172, 262

Courts (law), 13-14, 97, 107, 180, 193, 195, 197; see also Supreme Court

Criminals, 156, 180, 184, 196, 258, 310

Crusades, 149, 191-92, 195

Culture; see Acculturation, Greco-Roman culture, Literary (culture)

Customs, 191-92, 194, 196-98, 202

Daniel Deronda (novel), 215, 218-20, 227

Davidic Kingdom, 35, 150, 266

Dejudaization, 274-75

Democracy, 272-73

Dialetic, 77-78, 166, 169, 188, 190, 217

Diaspora, 25, 51, 159, 191, 211-12, 216, 242, 265, 289; see also American Jews, Central Europe, Eastern Europe, Ottoman empire, Spain, United States, Western Europe

Disease; see Illness

Divine influence (Halevi), 153, 155-56

Divorce, 202-4

Do>ar Ha-yom (periodical), 226

Don Carlos (poem), 226

Don Quixote (novel), 223

Dreams, 59, 132-33, 231, 248

Dr. Jekyll and Mr. Hyde (novel), 224

Dual Torah (as philosophical system), 68

Economic life, 30-31, 35, 97-99, 102-3, 108, 110, 132, 135, 138, 148, 157, 191-93, 195, 197, 200, 213, 215, 223, 244, 257, 260, 271, 291

Education, 14, 67, 192, 195, 197, 202-4, 211, 227, 239, 255-64, 266, 269, 273, 275, 279-87, 290-95, 300-10

Egotism, 199-200

Emanicipation, 250, 293; see also Political equality

Embryo, development and rights of, 163-65, 168, 170-72, 174-77, 179-83, 185, 187-89; see also Birth

Emirs, 147, 149, 159

English literature, 210, 212, 215-16, 218-21, 223-27

Enlightenment, 272, 277

Ensoulment, 189

Eschatology, 131-38, 160, 292-93

Esotericism, 31-34, 36, 39-40

Essays, 211-13, 216-17, 221-25, 236, 242, 244-46

Essenes, 93-94, 131, 136

Ethics, 161, 179-89, 227, 251-52, 256, 263-64, 266-67, 269-77, 309-10; see also Humanism, Judaic-Christian morality

Ethnocentrism, 94-98, 100, 102, 104-11, 155-61, 250, 266-73

Exegesis, 3, 6, 8, 14-15, 17, 22-23, 61, 239, 291; see also Hermeneutics

Existentialism, 144, 155

Experience, 165-66, 279-81, 283-87, 308

Faith, 290; development, 282

Fasts, 124, 128-29

Feminism, 226-27

Femme (novel), 226-27

Fertility rites, 118-19

Festivals; *see* Holy Days

Feudalism, 148, 150

Fish, 132, 174, 201

Foetus; *see* Embryo

Folklore, 5, 17-20, 22, 27, 32, 38-41, 43-44, 47-49, 69-70, 132, 143, 195, 265, 267, 269, 271-73, 280, 283; *see also* Miracles, Parables, Taboo, Tradition

Food, 267, 297; *see also* Kashrut

French literature, 210, 216, 221, 224, 226-27

Genetics; *see* Ancestry

Genitalia, 118-19

Gentiles, 13, 30, 34-37, 39-42, 47, 88-91, 93-111, 115-19, 135, 151, 155, 157, 159, 175-79, 183, 189, 192, 196-97, 201, 205, 219, 245-46, 250, 263, 268, 271, 273-75, 293, 296, 309; *see also* Christianity, Converts, Greco-Roman culture, Idolatry, Islam, Jewish-Gentile relations, Nineveh

Geography, 131-38

German language, 291, 309

German literature, 213, 216, 225-27; *see also* Freud, Sigmund

G'mara>, 11-12, 14-15, 124-25, 142, 240

G'nizah, 142

God (as philosophical concept), 63-65, 79-80, 88-91, 151-52, 171

God; *see* Monotheism, Theology, Theophany

Golden Age (Spain), 148, 158

G'>onim, 44, 142, 144, 197, 199-202, 302

Government; *see* Politics, Rulers

Greco-Roman culture, 65, 70-73, 75, 80, 86-91, 97, 119, 137, 157, 176-78, 201, 218, 237, 263, 271-73; *see also* Aristotle, Neo-Platonism, Plato, Plotinus

Ḥabad, 267-68

Haggadah, 141-45

Hagiographa, 44

Halakhah; *see* Law

Hammurabi, Code of, 175, 178

Ha-shiloaḥ (periodical), 236

Ḥasidism, 202, 233-34 *see also* Ḥabad

Haskalah, 202; *see also* Ahad Ha-Am

Ha-t'qufah (periodical), 212

Head covering, 201-2

Health, 184, 260

Hebrew language, 157, 202, 211, 215-21, 223-25, 227, 236-37, 266, 280, 291, 310; *see also* Literature (Modern Hebrew)

Hebrews, 246

Hellenistic; *see* Greco-Roman culture

Heresy, 241, 270, 296-98, 300

Index: Subjects

Hermeneutics, 278, 282-87; see also Exegesis

Hiawatha (poem), 224

History and historians, 31, 106, 119, 131. 136, 143-45, 150, 158-61, 165, 175, 198, 210, 214, 220-21, 232, 240, 246, 248-49, 253, 258, 272-74, 277, 283-84, 293

Holocaust; see Judeophobia, Nazis

Holy Days, 15-16, 23, 44-45, 48-49, 59-60, 96, 103, 105, 122, 141-44, 193, 196, 201, 241, 274, 276; see also Passover

Homicide, 175-76, 181; see also Murder

Homilies; see Midrash

Human rights; see Ethics, Humanism

Humanism, 177, 198, 203-4, 243, 252, 257, 259, 264, 272

Hylomorphism, 168

Identity, 94-96, 99, 102-11, 249-51, 261, 267, 269, 272

Ideology, 210, 213, 221, 225-27, 270, 272, 293, 299; see also Nationalism, Orthodoxy, Religion

Idolatry, 100, 108, 116-19, 170, 192-93, 247, 253, 273, 296-98, 300; see also Baal, Fertility rites, Gentiles

Illness, 182, 184, 189-90, 221, 243-44, 246, 248, 250, 260, 296, 301

Imagination, 22, 97, 142, 165, 174, 248

Imago (periodical), 245-46

Immigration to Land of Israel, 211, 215-16, 227, 265

Incest, 184, 266

Individuals, 176, 180, 194-95, 221, 225, 227, 230-32, 238, 248, 257, 262, 282-87, 296

Industry, 135

Infanticide, 176-79, 186

Informers, 196

Institutional framework; see Communal norms

Intermarriage, 107, 265-66

Islam, 147, 149-51, 154, 156, 158-60, 165-72

Jewish-Gentile relations, 191-93, 195-96, 201, 205, 250, 260, 265-76, 267, 271-75, 283, 290, 292, 309; see also Acculturation, Converts, Diaspora, Judaic-Christian morality, Judeophobia

Joseph Peretz (novel), 224

Journalists, 258, 263

Judaic-Christian morality, 186, 255-64

Judeophobia, 13, 25, 35, 40, 149, 151, 178, 183, 195, 260, 265, 272, 277, 290, 309; see also Crusades

Jurists; see Law

Justice, 257-59, 263, 304; see also Law

Kalâm, 166-68

Karaism, 160
Kashrut, 99, 134-35, 192, 197, 205, 293, 295, 297, 305
Kings; see Rulers
K'tuvim (periodical), 215, 226
Kuzari (Yehuda Halevi), 147-61, 234, 268
Laity, 201, 286, 294, 301
Language, 210, 212, 215-19, 221-23, 240, 274, 279, 281
Law, 26, 28, 33-36, 51, 86, 96-99, 102-3, 106-8, 118, 142, 149, 154-56, 175-76, 179-82, 184-89, 191-205, 227, 236, 238, 246, 249, 251-53, 258-59, 265, 269, 271, 273, 280, 284-85, 289-91, 294-310; of Return, 265
Levites, 133, 135-36
Liberalism, 268, 274, 277, 286, 293, 295-96, 301, 308, 310; see also Reform Jews
Libraries, 212, 222, 227
Life, inviolability of, 179-89; see also Piquah nefesh
Life Magazine, 263
Literary criticism, 219; culture, 209-27; narrative, 143-44, 224, 280; theory, 210-11, 223, 225
Literature, Modern Hebrew, 210-27
Liturgy, 12, 16-17, 44-56, 133, 141-45, 278, 291, 295-96, 298, 300-1; see also Prayer
Lovingkindness, 259-64; see also Ethics, Humanism

Magic, 231
Mahzor Vitry, 44-45, 48
Male chauvinism, 178
Manuscripts, 45-47, 126, 199; see also Scribal texts
Marriage, 27, 97, 111, 195, 197, 203-4, 265; see also Intermarriage
Masoretic texts, 115
Masses; see Communal norms, Poor
Medical matters, 132, 182, 187, 195; see also Physicians, Psychiatry, Psychoanalysis
Menstruation, 134
Messianism, 25, 31, 36-42, 47, 51, 131-38, 150, 153, 159-60, 210, 213, 241, 266, 293, 295-96
Metaphysics, 172, 174, 215, 267, 270
Middle Class; see Bourgeoisie
Midrash, 3-6, 10, 12, 17, 19-20, 22-23, 28, 35, 41-42, 118, 121-30, 173-75, 178, 184, 267, 306
Miracles, 141-45, 152, 154, 165-66, 168-71, 173-74, 190, 292
Miscarriage, 178
Mishnah, 11-12, 32, 35, 59, 63-91, 93-111, 117, 124-25, 128, 134-35, 142, 144, 173, 179-81, 183, 185, 188, 192-93, 240, 291, 302, 304, 307
Mission of Israel, 277

Index: Subjects

Mizpeh Publishing House, 216, 227
Modernity, 270, 274, 277, 283, 289-93; see also Enlightenment, Western civilization, Wissenschaft
Modern scholarship; see Wissenschaft
Modesty, 262-64; see also Ethics, Humanism
Moneylending, 193
Mongols, 159
Monotheism, 63, 89, 99-102, 105-6, 154, 172, 246, 263, 277
Morality; see Ethics, Humanism, Judaic-Christian morality, Law
Moreh (Maimonides), 118, 233, 235, 237, 239-41
Moses and Monotheism (Freud), 244-52
Murder, 179, 187, 246, 251
Music, 291; see also Cantors
Mysticism, 85, 150, 160, 183, 198, 201-2, 263, 267-68, 291; see also Esotericism, Ḥasidism
Myth, 144, 158, 161, 165, 249, 283
Narcissism, 179
Naśi>, 133
Nationalism, 215-16, 219, 221-27, 241-42; see also Patriotism
Naturalism, 165, 167, 169-71, 173
Nature; see Science

Nazis, 260, 265, 272, 309
Neo-Platonism, 65-72, 80, 82-90, 150-52, 165, 170, 172, 174, 237
Newspapers, 226, 299, 302, 307
New Testament, 94, 136, 154, 262, 275, 283
New York Times, 226
Nineteen Letters about Judaism (Hirsch), 292-93, 308
Norwegian literature, 210, 223
Nose, 114, 193
Novels, 210, 213, 215, 218-27, 246, 248
Occult; see Esotericism
Ontology, 64, 81-86, 89, 174, 183, 187, 190
Oral law; see Dual Torah, Mishnah, Talmud, Tradition
Oriental Jews, 224, 273
Orthodoxy, 33, 151, 153-61, 165, 185, 188-89, 191-205, 233, 235, 273, 277, 289-310; see also Monotheism, Revelation, Tradition
Pacifism; see Peace
Painting, 286
Parables, 121, 124, 127
Parents, 176-81, 184, 246, 257, 263, 271, 278, 280, 282, 286
Parochialism, 93-97, 99, 108, 218, 224; see also Ethnocentrism
Passover, 103-5, 141-45, 204

Patriotism, 292-93, 308
Peace, 109, 178, 194, 196, 278, 301
Pentateuch, 131, 143, 176
Periodicals, 212, 225-26, 245, 259, 263; see also Newspapers
Personalism, 263
Personality, 249, 306, 308
Pharisees, 26, 28, 94
Philanthropy, 125, 194
Philosophy, 63-92, 151-53, 155-58, 160-61, 163-68, 171, 175, 177-78, 188, 195-96, 201-2, 233-42, 261, 263, 266-67, 280, 284, 308; see also Rationalism, Science
Physicians, 149, 161, 175, 244, 251-53, 299
Pilpul, 201, 309
Piquaḥ nefesh (talmudic), 182, 188
Poetics, 211
Poetry and poets, 43-56, 70, 115, 137, 149-50, 155, 158-59, 161, 212, 221-26, 259
Polemics, 34-36, 129, 144-45, 151, 157, 272-73
Political equality, 290, 292
Politics, 26-31, 36-42, 158, 190, 221, 225-26, 231, 241, 257-58, 265, 272
Polygamy, 204
Poor, 258, 260
Potash, 138
Pravda (newspaper), 259

Prayer, 8, 12, 14, 16, 18, 21, 23, 52, 125-26, 194, 202, 271, 273, 276, 278, 292; see also Liturgy
Priesthood, 26, 58-61, 69-70, 77, 118, 132-35, 231, 285
Printing, 199
Prooftexts, 124, 126, 300, 307
Property rights, 188, 190
Prophets, 43, 45, 48-49, 51, 113-19, 121-22, 125-38, 152-54, 156, 165, 170, 174, 182, 230-32, 237-39, 241, 255-64, 268, 285, 292
Psychiatry, 244, 262
Psychoanalysis, 245-53
Psychology, 261, 282, 308; see also Freud, Sigmund
Publishing, 213, 215-16, 223, 225-27
Purity, 107-8, 135, 156, 185, 266, 268
Qabbalah; see Mysticism
Qidush, 142
Quran, 154, 167, 169
Rabbinical conferences, 191, 293, 308
Rabbis, 191-205, 219, 268, 271, 273, 289-310; see also Law, Midrash, Mishnah, Talmud, Tosefta>
Rationalism, 64, 71, 89-90, 152-53, 155, 157-58, 160-61, 163, 166-67, 171, 198-99, 201, 203, 233-42, 277, 284, 310; see also Science

Readership, 210, 213, 215-23, 225-27, 281-87

Reason; see Rationalism

Reform Jews, 227, 265, 290, 292-93, 297-301, 308

Religion, 75, 233, 235-41, 246, 249, 256, 258, 261, 263, 265, 273, 277-87, 302; see also Christianity, Conservatism, Faith, Greco-Roman culture, Islam, Orthodoxy, Reform Jews, Revelation, Spirituality, Tradition

Religious freedom, 289, 294, 308

Repentance, 121-22, 124-25, 128-29

Restoration, 296

Resurrection, 169, 172

Revelation, 89-90, 151, 154, 158, 172, 238-41, 249-50, 252, 277, 290; see also Sinai, Theophany

Reward and punishment, 9-11, 13, 16, 21-22, 125, 154

Rites of passage, 57-61

Rodef (aggressor), 180-81, 183, 187

Roe vs. Wade, 189-90

Romance (literary), 165; see also Novels

Romeo and Juliet (drama), 223

Rulers, 26, 35, 38-41, 52, 59-60, 77, 121, 124, 127, 133, 147, 149, 154, 159, 178-79, 183, 230-31, 246, 258, 266, 275, 282-83, 289, 293, 305-7, 310

Russian literature, 210, 216, 218, 220, 259

Sabbath, 103-4, 122, 133, 182, 192, 198, 201, 205, 227, 271-74, 300

Sacrifice, 7-23, 35, 37, 59, 101, 106, 134, 156, 231, 271, 293, 295-96

Sadducees, 26, 94

Salvation, 152, 249; see also World to Come

Sanctity, 132-36, 177, 186, 189, 278

Sanhedrin, 30

Schools; see Education

Science, 71, 77-79, 81, 165-68, 170-71, 174, 179, 188, 195, 197, 201-2, 214, 221, 245, 250, 259, 262-64, 272, 284, 302

Scribal texts, 115, 192, 199

Scribes; see Ezra

Scrolls, 131, 134-35

Sculpture, 75, 244-9, 251, 253

Secular studies, 195, 197-98, 202, 237, 272, 290, 302, 310; see also Haskalah, Medical matters, Philosophy, Science, Western civilization

Seder, 142-45

Sefardim, 197; see also Oriental Jews, Spain

Seljuks, 149

Separatism; see Hirsch, Samuel Raphael

Septuagint, 20, 114, 177-79, 183

Sexual activity, 107-8, 110-11, 117-19, 134, 169, 178, 189, 196, 225, 227, 252, 271

Sh'khol V'khishalon (novel), 220

Shrines, 230-31, 297; see also Temple

Shulḥan <Arukh; see Codes

Simon Wiesenthal Center, 260

Sicarii; see Zealots

Skirball Museum, 286

Slavery, 98, 104, 142-43, 178, 184

Social change, 26, 230-32, 236-39

Social classes; see Bourgeoisie, Poor, Rulers

Social intercourse, 107-8, 110, 157; roles, 261

Sociology, 218, 229-32, 269, 308

Soul, 81, 84, 88, 152, 189, 239, 268, 270

Spirituality, 277-87

Stoics, 178

Suicide, 178, 187, 244

Supreme Court (United States), 258

Synagogue, 48, 101, 196, 275, 293-94, 297; see also Prayer

Synods; see Rabbinical conferences

Taboo, 58-59, 70, 100-2, 118, 134

Talmud, 3-4, 6, 11-16, 19-23, 28, 31-41, 43, 49, 118, 122, 124-25, 127, 129, 134, 141, 171, 180-83, 185, 187, 192-203, 239, 256, 266, 269, 271, 273, 278, 285-86, 291, 295-300, 302-3, 305-7; see also G'mara>, Mishnah

Tanning, 138

Tanya> (Ḥabad), 267-68, 272

Targums, 4, 10-11, 13, 17-23, 43-45, 47-56, 114, 209, 227

Taxation, 29-30, 105, 289, 294

Technology, 262

Ten Commandments, 173, 247, 253, 297

Tent of Meeting, 136

Texts, 277-87; see also Masoretic, Scribal, Ugaritic

Thanksgiving Psalms, 136-37

Theology, 65, 91-92, 122, 131, 154-57, 165-74, 209, 233-39, 261-63, 267, 270, 272, 274, 280, 292, 308; see also Monotheism, Spirituality

Theophany, 18, 32, 154, 171

Time, sacred, 96, 100, 103, 108, 278; see also Holy Days, Sabbath

Tithing, 35, 102, 106

Tombs, 246-47, 253, 292

Torah; see Bible, Law, Pentateuch, Tradition

Torah <im Derekh >Ereẓ, 291, 301

Tosafists, 191, 193, 304

Tosefta>, 32-35, 93-111

Tradition, 4, 6, 10, 13, 16, 22-23, 26, 29, 34, 36, 39, 41, 64-65, 68, 80, 87, 89-91, 110, 134, 141-42, 155, 172, 177, 185-89, 191, 194, 196, 209-10, 224, 230, 235, 249, 258, 266-74, 277-87, 290, 304, 310; *see also* Communal norms, Customs, Orthodoxy

Translations, 5-6, 11, 14, 22, 43, 47-48, 51, 113-15, 126-27, 150, 165, 167, 202, 209-27; *see also* Septuagint, Targums

Turks, 159; *see also* Ottoman empire, Seljuks

Twelve Tribes, 133, 136

Ugaritic texts, 115, 117

Ummayyads, 147, 159

Utopia, 161, 286; *see also* Eden

Viticulture; *see* Wine

Voting Rights Act, 258

Webster vs. Reproductive Health Services, 189

Western civilization, 250, 270, 272-73, 290-310

Wilderness, 132, 154; *see also* Dead Sea

Wine, 98-99, 108, 192-93, 197, 201

Wissenschaft des Judentums, 290-91

Women, 27-28, 119, 125, 127, 134, 175-81, 183-88, 193, 196, 202-5, 226-27, 248, 263, 266, 272, 274-75

World to Come, 37, 242, 271

World War II, 258, 260, 272

Yaḥad; *see* Essenes

Yefet project, 218

Yiddish, 291

Yishuv̄, 210-27; *see also* Israel, Land of

Zealots, 26-29, 35-36, 38, 41, 93-94

Zionism; *see* Nationalism, Yishuv̄

Zohar, 183, 268

South Florida Studies in the History of Judaism

240001	Lectures on Judaism in the Academy and in the Humanities	Neusner
240002	Lectures on Judaism in the History of Religion	Neusner
240003	Self-Fulfilling Prophecy: Exile and Return in the History of Judaism	Neusner
240004	The Canonical History of Ideas: The Place of the So-called Tannaite Midrashim, Mekhilta Attributed to R. Ishmael, Sifra, Sifré to Numbers, and Sifré to Deuteronomy	Neusner
240005	Ancient Judaism: Debates and Disputes	Neusner
240006	The Hasmoneans and Their Supporters: From Mattathias to the Death of John Hyrcanus I	Sievers
240007	Approaches to Ancient Judaism: New Series, Volume I	Neusner
240008	Judaism in the Matrix of Christianity	Neusner
240009	Tradition as Selectivity: Scripture, Mishnah, Tosefta, and Midrash in the Talmud of Babylonia	Neusner
240010	The Tosefta: Translated from the Hebrew: Sixth Division Tohorot	Neusner
240011	In the Margins of the Midrash: Sifre Ha'azinu Texts, Commentaries and Reflections	Basser
240012	Language as Taxonomy: The Rules for Using Hebrew and Aramaic in the Babylonia Talmud	Neusner
240013	The Rules of Composition of the Talmud of Babylonia: The Cogency of the Bavli's Composite	Neusner
240014	Understanding the Rabbinic Mind: Essays on the Hermeneutic of Max Kadushin	Ochs
240015	Essays in Jewish Historiography	Rapoport-Albert
240016	The Golden Calf and the Origins of the Jewish Controversy	Bori/Ward
240017	Approaches to Ancient Judaism: New Series, Volume II	Neusner
240018	The Bavli That Might Have Been: The Tosefta's Theory of Mishnah Commentary Compared With the Bavli's	Neusner
240019	The Formation of Judaism: In Retrospect and Prospect	Neusner
240020	Judaism in Society: The Evidence of the Yerushalmi, Toward the Natural History of a Religion	Neusner
240021	The Enchantments of Judaism: Rites of Transformation from Birth Through Death	Neusner
240022	The Rules of Composition of the Talmud of Babylonia	Neusner
240023	The City of God in Judaism and Other Comparative and Methodological Studies	Neusner
240024	The Bavli's One Voice: Types and Forms of Analytical Discourse and their Fixed Order of Appearance	Neusner
240025	The Dura-Europos Synagogue: A Re-evaluation (1932-1992)	Gutmann
240026	Precedent and Judicial Discretion: The Case of Joseph ibn Lev	Morell
240027	Max Weinreich *Geschichte der jiddischen Sprachforschung*	Frakes
240028	Israel: Its Life and Culture, Volume I	Pedersen
240029	Israel: Its Life and Culture, Volume II	Pedersen
240030	The Bavli's One Statement: The Metapropositional Program of Babylonian Talmud Tractate Zebahim Chapters One and Five	Neusner

240031	The Oral Torah: The Sacred Books of Judaism: An Introduction: Second Printing	Neusner
240032	The Twentieth Century Construction of "Judaism:" Essays on the Religion of Torah in the History of Religion	Neusner
240033	How the Talmud Shaped Rabbinic Discourse	Neusner
240034	The Discourse of the Bavli: Language, Literature, and Symbolism: Five Recent Findings	Neusner
240035	The Law Behind the Laws: The Bavli's Essential Discourse	Neusner
240036	Sources and Traditions: Types of Compositions in the Talmud of Babylonia	Neusner
240037	How to Study the Bavli: The Languages, Literatures, and Lessons of the Talmud of Babylonia	Neusner
240038	The Bavli's Primary Discourse: Mishnah Commentary: Its Rhetorical Paradigms and their Theological Implications	Neusner
240039	Midrash Aleph Beth	Sawyer
240040	Jewish Thought in the 20th Century: An Introduction	Schweid
	in the Talmud of Babylonia Tractate Moed Qatan	Neusner
240041	Diaspora Jews and Judaism: Essays in Honor of, and in Dialogue with, A. Thomas Kraabel	Overman/MacLennan
240042	The Bavli: An Introduction	Neusner
240043	The Bavli's Massive Miscellanies: The Problem of Agglutinative Discourse in the Talmud of Babylonia	Neusner
240044	The Foundations of the Theology of Judaism: An Anthology Part II: Torah	Neusner
240045	Form-Analytical Comparison in Rabbinic Judaism: Structure and Form in *The Fathers* and *The Fathers According to Rabbi Nathan*	Neusner
240046	Essays on Hebrew	Weinberg
240047	The Tosefta: An Introduction	Neusner
240048	The Foundations of the Theology of Judaism: An Anthology Part III: Israel	Neusner
240049	The Study of Ancient Judaism, Volume I: Mishnah, Midrash, Siddur	Neusner
240050	The Study of Ancient Judaism, Volume II: The Palestinian and Babylonian Talmuds	Neusner
240051	Take Judaism, for Example: Studies toward the Comparison of Religions	Neusner
240052	From Eden to Golgotha: Essays in Biblical Theology	Moberly
240053	The Principal Parts of the Bavli's Discourse: A Preliminary Taxonomy: Mishnah Commentary, Sources, Traditions and Agglutinative Miscellanies	Neusner
240054	Barabbas and Esther and Other Studies in the Judaic Illumination of Earliest Christianity	Aus
240055	Targum Studies, Volume I: Textual and Contextual Studies in the Pentateuchal Targums	Flesher
240056	Approaches to Ancient Judaism: New Series, Volume III, Historical and Literary Studies	Neusner
240057	The Motherhood of God and Other Studies	Gruber
240058	The Analytic Movement in Rabbinic Jurisprudence	Solomon
240059	Recovering the Role of Women: Power and Authority in Rabbinic Jewish Society	Haas

240060	The Relation between Herodotus' *History* and Primary History	Mandell/Freedman
240061	The First Seven Days: A Philosophical Commentary on the Creation of Genesis	Samuelson
240062	The Bavli's Intellectual Character: The Generative Problematic: In Bavli Baba Qamma Chapter One And Bavli Shabbat Chapter One	Neusner
240063	The Incarnation of God: The Character of Divinity in Formative Judaism: Second Printing	Neusner
240064	Moses Kimhi: Commentary on the Book of Job	Basser/Walfish
240065	Judaism and Civil Religion	Breslauer
240066	Death and Birth of Judaism: Second Printing	Neusner
240067	Decoding the Talmud's Exegetical Program	Neusner
240068	Sources of the Transformation of Judaism	Neusner
240069	The Torah in the Talmud: A Taxonomy of the Uses of Scripture in the Talmud, Volume I	Neusner
240070	The Torah in the Talmud: A Taxonomy of the Uses of Scripture in the Talmud, Volume II	Neusner
240071	The Bavli's Unique Voice: A Systematic Comparison of the Talmud of Babylonia and the Talmud of the Land of Israel, Volume One	Neusner
240072	The Bavli's Unique Voice: A Systematic Comparison of the Talmud of Babylonia and the Talmud of the Land of Israel, Volume Two	Neusner
240073	The Bavli's Unique Voice: A Systematic Comparison of the Talmud of Babylonia and the Talmud of the Land of Israel, Volume Three	Neusner
240074	Bits of Honey: Essays for Samson H. Levey	Chyet/Ellenson

DATE DUE

BM 160 .B55 1993

37162

Bits of honey

HIEBERT LIBRARY
Fresno Pacific College - M. B. Seminary
Fresno, Calif. 93702

DEMCO